Railways

THE PIONEER YEARS

Railways

THE PIONEER YEARS

Researched and edited by
MALCOLM FLETCHER and JOHN TAYLOR

Chartwell
Books, Inc.

Railways: The Pioneer Years
is published 1990 by Chartwell Books Inc.
A Division of Book Sales, Inc.
110 Enterprise Avenue, Secaucus
New Jersey 07094, USA.

First published 1990 by Studio Editions Ltd.
Princess House, 50 Eastcastle Street
London W1N 7AP, England.

ISBN 1 55521 627 7

Printed and bound in Italy

CONTENTS

PREFACE
page 7

CHAPTER ONE
The First Fifty Years
pages 9 to 110

CHAPTER TWO
The Great Age of the Railways
pages 113 to 244

CHAPTER THREE

Railways between the Two World Wars

pages 245 to 306

CHRONOLOGY OF RAILWAY HISTORY
page 307

GENERAL INDEX
page 311

INDEX OF TYPES OF LOCOMOTIVE
page 319

PREFACE

Railways: The Pioneer Years is organised chronologically, but throughout the volume the sequence of carefully integrated text and illustrations examines on the one hand the technological achievements which made possible the building of railways, locomotives and rolling-stock, and a rapid improvement in performance, and, on the other hand, the social changes brought about when it became possible to move passengers and goods over long distances quickly, safely and economically.

The authors divide their treatment of railway development into three main periods. The first part deals with the years from the turn of the century up until 1860. This establishes the connection between stationary steam engines used in industry and colliery tramways, and the early experiments with steam locomotives for goods and passenger traffic which culminated in the Rainhill Trials of 1829 when Stephenson's *Rocket* achieved a speed of 29 m.p.h. By 1860 all the major European countries had well-established rail networks and by that date too the American railroad network had already pushed west of the Mississippi. Railways had also been established by then in South America, Africa, Australia and India.

The second part deals with the years 1860–1914. This was a period of consolidation and expansion during which rail travel became an everyday experience for many people. The industrialisation of the second half of the nineteenth century would not have been possible without the railway system to move coal and other raw materials from one region to another as well as the movement of foodstuffs and passengers which permitted the rapid growth of urban centres.

The final part of the book covers the period after the First World War. By the outbreak of the Second World War the essential features of the railway system that we see today were firmly established. Railway systems were already using or experimenting with the two alternative sources of motive power which were competing with steam – diesel and electric traction. Suburban networks and underground railways were well established, aerodynamics were being applied to the design of locomotives to improve performance, and there were considerable advances in the design of rolling-stock for reasons of safety and comfort, in particular in the design of restaurant-cars and sleeping-cars to cater for the increased expectations of the travelling public.

Although half a century has elapsed since the finishing date of 1939, during which time in certain respects the railway network has contracted and there has been competition for short- and long-distance travel from airlines on the one hand and the motor-car and motor-coach on the other, railways still provide an essential part of our social and economic fabric. Developments since the Second World War (some of which are dealt with in the chronology at the end of the book) have only built on the foundations which were already there. What this book provides is a fascinating survey of what might be termed the 'heroic age' of railways.

A number of themes run through the book as a whole. The first is concerned with the personalities involved – the engineering giants whose ingenuity made possible the rapid expansion of the railway system. The authors are quick to acknowledge the contribution of Britain and its pioneers – notably George and Robert Stephenson, Trevithick, and Brunel, though there are many others. In France, they pay tribute to the contribution of Marc Seguin, who is credited with the invention of the multi-tubular boiler. In the United States, Mathias Baldwin, William Norris and J B Jervis were among the innovators in locomotive design.

The authors clearly explain the significance of the many technological achievements which enabled the railways to improve their capabilities and performance. These include Jessop's 'fish-bellied' cast-iron rails, improvements in the development of boilers and cylinders, coupled axles, bogies, Stephenson's valve gear and Walschaerts' valve gear, the compound principle, superheaters, tenders, braking systems and water troughs.

Speed, of course, has always been an important indicator of performance, although it could not be divorced from considerations of safety and was itself related to improvements in the way in which steam power could be harnessed and transformed into the movement not only of the locomotive but of the train of carriages or waggons behind it. The speed of the *Rocket* at the Rainhill Trials in 1829 was improved on in somewhat macabre circumstances the following year, when William Huskisson MP, who had been knocked down at the opening of the Liverpool & Manchester Railway, was rushed from Parkside to Eccles on board Stephenson's *Northumbrian* at a speed which reached 36 m.p.h. By the 1840s speeds of 60 m.p.h. had been achieved, by the 1890s speeds of 90 m.p.h., and by the 1930s, under experimental conditions, speeds in excess of 120 m.p.h.

Railways have always been aware of the need to ensure the safety of travellers, particularly as speeds increased. Coach construction, signalling, alarm systems were all improved, though sometimes improvements only came in the wake of disasters. The authors deal with a number of accidents and catastrophes and relate these to the defects which led to them and the improvements which followed. They provide accounts of the first large-scale railway accident as early as 1842 when an express from Versailles to Paris crashed and 48 people burned to death, unable to escape through the compartment doors which were locked. The Tay Bridge disaster in 1879 in which the bridge collapsed while a train was crossing, with the loss of all 73 passengers and the crew of 5, is also investigated.

Safety was one concern of passengers, comfort another. The improvements in the construction of rolling-stock, including the introduction of corridors, heating, restaurant- and sleeping-cars are all dealt with. Changes in the design of goods waggons are also illustrated.

The engineering challenge posed by the construction of tunnels, bridges and viaducts, and cuttings and embankments is studied, as is station architecture, particularly that associated with the famous terminus stations such as Grand Central in New York, the Gare St Lazaire in Paris, and Euston and Waterloo in London.

Nor does the book overlook developments in ticket systems, the carriage of mail by rail, and other specialist features such as funicular railways, cable-cars, atmospheric and pneumatic railways, and metropolitan underground systems.

For illustrations, the book draws extensively not only on private collections but on those of specialist collectors such as Dendy Marshall, Pierre Lichtenberger and Laurent Seguin, grandson of Marc. It also draws on the archives of the Science Museum, London, the Bibliothèque national, Paris, the Conservatoire des arts et métiers, Paris, the Newcomen Society, London, the National Museum, Washington. A further source of historical illustrations were newspapers and magazines, notably *L'Illustration*, *Le Monde illustré*, *Nature*, *The Engineer*, *The Railway Gazette*, *The Sphere*, *The Times*, *The Illustrated London News*, and *Illustrirte Zeitung*. Many railway companies manufacturing locomotives and rolling-stock were also helpful in supplying illustrations. All these illustrations are individually acknowledged in the captions.

Stephenson's locomotives in the Hetton mines (1822)

CHAPTER I

THE FIRST FIFTY YEARS

THE ORIGINS OF THE RAILWAY

Railways are much older than locomotives. However, like the latter and like steam engines they began life in the mines. It would appear that tracks consisting of two grooves were to be found in Ancient Greece. These grooves had been made in the ground at a distance from each other which corresponded to the average distance between the wheels of a cart. They ran between slabs of stone placed end to end in parallel lines and allowed carts to run along them. Remains of these tracks can be seen on the road from the Piraeus to the Agora in Athens and in the region around Orchomenos where, according to M. Caillemer, the roads contain 'two grooves perfectly level with each other. The edges at top and bottom are clean-cut, and they are separated by quite deep holes.' The system passed from Greece to Rome where tracks are to be found 'on the roads which lead to the ruins of the oldest towns in Latium, namely Cora, Norba and Siguia home of the Volsci'. Such remains can similarly be found around Syracuse in Sicily.

In the centuries which followed, the use of stone grooves appears to have disappeared except perhaps in Scotland, but a granite grooved-road was built about 1826 in the quarry on Dartmoor,

Truck running along rails in the Leberthal mines in Alsace, from Sebastian Münster's *Cosmographiæ Universalis* (1550).

and is still in existence.

Although texts are not entirely clear on the matter, it is also possible that wooden rails were used to transport boats overland across the Isthmus of Corinth.

The earliest record of railways as we understand them appears in the fifteenth century. Different editions of Sebastian Münster's *Cosmographiae Universalis*, the first of which appeared in 1550 in Basle, describe the Leberthal mines in Alsace. Under the heading 'Instrumentum Tractorium', a wood-engraving clearly shows a miner pushing a truck along a gallery. Its small-diameter wheels are guided by a length of wood which is, in fact, a rail. The truck is described as being 'a cart with four small, iron wheels'. It is, therefore, likely that the use of rails was widespread in the German mines of the sixteenth century. Such rails, however, existed before this in Flanders, since a similar truck exists in relief on the old ceremonial silver chain of the Silversmiths' Guild in Ghent, a chain dating from the fifteenth century.

According to a study made by M.W. Grosseteste, the word 'rail' is possibly derived from *riceule* and *rieulet*, dialect words from the Hainault and Lille regions which were used to describe a bricklayer's rule. In Old French the latter was called a *rhil*, and in Low German it was referred to as a *regal*, *regchel* or *riegel*. Again, in Old French

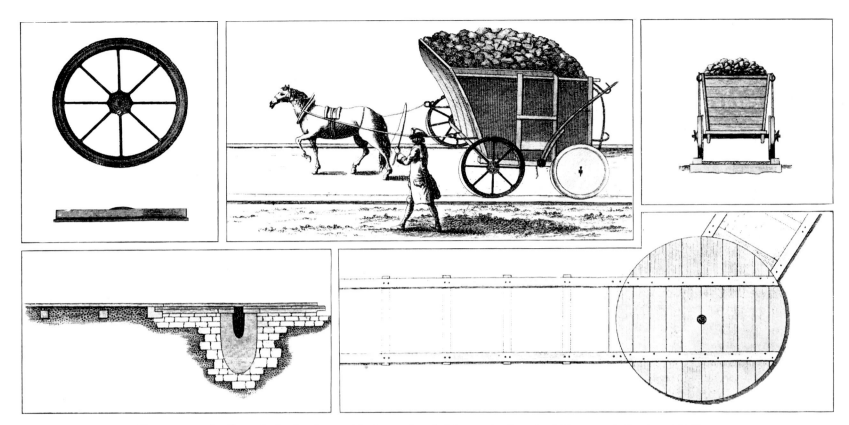

Waggon on rails, flanged wheel and turntable from mines in Newcastle, from Jars' *Voyages métallurgiques* (1765).
(Science Museum, London)

people talked of the *roye* of a meadow, and in Berry and Saintonge the words *raye*, *raiye* and *rege* were used. All these words may well stem from the Latin word *regula* which gave the French word *regle*. It would therefore be natural to use in French as in English the pronunciation *relle* rather than *raille* for the word 'rail' when it crossed the Channel from England around 1825.

Wooden rails appear to have been used frequently in the Nottinghamshire mines at the end of the sixteenth century. They were first used in the area around Newcastle about 1602 by Beaumont 'a man of great talent and rare ingenuity'. From among the 'many unusual machines not yet known in that area' he introduced 'horse-drawn carts which transported coal from the mines to the shipping stages'. According to some writers this was Huntingdon Beaumont from Nottingham; other writers claimed that Beaumont was a Frenchman.

The following description of the railways in the Newcastle area was given by Lord Keeper North in 1676: 'The system of transportation consists of laying perfectly straight and parallel wooden rails from the mine to the river. Stout trucks are built which run along these rails on four wheels; by this means transportation becomes so easy that a horse can pull four or five chaldrons of coal. This is a huge benefit to the coal merchant.' The value of this system is revealed by the fact that in 1690 a single mine had 600 trucks.

Desaguliers' *Cours de physique experimentale*, published in London in 1734, contains a detailed description and wonderful illustrations of the flat trucks used by Ralph Allen to transport stone from his quarries to the quayside of the River Avon near Bath. It is amazing to see how modern in appearance are these trucks which are more than 200 years old. In fact, they are no longer trucks with sides as used in the mines, but, rather, very strongly built, flat trucks.

A chassis made up of four oak beams 14 ft in length by 4 in. square supported a solid base consisting of reinforced oak timbers which were 13 ft long and 3½ ft wide. The tall sides which were detachable were fastened by hooks and rings to the front and rear ends which remained fixed in place. Beneath the chassis, two strong wooden beams 'bound with iron' carried a brass half-collar 'for the wheel axis, which being well-greased would then turn without friction. The axle is approximately 3 in. in diameter. One of its ends is square, the other rounded, and the wheels are positioned alternately on the two ends. In other words, the front wheel on the right-hand side is on the square end and the front wheel on the left-hand side is on the round end, while the rear wheel on the right-hand side is on the round end and the rear wheel on the left-hand side is on the square end. In this way, each of the wheels can stop independently, since, when the wheel on the round end is stopped the other wheel on that axle continues to turn; and when the wheel on the square end is stopped, the other wheel continues to turn normally on the stationary axle.' This particular feature overcame the problem of manoeuvring through tight bends. 'The wheels are made of smelted iron and are about 20 in. in

Waggon used in the Newcastle mines going downhill, from the *Recueil des arts et métiers* (1773).
(Science Museum, London)

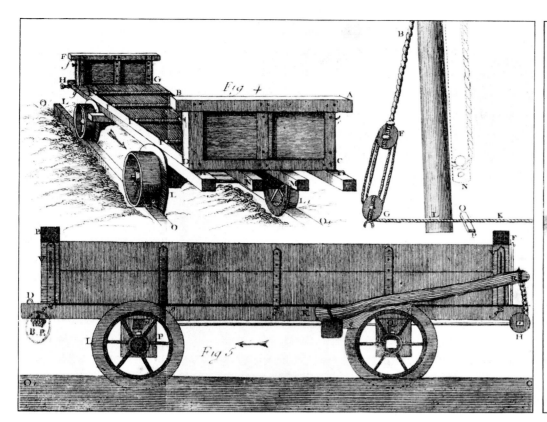

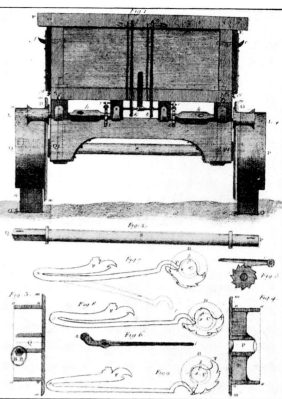

Waggon designed by Ralph Allen (1734), showing axles, wheels and brakes, from Desaguliers' *Cours de physique experimentale* (1734 and 1751).

(Bibliothèque nationale, Paris)

diameter and have a rim 6 in. wide. They are positioned next to the truck, which prevents them leaving the oak rails along which they travel.'

The brake was operated by a long, metal-clad, wooden lever which was pushed against one of the wheels by means of a chain attached to a roller bar with a ratchet wheel. This could be released by a lever so as to free the wheel. The braking system was completed by a bolt which could immobilise either of the wheels at the other end of the truck. The excellence of the workmanship in Allen's trucks is clearly to be seen. The total cost of each one was £30, 'a very reasonable price, given the quality of all the parts which have been so finely crafted'.

Desaguliers describes the use to which these trucks were put: 'Although these carriages are very heavy, even when empty, because of the rails along which they pass and the axles' brass collar which reduces friction considerably, not only can two horses pull them with great ease up a hill when they are empty, but they can also pull them on the flat when heavily laden. As soon as the carriages arrive at the top of the hill, the horses are unharnessed and one or more wheels are immobilised, the driver stationing himself at the rear in order to control operations as required.

'When the trucks have been loaded by the riverside and then, subsequently, unloaded, the horses are harnessed to the other end of the truck. In this way, what was the front of the truck when it went down the hill becomes the rear of the truck when it goes up the hill, a manoeuvre which avoids the problem of having to turn the trucks around.'

Seen in cross-section the 'wooden rails' are almost square. It was about this period (1738) in Whitehaven that the idea was conceived of nailing strips of metal to the wooden rails. Similarly someone thought of covering the oak rails with lengths of beech wood which would be cheap to replace. In 1765, Jars, in his *Voyages métallurgiques*, describes and illustrates the mine trucks to be found in Newcastle and tells us that the wheels, whether wooden and solid or with spokes and made of iron, were of different sizes so that the loads of coal would remain horizontal in trucks which always operated on gradients. These same trucks were in use in Cumberland. Jars also gives illustrations of turntables.

The first railway-lines to be made entirely of cast iron were laid in the Coalbrookdale mines in the county of Salop, and this led to a rapid expansion of railways. According to one account, the first metal line was laid between Horsehay and Coalbrookdale by Abraham Darby in the period 1750 and 1763; others claim it was his son-in-law, Richard Reynolds, who built a wide network of cast-iron lines between 1763 and 1768. Between 1768 and 1771 he laid another 800 tons of these railway-lines. It appears likely that it was Darby who brought wooden rails to the area, but that it was Reynolds who, after Darby's death, invented metal rails. These measured 6 ft in length and were 3¾ in. wide and 1¼ in. deep. By 1785 the network extended over a distance of 20 miles, each mile having cost £800.

In 1774, John Curr, who at the time was only

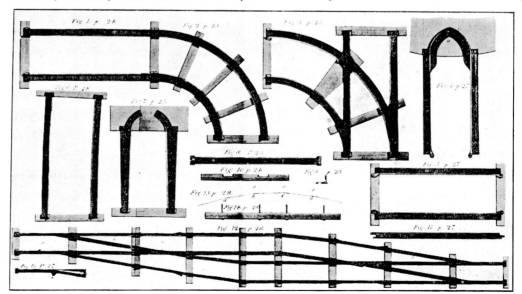

John Curr's metal tramways (1796).

(*Newcomen Society Transactions*, Volume XI)

Model of cast-iron rail laid on wooden supports (1767).
(Science Museum, London)

18 years of age, laid in Sheffield for the Duke of Norfolk a line which so irritated the local inhabitants that a serious riot broke out, and the line and a coach were destroyed and burned. Shortly after this, John Curr invented and laid the first 'tram-road'. This was a line which consisted of cast-iron rails with a projection on one side so as to be able to carry coaches with flanged wheels. These rails were laid on wooden sleepers which the local people destroyed. They were replaced by metal blocks and then by small stones which remained in use for a long time. Curr's rails, called 'plate-rails', were cast by James Outram, and it is thought that his name gives us the word 'tram-way'. John Curr had incorporated into his system bends, loop-lines, forks and derailers.

The third stage in the history of the railway-line begins in 1789 with Jessop's invention, the 'edge-rail', that is the modern railway-line, made entirely of metal and with a return to the flanged wheel.

At this period it was becoming increasingly common to use railways. Certain features of this increased use are of interest. In 1768, Lowell Edgeworth proposed a general system of railroads which the public could use. In 1782, following a visit to Le Creusot, Daubenton describes in a letter to Buffon the first use of railway-lines in France: 'Sections of wood mark out all the routes which are to be taken. These wooden lengths are covered in strips of metal, and it is these which carry the wheels of the trucks which transport the coal. Moreover, these wheels are directed in such a way that the truck cannot turn from its path, but is obliged to follow the way which is marked out for it. Thus, a single horse, even were it to be blind, could without the slightest difficulty pull four tons or more.' About 1788, railroads existed in Indret, while wooden rails 'as in Germany' were to be found in Anzin and in the lead mines of Poullaouen.

Tip-up trucks were in use in 1795 on the tram road which crossed Chat Moss near Liverpool. About 1791, Faujas de Saint-Ford on a journey to Newcastle described the lines, the trucks and the way they operated: 'Four-wheeled trucks car-

rying 8 tons of coal travel along an incline, drawn by their own weight, and as if by magic follow each other in single file to the sea. There, a strongly-built wooden structure of pleasing appearance extends the track by a distance of several feet above the water, at a height which allows ships with their masts lowered to pass beneath. A man, stationed on this platform, opens a trap-door. A kind of large, wooden hopper arrives and makes its way towards the vessel, the decks of which are open. The truck comes and stops above the trap-door, its conical base opens, and all the coal passes in an instant through the hopper and into the ship. The empty truck returns along a second line parallel to the first, followed by the other trucks, each of which has in turn discharged its load. In this way, and in a short space of time, the vessel is fully loaded. Only a few horses are needed to take the empty trucks along the second line, and these soon return with more coal. This operation is not only efficient, but economical, and offers a very handsome return on the investment which such a track necessitates'. (From *A Journey to England, Scotland and the Hebrides*.)

Finally, in 1802, Basil Hall provides an interesting detail in his *Scenes of Maritime Life*: 'Have observed coal trucks near Newcastle; the wheels are constructed in such a way that they descend the hill on chains into which the wheels engage: the horse follows the truck and pulls it back up when empty'.

At the beginning of the nineteenth century, in the area around Newcastle, there were 200 miles of track above ground and as many underground. There were 250 miles of track in Glamorgan, 30 miles between Cardiff and Merthyr Tydfil, and 18 miles on the Surrey Iron Railway which was opened on 26 July 1803. This was the first railway which the public could use to transport goods in return for a fee which had been authorised by Parliament.

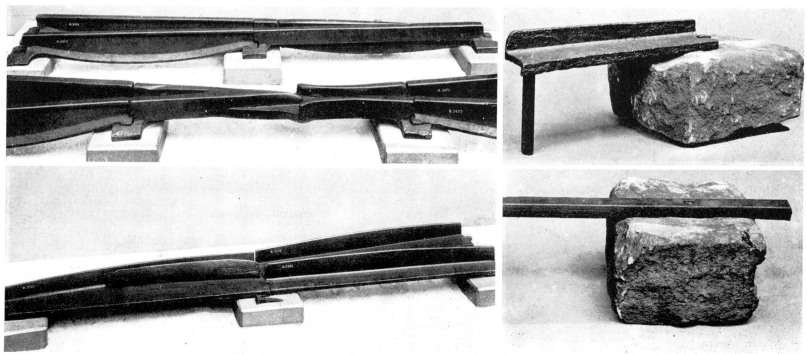

Top left: Jessop's cast-iron rail (the original dated 1793). *Bottom left*: Outram's flat, cast-iron tram rail (1799). *Top right*: Rail from the Surrey Iron Railway (1803). *Bottom right*: First rail made from malleable iron (1808). (Science Museum, London)

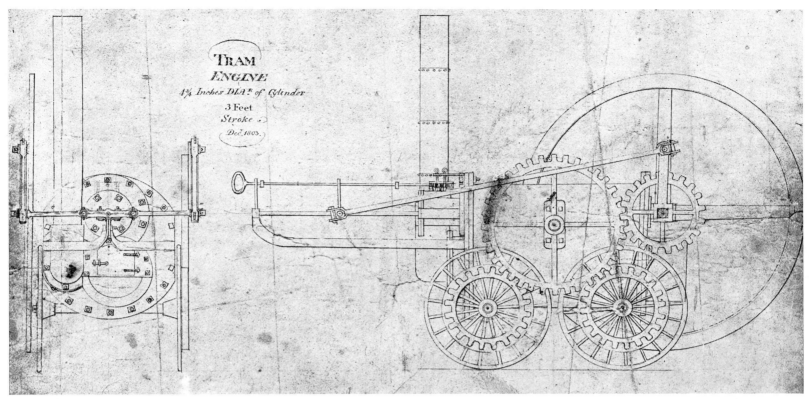

Richard Trevithick's first locomotive, built in 1803 and tested in 1804 at Merthyr Tydfil.

(Contemporary drawing by Llewellyn. Science Museum, London)

RICHARD TREVITHICK AND THE FIRST LOCOMOTIVE

The first locomotive was the work of Richard Trevithick. This fact alone ensures a place in history for this amazing man, the 'Cornwall Giant', one of the innovators of this great era of the machine. Born on 13 April 1771 in Illogan near Camborne, Trevithick soon revealed an interest in engineering together with an inventive and original mind. He had the build of an athlete, and was impetuous, dynamic, optimistic and extremely versatile. An indefatigable inventor, a man of intuition rather than instruction, his faith in his ideas was total, and it was this which marked him out from all other engineers. However, in spite of enjoying the adoration of the people of Cornwall and in spite of the enormous profits which the mining industry of his region made through his genius, he was unable during his lifetime to achieve wealth, being unable to persist for long in any one task, living for the future and often penniless in the present.

As a young 'captain of the mining industry' he turned his thoughts to the steam engine, in the hope of challenging the monopoly held by Boulton and Watt, and he found himself re-examining the ideas of Oliver Evans, the American pioneer of the high-pressure engine. From 1797 onwards he experimented with steam-carriages, giving a glimpse of what he would achieve later on. In 1802, with his cousin Andrew Vivian, he took out his famous patent for a high-pressure engine, and at the same time he was already constructing two road-carriages. From 1803 to 1808 he tested his first three locomotives, simultaneously develop-

ing the production of semi-stationary engines and high-pressure boilers. He then turned his attention to steam-boats and steam-dredgers, to propellors, pumps, engines, to the iron hulls and tanks of ships, and, finally, to the tunnel under the Thames. From 1816 to 1827 he lived a life of extraordinary adventure in Peru, Chile, Colombia and Nicaragua where he had been invited to work as an engineer. He returned home completely ruined and passed away in obscurity and poverty at Dartford, Kent on 22 April 1833.

As early as August 1802, in Coalbrookdale, the building of a locomotive was begun, but then abandoned. The first real locomotive was constructed by Trevithick to haul trucks laden with metal along a 9¾-mile track linking the ironworks of Penydarran near Merthyr Tydfil in

Wales to Abercynon on the Glamorganshire canal. This engine travelled for the first time along its track on 13 February 1804, and completed its first journey on 21 February.

As a result of contradictory statements by various writers, doubts exist about the appearance of this engine, but one can suppose, as did Richard's son, Francis, that the design on display in the Science Museum, London represents more or less the engine as it was, even though certain dimensions do not entirely correspond with the description. The boiler was a Trevithick boiler with a return tube to increase the heating surface. The horizontal cylinder, situated inside the boiler, was activated by means of a connecting-rod and a large flywheel. This engaged with a cog-wheel which, in turn, controlled the two left-hand

Trevithick's railway and locomotive *Catch me who can* in London, in 1808.

(From a drawing of about 1837. *Newcomen Society Transactions*, Vol. 1)

wheels, the right-hand wheels being free. These wheels were not flanged, thus enabling the engine to run on a tramroad.

Trevithick himself wrote to his friend Giddy an account of this great event: 'Yesterday our engine made its first journey: we pulled 10 tons of iron and 5 trucks with 70 men on board along the whole of the route. We covered about 9 miles in 4 hours 5 minutes, but we had to cut down some trees and remove several large rocks which were obstructing our way. The engine travelled at approximately 5 m.p.h. No water was added to the boiler from the time of departure to the moment we arrived at the end of our journey. Two hundredweight of coal was used. During the return journey at about 4 miles from Ironport one of the small bolts which connect the axle to the boiler broke, thus allowing all the water from the boiler to escape. As a result the engine was unable to return home until this evening . . .'.

The newspaper, *The Cambrian*, on 24 February 1804 completed its account of the experiment with this prophetic conclusion: 'There can be no doubt that the number of horses in our land will be considerably reduced, and that the machine has a potential use far exceeding anything imagined so far for this engine'.

This journey was repeated several times, in particular in March 1804 with a 25-ton load, but the weight of the locomotive was such that many rails were broken.

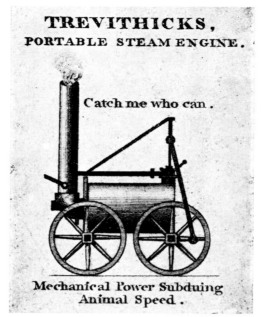

The locomotive *Catch me who can* (1808).
(Entrance ticket to the London demonstration.)
(Science Museum, London)

In Penydarran this first locomotive left behind it various rumours and myths. People say, among other things, that it was buried in a rubbish tip, and that it had a brick chimney. The latter is certainly not true, although it is possible that Trevithick used bricks in an earlier experiment involving the return fire-tube.

The following year, 1805, an almost identical locomotive, but with the cylinder at the rear, was built in Newcastle by John Steel. It had been requested by Blackett for the mine in Wylam. It was tested in Gateshead, but not put into service, and it was used as a stationary engine.

In 1808, Trevithick turned for one last time to the subject of locomotives and had Rastrick construct a small four-wheeled engine with a vertical cylinder which entered the rear of the boiler and was linked via a con-rod to the rear wheels. It was a very simple engine, similar to one of Trevithick's stationary engines, but set on wheels. To increase the draught, gases were expelled from the chimney which, as in the first locomotive, was fitted with a damper. This locomotive, named *Catch me who can*, was brought to London and ran on land close to Euston Square on a circular track surrounded by railings. From 19 July 1808 the public were admitted on payment of 5 shillings. For 1 shilling more, people could sit in the carriage which the locomotive pulled. This exhibition was advertised in the newspapers of the time, as was a race between the locomotive and horses. The attraction lasted several weeks, and then a rail broke, the locomotive left the track and overturned. Trevithick, disheartened and penniless, abandoned his experiments, and appears to have taken no further part in the development of the railways.

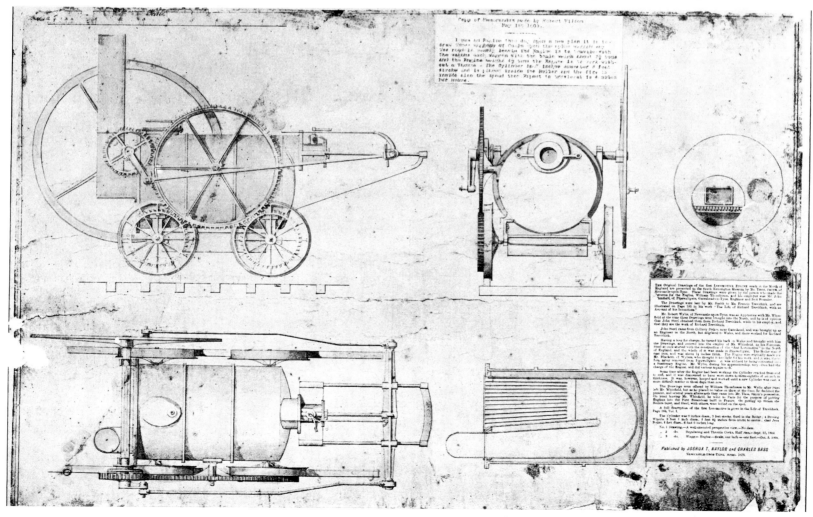

Original drawings of Trevithick's second locomotive, built in Newcastle in 1805.
(Science Museum, London)

Rack locomotive designed by Blenkinsop and built by Matthew Murray (1812).

THE FIRST INDUSTRIAL LOCOMOTIVES

The oldest engraving of a locomotive in service shows Blenkinsop's locomotive and a train of waggons at Middleton colliery in Leeds; in the foreground is a miner. The creators of that engine were John Blenkinsop who ordered it, and Matthew Murray who built it. Among the great pioneers of the locomotive both have equal merit, but in different ways.

Blenkinsop was the manager of Mr Brandling's mine in Middleton, Yorkshire and he wanted to use locomotives to pull trucks from that mine to Leeds, a distance of 3½ miles. These locomotives would work by means of a system invented by Blenkinsop in which cog-wheels would engage an outer rack running parallel with the rails. He had, in fact, patented this system in 1811. At Fenton, Murray and Wood's works in Leeds, he had four of these engines built to a design of Murray's. They were similar to Trevithick's *Catch me who can* locomotive but Murray had incorporated one of his own ideas: he introduced two vertical cylinders which activated, by means of two cranks set at right-angles to avoid dead points, two cogs which linked to the cog-wheel

axle. This was a considerable improvement on Trevithick's engine. The latter showed no interest in this new development, but received a sum of £30 in return for copyright.

The first test took place on 24 June 1812. The *Leeds Mercury* gave this description: 'At 4 o'clock the engine left Coal Staith on the top of Hunslet Moor with six, and later eight, coal waggons weighing 3½ tons each coupled to it. Pulling this enormous weight, to which was added the weight of about 50 spectators who had climbed on the waggons as it approached the town, the engine succeeded in returning to Coal Staith and completed the journey of about 1½ miles, mainly on the flat, in 23 minutes without the slightest problem.' These 4-horsepower locomotives weighing 5 tons were able to pull 27 coal waggons, that is a weight of 94 tons, at a speed of 3½ miles per hour. They could reach 10 m.p.h. with a light load. They cost £400, and remained in service for more than 20 years, which proves the quality of their design and construction. This was the first industrial, long-term application of traction by locomotive. It was also the first rack railway.

Costumes of Yorkshire, published in 1813 in both English and French, gives the following commentary against an engraving of Blenkinsop and Murray's engine: 'One can see in the background the engine invented recently by Mr Blenkinsop, the manager of the mine belonging to Mr Charles Brandling, near to Leeds. This engine hauls more than twenty trucks loaded with coal from the mine to Leeds. Two of these engines in constant use save the work and expense of more than fourteen horses.' Many visitors came to see these engines working, including most of the early railway engineers and, in 1813, the Grand Duke Nicolas, the future emperor of Russia. Two similar locomotives were built in 1813 for the Coxlodge mines, and others, built by John Daglish, were used in the mines at Orrell.

Two locomotives based upon those of Blenkinsop and Murray were built in Germany at the

Royal Foundry in Berlin. The first, built in 1816 and destined for the Königsgrave mines in Silesia, was abandoned after its first tests; the other was built in 1818 for Geislautern in the Saar, but never ran because of defects in its boilers.

In 1813 in Newbottle, William Brunton tested a locomotive which moved on two legs. These were operated by a piston, each leg in turn being in contact with the ground. The arrangement was inspired once again by fears about track adhesion. In fact, this engine, with its nickname 'Steam Horse', appears to have been in use until 1815 when it was destroyed by an enormous explosion. It seems another Brunton engine was used in the Rainton mines. With regard to these early locomotives, it is interesting to note how mine-owners in England favoured and gave encouragement to such inventions.

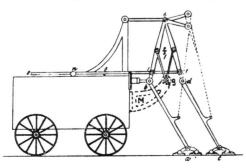

William Brunton's 'Steam Horse' (1813).
(*Newcomen Society Transactions*, Vol. II)

First locomotive in Germany (1816).
(Illustrated on a plaque from the Royal Foundry, Berlin)

GEORGE STEPHENSON
1781–1848

Engraving by T.S. Atkinson from the painting by John Lucas.

(Science Museum, London)

GEORGE STEPHENSON

Before describing in detail the life and works of George Stephenson we should mention some of the achievements which preceded his.

On 30 December 1812, William and Edward Chapman from Newcastle took out a patent for a warp locomotive, that is one which pulled itself along by means of a drum on a fixed chain. This patent also gave us the first description of a four-wheel bogie with a central pivot. This bogie must have been positioned at the rear and mounted on friction rollers. Mention was also made of the double bogie.

Chain-operated locomotives were tested in 1813 in the Heaton mines, and on 21 November 1814 on J.G. Lambton's mine track, but the system proved to have too many faults. Because of a long-standing error, William Hedley's eight-wheel locomotive has often been described as the work of W. and E. Chapman.

Christopher Blackett, the owner of the Wylam mine, had tested Trevithick's second locomotive, and had noted the possibility of direct adhesion of smooth wheels on rails. He replaced the weak wooden track by cast-iron rails and in 1812, following Blenkinsop's success, he decided to try steam traction once again. Not wishing to go to the expense of a rack line, towards the end of 1812 he instructed his inspector William Hedley to carry out tests on track adhesion. In order to determine the relationship which existed between the weight of an engine and the greatest load it could pull from a stationary position, Hedley built a truck the wheels of which were turned by men. The results were conclusive, and Hedley then had a cast-iron boiler, a cylinder and a flywheel mounted on this truck, thus creating a primitive working locomotive. Immediately thereafter, in 1813, Blackett had three locomotives built at Wylam by Hedley, assisted by Jonathan Foster and Timothy Hackworth. Two of these locomotives are still in existence, one nicknamed *Puffing Billy* being in the Science Museum, London, the other in the Edinburgh Museum. They ran until 1864.

The boiler, resting on a wooden chassis, was horizontal, made of rolled iron, and contained a return fire-tube, copied from Trevithick. The two vertical cylinders are at the rear on a central axle which connects to the four wheels by a system of gears. In working order the engine weighed just over 8 tons and could pull 50 tons at a speed of 5 m.p.h.

Apparently in 1815 these four-wheel locomotives were replaced by engines with eight wheels coupled by gears in order to spread the weight which otherwise destroyed the track. It appears that these wheels were not mounted on pivoting bogies. Later when stronger rails were laid these locomotives were converted back into four-wheel engines. Some quite important differences are to be found between the design of Hedley's eight-wheel engines and the two old locomotives to which changes had to be made.

These high-pressure engines produced huge clouds of smoke and were extremely noisy, hence their nickname 'Puffers'. They were also, as a result, the subject of numerous complaints, in

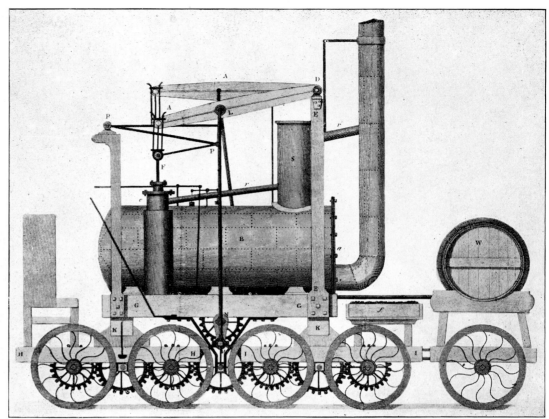

William Hedley's eight-wheel locomotive built at Wylam (1815).

particular because of the terror they inspired in horses. Hedley therefore conceived the idea of directing the exhaust fumes into a huge tank before releasing them through the chimney.

From 1814 to 1825 all the locomotives built were the work of George Stephenson. The life of this man was an admirable one. He was born on 9 June 1781 in Wylam, the son of a mineworker, and from his early years he had a happy disposition and an open mind, and showed an aptitude for engineering. When he was still young he was made responsible for the supervision of engines by Newcomen, and he there acquired invaluable knowledge of steam. Showing great resilience and being a tireless worker, he made every effort to make good the gaps left by a woefully inadequate early education. In 1810 he was made chief

engineer of the Killingworth colliery. In 1813 he suggested the construction of an engine 'which would travel', and Thomas Liddell (Lord Ravensworth), who was the main shareholder, approved this proposal. Later on we shall see the major role which George Stephenson played in the development not only of engines – for more than 10 years he remained the only pioneer – but also, and especially, of the railways themselves. One finds his name in the technical manuals used in almost all the great entrepreneurial works following his two greatest triumphs, the establishment of the Stockton to Darlington and the Liverpool to Manchester lines. However it was rather his son, Robert, born in 1803, who was responsible for the improvement of the locomotive. In 1828, George Stephenson handed over this role to his

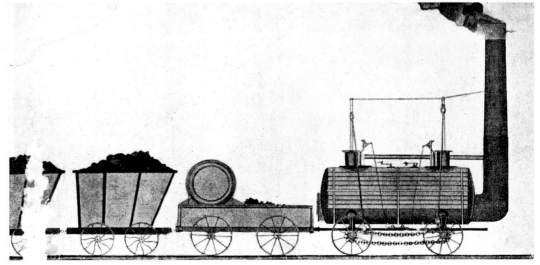

George Stephenson's Killingworth locomotive (1815).

(From a drawing attributed to George Stephenson: Science Museum, London)

ROBERT STEPHENSON
1803–1859

Engraving by T.S. Atkinson from the painting by John Lucas.

(Dendy Marshall Collection)

son, whom he had already been able to help as a result of his sound judgement and his unique experience as a man who had built engines from their very beginnings. Honoured and amply rewarded for his efforts, he died on 12 August 1848 in Tapton. Robert Thurston wrote of him: 'From any point of view, George Stephenson was an admirable man. He was simple, serious, honest, energetic, tenacious, as well as being clever. He was a charming, compassionate and gentle man. He will always be respected; for many years to come, when they read the story of this simple, but fascinating life, as it has been described by his biographer, Smiles, hundreds of young men will feel heartened and sustained by his noble example on that difficult path which leads to glorious fame.'

His son, Robert, had the same qualities. An engineer without equal, one of the greatest ever to have lived, he combined knowledge, inventiveness, practical sense and an agreeable temperament. He had also inherited from his father his courage and his impartiality. After playing a vital role in the history of the locomotive, he built countless engines and then went on, such was his amazing energy, to construct the greatest metal bridges the world had ever known. He died on 12 October 1859.

George Stephenson's first locomotive, called *Blücher*, was based upon Blenkinsop's, but power was transmitted to the wheels by gears. It ran from 25 July 1814. His next locomotive is known as the 'Killingworth's locomotive'. The cylinders, no longer next to each other, are positioned above the wheels which are driven by connecting rods. It made a successful debut on 6 March 1815. In the design and construction of this engine Stephenson was helped by Ralph Dodds. The two axles were coupled by a rod which was later replaced by a chain.

In 1816, George Stephenson and W. Losh took out a patent for a locomotive mounted on steam springs. The boiler sat on six steam-filled cylinders, the pistons of which were attached to the

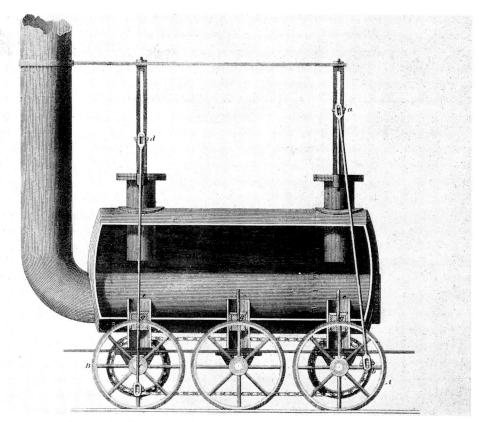

George Stephenson's and W. Losh's locomotive (1815).

wheel-bearings. In this way the engine was protected from violent shocks and the wheels gave an even downward thrust onto the rails. The six wheels were linked by two chains which ran over cog-wheels. Such an engine operated in Killingworth, and another was built for the Kilmarnock mine, the first ever to run in Scotland. From 1822 onwards, Stephenson built eight four-wheel, Killingworth-type locomotives for the mines in Hilton, Heaton, etc.

The first locomotive factory was built in 1823 in Newcastle by George and Robert Stephenson, Edward Pease and Michael Longridge. The first orders received in 1824 were for two of the locomotives for Hetton, and for two of the same class for the Stockton & Darlington Railway. Robert Stephenson had left for South America and did not return home until 1827, which was the year his father chose to entrust to his son's inventive genius, boldness and vision responsibility for continuing his life's work in the development of the locomotive. Since 1814 there had been little development in George Stephenson's technical approach to the locomotive: the cylinder arrangement required the use of long, connecting rods, but their vertical position caused the engine to shake considerably. The boiler in particular showed little improvement, since a simple firetube passed through it and gave such little heat to the water that the bottom of the chimney frequently glowed red. The production of steam was slow, ineffective and expensive and allowed only very moderate speeds, which were sufficient for mines but not for any system of transport with more widespread applications. Robert Stephenson set himself the task of simplifying the engine and increasing its speed. The result was that he built the *Lancashire Witch*, which made its first journey in July 1828 on the recently-opened Bolton to Leigh railway line. It was a vastly superior engine: the four coupled wheels were driven by two rear cylinders inclined at an angle of 39 degrees. Metal springs supported the boiler which had two fire-tubes. Boiler apart, this was the engine which directly inspired the *Rocket*. Meanwhile, Hackworth had built the *Royal George*, a fine six-wheel engine, which will be dealt with later. These two engines, the *Lancashire Witch* and the *Royal George*, came to the rescue of locomotives at a time when initial enthusiasm had given way to a certain disillusionment.

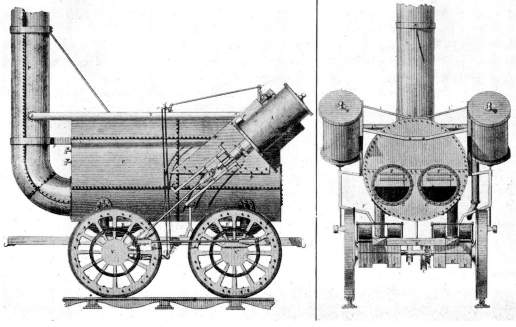

Robert Stephenson's *Lancashire Witch* (1828).

The oldest American locomotive, the *John Bull*, built in 1831 by Robert Stephenson for the Mohawk & Hudson R.R.
(National Museum, Washington)

Foster, Rastrick and Company's *Agenoria*, which
was in service at Shutt End mine from 1829 to 1864.
(Science Museum, London)

The Baltimore & Ohio R.R.'s *Atlantic* (1832),
under steam in 1927.
(Courtesy of Baltimore & Ohio R.R)

THE FORERUNNERS OF TODAY'S LOCOMOTIVES

Opening of the first steam passenger railway from Stockton to Darlington, 27 September 1825.

(From an original drawing by Dobbin: Science Museum, London)

THE FIRST
PUBLIC RAILWAY

One of the great dates in the history of the railways is 27 September 1825: that day saw the inauguration of the first passenger line. This ran for 24 miles between Stockton and Darlington, in Durham. The line was the creation of a remarkably far-sighted man, Edward Pease (1766–1858). In 1817, wanting further to exploit the rich coalfields of Darlington and Bishop Auckland, he requested permission to build this railway, which would be worked by 'men, horses or other means'. The Bill did not pass through Parliament until 1821, and was amended shortly afterwards to allow the use of locomotives. This was at the insistence of George Stephenson, who had been responsible for laying the track. The first rail was laid in May 1822 and the work was completed in September 1825.

The opening of the line was a solemn occasion with a train of 34 waggons drawn by the locomotive *Locomotion* and driven by George Stephenson. The train weighed more than 90 tons and no fewer than 600 people had taken their places in the coal trucks and the single passenger coach. A flag-bearing horseman preceded the convoy. Horses and locomotives combined to pull the train along, and on the Brusselton and Etherley gradients stationary engines were used.

In the early days, on payment of a fee, private individuals could use this line and, indeed, several others. They could use their own horses to pull their trucks, or couple their trucks to the regular trains. This type of use was based on the system operating on the canals, but it soon proved to have drawbacks. Trains for passenger use only did not run until after 1833.

The *Locomotion*, still in working order and carrying the No. 1 of the North Eastern Railway, is on display in Darlington Station. Restored, following an explosion, it ran until 1846. It is a 10-horsepower engine, and had an operating weight of 6½ tons. Its speed was limited to a few miles per hour, which was sufficient for transporting coal. Moreover, the lack of pressure in this class of engine often allowed drivers to sit on the embankment and quietly smoke a pipe. The low return on investment and the high cost of locomotives threatened the company in about 1827 and steam traction was almost abandoned.

George Stephenson's *Locomotion* (1825).

(Preserved at Darlington station)

The oldest locomotive in the world: William Hedley's *Puffing Billy*, built at Wylam in 1813 and still in service in 1864.

Left, rear view; *right*, front view. (Science Museum, London)

Two locomotives from the Rainhill Trials (1829), preserved in the Science Museum, London.

Left, Robert Stephenson's *Rocket*; *right*, Timothy Hackworth's *Sans Pareil*.

THE FORERUNNERS OF TODAY'S LOCOMOTIVES

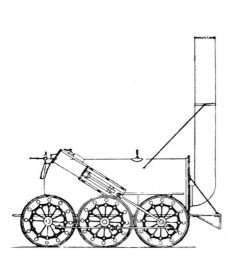

Robert Stephenson's first *Rocket* (1829).

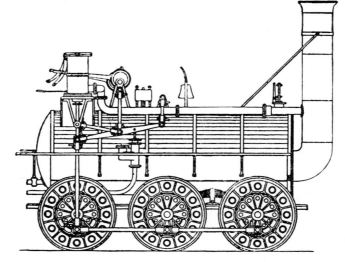

Timothy Hackworth's *Royal George* (1827).
(*Newcomen Society Transactions*, Vol. II)

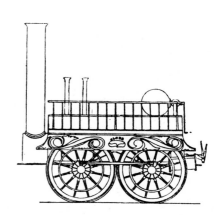

Timothy Hackworth's *Globe* (1830).

THE DEVELOPMENT OF LOCOMOTIVES

Major developments in locomotives occurred in England in the period between the opening of the Stockton & Darlington Railway and the Rainhill Trials, that is from 1825 to 1829. The two great pioneers who produced the most interesting work were Timothy Hackworth and George Stephenson, the latter being replaced in 1828 by his son, Robert, who had returned from America.

For a long time, railway historians ignored the part played by Hackworth. As an engineer with the Stockton & Darlington Railway he had collaborated with George Stephenson and had certainly influenced Stephenson's designs of the engines built from 1825 onwards.

In 1827 it was Hackworth who was given the task of making use of the boiler of the *Chittapratt*, an experimental engine built by R. Wilson. It had been the first engine to operate with four cylinders, but had not been a success. Using this boiler he built the *Royal George*, which was the most powerful engine of its time and offered features of particular interest: it was the first engine with six wheels coupled by external rods, the first whose rods were linked directly with the wheels and the first whose exhaust tube had a narrowed end to increase the steam blast and thus activate the draught. In spite of its faults, in particular its vertical cylinders, the *Royal George* was a success and a timely one, since the Stockton & Darlington Railway Company had been preparing to abandon the locomotive as a result of the inefficiency of its earlier engines. The *Royal George* operated up to 1842.

Later, Hackworth built many engines, all of which embodied the impressive features of the *Royal George*. He remained faithful to the return tube with the result that until about 1840 his engines had two tenders, one near the chimney for the coal and the fireman, the other at the opposite end for water and the driver. During the same period, Foster and Rastrick of Stourbridge produced several engines of the Killingworth balance-wheel type. One of these was the *Stourbridge Lion* which was sent with two others to America, and another was the *Agenoria* which worked until 1864 and still exists.

The first two locomotives to operate in France are not well known, but arrived from England in March and April 1928: following a journey to England by Marc Seguin, the Saint-Etienne Railway Company in Lyons bought from Stephenson two second-hand engines which do not seem to have been the best which England produced. The idea was to obtain engines with a view to building them in France. The two locomotives with their tenders cost £550 each. One was sent to the Hallette workshops in Arras. Judging from a drawing which must have represented a design project of some description, this engine was extremely basic, with two vertical cylinders at the rear operating two semi-balance wheels which were as long as the boiler. These drove the rear wheels which in turn were coupled to the front wheels by a system of gears. The second engine was sent to Marc Seguin in Lyons, and clearly inspired all his early locomotives: it had two vertical cylinders positioned in the middle of the engine and fairly low-down, with rods on each side which connected to a balance-wheel. This in turn was linked at each end by a con-rod which drove the wheels, the latter being coupled by another rod. The firebox was at the front. This locomotive must have been in experimental use on the Stockton & Darlington Railway, and it served as such in France.

It appears quite probable that the drawing which was found is not that of the engine Hallette received, but rather a design for a locomotive which was never built. The two engines bought from Stephenson must have been similar, in fact like the one we see in the other drawing.

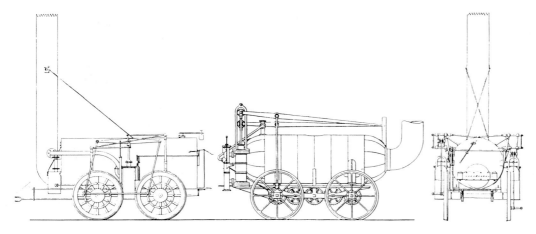

The first locomotives sent to France (1828) for the Saint-Etienne–Lyons Railway.
Left and right: engine built by G. and R. Stephenson and sent as a model to Marc Seguin in Lyons;
Centre: drawing presumed to be of engine sent to Hallete in Arras.
(*Newcomen Society Transactions*, Vol. III)

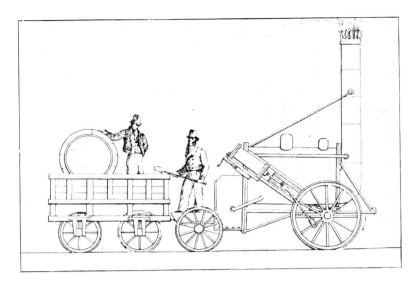

Rainhill Trials' locomotives (1829) in their original state.
Left: Robert Stephenson's *Rocket*, the winner of the competition. *Right*: Ericcson and Braithwaite's *Novelty*.

THE RAINHILL TRIALS

The decisive event which was to create the locomotive with all those features which characterise steam railways in the 1930s was the Rainhill Trials. The directors of the Liverpool & Manchester Railway were unsure about the future. Various commissions had failed to enable them to reach a decision in the choice between stationary engines and locomotives. The practical applications of the latter seemed limited. Nevertheless, the directors came to the conclusion that they offered more scope for development than stationary engines, and on 25 April 1829 they published details of a competition offering a prize of £500 'for the most improved form of locomotive'. The conditions were: the track would measure 4 ft 8½ in. in width, the engines were to be six-wheel engines fitted with springs and weighing not more than 6 tons; engines not exceeding 4½ tons were allowed to have only four wheels; the 6-ton engines were to pull on a level track a 20-ton train at a speed of 10 m.p.h. The competition took place from 6 to 14 October 1829 on their own line at Rainhill. The engines were to travel a distance of 1¾ miles.

In spite of the huge interest created by this decisive trial there is no contemporary picture of it. On the other hand there is no shortage of newspaper accounts. In the *Liverpool Courier* of 7 October we read: 'Spectators lined both sides of the track for 1½ miles. It is difficult to estimate the number of people, but at a modest estimate there cannot have been fewer than 10,000. Some gentlemen even claimed there to be 15,000. However that may be, never probably has the number of scientists and engineers meeting together in one place exceeded yesterday's gathering. The interesting, important nature of the tests brought them from every corner of the country to witness a demonstration which could well change fundamentally communications within our land . . . '.

Five engines took part. Ericsson and Braithwaite's *Novelty*, built in seven weeks, was mounted on four wheels with suspension, one pair of the wheels being driven by two vertical cylinders. The boiler, 10 ft long and 13 in. in diameter, had a fire-tube which ran the length of it three times. Air was fed into the closed firebox by two bellows. With its supplies of water and coke the locomotive weighed nearly 4 tons.

Timothy Hackworth's *Sans Pareil* also had four wheels and two vertical cylinders. A return tube ran from the firebox to the chimney, both of which were on the same side of the engine. The *Sans Pareil* was allowed to run even though its weight of 4.77 tons exceeded the limit (4.60 tons).

Timothy Burstall's *Perseverance* was a small, four-wheel engine with a vertical boiler, and weighed only 2.85 tons. The picture reproduced here is taken from the only drawing of it which exists.

The *Rocket* is the prototype for all subsequent models. It was entered by George and Robert Stephenson and Henry Booth, but was the personal work of Robert Stephenson. However, Booth, who was the company secretary, suggested the use of the tubular chimney. It appears certain that this was quite simply a copy of Marc Seguin's chimney. The *Rocket* had two driving wheels at the front, 4 ft 8 in. in diameter, and two 2 ft 6 in. carrying wheels at the rear. The cylinders were positioned at the rear and inclined at an angle of 35 degrees. The boiler contained 25 brass tubes each with a diameter of 0.30 in. The operating weight was 4¼ tons.

Brandreth's *Cycloped* was not allowed to compete. This was an engine pulled by two horses walking on a moving platform of the treadmill type.

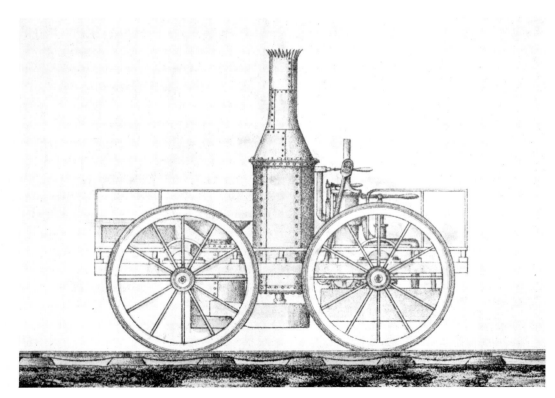

Timothy Burstall's *Perseverance*, which took part in the Rainhill Trials (1829).

№ 2.

LIVERPOOL, OCTOBER 5, 1829.

A LIST OF THE ENGINES

Entered to contend at RAINHILL, on the 6th of OCTOBER instant,

FOR

THE PREMIUM OF £500,

OFFERED BY

The Directors of the Liverpool and Manchester Rail-road,

FOR THE

BEST LOCOMOTIVE POWER.

No. 1.—Messrs. Braithwaite and Erickson, of London; "The Novelty;" Copper and Blue; weight 2T. 15CWT.

2.—Mr. Ackworth, of Darlington; "The Sans Pareil;" Green, Yellow, and Black; weight 4T. 8CWT. 2Q.

3.—Mr. Robert Stephenson, Newcastle-upon-Tyne; "The Rocket;" Yellow and Black, White Chimney; weight 4T. 3CWT.

4.—Mr. Brandreth, of Liverpool; "The Cycloped;" weight 3 Tons; worked by a Horse.

5.—Mr. Burstall, Edinburgh; "The Perseverance;" Red Wheels; weight 2T. 17CWT.

The Engines to be ready at Ten o'Clock on Tuesday Morning. The Running Ground will be on the Manchester side of the Rainhill Bridge.

The Load attached to each Engine will be three times the weight of the Engine.

No Person, except the Directors and Engineers will be permitted to enter or cross the Rail-road.

J. U. RASTRICK, Esq., Stourbridge, C.E.
NICHOLAS WOOD, Esq., Killingworth, C.E. } Judges.
JOHN KENNEDY, Esq., Manchester,

Rail-way Office, Liverpool, 25th April, 1829.

STIPULATIONS AND CONDITIONS

On which the Directors of the Liverpool and Manchester Rail-way offer a Premium of £500 for the most improved Locomotive Engine.

1st.—The said Engine must "effectually consume its own smoke," according to the provisions of the Rail-way Act, 7th Geo. IV.

2d.—The Engine, if it weighs Six Tons, must be capable of drawing after it, day by day, on a well-constructed Rail-way, on a level plane, a Train of Carriages of the gross weight of Twenty Tons, including the Tender and Water Tank, at the rate of Ten Miles per Hour, with a pressure of steam in the boiler not exceeding 50lb on the square inch.

3d.—There must be two Safety Valves, one of which must be completely out of the reach or control of the Engine-man, and neither of which must be fastened down while the Engine is working.

4th.—The Engine and Boiler must be supported on Springs, and rest on Six Wheels; and the height, from the ground to the top of the Chimney, must not exceed Fifteen Feet.

5th.—The weight of the Machine, with its complement of water in the Boiler, must, at most, not exceed Six Tons; and a Machine of less weight will be preferred if it draw after it a proportionate weight; and if the weight of the Engine, &c. do not exceed Five Tons, then the gross weight to be drawn need not exceed Fifteen Tons; and in that proportion for Machines of still smaller weight—provided that the Engine, &c. shall still be on six wheels, unless the weight (as above) be reduced to Four Tons and a Half, or under, in which case the Boiler, &c. may be placed on four wheels. And the Company shall be at liberty to put the Boiler, Fire Tube, Cylinders, &c. to the test of a pressure of water not exceeding 150lb per square inch, without being answerable for any damage the Machine may receive in consequence.

6th.—There must be a Mercurial Gauge affixed to the Machine, with Index Rod, showing the Steam Pressure above 45 pounds per square inch; and constructed to blow out at a Pressure of 60 pounds per inch.

7th.—The Engine to be delivered complete for trial, at the Liverpool end of the Rail-way, not later than the 1st of October next.

8th.—The price of the Engine, which may be accepted, not to exceed £550, delivered on the Rail-way; and any Engine not approved to be taken back by the Owner.

N.B.—The Rail-way Company will provide the Engine Tender with a supply of Water and Fuel, for the experiment. The distance within the Rails is four feet eight inches and a half.

List of engines taking part, and rules of the Rainhill Trials in 1829.
(Dendy Marshall Collection)

The *Rocket* and the *Sans Pareil* were the first to be tested on 6 October. Then it was the turn of the *Novelty*. This engine made a more favourable impression on the spectators than the first two, and even after the *Rocket*'s victory it seems that the engineers present were disappointed. One spectator made the comment: 'Braithwaite and Ericsson's engine was generally accepted as being in appearance and line the "ideal shape" for a locomotive. Its speed surprised, amazed and excited all those present. It seemed to be in flight, and offered us one of the most sublime examples of the genius and courage of man that the world has ever witnessed.' Its speed was 28 miles per hour. However, the following day, it suffered a burst bellow.

On 8 October, the judges requested that the engines cover virtually non-stop a distance of 70 miles at an average speed of at least 10 miles per hour. The *Rocket* completed the test at an average speed of 16 miles per hour and with a maximum speed of 29 miles per hour.

On 10 October, after a bitter argument, the *Novelty* continued the trials, but not without problems. It did, however, succeed in pulling at a speed of 30 miles per hour a coach containing 45 people who, at that speed, could 'scarcely see the objects they passed'.

On 13 October, the *Sans Pareil* attempted the test, but was hindered by various problems, one of which was its extremely high coke consumption. The next day, the *Novelty* was forced to abandon the trials, as was the *Perseverance*.

The prize was awarded to the *Rocket*, and the engine was bought by the company. Some time later, the *Rocket* travelled 4 miles at a speed of almost 53 miles per hour, and proved itself capable of climbing average gradients. It owes its success primarily to the tubular boiler, but also to the clever positioning of the firebox.

Brandreth's *Cycloped* (1829): drawing taken from the original patent.
(Science Museum, London)

The race between Peter Cooper's *Tom Thumb* and the horse-drawn waggon on the Baltimore & Ohio R.R. in 1830.

(Taken from a drawing by Brown)

HORSE TRACTION

In the early years of the railways, horses were still the normal means of traction and on certain lines this system was maintained for a long time. When locomotives were first being developed, lines were used for mechanical and animal traction, both because of a lack of confidence in the new machines and also because they were anyway in short supply.

The first railway-line to operate on the European Continent was the line running from Budweiss to Linz in Austria. Franz Anton von Gerstner obtained the concession for this line on 7 September 1824, after tests carried out on a small track between Vienna and the Prater. In this way he put into practice the ideas of his father, Franz Josef von Gerstner, who in 1813 had published a plan to link the Danube and the Moldau by rail.

The first section, from Budweiss on the Moldau to Trojanov, ran for at least 33 miles which, at that time, was by far the longest railway in the world. It was inaugurated on 7 September 1827. Von Gerstner then left for Russia but the work was continued by Mathias von Schönerer, and the line reached Mauthausen on the Danube and was then extended to Linz. This line was used principally to transport salt but passengers and other

Detmole's *Flying Dutchman* on the
South Carolina R.R.

(Drawing by Brown)

goods were also carried on it. On 21 July 1832, the Emperor Francis and the Empress Caroline Augusta travelled on this railway-line from Magdalena to Anhof. A passenger-coach of the time can be found in the Technisches Museum in Vienna. This coach, which is the ancestor of all subsequent railway-coaches, bears a strange similarity to a post-chaise. Although it is difficult to believe, animal traction continued up to 1856 on the Linz-Gmunden section and up to 1872 between Budweiss and Linz. This delay in implementing the work of Gerstner, a true railway pioneer and a keen supporter of locomotives, is quite astonishing. However, from 1829, the development of this line as far as Gmunden continued under the engineer Franz Zola, the father of novelist Emile Zola.

In Austria, the horse-traction network of lines was extensive. In 1836 it covered 158 miles. On 20 August 1827, the first animal-traction railway-line in Hungary was opened between Pesth and Kobanya. It was used to transport material from a quarry but, after several months, the line was closed. In Germany in 1825, at Nymphenburg near Dresden, Counsellor Baader built a line to demonstrate horse traction.

In the United States, animal traction was extremely common on all the early wooden and iron railroads. In fact, the early locomotives could

A view of the first Austrian railway, from Linz to Budweiss, in 1839.

The first horse-railway passenger service from Linz to Budweiss (1832).

(Courtesy of the Œsterreichischen Bundesbahnen)

Horse-drawn goods train on the Saint-Etienne–Lyons Railway (1832).
(A lithograph by Engelmann: Jean de Montgolfier Collection)

not be used on certain lines, because the tracks had been built quickly and flimsily with horse traction only in mind.

The first line in the United States was built in 1826–27 at Quincy, Massachusetts, and it ran for 3 miles between a granite quarry and the river Neponset. In 1827, a further line, 9 miles long, was laid between the coal-mines of Monch Chunk in Pennsylvania and the river Lehigh, and then, in 1828, another line was laid from Carbondale to Honesdale, taking coal along the Delaware Canal to the Hudson. But the company which led the way in the United States was the Baltimore & Ohio. It was this company which persuaded America to develop its railroads, and it was on the company's own line in 1830 that the famous race between a horse-drawn waggon and Peter Cooper's small experimental locomotive *Tom Thumb* took place. The race was won by the horse. Nevertheless, the advantages of steam had been clearly demonstrated, and this ensured the rapid development of the locomotive throughout North America. At the same time, engines such as Brandreth's 'cycloped' continued to operate, in particular on the Baltimore & Ohio and the South Carolina lines. In fact, in 1829 the latter company offered a prize of 500 dollars for the best horse-drawn engine. This was won by A.C. Detmole with the *Flying Dutchman*. This engine, carrying

The oldest passenger-coach in the world: horse-drawn coach from the Linz-Budweiss Railway (1832).
(Technisches Museum, Vienna)

12 passengers, travelled at a speed of 12 m.p.h. on the Charleston-Hamburg line.

In France, horse traction hardly existed, except on the lines running from Saint-Etienne to Lyons, Andrézieux and Roanne. From 1827 to 1844, horses were the only means of traction on the line running from Saint-Etienne to Andrézieux, as they were between 1830 and 1832 on the Saint-Etienne-Lyons line. For two or three years after that date they continued to operate alongside the locomotives. In Belgium, horses were still used in the coal-mines and both horse traction and locomotives operated in 1835 and 1836, the first years of the German and Russian railways.

Apart from the lines used by certain mines and canals, the first railway-line in England requiring an Act of Parliament was the Surrey Iron Railway, which ran from Wandsworth to Croydon. This line came into service on 26 July 1803 and was a horse-traction line. In England, a curious feature of the early horse-traction lines, such as the Stockton & Darlington Railway, was that private individuals could use the track for their own private transportation, making use of their own stock, providing they fulfilled certain conditions and paid the necessary fee. This system, based largely on the rules and conditions governing the use of canals, was also adopted in France.

The horse locomotive of C.A. Steinheil of Berlin, tested in 1853.
(Railway Museum, Utrecht)

Photograph of a horse train on the Linz–Budweiss line, still in service about 1872.
(Courtesy of Ceskoslovensky Zeleznickni)

The first train pulled by Miller's *Best Friend* on the South Carolina Railroad (1830).

(From a drawing by Brown)

THE FIRST LOCOMOTIVES IN AMERICA

In 1812, John Stevens spoke in favour of the establishment in the United States of railways which would use steam traction, and he predicted that such engines would achieve high speeds. In 1825, in Hoboken, he gave a demonstration using a tiny locomotive which had smooth wheels and was guided by a lug between two central rails. In 1828, Horatio Allen, an engineer with the Delaware & Hudson Canal, bought four British engines, three from Foster & Rastrick and one from Stephenson. Rastrick's *Stourbridge Lion*, which was tested in Honesdale on 8 August 1829 on a line built by Jervis, was the first real locomotive to run in America, but the track broke beneath its weight and it was not used again.

Mississippi, for the Natchez & Hamburg R.R. (1834).

(Photo: Moore)

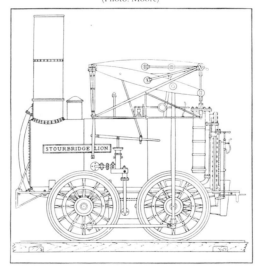

The Baltimore & Ohio Railroad was the first great American railroad company. The laying of its line began on 4 July 1828, and it was only 14 miles long when, in September 1829, it was used to test the first locomotive built in the United States, Peter Cooper's *Tom Thumb*, a vertical-boiler locomotive. This test ensured the future development of locomotives in America and, in 1831, the B & O offered a 4,000 dollar prize which was won by Phineas Davis' vertical-boiler engine the *York*. The B & O still has its 1832 *Atlantic* in working order.

In 1830, the South Carolina Railroad used Miller's *Best Friend*, and, in 1831, the Mohawk & Hudson Railroad, managed by Robert Stevens, took possession of Jervis' *De Witt Clinton* and Stephenson's *John Bull*. In 1832, Jervis and Baldwin built the first American-style locomotive, with a pivoting bogie at the front.

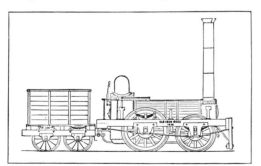

Baldwin's first locomotive, *Old Ironsides* (1831).

Foster and Rastrick's *Stourbridge Lion* – the first locomotive to run on rails in America (1829).

(*Newcomen Society Transactions*, Vol. IV)

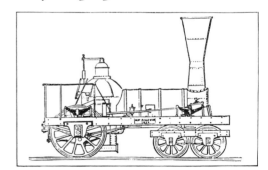

Baldwin's *E-L Miller* (1834).

The first train to run in New York State on the Mohawk & Hudson R.R., pulled by the locomotive *De Witt Clinton* (1831).

(National Museum, Washington)

The Gier Valley, showing Saint-Etienne–Lyons railway trains moving by force of gravity,
and, on the left, a mine railway using stationary engines.

THE FIRST RAILWAYS IN FRANCE AND MARC SEGUIN

Apart from a few tracks for coal-mines, there was no railway in existence in France when, sometime prior to 1804, James Henderson suggested to the First Consul a 'plan to build iron roads with steam trucks'. In 1814, the mining engineer, Moisson-Destroches, sent to Napoleon a memorandum on the possibility of shortening distances by 'the creation of seven great iron ways'. Finally, in 1818, his colleague, de Gallois, published in his *Annales des Mines* a memorandum on the railways and tramways in England.

It was in the area around Saint-Etienne that railways were first developed in France, not only the tracks themselves, but steam traction as well. Three lines were built almost simultaneously. On 5 May 1821, on the initiative of the engineer, Louis-Antoine Beaunier, a company consisting of Messrs Lur-Saluces, Milleret, Bricogne, Hochet and Boigues applied for the concession for a railway to run from Saint-Etienne to the Loire and this was granted on 26 February 1823 by Royal Decree. The line would simply be used for the transportation of coal, coke and goods. In spite of 'the most determined and backward-looking opposition' from the owners of land along the route, the line was opened between Saint-Etienne and Andrézieux towards the end of May 1827. The line was 178 miles long and had cost in total 1,554,000 francs, including 230,000 francs for tools and equipment. Until 1844, only horse traction was used on this line. On 21

August 1827, Countess Bertrand travelled the whole length of the line on a truck, and on 1 March 1832 a public passenger service was inaugurated.

On 27 March 1826, the Highways Department granted to a company whose members included the Seguin brothers and Edouard Biot permission to build and run a railway between Saint-Etienne and Lyons. Marc, Camille, Paul and Charles Seguin were the nephews of the Montgolfier brothers, celebrated balloonists. All were skilled engineers. Marc Seguin, the eldest of the brothers, was born on 20 April 1786 in Annonay and died on 24 August 1875 in Varagnes. In the history of the railways, he played a major role. Not only was he the pioneer of mechanical traction on the Continent but he invented the tubular boiler for the locomotive. He was a fascinating man, not only an inventor and an engineer but also an intellectual who loved science for its own sake. He was responsible for the theory of the mechanical equivalent of heat (1824), the construction of the first suspension bridges (from 1823 onwards), and the building of the first great tunnels (about 1827). Edouard Biot was the son of the scientist J.B. Biot.

Twenty-three people, almost all from Paris, invested in the company some investing more than 2,000,000 francs, a remarkable fact at a time when little was known about the railways and 'the company spirit was not understood or widely practised'. It is true, on the other hand, that some speculators were simply waiting for share prices to rise in order to sell their investments. Work began on 28 June 1826, and was long and difficult, the route being an extremely complicated one. It was initially estimated that the cost of buying the

land would be 120,000 francs. This then increased to 600,000 francs, that is about 1 franc per square yard, and finally rose to 3,633,310 francs. Ninety per cent of landowners accepted the price offered but others held out and obtained huge sums of money. An embankment was built which required over 2 million cubic feet of soil, and the Terrenoire (nearly a mile long), Rive-de-Gier, and Lyons Tunnels were constructed with the primitive equipment of the time, but using the highly skilled workers demanded by the Seguin brothers. The company then ran into severe financial problems and was further troubled by the 1830 Revolution.

Marc Seguin wrote: 'On 25 June 1830, the second section of the railway running from Givors to Rive-de-Gier was completed and opened to the public, with 100 coaches which run daily. On 3 April 1832, the first Lyons to Givors section was completed and opened to the public, and coaches ran regularly providing a passenger and goods service. On 18 October 1832, the third section from Rive-de-Gier to Saint-Etienne was opened to the public but only for the carrying of passengers. On this section the carriage of goods did not begin until 25 February 1833. Up to 31 October 1835, this railway had cost the sum of 15,340,000 francs'.

Seguin had decided not to use stationary engines. He had several times visited English railways and had studied the locomotives, and in 1828 he bought the two engines already mentioned. Meanwhile, having realised the need to produce more steam, he conceived the idea of a multi-tubular boiler. Such a possibility had already been suggested by certain inventors, and a small-scale rough model had been built as early as

MARC SEGUIN
1786–1875

Painting by W. Bennett (1822).
(Courtesy of M. Roger Seguin)

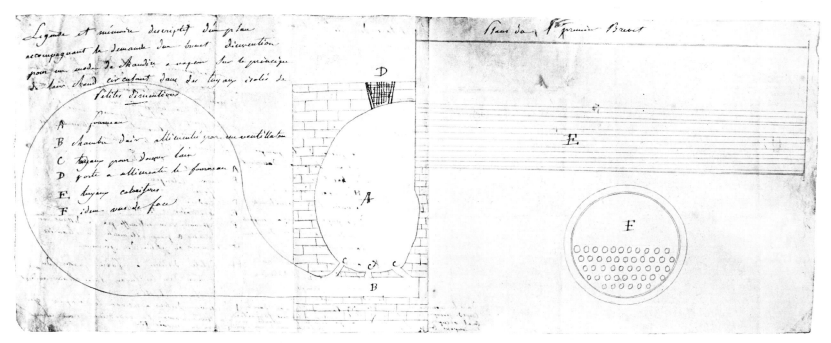

An original drawing taken from Marc Seguin's tubular-boiler patent, 12 December 1827.
(Office national de la propriété industrielle)

1784 by the Marquis de Jouffroy though a large-scale version had never been tested. In 1827, Marc Seguin built a fixed boiler measuring 10 feet long by 32 inches, with an outside firebox and containing 43 horizontal parallel tubes 1½ inches in diameter. These provided 2645 lbs of steam pressure per hour, with the draught being forced through by a fan. On 12 December 1827, he applied for a patent, which he received on 22 February 1828.

The purpose was clear. Seguin had built his boiler for a locomotive and, in May 1829, he had one in an advanced state of construction in his Perrache workshops. Work started on the *Rocket* at about the same time, but it was completed more quickly and the *Rocket* underwent its first tests between 1 and 5 September, in order to take part in the Rainhill Trials on 6 October.

Seguin's locomotive was finished on 1 October. On that date, he wrote from Lyons to his wife: 'I arrived here and I found my engine completed. I immediately lit the fire and it completely fulfilled all my hopes'. Unfortunately, he did not give sufficient details for us to be sure whether the engine actually completed a journey on that date. It is likely that he was simply referring to tests carried out on the boiler. The first confirmation of an actual test run, although at a later date than the *Rocket*'s, is found in a report given by Humblot-Conte to the French Parliament on 21 December 1829:

'Two tests have taken place, one on the 7th November, the other on the 12th. In the first, the fire in M. Seguin's engine was lit at half-past-eleven and at six minutes past mid-day it commenced manoeuvring on a test railway approximately 140 metres [about 150 yards] long. This track was built in the Perrache yards and it presents the greatest problems which an engine could encounter on an actual line, namely a 16mm [1 in 63] gradient and a bend with a 500-metre [about 1600 feet] radius. The engine pulled four waggons laden with 15 tons of cast iron. There-fore, if we add the weight of the load to the weight of the waggons, it pulled 19 tons up a slope. This manoeuvre was effected with the greatest of ease. The engine was then stopped in the middle of the steepest part of the slope so as to verify that it could overcome this problem without being assisted by its momentum. After a few seconds rest, it set off once again without the slightest difficulty. The manoeuvres continued for almost an hour with the same degree of success. Uphill, it moved at a speed of 2 metres [about 6 feet] per second. Two men standing on the first truck were sufficient to work the engine.

'On the 12th, with all my inspectors present, the test was less successful. It was, in fact, our presence which was indirectly the cause of this. Because we were expected, everything had been greased with the greatest care and in fact more than was required. The warmed grease flowed on to the wheels of the engine and on to the rails in such a way that the wheels, instead of being helped by the friction to set the trucks in motion, slipped on the rails. Although they tried to clean the grease off, its effect was felt during the whole of the test. In spite of this inconvenience, how-ever, they were able to increase the number of trucks pulled to six, and the weight of the load to 17½ tons, but the engine speed was slowed by this load and it could not pull the six trucks when the load was increased to 18 tons.'

A second engine was completed in June 1830, shortly after a second patent was taken out, dated 25 March 1830, describing the tubular boiler with particular reference to locomotives, but Seguin himself tells us that 'some faults in the building of the boiler prevented the engine from providing a regular service. The engines did not begin to operate a service until January 1831.'

Seguin's locomotive was built with a return fire-tube. Air entered the firebox by means of two fans which were coupled to the wheels of the tender, this arrangement allowing him to shorten the smoke-stack. The water-feed was contained in the area around the firebox and the bottom of the boiler. The positioning of the cylinders and of the wooden wheels was borrowed from Stevenson. Marc Seguin built twelve engines of this type, increasing the height of the smoke-stack in order to avoid the need for fans. The first weighed only six tons but Seguin was forced to strengthen them to compensate for the lack of care taken by his French workforce.

A passenger service preceded the date given by Seguin, because as early as 20 December 1831 we read in a report: 'In the last six months we have taken receipts of 3,233 francs and 8 centimes from the conveyance of passengers. That is not to say that the passengers were given well-prepared carriages in which to travel; they were in fact simply a few empty waggons, often the ones used to carry coal, and the number of centimes which we have taken shows quite clearly the cost of a journey. It was not the upper class whom we carried but the working people and it is the working people who make the greatest use of this kind of transport'. It must be added that the railway quickly provided attractive covered carriages with an upper and lower deck for both first- and second-class passgners.

Following a series of disagreements, Seguin left the company in 1834. Under the terms of its agreement, the company could change its prices as it saw fit and it became very unpopular. The third railway was built between Andrézieux and Roanne by Mellet and Henry, two of the most active of the early French engineers. The purpose of this railway was to extend the earlier line to a navigable point on the Loire. The concession was granted in 1825 and the work carried out between 1829 and 1833. Transport was provided by two English locomotives as well as by horses. However, the company became bankrupt following financial difficulties. Reformed with a loan from the State, it struggled along until it merged with the railway company which linked the Rhone and the Loire.

Voitures pour voyageurs descendant sans chev

Convoi de waggons chargés de houille

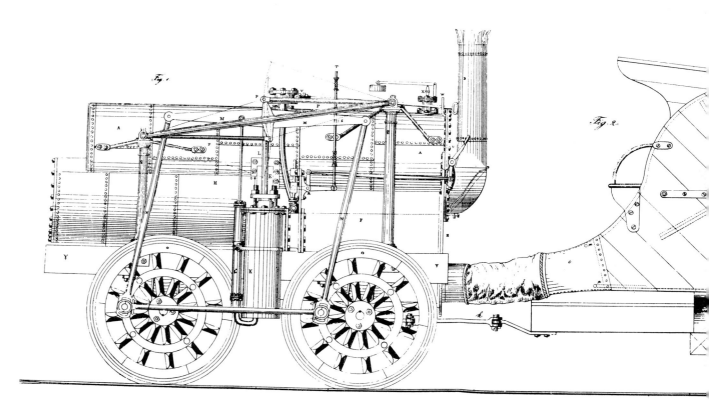

FIRST RAILWAY IN FRANCE,
BETWEEN SAINT-ETIENNE AND LYONS,
BUILT BY MARC SEGUIN

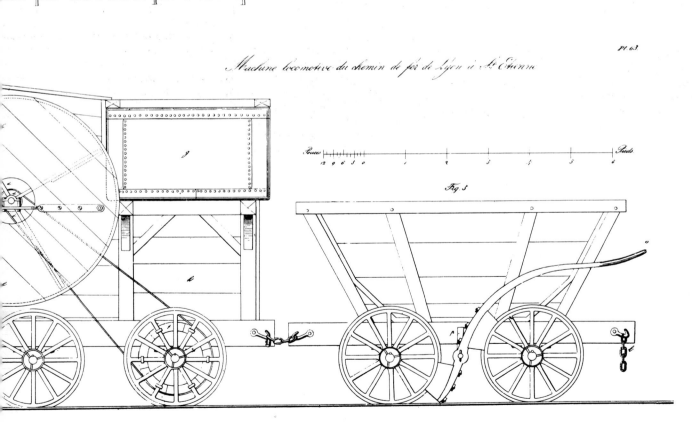

Above: Passenger-coaches without horses or engine proceeding downhill by gravity
from Saint-Etienne to Givors, and coal waggons hauled by a Seguin locomotive.

(Lithograph by Engelmann: Jean de Montgolfier Collection)

Below: Marc Seguin's first tubular-boiler locomotive.

(From the *Bulletin de la Société industrielle de Mulhouse*, Bibliothèque nationale, Paris)

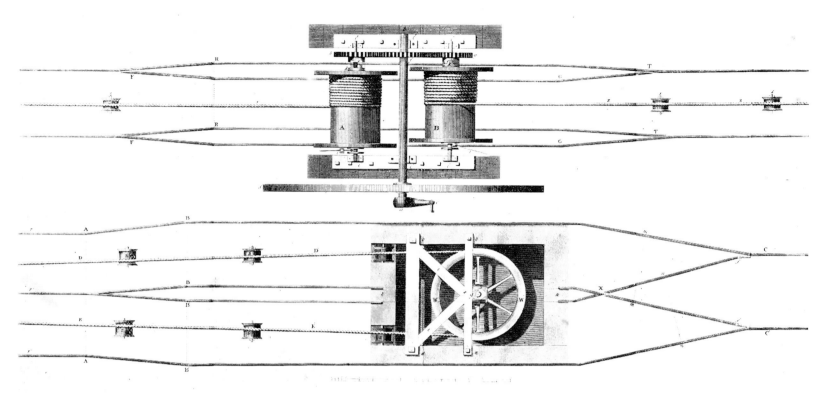

Above: stationary engine placed at the top of a double slope to haul two trains simultaneously. Used about 1825, near Newcastle.
Below: stationary engine used to haul wagons up and let others down simultaneously on a single slope.

TRACTION BY STATIONARY ENGINE

Until 1830, lack of power in the early locomotives, the weakness of the rails themselves which often broke, and fear of the lack of adhesion, caused railway entrepreneurs to use funicular systems based upon gravity or upon the use of stationary engines to move trains along sloping tracks.

The gravitational system has already been described. To avoid the use of horses to pull trucks back up the slope, another system was devised in Britain at the end of the eighteenth century. Under this system, the loaded trucks went downhill along the track, pulling a rope which passed through a pulley at the top of the slope. By this means, and without any further energy being

expended, the convoy of empty trucks was hauled back up the hill along a parallel track or even along the same track fitted with loop lines. The pulley was fitted with brakes to control the speed of the descent.

In 1808, in Birthy Fell in County Durham, S. Cooke was the first to build a stationary steam-engine to haul mineral trains up the hill from the mine in Inpeth. Since then many similar engines have been built near Newcastle and on the Continent. These engines positioned at the top of the hill worked in two ways. Either they turned two drums which simultaneously drew in up both slopes ropes which, passing through guide pulleys, hauled up the trucks, or they operated a length of rope which turned continuously in a full circle, the trucks being attached to it. This idea was used once again some years ago in Paris on the Belleville funicular railway. To achieve a constant level of tension and counter the differences in humidity, a shaft was sunk. The rope was

fed into the shaft and with the help of a pulley it supported a weight which maintained the correct tension. In 1833, Saxton suggested that the circulating rope should be fed on to a drum fixed to a vehicle so that it could drive one of the wheels.

The most noteworthy of these engines were the ones built on the major lines, such as the Brusselton and Greenfield lines and the Stockton & Darlington line, and, of course, the engine used in the Liverpool Tunnel on the Liverpool–Manchester line. In practice these engines were soon replaced by locomotives. In 1838, Maudslay built and installed one of these engines in Camden Town on the London–Birmingham line, to pull trains up the slope out of Euston. Then, in 1840, he constructed two more pairs of stationary engines at Minories on the London–Blackwall line. Some idea of the performance of these engines can be gauged from the following figures: rope traction was 224 horse power, train traction 73 h.p., and friction 26 h.p., giving a total of 323 h.p.

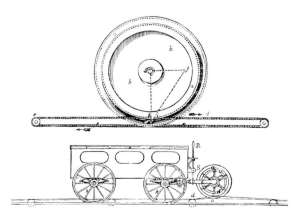

Saxton's stationary engine-cable turns a driving-wheel (1833).

Brusselton's stationary engine on the Stockton & Darlington Railway (1825).
(Science Museum, London)

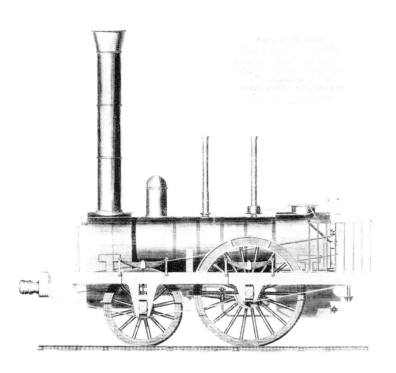

Robert Stephenson's four-wheeled *Planet* (1830).

Robert Stephenson's four-wheeled *Samson*. From a model by Clair (1833).

(Conservatoire des arts et métiers)

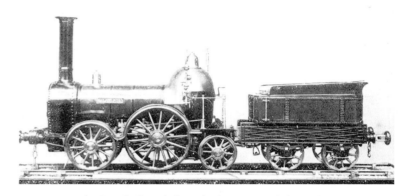

The *Bury*, built with four wheels in 1832 and changed to
a six-wheeled locomotive about 1840.

(Model from Science Museum, London)

FROM FOUR WHEELS TO SIX WHEELS

The modern steam locomotive, although a much improved version of Robert Stephenson's locomotive, is still built on the same principles.

In 1830, in the *Northumbrian*, we find the oldest example of the modern boiler, that is, a multi-tubular boiler with 132 tubes and incorporating a firebox and a smokebox. Moreover, its cylinders were almost horizontal. *Invicta*, built in the same year for the Canterbury & Whitstable railway, is the oldest locomotive to have its cylinders at the front of the engine but still at a very inclined angle.

Immediately after 1831, Robert Stephenson combined these ideas to create the design which is still in use today. In 1831, he put into service on the Liverpool–Manchester line locomotives of the *Planet* and *Samson* types. The *Planet* type had a driving-wheel and a carrying-wheel of unequal diameter, the *Samson* type had wheels of equal size, in some instances coupled and with a rear driving-axle. In both types the cylinders were horizontal.

These two types of locomotives are the precursors of six-wheel engines. The instability of four-wheel engines, and the considerable load on each axle, soon caused Robert Stephenson to add a carrying-axle to the rear of the firebox. Thus, in December 1833 he built goods engines of the 0–4–2 class, and in the same year produced the

first express locomotive of the 2–2–2 class, the *Patentee*, which proved to be a model copied all over the world and used in England up to 1894. A strange and not widely known feature of these engines was that their driving-wheels were not flanged, which enabled them to negotiate bends more easily. In 1834, Forrester's *Vauxhall* was the first engine to have outside horizontal cylinders placed at the front of the engine.

Thus, in a period lasting not more than five years the locomotive had found its permanent shape. The illustrations on this page show how this change occurred, as the locomotive evolved from the *Planet* type to the six-wheeled express locomotive, and from the *Samson* type to the goods engine.

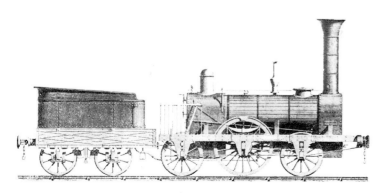

Stephenson's six-wheeled *Patentee* (1834).

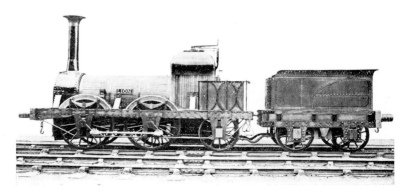

Todd, Kitson & Laird's six-wheeled *Lion*, built in 1838, restored about 1930.

(Photograph: Moore)

LOCOMOTIVES BUILT BY ROBERT STEPHENSON FOR THE LIVERPOOL & MANCHESTER RAILWAY IN 1831

Above: Planet. Below: Northumbrian.

Opening of the Liverpool & Manchester Railway, 15 September 1830.
The official train stops in front of the Moorish Arch in Liverpool station. (Engraving by I. Shaw.)

THE DEVELOPMENT OF THE RAILWAYS IN BRITAIN

The first main line and the precursor of all other lines in terms of rolling stock and use was the Liverpool–Manchester railway. The idea for this steam railway belongs to William James (1771–1837), a man full of enterprise but unable to put his ideas into practice, and to Sanders, who was the first to finance this railway. A company was founded in 1824 in Liverpool. At the time it was envisaged that the line would be used principally to carry goods, passengers being only briefly mentioned in the initial prospectus and locomotive traction not at all. Various routes were drawn up by George Stephenson and by the Rennie brothers and Vignole, but all met with opposition from landowners, and detours had to be made to avoid the properties of the most hostile opponents.

In 1826 George Stephenson was appointed Chief Engineer. 'It would not be an exaggeration to say that without his fierce determination the success of the locomotive would have been delayed several if not many years. Had he not argued constantly in favour of this means of transport, the directors of the Liverpool & Manchester Railway would probably have looked elsewhere and spent huge amounts of money on stationary engines. He is one of the greatest, self-taught geniuses the world has ever seen.

Nevertheless, too much was often asked of him both as an inventor and an engineer. The Liverpool & Manchester Railway remains, however, a magnificent achievement, when one considers that it was the first of its type and that Stephenson had no predecessor to instruct or to guide him, and the quality and implementation of the plans in all their details is due almost entirely to him alone.' (Dendy Marshall)

To build this line, George Stephenson had to solve all the familiar engineering problems: traction, track, viaducts, tunnels, deep cuttings and a passage across swampy land. To overcome this last problem on Chatt Moss, he had to build a kind of floating road made up of brushwood, tar barrels and sand. The Mount Olive cutting, which is 2 miles long, very narrow and more than 90 feet high, is hewn out of rock, and leads to a tunnel 2200 yards long built beneath the city of Liverpool. It is one of the oldest tunnels in the

Liverpool station and tunnels in 1830.
(Engraving by Ackermann: Dendy Marshall Collection)

FIRST CLASS

SECOND

CATTLE AN

DIFFERENT TYPES OF TRAIN ON THE LIVERPOOL TO MANCHESTER RAILWAY IN 1832

Top: First class passengers pulled by Stephenson's *Northumbrian*
Middle: Covered second class coaches pulled by Stephenson's *Jupiter*
Above: A goods and livestock train pulled by *Liverpool* built by Bary

Gravure print by W. Grane of Chester, from Sir David Solomons' collection

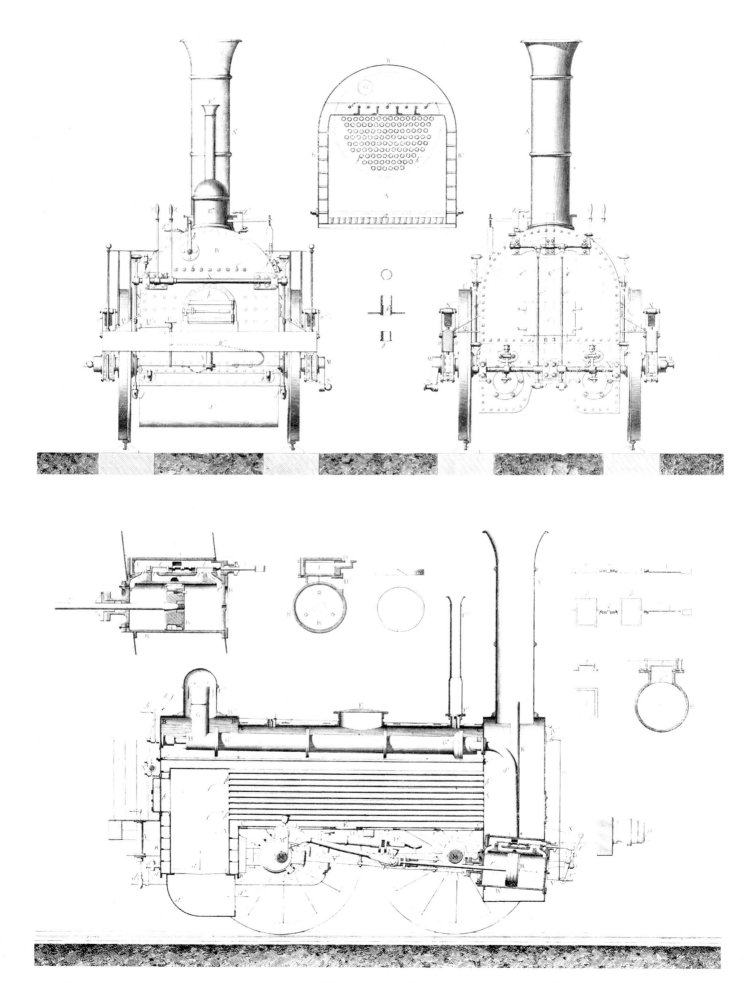

Front and rear elevations and cross-sections of an 1831 *Samson*-class Stephenson locomotive, with details of the tubular boiler and the system of steam distribution.

world. Sixty-three bridges were built either above or beneath the line to avoid wherever possible having to construct level-crossings. Two of these bridges in particular should be mentioned, the stone Rainhill bridge, the first skew bridge in the world, built at an angle of 34 degrees, and the great 9-arch brick viaduct built above the Sankey Valley. The entire line cost £800,000, including £100,000 for bridges, £200,000 for cuttings and embankments, £100,000 for the land, and £28,000 for costs incurred in connection with Acts of Parliament.

Locomotives had hardly figured in plans for the construction of the line, but after the success of the *Rocket* they occupied place of honour in the inauguration which took place on 15 September 1830. A procession of eight trains was formed up in Liverpool. The first, pulled by the *Northumbrian*, the best engine, was driven by George Stephenson himself. It consisted of a carriage in which was seated an orchestra, and the eight-wheel 'state carriage', gilded and richly ornate, in which the Duke of Wellington had taken his seat. At 10.50, the 'splendid cavalcade' set off. Unfortunately, when it reached half-way and stopped at Parkside, William Huskisson, the MP for Liverpool and a keen supporter of the line, got out of his carriage and was chatting with the Duke of Wellington when he was surprised by the *Rocket*. He was knocked down and his leg was crushed. He died that same evening, but this dramatic death at least provided an opportunity to demonstrate the value of locomotives. Placed immediately in a carriage drawn by the *Northumbrian*, the first victim of the railways was taken to Eccles at almost 36 m.p.h. All the festivities were cancelled, but the procession continued for the sake of the future of the railways, and to calm the excited inhabitants of Manchester, who had been made impatient by the delay. Because of traffic prob-

Opening of Shoreham station on the London & Brighton Railway (1840).
(M. de Clermont-Tonnerre Collection)

lems, the trains had to return to Liverpool by night, and they were preceded by the *Comet*, which was sent on ahead to check the line and to indicate the presence of any obstacles by the waving of a length of rope which had been covered in tar and lit.

Branch lines linked this main line to Bolton and Warrington and then to Birmingham. In the years which followed, a considerable number of smaller lines were opened: in 1830, the Canterbury & Whitstable line; in 1831, Glasgow & Garnkirk; in 1832, St Helens & Runcorn; in 1832, Leicester & Swannington; followed by Newcastle & Carlisle, and Leeds & Selby.

In Ireland, the railways began with the Dublin–Kingstown line, the concession being granted in 1831 and the line opened on 17 December 1834.

The first railway in London did not operate until 1836, and this was a section of the Greenwich line. On 4 July 1837, the Grand Juction

linked Liverpool and Manchester to London via Newton and Birmingham. In 1839 to 1840, the capital was linked to Southampton and Portsmouth and then to Dover and Brighton, thus connecting with steamboats to the Continent.

Construction of the Great Western Railway to link London and Bristol, the port which competed with Liverpool for travellers going to America, commenced in 1833. With Brunel's 7 ft-gauge track, this line was opened between Paddington and Maidenhead on 4 June 1838, and then extended as far as Bristol in 1841. In the development of the railways, this company played an important role because of the advanced ideas of its technical directors, Isambard Kingdom Brunel and Daniel Gooch.

In 1840, in Britain, there were 76 railway companies and 2,236 miles of track, 634 of which were completely finished, 298 partially opened, and 1,304 under construction.

Opening of the Glasgow to Garnkirk Railway in 1831.
(Science Museum, London)

Opening of the first Belgian railway, 5 May 1835: the trains leave Brussels for Malines.
(Formerly Sir David Salomons Collection: Bibliothèque nationale, Paris)

THE EARLY YEARS OF RAILWAYS ON THE CONTINENT

Belgium was the first country to plan and build a complete network of railways which would answer the needs of a developing country. This was to be achieved by the careful planning and building of a national system of trunk lines. Other countries, including Britain, had simply allowed private enterprise to build isolated sections of track which answered local needs. Mine tracks had existed in Belgium since the fifteenth century, but the first horse-traction line, which was 11½ miles long, opened in May 1830 and was fully completed in February 1831, running between Hornu and Saint-Ghislain and linking a coal-mine to the Mons Canal at Conde.

After the 1830 revolution, the Government was worried that Holland might hinder commercial links between, on the one hand Antwerp and the Meuse, and on the other hand the Rhine and the sea. It therefore decided in 1831 that the possibility should be studied of building a railway to link the great port of l'Escaut with these two rivers. This task was entrusted to the engineers Pierre Simons and Dr Ridder. On 1 May 1834, King Leopold I gave approval to a law which defined the principles which still govern the Belgian network: 'A railway system will be established throughout our Kingdom. Its central point will be Malines and it will extend eastwards to the Prussian frontier, passing through Louvain, Liége and Verviers. It will run north to Antwerp and west to Ostend via Termonde, Ghent and Bruges. Its southern path will take it to Brussels and France.'

The first line was built between Malines and Brussels, and was completed within a year. On 5 May 1835, three locomotives provided by Robert Stephenson, the *Arrow*, the *Stephenson*, and the *Elephant*, left the Allee-Verte station in Brussels and set off for Malines with 900 guests on board, one of whom was George Stephenson. One year later, on 3 May 1836, the Malines-Antwerp section was opened. Ghent was linked to Termonde in 1837 and to Courtrai in 1839. In 1842, the network was linked to the French railway system by the junction at Mons on the frontier, and in 1843 the section from Verviers to Aix-la-Chapelle was opened, linking Belgium to Prussia. In 1841, a line was built between the North station in Brussels and the South station, and in 1846 the line from Brussels to Paris via Lille was completed. In 1840, however, there were still no night trains running anywhere in Belgium. Up until 1844, all Belgian main lines were state-owned. From that year onwards, however, concessions were granted to private companies. The Belgian network expanded very rapidly. In 1840, there were 204 miles of track. By 1860, there were 465 miles, 352 of which had been built by the State.

The first German railway was built in Bavaria between Nuremberg and Furth. It was opened on 7 December 1835 by the locomotive *Adler*, again

Opening of the first German railway, 7 December 1835, the Nuremberg to Furth line.

The first steam railway in Austria (1837): train leaving Vienna for Wagram on Kaiser Ferdinand's Nordbahn.

provided by Robert Stephenson. The inauguration of this line was marked by a huge production of lithographs for children's books and of toys manufactured in Nuremberg itself. The line had been built in 8 months by Paul von Denis. Animal traction was used until 1860 for morning trains 'for economic reasons'. On 29 October 1838, the Berlin–Potsdam railway was inaugurated. On 24 April 1837, a section of the Leipzig–Dresden line was opened to traffice but the line was not fully completed until two years later. Initially, the *Comet*, provided by Rothwell of Bolton, ran on this line, but it was replaced in April 1839 by the first German locomotive, the *Saxonia*. This was a class 0–4–2 and was built in the workshops at Ubigau near Dresden. In 1842, the Cologne-Aix-la-Chapelle line linked Germany with the Belgian frontier. On 1 April 1847, the first night train in Germany ran between Berlin and Hamburg.

Russia took an early interest in this new means of transport, as it had in the case of steamships. On 27 April 1836, Emperor Nicolas I authorised the building of a line between St Petersburg, Tzarskoie Selo and Pavlosk. It opened as an animal-traction line on 9 October 1836, and as a steam line on 30 October 1837. In the early stages, this line operated in a rather strange way, horses being used while they awaited delivery of a Hackworth locomotive; even when locomotives were delivered they were used only when there were more than 40 passengers, failing which a horse-drawn wagon was used. Trains stopped only at main stations. From there, passengers were taken to smaller stations by horse-drawn wagons. This was the first practical application of the service provided subsequently by railcars. On the Emperor's orders, locomotives were equipped with 11 horns and a trombone to warn the public of an approaching train!

In 1833, the engineer Tcherepanov built a locomotive in Russia. The Great Nicolas railway was built by the State and ran from St Petersburg to Moscow. Work was begun in 1842, and the line was opened on 7 May 1847. In accordance with the wishes of the Emperor, it ran in an almost straight line. It was 372 miles long and cost 75,000,000 francs. The track was 5½ feet wide and this gauge was adopted throughout Russia.

Between 2 June and 14 June 1845, trains began to run on the Warsaw–Vienna line. The Warsaw–Bromberg line, which linked Russia and Prussia, was not opened until 1862. In 1864, Kiev and Odessa were linked by a major line on which luxury-class stock provided by Germany was used.

In Austria, steam traction was first used on 17 November 1837. This was the date on which the Florisdorf–Wagram section of Kaiser Ferdinand's 'Nordbahn' opened. It was to link Vienna with Galicia via Cracow and the concession for it had been granted in 1836 to Salomon de Rothschild. The first Robert Stephenson *Planet*-type locomotives used on this line were called *Vindobona*, *Austria*, and *Moravia*. Subsequently other engines were acquired in America from W. Norris of Philadelphia. This last class of engine was copied

First steam train in Russia, 30 October 1837, on the St Petersburg–Pavlosk line.
(Engraving from an 1837 almanac, courtesy of Madame Maurice Chotard)

Railway viaduct across the lagoon in Venice; construction started in 1841.
(Charles Dollfus Collection)

Stephenson rear-cylinder locomotive used on the Antwerp-Ghent Railway
(1840): seen here in its present state.
(M. Lengelle Collection)

The *Saxonia*, the first passenger locomotive built in Germany,
in 1839, at Ubigau.
(Verkehrsmuseum, Nuremberg)

in Austria and used widely on the early networks.

The 'Sudbahn' was inaugurated in 1844 between Vienna and Graz, but, generally speaking, railways in Austria developed slowly and experienced serious financial difficulties. The mountain locomotive trials in 1851 for the Semmering line saw the development of powerful, articulated engines. This line, from Vienna to Trieste through the Semmering Pass, was the first to cross the Alps. It was built by the engineer Carl von Ghega and was opened on 17 July 1854. Prague was linked in 1845 to Olmutz and Vienna, and in 1851 to Dresden.

The first railway in Italy, which at the time was divided like Germany into many states, was opened on 4 October 1839. It was built by the Bayard brothers between Naples and Portici. The Naples–Caserte line was opened in 1843 and extended to Capua in 1844.

The Austrian Emperor gave permission to build the Milan–Monza line in the provinces of Lombardy and Venezia, and it was opened in 1840. The Milan–Venice line was opened in 1842.

A model of the *Hercules*, a locomotive
used on the Rhine Railway (from
Amsterdam to the Prussian border),
1843.

(Railway Museum, Utrecht)

Trains ran in 1847 in the Grand Duchy of Tuscany between Pisa and Livorno, in 1848 in Piedmont, between Turin and Moncalieri, and in 1859 in the Papal States, between Rome and Civita Vecchia. In the early years, English engines were used, and these were the first in Europe to provide a cab for the driver.

In the Netherlands, the first line was opened on 20 September 1839, between Amsterdam and Haarlem. The Dutch Government and industry proved to be hostile to this new means of transport, and it was King William himself who had to fund the building of the railway which ran from Amsterdam to Prussia.

In the Scandinavian countries, the first lines were opened in 1856 between Goteborg and Joosered and between Malmö and Lund.

In Switzerland, locomotives ran for the first time in 1841 on the Strasbourg–Basle line but the oldest internal Swiss line is the one which links Zurich and Basle, and this was opened on 9 August 1847.

A train on the Strasbourg–Basle line passing the villages of Wattviller and Bollwiller in 1844.

(Lithograph by E. Simon Jr & Thomas Muller published in the *Panorama des Vosges et du Chemin de fer de Strasbourg à Bâle*: courtesy of M. Armand Boeringer)

THE DEVELOPMENT OF RAILWAYS IN FRANCE

In France, railways developed fairly slowly. After considerable discussion, the concessions for the two lines running from Paris to Versailles were granted on 24 May 1837, with a 99-year lease. The concession for the line to run along the right bank of the Seine was given to M. de Rothschild, and for the left-bank line to M. Fould. For this line, a new station called the gare de l'Ouest was built in the Montparnasse district. The route taken by this line required the building in Meudon of a remarkable viaduct which is still in existence. The work was interrupted by frequent land slips and was completed by Seguin.

The right-bank line opened on 2 August 1839 and the left-bank line on 10 September 1840. Financially, the first was moderately successful, whereas the second was a disastrous operation, worsened by the catastrophe of 8 May 1842. In fact, for Emile Pereire, the value of the Saint-Germain railway was principally symbolic. Like the Versailles lines, it could not be used to transport goods. Later, the Paris–Rouen and Paris–Orleans lines were to arouse considerable interest. The decision to build them was taken on two consecutive days, 6–7 July 1838, with inauguration ceremonies on 2–3 May 1843.

These achievements, however, were preceded by the building of the Alsace railway, running from Mulhouse to Thann and from Strasbourg to Basle. This was built to a very high standard based upon the best principles of English railways. They were the first lines to be built in France which would provide a high-speed link between farming areas, and centres of commerce and industry. In May 1837, a famous industrialist from Mulhouse, Nicholas Koechlin, had accepted the offer 'to build at his own expense, risk and peril, a railway from Mulhouse to Thann'. On 1 September 1839, the first train ran between these two towns and was pulled by the locomotive *Napoléon*. This had been built by André Koechlin in Mulhouse itself. It achieved a remarkable speed. The outward journey of just over 12 miles was completed in 25 minutes and the return journey in 15 minutes; in other words, at speeds of about 30 and 50 miles per hour respectively.

Nicholas Koechlin and his engineer, Bazaine, were keen to use French rolling-stock to 'create in our country a new industry which soon will be of great importance. Of the 29 engines used on the Alsace railway, only 3 will be from England, the other 26 will have been made in France and 25 of these in Alsace.'

Following the technical and financial success of this line, Koechlin undertook to build the much longer railway from Strasbourg to Basle. It was to cross the Alsace plain over a distance of 87 miles at a time when there were only 174 miles of track in the whole of the French network. This line, which was at that time the longest on the Continent, was the first in the world to link two states by crossing the border between them. It was opened to the public on 19 September 1841, but financially it was not a success.

By March 1839, other lines had opened, notably between Alais and Beaucaire, between Epinal and the Burgundy canal, and between Montpellier and Cette. The feasibility of the Montpellier–Cette line had been studied by a local committee, and the line itself had been built by Mellet and Henry. The information concerning the Montpellier–Cette railway gives interesting details about the life of this small line: 'Engines – there are 5 locomotives, each with its own tender, built to the most modern design in the workshops of Messrs Fenton, Murray and Jackson of Leeds, England. They were brought first of all to Le Havre and from there to Cette. The first three were off-loaded from their ship in October 1838 and taken on a tender along the Athon canal and the Lez river as far as Port-Juvenal. As for the other two, they arrived in Cette in April 1839 aboard the *Amélie*. They were then taken by rail to Montpellier. These locomotives are the *Notre-Dame-des-Tables* (the patron saint of Montpellier), the *Hérault*, the *Montpelliérenne*, the *Cettoise*, and the *Rosine*. They weigh nearly 8 tons and are all capable of 20 h.p.

The same authors write of the 'many thoughts and delights which this extraordinary means of communication inspire in us all'. 'Having bought our ticket let us first of all enter the station's waiting rooms. There all the passengers meet and greet each other with a smile. Naive curiosity is visible on every face. One senses a feeling of general happiness, almost of festivity. Soon the bell gives the signal. The door opens. The passengers rush into the huge station where the coaches await. Five or six hundred people enter the train but there is no confusion, no panic, everybody taking the seat numbered on his ticket. The passengers sit down and hand in their tickets. An elegantly dressed train driver, standing on the top deck of the front coach, sounds a horn, a guard at

Roasting the ox served at a banquet for the 600 workers who completed the Maisons-Laffitte bridge (May 1843).

(*L'Illustration*, 6 May 1843)

The first Northern Railway lines were the trunk lines running from Paris to Douai and Lille in 1846, with a branch line to Courtrai and Ghent and from Douai to Valenciennes and Blanc-Misseron.

In 1847, the Amiens-Boulogne line was opened, and in 1850 the Saint-Quentin line, which was then extended in 1856 to Erquelines. In 1852, the Eastern Railways completed the Paris–Strasbourg main line with branch lines to Reims and Metz. This linked up with the Montereau–Troyes line which had been built earlier by the State. The P-L-M network of the 1930s represents a merging of separate companies, in particular of the Saint-Etienne lines, the Marseilles–Avignon line, which was opened in 1849, the Paris–Dijon line (1851), extended to Lyons (1854) and to Marseilles (1856), the Lyons–Geneva line (1858), and the Dijon–Belfort line (1858). The Paris–Lyons company and the Lyons–Mediterranean company were separate. A third network, called the Grand Central, extended from Lyons to Roanne, Saint-Germain-des-Fossés and Brassac. This was the only attempt to create an east-west link running between Lyons and Bordeaux. In 1855, apart from a few unimportant lines, all the main lines radiated out from the capital, forming a kind of star-shape whose central point was Paris.

Top: Footbridge near the Château de Trousseau, on the Paris–Orleans line.
Centre: The Rolleboise tunnel on the Paris–Rouen line.
Bottom: The Maisons-Lafitte bridge on the Paris–Rouen line.

the rear answers him, and suddenly the train gives a judder. The engine moves, taking with it effortlessly the 15 or 20 coaches which it is pulling. At first the speed is gentle, but soon it increases, and the carriage moves more and more rapidly, hardly giving you time to breathe.'

On 2 May 1843, four trains, one of which had on board the Dukes of Nemours and Montpensier, left Paris for Orleans and returned the same evening, having completed the first major journey to leave the capital. In 1840, the company had already opened the Corbeil line, and in under 2½ years all the work on the 75-mile line between Paris and Orleans was completed.

The following day the Princes inaugurated the Paris–Rouen line, again built at amazing speed in under two years. The opening of the line was celebrated in a curious manner. 'A whole beef was roasted and served to the 600 workmen who had just put the finishing touches to the Maisons bridge. M. Laffitte presided at this banquet.'

By 1846, a cheap-rate night train was in operation. The normal fares from Paris to Rouen were 16, 13 and 10 francs in 1st, 2nd and 3rd class respectively, and from Paris to Mantes 6 francs, 4 francs 50 centimes, and 3 francs 25 centimes. The line was extended to Le Havre and completed on 22 March 1847, and a branch line to Dieppe was opened. The Western Railway was completed with the opening of the lines from Paris to Le Mans in 1854, to Rennes in 1857, to Caen in 1855, and to Cherbourg in 1858.

Buddicom workshops at Sotteville near Rouen, about 1845.
The figure in the centre is thought to be William Buddicom.

THE MEN WHO BUILT LOCOMOTIVES

The first company to build locomotives for customers was the firm of Fenton, Murray and Jackson in Leeds in 1812. It stopped production about 1843, but the oldest company which built specifically to meet customer demand was the firm created by George Stephenson in 1823 in Newcastle. This famous firm still existed in the 1930s under the name of Robert Stephenson and Company. Its locomotives brought steam traction to France, Belgium, Germany, Austria, Canada, Egypt and Australia. Its first rival was the firm of Edward Bury and Company in Liverpool, a firm which specialised in 4-wheel engines but which stopped production in 1850.

One of the most famous firms of this period was Sharp, Roberts and Company of Manchester. Following various mergers, it still existed be-

The Maffei workshops in Munich.

tween the two world wars under the name of the North British Locomotive Company. It built excellent locomotives, which were often used as models by foreign railways, particularly in France and Germany.

In 1832, Robert Stephenson and Charles Taylor created another company in Newton-le-Willows under the name of Taylor and Company. In 1847, this became the Vulcan Foundry and it continued in production a century later. Other pioneer builders of early locomotives were Forrester, Mather, Hawthorn, B. Hick and Sons, Kitson and Laird, and Kitching. Later, near Manchester, the famous Beyer Peacock factory was set up. Several railway companies built their own workshops, the best known being the London & North Western workshops, built in Crewe and managed by Alexander Alan, and the Great Western workshops, built in Swindon and managed by Daniel Gooch. Crewe, in particular, produced a considerable number of engines and these have re-

mained famous because of their speed and their durability. A similar reputation is enjoyed by the marvellous engines built in Swindon.

About 1840, there were 30 engineers building locomotives in Britain. Twenty years later, however, apart from the workshops of five companies, there were only four well-known and five or six lesser-known engineers involved in this work. All British locomotive-builders were concerned to give their engines that elegance and that shape which have always characterised British locomotives and which for them and the public is a sign of quality.

In America, the building of locomotives took place mainly in the Eastern states, and was initially entrusted to a variety of firms, such as Davis and Gartner in York, Pennsylvania, the West Point Iron Works, Stevens Workshops in Hoboken, and various smaller engineering companies. In 1832, in Philadelphia, two famous companies specialising in the building of locomotives were formed. The most famous was Mathias W. Baldwin. This was the company responsible for the building of an engine for the Germantown line in Philadelphia. This locomotive was inspired by Stephenson's *Planet*. It cost $3,500, and bore the name of *Old Ironsides*. In 1834, Baldwin built the *E.L. Miller*, which proved to be the prototype of all subsequent American locomotives. It had a long boiler connected to a domed smokebox, a wooden underframe, which rested at the front end on a 4-wheel bogie (this design being based upon an idea by Jervis), and at the rear it had two large driving-wheels which were positioned behind the firebox. In the years 1836 and 1837, Baldwin built 80 locomotives, which gives some idea of the importance of this new industry. At the same time, William Norris opened his new workshops, and he built, with the collaboration of J.B. Jervis, a class of locomotive which became very popular in Europe and was used on the Austrian railways and by a variety of companies

Building a boiler in the Great Western Railway workshops in Swindon in 1854.

in Britain, France and Germany.

The development of this new industry in America was slowed down considerably by the economic crisis of 1837–40. Nevertheless, workshops continued to be built; for example, the workshops of Ross Winans in Baltimore and of William Mason, who about 1856 created the 4–4–0 class of engine which was to become the standard design for all the great American locomotives. It embodied all the principal features which were to last for 50 years. The most famous factory for passenger-coaches was Pullman's in Chicago.

In Continental Europe, France was the first country to have a locomotive construction industry. Between 1829 and 1832, Marc Seguin built 12 engines in Lyons-Perrache at the Saint-Etienne railway workshops, but the first custom-built industrial production of engines took place in Paris at the Chaillot Ironworks managed by Edwards. In 1833, he bought from Robert Stephenson a *Samson*-type locomotive and built many others based upon this design. This type was known throughout France and Belgium as the 'Chaillot Engine'. The ironworks where these engines were built was a neighbour of the Perier brothers' factory, and it soon took over their engineering workshops. Later, it changed its name to Derosne and Cail, and from 1849 onwards it specialised in building Cramptons. These workshops were then transferred to Javel under the company name of J.F. Cail.

The Le Creusot Company was bought in 1835 by M. Schneider, and in 1838 it produced its first locomotive, the *Gironde*, for the Versailles railway. In 1839, the Alsace workshops of André Koechlin, Stehelin and Huber began production.

In 1842, two English engineers, William Allcard and W. Buddicom, were appointed by the Rouen railway to build engines for its line at Sotteville. They built many high-quality engines, and when Buddicom became sole head of the workshops he produced locomotives which remained in service on the Western Railway for 70 years.

In the provinces, other workshops were built, the best known being Hallette's in Arras and the workshops of Verpilleux, Clément Desormes, and Parent and Schaken, in Lyons. In 1866, Parent and Schaken set up new workshops in Fives near Lille. In the Paris region, Cavé, Claparède, and Ernest Gouin in Saint-Denis produced many locomotives.

In Belgium, construction began in 1835 in the large workshops of John Cockerill, a British industrialist living in Seraing. His first locomotive was called the *Belge*. Later, the very important factories of Couillet, Tubize, and la Haine-

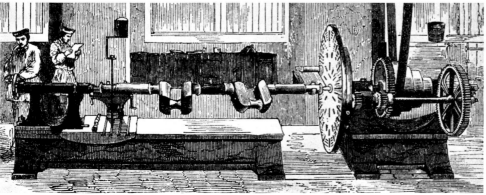

The Great Western workshops in Swindon in 1854. Engine and axle assembly area.

Saint-Pierre were built.

Germany's first locomotives were built in 1839 in Ubigau in Saxony. The Borsig workshop in Berlin produced their first locomotive in 1841. About the same period, Maffei began production in Munich, Vohlert in Prussia and Kessler in Karlsruhe.

In Austria, the first locomotive-factory was built by the Sudbahn Company in Vienna under the management of Mathias von Schönerer. It used W. Norris's *Philadelphia* as a model for its engines. In 1844, Norris himself formed a subsidiary company in Vienna which later became the G. Sigl Company. Günther opened a factory in Wiener Neustadt.

From 1845, Russia built locomotives in workshops in Alexandrovsk near St Petersburg. In Italy, the first man to build engines was Ansaldo in San Pier d'Arena.

One unusual feature of this new industry was the emergence of the steam-engine builder-entrepreneur. To begin with, several companies had awarded concessions to engineer-entrepreneurs who paid the company according to the tonnage of the engine. The system replaced a similar one operating in the days of horse-traction. Thus, in France, Verpilleux held a concession for the Saint-Etienne railway. In England, in 1833, Hackworth held the concession for the Stockton & Darlington line, as did Bury in 1836 for the North Western Railway, and Crampton

Construction of Crampton locomotives in the Derosne & Cail workshops at Chaillot in 1849

for the London, Chatham and Dover railway.

The first locomotive testing-plant was built in Leeds at Fenton, Murray and Jackson's workshops, for engines which would operate on the Great Western line.

About 1845, locomotive-builders started to produce, not only engines which they themselves had designed, but also engines which had been ordered from them to a design which was not their own. This close collaboration between the drivers, the engineers and the builders of locomotives still exists today.

Construction of a McConnell locomotive for the London & North Western Railway in Fairbairn's workshops in Manchester in 1852.

Stephenson's locomotive for the railway from Montereau to Troyes.

Model of locomotive (1841).

(Conservatoire des arts et Métiers)

Model of a Stephenson long-boiler locomotive (1845).

(Charles Dollfus Collection)

Buddicom locomotive for the Paris and Rouen line (1843).

(Conservatoire des arts et métiers)

Locomotive by André Koechlin for the Strasbourg-Basle line (1847).

(Photo taken in 1867: Fortant Collection)

Kitching's passenger locomotive *Woodland* for the Stockton & Darlington Railway (1848).

(Photo: Moore)

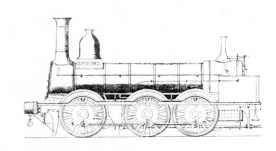

Goods engine *Sphynx*, made by Sharp Brothers for the Manchester & Lincolnshire Railway (1849).

(After *The Engineer*)

SOME TYPICAL LOCOMOTIVES (1840–1850)

Timothy Hackworth's double-tender locomotive *Wilberforce* for the Stockton & Darlington Railway (1838).

Galloway Bowman's *Manchester* for the Liverpool & Manchester Railway (1831).
(Dendy Marshall Collection)

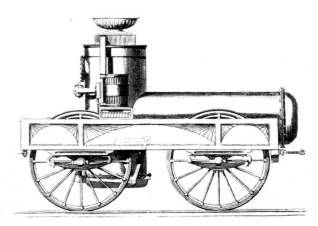

Braithwaite & Ericsson's *William IV* for the St Helens & Runcorn Railway (1830).

The *Caledonian*, built for the Liverpool & Manchester Railway (1832).
(Pierre Lichtenberger Collection)

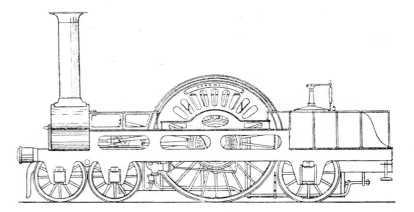

Trevithick's *Cornwall*, built for the London & North Western Railway (1847).
(From a drawing by Ahrons)

Blavier and Larpent express locomotive, *L'Aigle*, built by Ernest Gouin for the Western Railway in France (1855).

EXPERIMENTAL LOCOMOTIVES (1830–1855)

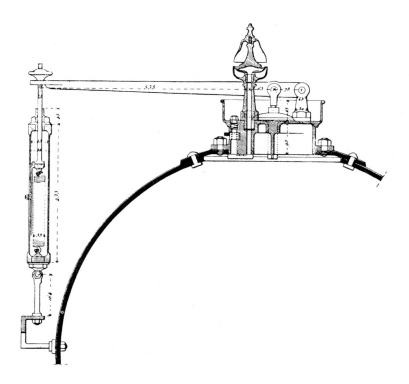

Firebox dome with valve and whistle on a French Northern Railway locomotive (1846).

Steam dome and valve on a Lyons Railway locomotive (1850).

LOCOMOTIVE ACCESSORIES

The steam dome was used to prevent water entering the cylinders. It first appeared about 1830 on Robert Stephenson's *Northumbrian* and *Planet* engines, and on Hackworth's *Globe*. It took its name from the spherical shape of its brass dome.

Valves were originally based upon Papin's model, with its lever and weight. Edouard Biot wrote in 1834: 'When the engine is moving, even though it may be fitted with springs, every sudden jerk causes the lever to move and opens the safety valve, so that pressure is intermittent and steam rapidly escapes. This problem is so serious that, on the railways around Newcastle, it

was the custom to use a moveable iron block to immobilise the valve's lever arm while the engine was moving. The iron block was disconnected when the engine was stationary.' In fact, as early as 1815, Matthew Murray had fitted Blenkinsop's locomotive with direct spring valves.

The first locomotive did not have a whistle. Locomotives on the Stockton & Darlington line were fitted with a bell. On the Liverpool–Manchester line the fireman had a trumpet. It was the Leicester & Swannington Railway's *Samson* which was fitted in 1833 with the first whistle, following a request made to George Stephenson by the director Mr Bagster. On the Liverpool & Manchester line, the whistle was probably first used by Fyfe in 1835.

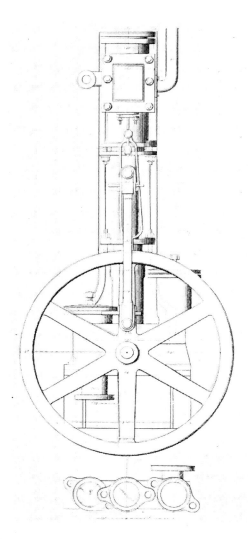

The 'donkey' water-feed pump
(1855).
(Charles Dollfus Collection)

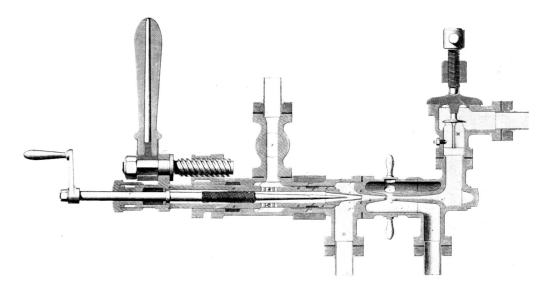

Cross-section of the 1860 Giffard injector.
Steam enters the adjustable jets via the central pipe and draws water from pipe (H). The water is then injected into the boiler through pipe (M). Excess water is ejected through the lower, right-hand pipe.

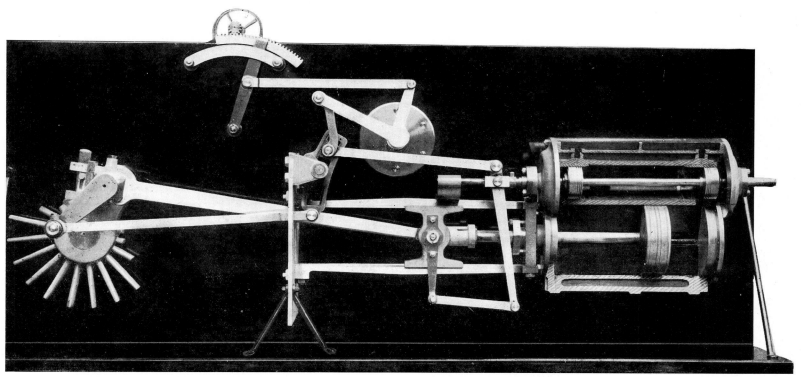

Model of Walschaerts' valve gear, invented in 1844 and modified in 1859.

(Science Museum, London)

Steam distribution plays an important role in the working of a locomotive. On early engines, the slide-valve was driven by an eccentric fixed to the shaft. The steam operated, therefore, under full pressure. In 1838, the slide-valves were modified to reduce admission. This allowed the steam to expand and thus avoided counter pressure. There was a 25 per cent drop in steam consumption, and engine speed increased.

The so-called 'Stephenson's link motion' was, in fact, invented in 1842 by W. Howe. Intended for use as a steam reversal control, this device proved to be much more important in that it enabled the driver to control steam admission. It consists of two eccentrics placed on the axle, one at the angle required to regulate forward movement, the other at the angle necessary to control reverse. The two eccentrics are connected by a rod at one end of a curved link. A dye block slides along this curved link and is connected to the slide-valve control. The link can be raised or lowered so as to activate the valve by means of one or other of the eccentrics. In the intermediate

setting, the valve is controlled by the combined movement of both eccentrics. Various modifications were proposed in 1843 by Daniel Gooch and then in 1844, in Belgium, by Walschaerts.

Water-feed had for a long time been a difficult problem. Early engines were fitted with a pump which was driven by the wheels during movement. When the engine was stationary it was necessary first to uncouple it and then to move it forwards and backwards to drive the pump. To avoid this problem a small steam-pump was fitted. This was called in England a 'donkey' and in France a 'little horse'.

In 1858, Henri Giffard took out a patent for his injector. This device, which contains no moving parts, has since been fitted to all locomotives. It is based upon the capacity of a jet of steam to absorb water. As the steam passes along a suitably shaped tube, it takes in water. As the water condenses, the steam causes it to move at sufficient speed for the liquid mixture to enter the boiler in spite of internal pressure.

The large water-consumption by express en-

gines led Ramsbottom in 1860 to develop a system of filling the tender when the train was still moving. A water-filled channel ran down the middle of the track, and as the tender moved along, a scoop at the end of a large pipe was lowered into the channel.

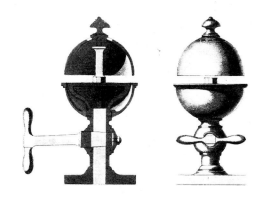

Locomotive whistle, about 1848.

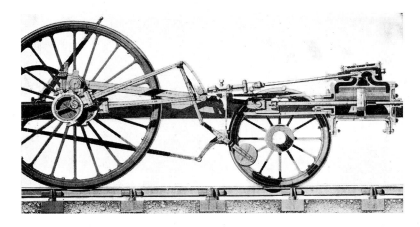

'Stephenson's link motion' for Crampton locomotive.

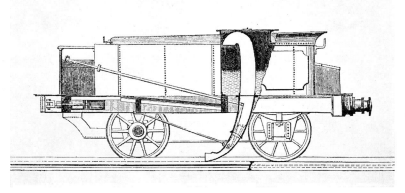

Ramsbottom's water-intake tender (1862).

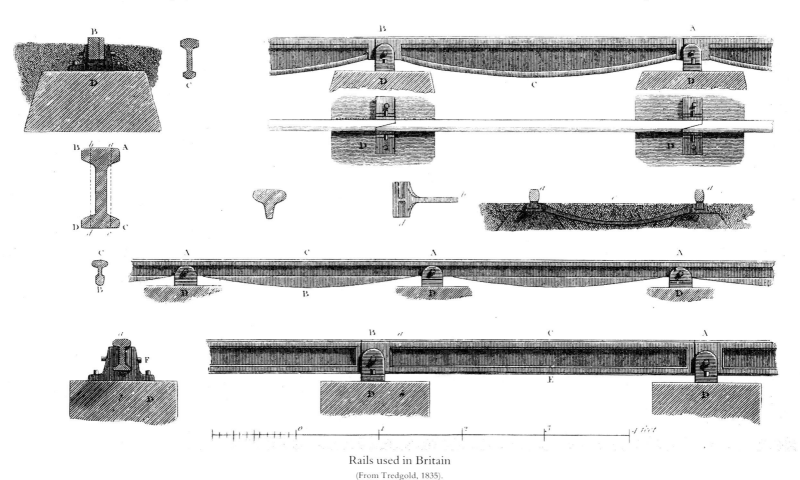

Rails used between 1780 and 1855

Left to right: 1. Early flat iron rail; 2. Tram-rail; 3. Semi-flat rail; 4 & 5. Rails used on the Saint-Etienne to Lyons and Roanne lines; 6. Bull-headed rail; 7. Rail from Paris–Versailles line; 8. Coste rail used on the Saint-Etienne–Lyons line; 9–11. Single-headed rail; 10. Nord; 12. Stevens and Vignole rail used on German lines; 13. Brunel's bridge rail.

Camden & Amboy R.R. track in 1837: rails on pillar supports for use in marshland.

(National Museum, Washington)

THE TRACK

The quality of the track has always been as important as the quality of the locomotive.

Jessop's cast-iron edge-rail was invented in 1789 and first laid in Loughborough. It was made up of parts of equal strength and durability, with a curved lower edge often described as 'fish-bellied'. Each part of these curved rails was fixed by bolts directly to a block of stone or of wood.

In 1797, in the coal-mines owned by Lawson, Barnes used straight rails fixed for the first time by T-shaped chairs. A short time later, fish-bellied rails were used on the Welsh tram roads. In 1816, George Stephenson and Losh took out a patent for a system of chairs with a base plate and raised rail. This rail, looking very much like our modern track, was used in 1825 on the Stockton & Darlington line.

Progress made in metallurgy and steam-rolling allowed rolled-iron rails to be manufactured.

These were first seen in use in 1811 in Lord Carlisle's quarries, but it was John Birkinshaw who, from 1820 onwards, popularised the use of the rolled-iron rail. He designed a rail with a convex upper edge which would reduce friction. Very quickly this type of rail came to replace the cast-iron rail, which disappeared completely once the use of steam-traction became widespread. The laying of rails on stone blocks remained the practice for many years. Mark Seguin introduced into France the single-headed rail, with a bottom flange and a straight base. This allowed variation in the distance between the support blocks. His rails were manufactured at Le Creusot by Manby & Wilson, the predecessors of Messrs Schneider. The rails which formed the track running from Andrézieux to Roanne were made in the Terrenoire forges, which produced nearly 2000 tons of them. The 60,000 chairs used on this line were made in the ironworks of Lyons and Fourchambault. These statistics are among the earliest we have in the history of the French locomotive

Rails used in Britain

(From Tredgold, 1835).

Top to bottom: sectional, side and plan view of Newcastle 'fish-bellied' cast-iron edge-rail; sectional view of the Penrhyn Quarry track with cast-iron sleepers fixed to heel of rail; front and sectional views of Birkinshaw's curved laminated iron rail on stone blocks; straight rail. (Charles Dollfus Collection)

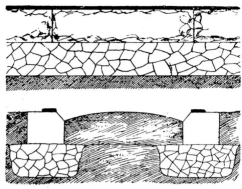

Baltimore & Ohio R.R. track in 1833:
flat rails on stone blocks and ballast.

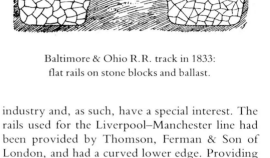

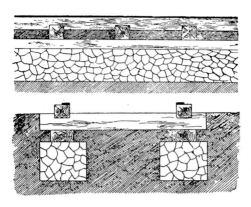

Albany & Schenectady R.R. track in 1837: rails made
of wood, and iron sleepers laid on wooden beams.

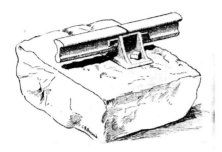

Top: stone block and joint from the Camden
& Amboy R.R. in 1831. *Above*: stone block
and chair from the Old Portage R.R. in 1832.
(National Museum, Washington)

industry and, as such, have a special interest. The rails used for the Liverpool–Manchester line had been provided by Thomson, Ferman & Son of London, and had a curved lower edge. Providing equipment and tools for the railways of Britain gave a dramatic and much-needed boost to the iron industry, which was experiencing a crisis about 1830.

About 1835 the use of stone blocks became less common because they had a tendency to allow the rail to move and break.

In 1825, on the Stockton & Darlington line, the weight of track was nearly 9 lbs per foot. In 1827, on the Saint-Etienne–Lyons line, it was nearly 19 lbs per foot and, in 1830, on the Liverpool–Manchester line, it was about 11 lbs per foot.

In America, tracks were very light, considerable use being made of wood because of its low cost and availability.

When the single-headed rail had a symmetrical cross-section, it could be turned round after one edge had worn, placed end to end, and used again. With the invention of the bull-headed rail, there was the extra facility of being able to turn the rail over and use the other edge, but this advantage proved to be more theoretical than practical since the strength of the worn rails had been considerably reduced.

The single-headed rail with a tieplate was invented in 1830 by the American engineer, Robert Stevens, during the crossing from America to England on a visit to study railways. He wanted to find a replacement for chairs since these were difficult to manufacture in America. The rail with its tieplate was laid directly on to the stone blocks or the sleepers, and the joints were covered by a riveted iron strip. His first rails were made by

Messrs Guest in Wales for the Camden & Amboy Railroad and sent to America in 1831. They were then introduced into Britain by Vignole, to whom they have been incorrectly attributed.

Another interesting type of rail was invented about 1850 by I.K. Brunel for the Great Western Railway. This was the bridge rail. It had the shape of an upturned gutter and was fixed to the sleepers by a double tieplate. Barlow's bridge rails, which were wider at the base, were laid directly on to the ground and partly covered in ballast. To reduce stress on the joints, some American lines used rails consisting of two parallel units which were laid side by side and overlapped. Other types of rails consisting of three units were tested but were not manufactured. The first steel rails were made in 1857 by the Ebbw Vale Company and laid near Derby.

Many ways of fixing rails were suggested, including a variety of shapes of tieplates, plates joined by a rod, as, for example, on the Strasbourg railway, and bells sunk into the sand as in Alexandria.

Similarly, many different kinds of points were invented, and these came to be used widely once railways started to develop. In the early years, the pointsman had to hold a lever as the train passed by. The dangers involved in such a manoeuvre disappeared with the invention of the swing-bob lever. Sometimes points were controlled by an eccentric which was turned by a crank. Stevenson developed an early points system in which a length of track was mounted on a pivot and could turn and guide the wheels to one of the two or three tracks. Although difficult to construct, this system had the advantage of allowing a single track to divide into several tracks.

Les fig. 1 et 2 représentent une coupe du rail dans le sens transversal et une dans le sens de sa longueur.

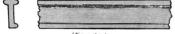

(Fig. 1 et 2.)
Les fig. 3 et 4 représentent, l'une l'élévation, et l'autre la base du coussinet.

(Fig. 3.)

(Fig. 4.)

(Fig. 5.)
La fig. 5 représente l'ensemble du rail, du coussinet et du dé en pierre posés l'un sur l'autre.
Enfin la fig. 5 bis représente un chemin de fer tout construit.

(Fig. 5 bis.)

Early rails from the Saint-Etienne–Lyons line.
(*Magasin pittoresque*, 1833)

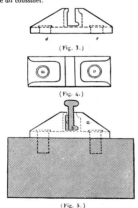

Left to right: Baltimore & Ohio R.R. compound rail, 1848; simple and compound chairs, France, 1858: Brunel rail from the Great Western Railway, 1858: compound rail from the New York Central R.R., 1855 Stevens rail (shaded – the original design from 1830; unshaded – laminated rail made in 1831); Vignole rail from the Western Railway in France, 1855; cast-iron chair from the Philadelphia & Reading R.R., 1837; Stevens rail from the Royal Swedish Railway, 1854; Vignole longitudinal rail for Great Western Railway broad gauge, 1858. (National Museum, Washington)

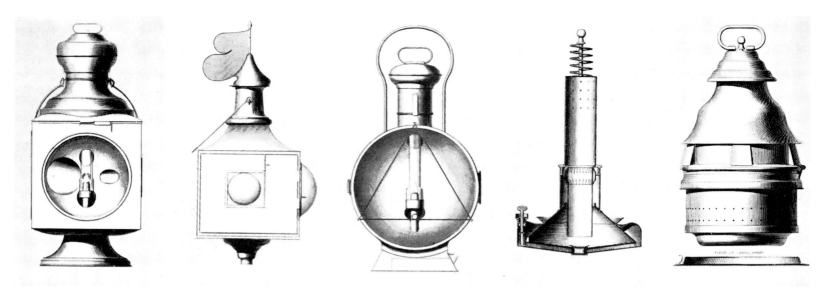

Railway lamps (1859).

Left to right: two four-way track signal lamps with optical glass; locomotive headlamp; interior coach lamp, and lantern. (Charles Dollfus Collection)

Alarm signal used on
Great Western Railway tenders.
(Great Western Railway Collection)

LIGHTING, HEATING AND SAFETY

For a long time, carriages were lit by oil lamps fastened to the ceiling. In first-class carriages, oil lamps gave such a poor light that about 1850 passengers could purchase at stations a cheap individual lamp containing a candle. One of these lamps has been conserved by the Great Western Railway in Paddington.

In 1840, Bideau wrote: 'on the London to Birmingham railway the carriages have internal lighting and the lamps are lit even during the daytime to counter the darkness of tunnels'. This was not a widespread practice, because on the Great Western Railway ceiling lights were not used until 1842 and then for first-class compartments only. Third-class carriages remained in darkness. In America, the long carriages were lit at each end by glass-covered lamps which ran off oil or candle. About 1860, compressed gas was frequently used to light carriages but in Britain such a system was not tried until 1857. In France, compressed gas was used for the first time on the Paris–Orleans railway in 1848 by Fortier-Hermann but only to light the front and rear ends of the train. Luxury and ceremonial coaches were fitted on the inside with wall-mounted lamps and on the outside with a courtesy light at each corner of the carriage.

From the earliest days in America, carriages were heated by a stove. In Europe, third-class passengers in open carriages had to make do with a litter of straw. In France, in 1855, only first-class coaches were heated by means of 'hot-water bottles'. This remained the custom for about 60 years.

The guard at the rear of the train was able to communicate with passengers and the driver by means of a rope with a bell on the end. Many companies were frightened that this system might be misused and refused to equip their trains with such a device. The electrically-operated alarm bell was first seen in France in 1866 on the Northern and Southern lines.

Lamp for individual use sold to
passengers (1850 to 1860).
(Great Western Railway Collection)

Lamp for use on outside of Pope
Pius IX coach (1858).

Interior light for Napoleon III
saloon-car manufactured in
1860 by Chatel.

Postmaster's comment at the sight of locomotives: *'All those railway passengers. We've been beaten by at least a nose!'*

CARTOONS AND ART

Cartoonists, of course, frequently turned to the railways for material, without, however, ever showing great hostility towards this new invention. In Britain, France and Germany cartoons often expressed the bitterness of postmasters and the happiness of horses. Daumier tended to criticise administrators and lampooned with good reason the many inconveniences and dangers involved in travelling by third-class open carriage or on the upper deck. Other cartoonists, such as

Cham and Bertall, satirised speculators and described the misfortunes which befell many railway shareholders.

The railways also provided inspiration for some great artists. In 1844, Turner took steam and speed as his theme and produced a famous painting. Although very elderly by then, the great master of light understood and captured the dynamic poetry of a moving train as it sped through a countryside where sun and rain vied with each other. From 1830 to 1850, minor art forms expressed popular enthusiasm for this new means of

transport. For example, in Britain, decorative pottery was manufactured featuring trains on the Liverpool–Manchester line and on the Grand Junction line. In 1843, in France, factories in Choisy-le-Roi and Gien celebrated the Rouen and Orleans railways with a series of delightful plates. Toselli coffee-jugs were made in the shape of locomotives and a variety of smaller objects were decorated with pictures taken from the railways or made in the shape of a locomotive: cigarette-holders, porcelain jugs, iron and wooden containers, seals, trinkets and writing pads.

A cartoon by Daumier (1843).

'Gentlemen, we are about to enter a long, narrow tunnel. Please do not move while we are inside. Someone always loses an arm or a leg or a nose and as you must realise the company can't go looking for them in such a dark passageway six miles long!'

(Bibliothèque nationale, Paris)

'The problems of travelling on the top deck: bad weather and tunnels.'

Unsigned cartoon.

Daumier's impressions of a journey by train (1843).

'Ah, mercy be, we're finished.' 'No we're not, it's just the train setting off again. Whenever the train goes forward passengers go back – everybody knows that.'

(Bibliothèque nationale, Paris)

A pleasant journey from Paris to Orleans, by Daumier (1843).

'My God, we're getting soaked. Next time the sky is covered in cloud, the carriage should be covered too.'

(Bibliothèque nationale, Paris)

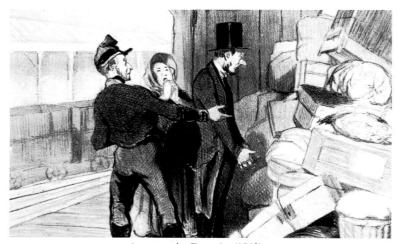

A cartoon by Daumier (1843).

'Are you looking for your trunk, sir? It's somewhere there and so is your wife's hat box.'

(Bibliothèque nationale, Paris)

A cartoon by Granville.

'I say, Dobbin, just look at them. They're taking their carriage by rail now.'

An ivory ticket from the
Liverpool & Manchester Railway
(Dendy Marshall Collection)

Leicester & Swannington Railway
brass ticket (1832).
(Science Museum, London)

Brass ticket from Montreal &
Lachine R.R. (1848).
(Dendy Marshall Collection)

TICKETS

Initially, tickets were forms on which were written in longhand the date, the destination, the name of the purchaser and the number of the coach and seat. Everything was written in triplicate, one copy being for the passenger, one for the guard, and the third for the issuing office. This had been the system which had operated in the days of the stage-coach, but it proved to be too complicated given the huge increase in numbers of passengers. In 1832, the Leicester & Swannington Railway was the first to use an 8-sided metal ticket bearing the destination and number of the passenger. The tickets were issued to the passenger upon payment of the fare and they were handed in on arrival. In England, passenger-tickets were, for a long time, ivory discs.

One of Edmonson's first cardboard tickets.

Furth-Nuremberg ticket (1835).

Cardboard tickets appeared in Germany about 1835, but it was Thomas Edmonson (1752–1851), the station-master at Milton on the Newcastle & Carlisle railway, who in 1836 invented the modern ticket, both in respect of its size and the information it contained – details and class of journey, fare and ticket number. He also invented a machine which would issue tickets in numerical order and a machine which would stamp the date on the ticket issued.

For passengers who could not read, certain lines, such as the Manchester & Leeds, issued tickets which had pictures on them – for example, a sack of cotton to represent Manchester and a woollen fleece to represent Leeds.

Platform tickets were first issued in France, and season tickets in Britain, the latter being found even on the very first railways.

An 1860 date-stamping machine.

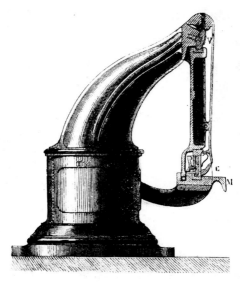

The first date-stamping machine by Thomas Edmonson.
(Indian State Railway Magazine)

A ticket-counting machine, 1860.

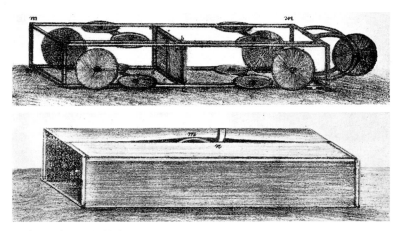

Medhurst's first atmospheric railway design (1827).

Left: A side view of the moving coach; *Right*: The piston truck, and a section of the tube as the truck passes over it.

ATMOSPHERIC RAILWAYS

The idea of using a vacuum as a means of transportation is a very old one. In 1687, Denis Papin first thought of the possibility when he suggested transmitting remote motor-power by means of a tube in which a vacuum would be created. The vacuum would pull a piston which in turn would draw on a rope. The state of technology at the time did not allow him to apply this very early idea for remote-power transport.

The real inventor of pneumatic transport was the English engineer, Medhurst. In 1810, he took out a patent to carry mail in towns, using a truck which would run along a track. The truck was connected to a piston which was moved along a tube by means of a suction pump. He then thought of carrying passengers by the same system along a tube 6 ft high and 5 ft wide.

In 1824, Vallance developed this idea and carried out a full-scale test near Brighton in a wooden tunnel with a diameter of 6 ft.

In 1827, Medhurst returned to his idea and, to avoid the practical difficulties of such a large tube, he invented a system which was used by all his successors. He described this system in *A New System of Inland Conveyance*. Basically, it consisted of an iron tube laid between rails with a slot running along its top edge. At each end were two vertical lips which entered a water-filled channel. A piston with a curved arm moved along the inside of the tube, the arm projecting out of the slot and being attached to the waggon. In this way the water created an airtight seal, but because the system involved the use of water it could only be used on a flat track. To solve this problem, Medhurst suggested using a square tube with a top face which could be partially opened. As the trolley with its piston passed down the inside of this tube, an arm connected to a waggon on the outside protruded from the slot. Although Medhurst was not able to build a full-scale version of this device, his name will be remembered not only for this invention but also because he was the first to create a streamlined shape – which today would be termed aerodynamic. He described the vehicle in these terms: 'The carriage will be 20 ft long and no more than 3 ft wide, with a vertical edge before and behind in such a way that it can pass through the air with the least resistance from opposing winds or the pacific atmosphere'.

The first practical test of an atmospheric railway was made in 1835 at Wormwood Scrubs by Pinkus on a track three miles long. The system was a practical application of Medhurst's ideas but the traction carriage was outside the tube and had a piston and two wheels inside the tube. The trolley opened and raised fully a cord-valve joint which covered the slot. The same system was later used by Clegg and Samuda, who replaced the cord by a leather strip. Two plates held the strip in place at the front and rear ends of the trolley. To simplify the system they moved even closer to Medhurst's invention and used a hinged leather strip as a valve joint. They then applied a wax and resin sealant to form an airtight joint and the leather strip was pressed against this. A small heater was used to improve adhesion!

In Ireland, Clegg and Samuda built a complete

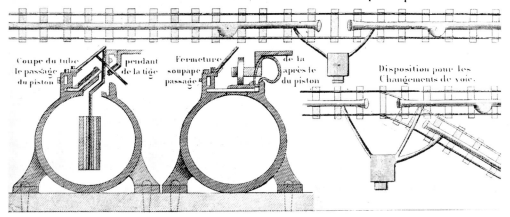

Plan à vol d'oiseau du chemin de fer atmosphérique.

The track, section of tubes, and junction used in Clegg and Samuda's system (1847).

A Clegg and Samuda coach used on the Saint-Germain atmospheric railway.

At the rear, can be seen the compressor-wheel and the heater.

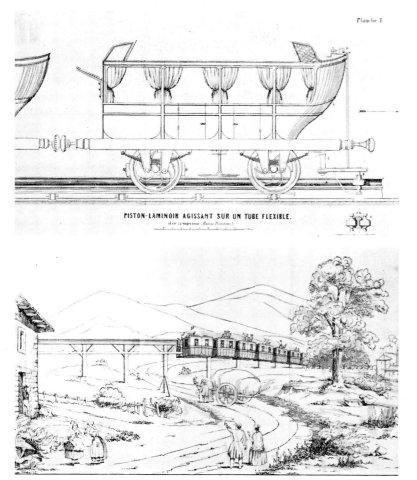

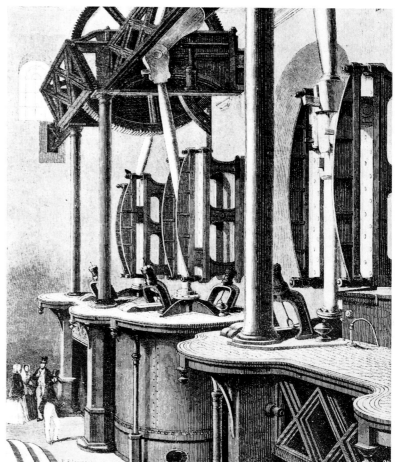

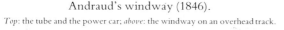

Andraud's windway (1846).

Top: the tube and the power car; *above*: the windway on an overhead track.

Air pumps in the station at Saint-Germain.

railway which was opened on 19 August 1843 between Kingstown and Dalkey. However, it never operated regularly.

In France, this idea was greeted with great enthusiasm because it meant that locomotives with their boilers and their weight would no longer be needed, and the Government loaned 1,790,000 francs to the Saint-Germain railway to build such a line. A tube 2 feet in length was laid over a distance of nearly 1½ miles between Vesinet Woods and Saint-Germain. Over the full length of the track there was a rise of nearly 170 feet and an average gradient of 1 in 43. Although the line was technically successful, it was a financial disaster. It operated from 14 August 1847, but it had cost more than 6 million francs. The huge machines built in Saint-Germain station could operate for only 3 minutes per hour. Meanwhile, locomotives had made such progress that the *Antée* and the *Hercules* could now haul heavy loads up slopes which in the past had been thought of as impossible. The atmospheric system therefore lost its only advantage; nevertheless it lasted until 1859.

In 1845, the Croydon Railway had also built a line of this type between Forest Hill and West Croydon. Brunel who, unlike the two Stephensons, was an ardent supporter of such a system, opened a similar line in 1847–48 on the South Devon Railway between Exeter and Newton Abbott. It proved, however, to be a disaster. By 1848, both in Britain and Ireland, all atmospheric

railways had completely disappeared. Their many problems had proved insuperable: a single speed, difficult and costly maintenance, and all the faults normally found in fixed engines. Nevertheless, a speed of 50 miles per hour had been achieved in Ireland with a train weighing 30 tons.

Left: Cross-section of Hallette's tube when closed (1844).
Right: Hallette tube as the piston passes.

Different systems were tested in France – by Hallette in Arras in 1844, by Chameroy in Paris in 1844, and by Hediard in Saint-Ouen in 1848. Hallette invented and tested an interesting valve system; along the edge of the slot ran two rubber tubes which were inflated under pressure and which pushed against each other on a reinforced metal face. The piston arm pushed the tubes away

from each other but they immediately came together again after the arm had passed by. These various systems were tested only over short distances. Many other inventors created alternative systems, which indicates how interested people of the time were in this idea. In Chameroy's system, suction drew the piston along the tubes and this drove the carriage. Pecquer's compressed-air railway operated in the opposite way, the engine passing over a series of distributors placed between the rails. A curious invention which never got beyond the theoretical stage was Andraud's 'wind railway'. A rubberised cloth tube ran the length of a central rail. Compressed air was injected into it and this gave a forward motion to two bars which pressed onto the tube and which were connected to the waggon. To operate his system in towns, Andraud designed a raised track similar in some ways to Palmer's invention. A small-scale test was carried out in Paris in 1856 on empty land near the Champs-Elysées.

In London, in 1865, the Post Office agreed to the building of underground pneumatic lines to carry mail. The tube was sufficiently large to allow a medium-size truck to be driven along it. This system, which had been thought up by Latimer Clark, operated for many years. Shortly afterwards, a pneumatic line for passengers was opened between London and Sydenham, with the carriage passing along the inside of the tube. In New York, in 1872, the underground system was similar but this was the last atmospheric railway.

COMPRESSED AIR AND ELECTRICITY

The weight of locomotives and the fear that these 'travelling furnaces' might explode caused inventors to look for other sources of motive power.

It was the great French engineer, Andraud, the inventor of the wind railway, who studied the many problems raised by compressed air. He developed the idea of obtaining power from natural sources, such as water and wind, and applying it to transport. In 1840, with his colleague, Tessié du Motay, he built in the Chaillot ironworks a carriage driven by compressed air and on 9 July of that year this was tested successfully on an experimental track. It was an 8-seater coach, fitted underneath with tanks which connected to a regulator and an expander, that is to say, a heating device which would increase air expansion within its two cylinders.

On 21 September 1844 on the Versailles left-bank track, Andraud tested a six-wheel locomotive driven by compressed air and weighing 5 tons. It was fitted with a 106 cubic foot tank which contained air pressurised to 300 lbs per sq. in. On its first test, it covered a return journey of just over 2 miles at a speed of between 17 and 20 miles per hour.

In Britain, about 1830, Brown tested a gas-driven locomotive and, in 1862, in London, Gallardo's model for a hydrogen-powered locomotive was on display.

Electro-magnetism applied to rail-traction is older than people think. In 1839, when Jacobi was testing it on his boat, Robert Davidson described an electric locomotive which was built and tested on the Edinburgh & Glasgow railway in 1842. It had an underframe and four wheels measuring 3 ft in diameter. Each of the axles was fitted with soft-iron armatures which turned between two pairs of fixed electro-magnets. The machine had its own batteries, weighed 5 tons, and could pull a load of 6 tons at a speed of 4 miles per hour with less than 1 h.p.

In 1851, the Count of Moncel and Géraldy unsuccessfully tested an electric locomotive. At

Andraud's first compressed-air locomotive (1839).

Robert Davidson's electric locomotive (1842).
(*Railway Gazette*, 1934)

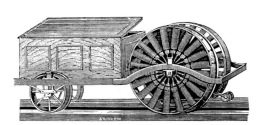

Bellet and Rouvre's
mail-carrying electric locomotive (1864).

the Paris exhibition in 1855, Roux exhibited a model of a locomotive with a motor consisting of two soft-iron plates oscillating around electro-magnets. In 1864, Bonelli suggested that an electric conduit tube should be laid the length of the railway track, and in 1865 Militzer presented to the Science Academy in Vienna a design for an electrified track whose two rails would be separate so that current could pass between them only via the electro-magnets on the locomotive's engine.

But in December 1864, a much more interesting experiment was carried out in Versailles by Louis Bellet and Charles de Rouvre. They built the first electric locomotive to be powered by a battery transmitting its charge through a central rail or through two wires running alongside the rails. This was an important moment in the history both of railways and of independent power transmission. The locomotive was designed solely to carry mail and was of a modest size.

Henri de Parville's *Causeries scientifiques* gives the following description of this locomotive: 'Two large wheels at the front of the vehicle and two small wheels at the rear make contact with the iron rails. Only the front wheels are driving wheels and they are turned by an electric current. To this end each of the large wheels has 20 spokes at the end of which are electro-magnets which fit onto the rim of the wheel. Let us consider one of the spokes whose end is in close proximity to the rail. Let us send a current into the electro-magnet at the end of the spoke. Immediately magnetisation occurs and the wheel pulls the rail to it. Since the rail cannot move it is the wheel which must move and as it moves it brings the spoke into contact with the rail.' Current was provided by a central rail along which ran a tiny 2-wheel trolley. The driving wheels were made of brass and fitted with 20 horseshoe-shaped spokes.

At the 1867 Paris exhibition, Gaiffe's demonstration model was on display. It had two electro-magnets which alternately attracted two armatures. These were fixed to a frame fitted with two cog-wheels which drove a ratchet-wheel. The ratchet-wheel was on the driving-wheel axle.

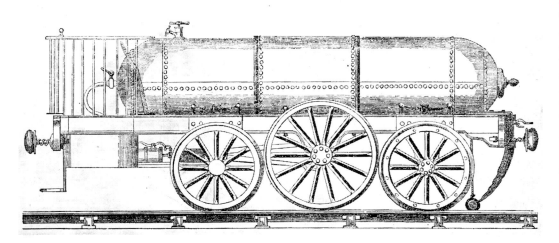

An Andraud compressed-air locomotive (1844).

Celebration in Nantes for the opening of the Angers-Nantes Railway, 17 August 1852.

OPENING CEREMONIES

In France, under the Second Republic and at the beginning of the Second Empire, the opening of many new lines was marked by solemn inauguration ceremonies, with not only the clergy and the local authorities present, but often Napoleon III himself, not simply in his capacity as Emperor of France, but also because he was very concerned to demonstrate the interest he took in the development of industry and transport. Where railways were concerned, this interest appeared geniune.

Opening of the Paris-Strasbourg line, 18 July 1852: the Archbishop of Strasbourg blessing the locomotives.

(*Illustrated London News*, 31 July 1852.)

The first Cuban Railway: Puente del Almadares on the Havana-Matanzas line.

RAILWAYS OUTSIDE EUROPE

The development of railways outside Europe was an interesting one. It frequently opened up new possibilities for those countries and was often a source of wealth, since it encouraged industry to expand. In Canada, the railways are by their nature similar to those found in the United States, but they developed much more slowly. The first was opened in July 1836 on the St Lawrence river opposite Montreal, between St John and Laprairie. It was initially a horse-traction line but in 1837 the first locomotive in Canada ran along it. This was a *Samson*-class engine as built by Robert Stephenson, who himself had arrived in Canada in 1836. Hackworth's three engines were put into service in 1838 on the Albion coal-mine line in Nova Scotia.

The second great line in Canada was opened in 1848 between Longueil in Montreal and Saint-Hyacinthe. This was followed, in 1850, by the lines running from Montreal to Lachine, from Quebec to St Andrews and from Quebec to Richmond. Until 1853, all the locomotives were bought from Britain, but in that year James Good in Toronto began building Canada's first locomotives. The Grand Trunk Railway was opened in 1856 between Montreal and Toronto.

In 1845, Jamaica was the first British colony to have a railway system. The first four locomotives were provided by Sharp, Roberts and Company.

Britain was keen to develop a large network of railways in India, but construction did not begin for some time. The first line, the Great Indian Peninsula Railway, was opened on 16 April 1853 between Bombay and Thana, the locomotives having been sent out in 1852 by the Vulcan Foundry. Initially it had been thought that there would be a delay of 18 months between the construction of the engines and their being put

Saint-Michel station in Oran during the opening of the Oran-Relizane Railway in 1868.

Touring locomotive built in 1859 by R. Stephenson & Company for the Viceroy of Egypt.

into service in India.

The East Indian Railway was the work of Rowland MacDonald Stephenson. It was started in 1851, and opened in 1855 between Calcutta and the Raneegunge coal-mines 120 miles away. It was then extended to Cawnpore, a distance of almost 600 miles. In 1857, it was used to transport troops during the Indian Mutiny. The Geelong Railway opened in 1855 and the Madras Railway in 1856. In 1858, the Great Indian Peninsula Railway opened a mountain line across the Ghat with Wilson's double locomotives. From the earliest years, carriages in India had the particular feature of being fitted with blinds to protect passengers from the sun.

In Australia, it was as a result of private enterprise in New South Wales that the first line from Sydney to Liverpool, a distance of 24 miles, was built. Work began in 1850, but on 3 September 1855 the Government was forced to take responsibility for this line, and it was inaugurated 23 days later. The locomotives which ran along it were built by Robert Stephenson. In Victoria, the Geelong Railway was opened in 1855, and in South Australia the Adelaide-Gowler Bridge Railway opened in 1859.

The building of railways in South America often proved a difficult task because of the mountainous nature of the terrain and the marshy ground. The first trains to run were on the Copiapo Railway in Chile. Work on this line was begun in 1848 and completed in 1850 by an American industrialist, William Wheelwright, who played a considerable role in the development of railways in South and Central America. It was Wheelwright who promoted the Trans-Andes line and also the line from Valparaiso to Santiago which was built by the great engineer H. Meiggs.

On the line from Copiapo to Caldera, British engines were used, but because of the curves and weakness of the track they had to be built with bogies and a large number of axles and thus, in 1860, the first 4–6–0 class locomotive was built.

In 1854, in Brazil, a rich banker, Baron de Mana, built at his own expense the Mana Railway, a small line linking Rio de Janeiro and Petropolis. A larger line was built later and called the Don Pedro II Railway. The first section from Rio de Janeiro to Queimadas was 25 miles long and was opened on 29 March 1858. Branch lines

The first Brazilian railway: an old photograph of a locomotive depot.

(Photo: Moore)

The *Sindh*, built in 1856 by Kitson for the Indian Midland Railway.

(Photo: Moore)

Inauguration of 'Don Pedro's Railway': ceremony in Rio de Janeiro station, 29 March 1858.

to São Paulo and Minas Geraes were also built. The same year saw a line opened in the province of Pernambuco and work begun in the province of Bahia. At the same time, the Campos and Cantagallo lines were started, as was a network in São Paulo. Generally speaking, railways in Brazil consisted only of isolated sections of track.

In Argentina, the South Argentine Railway began work on the first line on 7 March 1861. On 20 April 1863, the line from Rosario to Cordoba was started. The Central Argentine Railway, which was inaugurated in 1865, is also the work of Wheelwright, and his colleague, Brassey. They also built the line from Buenos Aires to the port of La Ensenada.

On 11 September 1866, the Ferro-Carril Del Oeste Railway was inaugurated, a line 100 miles long, linking Buenos Aires and Chivilcoy and built by Manuel G. Gonzales. The first locomotive to run on it was called *La Portena*. On 9 July 1866, the Gualeguay Railway was opened. In Peru, railways started in 1868–69, with the lines from Mejia to Arequipa, from Pisco to Yca and with the coal-mine railway from Pasco. In 1870, Meiggs began work on the sections from Callao to La Oroya and from Arequipa to Puno.

A line crossing the Panama Isthmus was planned as early as 1844. Once again Wheelwright is

among those who helped build this railway. On 28 January 1855, the line, which linked the Atlantic to the Pacific, was opened. 'Originally it took 17 days to cross the Isthmus. This, thanks to other means of transport, became a tiring three-day journey. Now it is completed in six hours.' (A. Perdonnet, 1855).

Where railways were concerned, Cuba was considerably ahead of Spain. Construction work began in 1834, and by 1855 a total of 375 miles of track had been laid whereas Spain at that point had no more than 70 miles.

Mexico, which already had the Panama Railway, began work in 1855 on the building of the great line which was to link the Gulf to the capital, Vera Cruz to Mexico. Mexican railways made particular use of Fairlie locomotives, that is, locomotives with a double boiler and two groups of 12 driving-wheels.

In Asia Minor, railways appeared as a result of British influence and because of Britain's links with India. The first line was built between 1857 and 1859 from Smyrna to Aidin and operated with ten of Robert Stephenson's locomotives. The Seguin brothers had drawn up a very detailed and interesting plan to link Europe and the Far East. The first section was to be a line running from Turkey to Basra and then extending to

India. Although it had the full support of Napoleon III, their project came to nothing.

In the Far East, the first railways were built in Japan on a narrow-gauge track, approximately 3½ feet wide, which linked Tokyo to Yokohama. This line was planned in 1868, work began in 1870, and it was inaugurated in 1872. By 1873, it had already carried 1,223,000 passengers.

In Africa, the first railway was built in Egypt by an English company. It linked Alexandria and Cairo. It was only inaugurated on 1 January 1857, but work had already started by 1852, and the first locomotive, a Robert Stephenson engine, had already run on it. Sometime later, this line was extended from Cairo to Suez and provided a connection with the steamships to India. Because of its vested interests, this railway company opposed very strongly the building of the Suez Canal. Egyptian locomotives were always painted in bright colours and consequently had a quite unusual appearance.

In Algeria, in 1857, an Act of Parliament authorised the building of railways, and as a result various lines were opened in the years that followed. The line from Oran to Relizane was operating in 1868 and later was extended to Algiers, which was already linked to Blida. Algerian lines were narrow gauge.

RAILWAY STAFF

As the railways developed, the jobs of many people who worked on the roads, in horse-transport, and in hotels and inns which relied on coaching traffic, disappeared. The railways, however, also created a large number of new jobs, and the people who are employed on them form an important group of workers in every country.

Among them, the technical staff – drivers and firemen – are a group of people with particularly important responsibilities. In the early years of the railways, good engineers hardly existed in France apart from the locomotive-builders themselves, since the use of steam-engines had remained very localised and had hardly developed by comparison with Britain or the United States. Marc Seguin wrote of the difficulties he had in training 'careful and intelligent workers' such as could be found in Britain. He was, therefore, forced to build the sort of engines which could be assembled and maintained by relatively unskilled workers. He said much the same thing about employees responsible for the maintenance of waggons. 'In England a worker needs to be told only once. He will then be able to carry out his task without further prompting.' In France, however, each worker wished to work as an

individual. As a result, the necessary technical discipline suffered. Initially, and in many cases for several years, all companies employed English mechanics. They were sent with the engines by the British locomotive-builders and they trained the French work-force and oversaw maintenance of the engines. The same happened in Belgium. In return for the sum of 3,000 francs per year, the American engine-builder, Norris, guaranteed for 10 years the running order of his engines which he exported to Europe, providing an American engineer was given responsibility for their maintenance. In 1832, on the Andrézieux–Roanne line, English mechanics were paid 325 francs per month. In England, about 1845, their wages were 35 to 40 shillings per week. In Belgium, at the same time, the wage was between 2,000 and 2,200 francs per year. They were required to work a 10-hour day and this was divided into 4 sessions,

Rhymney Railway	Taffvale Railway
Barry Railway	Cardiff Railway
Boulogne Railway	Marseilles to Avignon line

UNIFORM BUTTONS

the men being paid for every 2½ hours of work fully completed. In England, about 1845, firemen were paid between 25 and 30 shillings per week, and in Belgium they were paid 2 francs 50 centimes per day, that is, 900 francs per year. On colliery locomotives, drivers were paid according to the tonnage hauled at the rate of a farthing per ton per mile. Out of his own wages, the driver had to pay his fireman and provide fuel.

In Britain, railway-workers had a particular status in the early years. They belonged, not to the company work-force, but to the police, and their job was to guard the track in much the same way as police supervise traffic in towns now.

In February 1841, their role was described in these terms: 'The duties of the police may generally be defined as maintaining order in stations and on the railway lines. They must give and receive signals. They must ensure that the track is

A level-crossing guard about 1845

free of obstacles whether they have been placed there deliberately or not. They must give assistance in the event of an accident. They must warn people about the dangers of the railway. They must remove all unauthorised persons and supervise and operate crossings and points. They must give information about arrivals and departures and direct people at the entrance to the station and on the platforms. They must be on the lookout for land slip on embankments and in cuttings. They must inspect rails and sleepers. They must guard and watch over the company's property, and inform their superior without delay if any object requires attention.' In fact, apart from the men who worked on the trains themselves and porters and ticket-office staff, all employees belonged to this police force. They carried a constable's truncheon just as police do today. The nickname 'bobby' was used to describe the pointsman.

The first trains were manned by a large number of guards, whose job it was to supervise the train, to operate the brakes, and to give help to passengers. Between 1835 and 1850, in France and Belgium, railway employees were not allowed to accept tips from passengers, unlike on the stage-coaches where tipping was a widespread practice.

From the inception of the railways, staff have always worn uniforms.

Knife issued to guards on the Saint-Germain and Versailles Railway (about 1840).
(Moutier Collection)

Clavières' loop railway at Le Havre in 1846.

STRANGE RAILWAYS

There were many inventors who tried to get away from the standard type of track and rolling-stock. About 1820, for the transportation of building material, the English engineer, Palmer, devised a system which would solve the problem of the friction caused by litter and debris which frequently blocked tram lines. This system, the suspended monorail, could operate whatever the terrain. It consisted of trestles supporting a rail along which passed trucks with only one wheel. On each side of the truck was a kind of bucket fitted with guide wheels. These in turn ran along a further rail, which also had the advantage of

Cham's cartoon of the loop railway.

reinforcing the trestle structure. The largest trucks had two pairs of wheels. The idea was developed, and it was Palmer's system which was used on excavation work in the Bois de Boulogne and on the fortifications of Paris. In 1825, in Hertfordshire, a Palmer railway was used to carry bricks across the marshy land of the River Lea. In 1824, arising out of Palmer's system, the idea of sail propulsion was suggested by Luke Herbert to carry fresh fish from Brighton to London!

Sail-propulsion for carriages and sledges had existed in Holland from the beginning of the seventeenth century. About 1837, sail waggons ran in Sunderland, and before this, in 1829 and 1830, between Charleston and Hamburg on the South Carolina Railway, a sail-wagon with 15

Girard's hydraulic sliding railway (1869).

The Duke of Buckingham travels on a pneumatic mail train in London (1865).

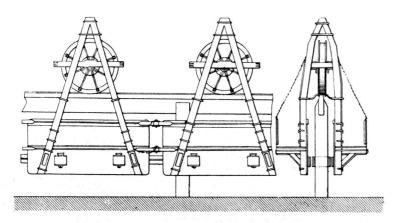

Palmer's monorail railway (1820).

Sails used on Palmer's monorail (1824).

passengers on board reached a speed of 15 miles per hour. On one occasion, the wind destroyed the mast and the sail and caused several passengers to fall out of the truck. However, the journey was completed with a makeshift mast.

In 1846, a railway was developed in France which had no serious practical possibility and which was used simply as a form of entertainment. It was to be the precursor of all those looping-the-loop machines which became so popular in funfairs at the beginning of the twentieth century. This system, devised by Clavières, was first exhibited in August 1846 in Le Havre in the Frascati gardens. The Le Havre newspaper said: 'We call this an airway because the departure point is 30 feet above ground level. Over a distance of 100 feet the track descends at a rate of 5 inches per foot. At this point, the car enters a loop 13 feet in diameter, travels round it at incredible speed, and then for 60 feet runs up a slope which rises at the rate of 3 inches per foot. One cannot imagine a stranger sight, a more interesting spectacle. The car carrying two sacks filled with 66 lbs of sand set off at a terrifying speed and after passing through the circle it came to a stop beneath the first-floor windows of the house occupied by Madame Aguado, with such accuracy that a bunch of flowers could not have landed more gently at the feet of this noble lady. M. Thiers himself was witness to this experiment.'

The same article appeared in L'Illustration, with a further paragraph: 'At the end, one of the workmen insisted on undertaking this short journey which proved to be more dangerous in appearance than in reality. He set off from the highest point at 1.00 pm and arrived at the other end, a distance of 246 feet, at 1 o'clock and 8 seconds. As he stepped out of the car he appeared to be very happy with his journey. Two collections were made for him, the first producing 120 francs, the second 60 francs.'

An airway had been exhibited already in London but passengers had not been allowed on it. Clavière's airway was later set up in the Paris Hippodrome and passengers were allowed to ride on it.

Another strange device to stem from Palmer's system was the suspended monorail called the William IVth Royal Car. This was exhibited in

Suspension railway exhibited in London about 1835.

Truck with sail on the South Carolina R.R. (1829–30)
(History of American Locomotives)

The Ostend to Bruges dog-operated mail truck.

1835 in London at the Royal Panarmonion Gardens, and consisted of a basket fastened to two sets of wheels and pulled by a kind of velocipede which was itself also suspended.

In 1845, L'Illustration, quoting from the Bruges Journal, described the 'canine railway': 'In Belgium, two Englishmen and their associates have built from Blankenberg to Bruges a canine railway which will be used to carry fish. Four dogs are harnessed to a light carriage which has two barrels of fish on board. The dogs have not been fed and a piece of fresh meat dangling a few inches in front of their noses causes them to run. The meat is held in position by a rod which is fastened to the carriage. When mail is to be carried, since this must be delivered more quickly, two greyhounds will be used. Another system could be to replace the piece of meat by a dead or stuffed hare which will seem to be running away from the hungry dogs.'

The great export on hydraulics, F.D. Girard, devised some new and interesting systems. In the first system, waggons fitted with base plates would slide along a film of water lying between the plates and flat rails of the same width. The train would be propelled along by a series of jets positioned horizontally on the track. These would project water onto blades fixed to the carriage. These blades were a kind of early forerunner of the turbine.

At the 1852 Paris exhibition, Girard applied this idea to the propulsion of ordinary trains. In 1854, he devised another system in which the train was propelled along on a cushion of compressed air. He later replaced the air by water. In 1862, on his land at La Jonchere, he built a hydraulic propulsion track which was 130 feet long and had a gradient of 1 in 20. On the basis of the results, he applied to build a line from Calais to Marseilles, and the concession for this was granted in 1869. However. war broke out and Girard was killed in January 1871. Nevertheless, his work was continued and a hydraulic railway based upon his system operated in Paris during the 1889 exhibition.

Latimer Clark built a pneumatic postal railway in London to link the main post offices by underground tube. It also carried a number of passengers curious to see how it worked, one of these being the Duke of Buckingham in 1865.

The Fampoux disaster on the French Northern Railway (1846).

ACCIDENTS

The first deaths caused by this new means of transport occurred when a locomotive, a modified Brunton engine, exploded at the Newbottle Mine near Newcastle on 31 July 1815. The driver, a man, and a small boy were killed instantly. Fifty people were seriously injured and several of these died shortly afterwards. Between 1825 and 1833, on the Stockton & Darlington Railway, two other engines exploded, one of which was the *Locomotion* in 1828, and two drivers were killed. In America, the locomotive *Best Friend* also exploded.

The first person to be run over by a locomotive was, as we have already noted, William Huskisson, the MP for Liverpool. On 15 September 1830, the inauguration day of the Liverpool–Manchester line, he was struck by the *Rocket* and crushed beneath its wheels.

The first derailment to cause the death of passengers occurred on 3 December 1830, on the Newcastle–Carlisle line. A train left the rails at Great Corby and three people were killed.

The accident which most shocked the public in the early railway era took place on the Versailles left-bank railway. On 8 May 1842, at the Pave des Gardes level-crossing in Meudon, a train overloaded with passengers was coming back from Versailles pulled by two locomotives. An axle fracture caused the first locomotive to turn over, and the second one mounted on top of it. The carriages piled into the two locomotives, and the wooden coaches immediately caught fire. As was the custom in those days, the passengers had been

William Huskisson (1770–1830),
killed by the *Rocket*, 15 September 1830.

locked in their carriages as a precaution and they were unable to escape. The scenes that followed were horrific. Officially there were 57 deaths, but the actual number may well have been much higher.

Another famous disaster occurred in 1846 in Fampoux on the Northern Railway when a train was derailed and fell into a river.

A survey of accidents in France from the very beginning of the railways up to 1 January 1854 produced the following report. 'In this period, the number of passengers carried on all railways in France was 158,399,924. The total number of accidents of any description, even accidents where nobody was injured or killed, was 1,869. The number of people killed or injured as a result of their own carelessness is 1,754. Of these, 1,112 were injured and 642 were killed. The number of people killed is, therefore, 4 per million passengers and the number of people injured is 7 per million passengers. If we consider the number of accidents caused through some fault of the management of the railway, we find that there were only 124 deaths, in other words, less than 1 death per million passengers carried. There were only 473 people injured, that is to say, 3 per million passengers. Moreover, we have not included in the number of people injured or killed, members of the companies themselves.' (A. Audiganne)

Between 1835 and 1856, out of a total of 224,345,769 railway passengers in France, there was only 1 death per 2,021,133 and 1 person injured per 558,071 passengers. By contrast, for horse-drawn coaches the figures were as follows: 1 death per 355,453 passengers and one person injured per 29,871 passengers.

In Belgium, the rate was 1 death per 8,861,804 passengers and in Britain 1 per 5,256,240. In the United States, the number of accidents was higher and the accidents themselves tended to be much more serious, since frequently they involved the collapse of a bridge or the explosion of a boiler.

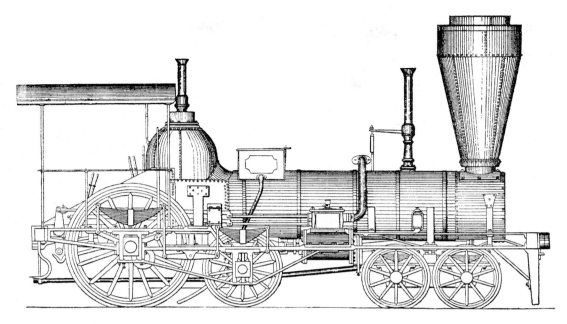

American passenger locomotive (1855).

The *Catawissa*, built about 1837, and a waggon from the Little Schuyhill R.R. and Canal Company.

One of the first locomotives in Canada, the *Samson*, built by Hackworth for the Albion Coal Mining Company in Nova Scotia (1838).

(Photo: Moore)

AMERICAN LOCOMOTIVES

From 1835 onwards, the American railway network expanded rapidly. Track was laid extremely quickly and straight onto the ground, without using ballast, and complicated projects, especially tunnels, were avoided as much as possible. American engineers did not hesitate to build tracks that curved, following the contours of the landscape, and this influenced the design of their locomotives. The first American locomotive was built by Baldwin in 1834, and about 1855 almost all the locomotives running in America were based upon his design. For 80 years, they were characterised by their long boiler built on a very flexible underframe to withstand the unevenness of the track. There were invariably at the rear of the engine one or two pairs of driving-wheels and, at the front, a four-wheel pivoting bogie. Sometimes another carrying-axle was positioned in front of the driving-wheels. Wood was generally used to fuel the engine, as was still the case immediately after the First World War. The cylinders were always on the outside. Certain minor features completed the appearance of what was to become the typical American type of engine: the cab, the cow-catcher at the front of the engine to remove from the track any animals which may have strayed there as a result of the lack of fencing, the flared chimney designed to hold in any fragments of burning wood, the large lantern used to illuminate the unguarded track, and, finally, the bell which warned that the train was approaching.

The United States quickly freed itself from European influence and exported engines to countries whose terrain required the use of articulated locomotives. Their locomotives were lighter and cheaper than those in Europe, and Americans remained justifiably proud of them.

Crampton locomotive built by Derosne & Cail at Chaillot in 1849 for the French Northern Railway.

EXPRESS TRAINS

Speed, a new element in the life of man at that time, was first demonstrated at the Rainhill Trials in 1829. Shortly afterwards, Robert Stephenson travelled 30 miles in one hour using a *Planet* locomotive, and at the beginning of 1835, 'on the Liverpool to Manchester railway a Sharp and Roberts locomotive travelled one mile in 57 seconds, one league in 2 min. 22 secs. and 25 leagues in an hour'. This was the first mechanised journey completed at 60 m.p.h., a speed subsequently recognised as a yardstick for all other attempts to establish records.

In 1839, the Grand Junction trains frequently travelled at 56 m.p.h. and on the South Western Railway a 46-ton train achieved a record speed of 50 m.p.h. The normal average, however, for a 50-ton train was a speed of 20–25 m.p.h. The inadequacy of this speed led Brunel in 1835 to introduce a broader gauge of 7 feet for the Great Western Railway: in this way he could use engines which had a very large heating surface and were very stable and he could reduce traction resistance by using coaches with wheels of larger diameter.

The first fast train on Brunel's track, the *North Star*, was built by Robert Stephenson in 1837. Based on a 2–2–2 wheel arrangement, with driv-

ing wheels 7 feet in diameter, it weighed 21 tons and had a heating surface of about 700 square feet.

However, Stephenson was concerned to increase engine power while at the same time retaining standard-gauge track, and in 1841 he patented the long-boiler engine. Without increasing the diameter of the engine body, thus avoiding raising the centre of gravity, he lengthened it, but being forced to retain the distance between the end axles in order to make use of existing turntables, he positioned the three axles between the smokebox and the firebox. The result was an engine with sleek and delicate lines, economical on fuel, but unstable because of its length.

In 1845, a Royal Commission was set up to settle the question of gauge. The decision, which was probably a bad one in the long term but difficult to avoid taking given the number of lines already in existence, favoured standard gauge. However, some very interesting, comparative tests were carried out with locomotives of both types.

The struggle, keen and filled with incident, ended with victory for broad gauge where speed and weight of load were the main considerations, but victory for standard gauge where capacity to generate steam was the principal concern. Doubts about the latter decision persist as a result of some shrewd, but dubious, practices introduced into the tests. The competitors were permitted to raise the water temperature in advance, and it appears that supporters of standard gauge went far beyond what had been intended.

Between London and Didcot (a distance of 53 miles) the broad-gauge *Ixion* achieved average speeds of 50 m.p.h. with an 81-ton load and 55 m.p.h. with 71 tons, reaching a maximum speed of 60–62 m.p.h. A standard-gauge long-boiler, modified by placing the driving-wheels at the rear behind the firebox, pulled 50 tons at 47 m.p.h. and 80 tons at 43 m.p.h. with maximum speeds of 58 and 52 m.p.h. respectively.

Daniel Gooch built the *Great Western*, the first

Gooch's express locomotive *The Lord of the Isles*, built for the Great Western's broad-gauge track (1851).

(Photo: Moore)

The French Northern Railway's Crampton locomotive of the 1–12
and 165–170 class (1849).

(Bibliothèque nationale, Paris: photograph taken in 1866)

Crampton locomotive class 122–133, built by Derosne & Cail in 1849.

(Bibliothèque nationale, Paris: photograph taken in 1866)

of his famous locomotives with driving wheels 8 feet in diameter, in only 13 weeks; in June 1846 it travelled with a load of 100 tons from London to Swindon at 59 m.p.h. Fierce competition existed between companies favouring either broad gauge or standard gauge, and although in 1847 a modified Stephenson long-boiler pulling a special train travelled from London to Birmingham at 56 m.p.h., reaching a maximum speed of 75 m.p.h. and covering the last 20 miles at 60 m.p.h., the broad-gauge networks also saw the introduction of marvellously powerful and impressive engines. The most famous of these was Gooch's *Lord of the Isles*, which was introduced in 1851 and travelled 79,000 miles in 32 years. These engines of the *Iron Duke* type achieved amazing performances: about 1850, the 77 miles from London to Swindon were covered in 1 hour 12 mins. at a speed of 63 m.p.h. The normal time for the journey of 53 miles from London to Didcot was, on the timetable, 55 minutes, representing a speed of 57 m.p.h. A train pulled by the *Great Britain* on 11 May 1848 in fact completed the journey in 47½ minutes at a speed of 67 m.p.h. The normal return journey

time was 57 minutes. The name given to this express was the *Flying Dutchman*, the name of the horse which won the Derby in 1849, and it has remained a classic.

In 1853, the Bristol and Exeter line operated with fast engines equipped for greater stability with ten wheels only, one pair of which were driving-wheels of 9 feet diameter. But as early as 1838 the wheels of the *Ajax*, constructed from metal plate and solid, had a diameter of 10 feet.

Where speed was concerned, designers of French locomotives had no reason to be envious of their English counterparts: the great English engineer T.R. Crampton built in France a type of locomotive whose name is still in use and which stands as a symbol for speed. A modified version of the long-boiler, the Crampton was a thoroughbred: very long and very low with a lowered centre of gravity and, as in Gooch's engines, steam admission through an internal tube, it had two carrying-axles and a driving-axle behind the firebox. The driving wheels had a diameter of between 7 feet and 7 feet 6 inches. These engines had great stability at all speeds. Almost 300

Cramptons were built between 1849 and 1864, notably by Derosne and Cail for the Strasbourg, Lyons and Northern Railways, and also in Germany. At trials in 1889, organised by the PLM Railway, an old Crampton with a load of 157 tons reached a speed of 90 m.p.h. It was with such an engine that Napoleon III beat a record which still stood 80 years later: in 1855 he returned from Marseilles to Paris at the timetable speed of 60 m.p.h. in a two-carriage train weighing 7 tons and hauled by Cramptons. At the present time [1935] the world record over 272 miles is 68 m.p.h. (London–Newcastle).

Various attempts were made to increase speeds still further. One of these featured Francis Trevithick's strange engine, the *Cornwall*, the boiler for which was to be found beneath the axle of driving-wheels measuring 6 feet 6 inches and which travelled in 1867 at 78 m.p.h. Another, in 1855, involved the locomotive of Blavier and Larpent which had four driving-wheels with a diameter of 9 feet 4 inches. This engine was tested on the French Western Railway and did not give good results.

Robert Stephenson's *North Star*, built for the Great Western's
broad-gauge track (1837).

(Reconstruction made in 1925: Great Western Railway archive)

Rothwell's broad-gauge locomotive for the Bristol & Exeter Railway (1853).

(Photo: Ahrons)

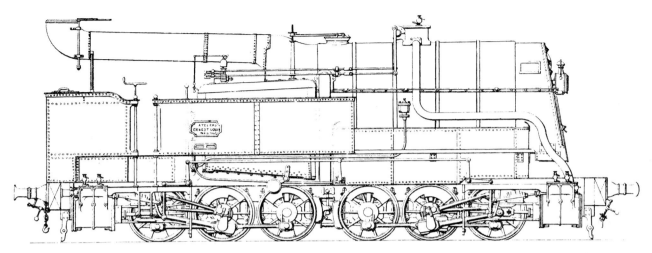

Petiet's four-cylinder and twelve driving-wheel 'camel' locomotive for goods trains on the French Northern Railway (1862).

POWER LOCOMOTIVES

Routes through Central Europe, and the increased traffic they generated, led to the building of special locomotives for mountain journeys and to pull heavy loads. Power had to be increased and at the same time track adhesion and flexibility had to be retained so that the locomotive could negotiate curves.

The steep gradient from Le Pecq to Saint-Germain had convinced Flachat of the need to adopt the atmospheric railway. Nevertheless, this great engineer later tried to devise a means of climbing this incline with a gradient of 1 in 28 by using steam-traction. In 1849, he built the *Hercules* and the *Antée*, both with six coupled wheels measuring 4 feet in diameter. The latter succeeded in pushing up this incline a load of 93 tons on top of its own weight of 26 tons and a 9-ton tender.

In 1842, J.C. Verpilleux had been the first to think of using the weight of the tender to increase adhesion without overloading the rails and to retain overall flexibility. He fitted the tender with

Flachat's *L'Antée* for the Saint-Germain gradient (1849).

An Engerth-type French Eastern Railway's goods locomotive (1835).

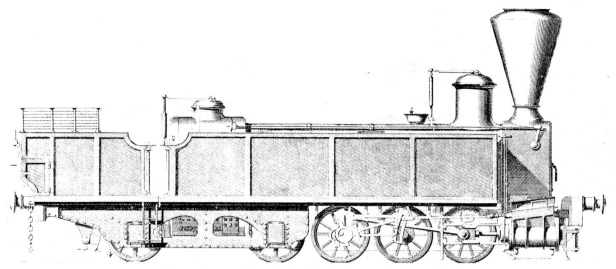

Engerth geared locomotive for the Semmering Pass (1854).

two cylinders which drove the four coupled wheels. This gave an engine with four cylinders and eight coupled wheels divided into two groups. Steam was transmitted to the tender via flexible brass tubes. From 1843, onwards, several Verpilleux engines were used on the Saint-Etienne–Lyons line but this early initiative was not copied.

The first mountain locomotive came into operation in Austria in 1851. Matthias von Schönerer had urged that there should be a competition to build a class of engine capable of crossing the Alps between Vienna and Trieste through the Semmering Pass up gradients of 1 in 40 and round curves with a radius of 625 feet. Four locomotives took part. Maffei's *Bavaria* was an eight-wheel engine. Its third axle, a driving-axle, was linked by a chain to the two front axles. These were coupled by a rod to a fourth axle which, in turn, was connected by a chain to the front-axle of the tender. The tender's six wheels were coupled by a rod. This gave a fourteen-wheel track adhesion and flexibility with the wheels which were divided into three groups. Günther's *Wiener Neus-*

Verpilleux locomotive with a driving tender (1842).

The *Bavaria*'s chain coupling (1851).

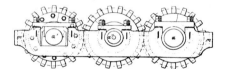

Engerth's gear coupling (1854).

tadt had four cylinders which drove in pairs two sets of four coupled wheels. Cockerill's *Seraing* had a similar arrangement, but with a double boiler like Miller's locomotive in 1830 and later Fairlie engines. Finally, the *Vindobona* was an eight-wheel engine, but not articulated. The winner of the competition was the *Bavaria*, and the tests gave the Austrian engineer Engerth the information he required to build an engine whose tender was connected to the boiler and bore the weight of the firebox, the size of which could therefore be increased. Moreover, Engerth connected the tender to the driving-wheels by a system of gears. At Le Creusot they replaced Engerth's gears by eight coupled wheels and this modified version was used by several railways in France to pull trains weighing between 400 and 665 tons.

About 1860, on the Northern Railway, Petiet built a strange kind of engine-cum-tender with four cylinders and twelve wheels divided into two sets of six. The high position of the boiler required the use of an horizontal chimney and this earned the engine the nickname of 'The Camel'.

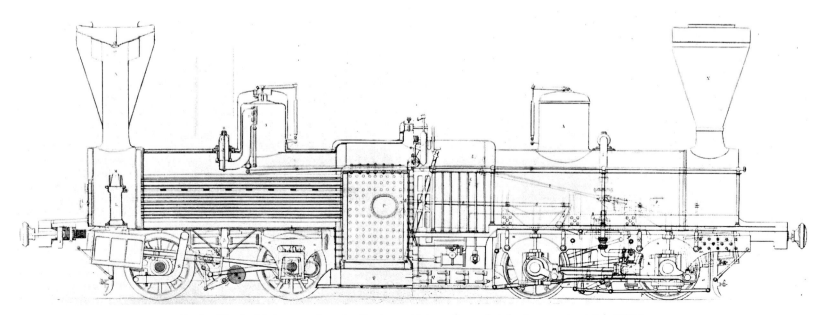

Cockerill's double locomotive, the *Seraing*, which performed at the Semmering trials (1851).

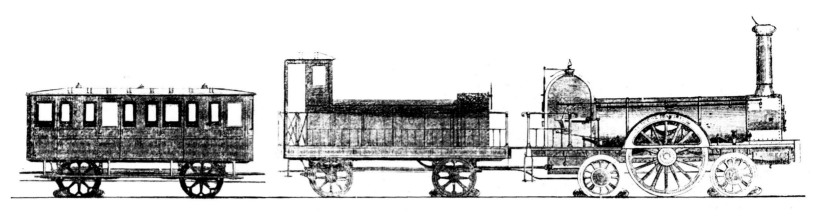

Sceaux Railway's articulated locomotive, tender and waggon, based on design by Arnoux (1846).

(L'Illustration, 6 June 1846)

ARTICULATED TRAINS

On European rail networks, a great deal of study has been directed at the problems posed by curves in the track. In various countries, and particularly in Austria, Norris's American locomotives were used in the early years. These engines had a front bogie which allowed them to negotiate gentle curves. In France, in 1846, Arnoux, an engineer working for the Sceaux railway, built an articulated train which ran on this line for almost 50 years. The coaches' underframe rested on two sets of wheels which were similar to the front set of wheels on a normal coach, with each axle pivoting on a pintle, and the wheels turning freely on their spindles. The coaches were coupled together by a rigid rod. The front set of wheels of the leading coach had four offset guide wheels which made contact with the rails and turned the axle according to the direction of the track. This axle transferred a corresponding direction to the rear

axle by means of a crossed chain passing through two pulleys which were of equal diameter and fixed to each axle. The direction to be taken was then transmitted to the second wagon by a crossed chain which passed over two pulleys, one of which had twice as large a diameter as the other. The system was then repeated along the full length of the train. Because it transmitted simultaneously a different angle of direction to the two axles of the coach, the second axle changed its angle just before it entered the curve, and, when the direction had been transmitted to the axles of the following coach, the angle of these axles was adjusted in time to guide the coach through the curve. These locomotives were fitted with four offset wheels. Shortly afterwards, Arnoux built locomotives whose coupled wheels had a strange arrangement. The two sets of right-hand and left-hand wheels were independent of each other and driven by two cylinders. Later, Arnoux's son simplified the process by replacing the chains

with a system of diamond-shaped articulated rods. Arnoux's offset wheels had already been tested on a small scale, in London in 1844, by Prosser on his wooden railway.

Flachat tested a train on which every waggon was a driving waggon with its cylinders connected to the locomotive's boiler. This development of Verpilleux' system was not successful because the steam did not reach the cylinders furthest away from the boiler.

The building of articulated locomotives led to some interesting designs, apart from those already mentioned as having taken part in the Semmering trial. Rarchaert's articulated locomotive had two bogies, each with four coupled wheels. The two inside crank-axles were driven by an untrue central axle by means of rods which had some play in them, whereas the rods connecting the pistons to the untrue axle remained rigid.

Haswell's engine, the *Steierdorf*, based upon Engerth's engine, had six coupled wheels at the

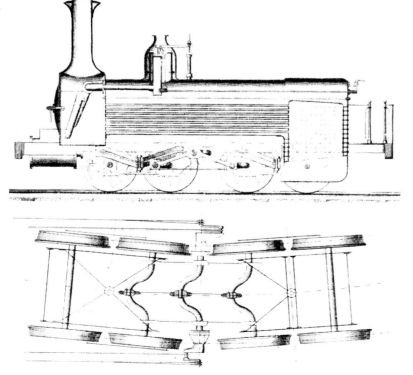

Rarchaert's articulated locomotive (1866).

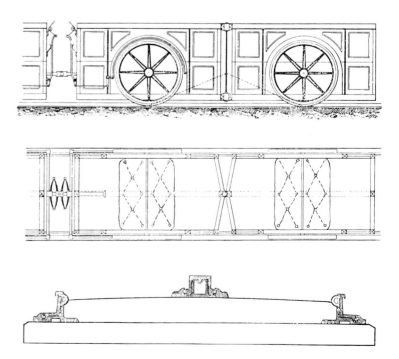

Jouffroy's articulated monorail railway (1844).

Side and plan view of track and waggon

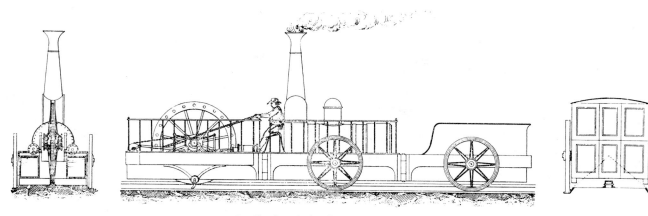

Jouffroy's articulated monorail railway (1844).
Front and side view of the locomotive, rear view of waggon

front connected to the pistons and four coupled wheels at the rear, the two sets of wheels being independent. Transmission was by means of an untrue axle and a vertical rod. In Germany and Austria, between 1855 and 1860, many different systems of balanced wheels and untrue axles, often very complicated, were tested. Shortly afterwards, in France, Beugniot, an engineer working for André Koechlin's firm (which later became the Alsace Mechanical Engineering Company), designed articulated locomotives which remained flexible by means of a 1½ inch sideways play in the axle. This movement in the axles, which remained parallel to one another, was made possible through a system of ball-joint supports. Polonceau achieved the same sideways play by using triangular-shaped parts which allowed the axle-collars to move.

About 1840, Jouffroy invented a system which attracted a great deal of interest, although it was only ever tested on a small-scale model. To increase track adhesion and be capable of negotiating any curve, Achille de Jouffroy designed a locomotive which would consist of two waggons with hinged articulation. Two of the waggons would have carrying-wheels which would run on flat rails, and one would have a large driving-wheel with a wooden rim which would run along a central grooved rail. The waggons themselves were divided into two sections with hinged articulation. Jouffroy had failed completely to understand the principles which govern track adhesion in heavy and powerful engines. In spite of the support of important people in the world of science his idea was never successful.

Nevertheless, about 1868, between Montfermeil and Le Raincy, a system not dissimilar to Jouffroy's operated effectively. It had been built by Larmenjat. The guide-wheel of the locomotive ran along a single central rail while the two driving-wheels, like the wheels of the coaches, ran along the ground.

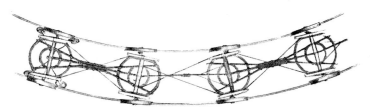

Plan view of Arnoux's articulated system (1846).

Right: Haswell's articulated locomotive, the *Steierdorf* (1862).
(Pierre Jacquet Collection)

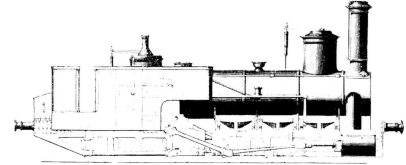

Larmenjat's monorail railway which ran from Montfermeil to Raincy (1868).

Excavation work on the Clamart Cutting (1840), on the Paris-Versailles line.

EXCAVATION WORK

The building of the railways led civil engineers to carry out excavation work on a scale hitherto unknown. Canals had always been built on the same plane. Roads generally made detours and did not require the huge earth works demanded by the railways since the latter had to avoid, wherever possible, bends and inclines. There was also the question of time, since railways had generally to be built far more quickly than roads or canals. This developing industry learned very quickly how to help itself and often, as work advanced, its wagons carried the earth which had to be moved.

In Britain, in the earliest years of the railways, a group of entrepreneurs quickly came together to supervise and direct all the civil engineering work involved, much as George Stephenson himself had done. They came to specialise in large-scale excavation work, and succeeded both in training a skilled work-force and in developing methods and equipment which they felt would be of use for a long time to come. 'Not only through their wealth but also through their skill and intelligence these men made huge improvements in the branch of industry in which they worked.' (A. Perdonnet)

On the Continent, things were, however, quite different. Railway engineers were unable to find entrepreneurs with any knowledge of the task in hand, and they had themselves to supervise all the earth works and the training of teams of workers. The equipment did not exist. Companies were only prepared to supply the rails along which the trains would later run.

British entrepreneurs collaborated with en-gineers on the Paris–Rouen line, while two Belgian engineers, Parent and Schaken, came to France to help build parts of the Strasbourg, Lyons and the Northern lines, and lines running from Lyons to Avignon and from Paris to Mulhouse.

Excavation work for railways took three forms. First, earth from cuttings was used in the building of embankments. Second, the soil excavated was spread over neighbouring land. Third, embankments were built by taking land from nearby areas. The first system did not affect neighbouring properties but was slower than the other two. Using rail waggons rather than road waggons proved faster in certain respects, but had serious disadvantages. Rail waggons operate only as part of a train and are loaded and unloaded at one end of, or at the side of, the track. Road waggons, however, can operate in far greater numbers and go virtually anywhere. Since those early years, however, the use of narrow-gauge railways has changed the situation considerably. Round about 1830, Palmer's monorails were used to excavate and move huge amounts of earth.

Tip-up trucks were first used in 1795 on the tram road across Chatt Moss. At the beginning of the nineteenth century, the tip-up truck was to become a common sight wherever earth was being excavated.

In Britain, the idea was conceived of using horses to help men pull wheelbarrows. The horses pulled on a rope which passed through a return pulley and was attached to the wheelbarrow. The amounts of earth moved by relatively primitive means in the course of building the original lines makes interesting reading. In the Tring cuttings on the London–Birmingham line, 1,400,000 cubic yards were moved, in Gadelbach, on the Ulm to Augsburg line, 1,300,000 cubic yards, in Tabatsofen 1,100,000, in Cowran on the Carlisle railway 900,000, in Pont-sur-Yonne, on the Lyons line, 600,000, in Poincy on the Strasbourg line, 650,000, in Clamart on the Versailles left-bank line 520,000 cubic yards. The Saint-Romain embankment on the Saint-Etienne–Lyons line required nearly 80,000 cubic yards of earth.

Excavations in England at Boxmoor, about 1850.

Station in the place Valhubert in Paris: boarding point for the Orleans Railway, about 1850.
(Paris–Orleans Railway Collection)

Boarding point for the Saint-Germain atmospheric railway, in 1846.

PASSENGER STATIONS

The history of stations reveals great differences in concept. A striking example of this is provided by engravings which show, in Paris, the modest Orleans station in the Place Valhubert, and the quite remarkable Saint-Germain, Versailles and Rouen station built in Rue Saint-Lazare from which it gets its name. The Saint-Lazare station survived almost unchanged for more than forty years until its transformation in 1886, and its internal design and facilities would still grace many stations today. On the other hand, the stations at Rouen and Le Havre on the same network remained until the 1930s in the same primitive state as they were in the reign of Louis Philippe. One is also struck by the unfinished appearance of the Midi station in Brussels, at the time when the trunk line to Paris was opened in 1846.

The British influence on the men who built the

Interior of Bristol Temple Meads Station in 1840.
(Great Western Railway Collection)

Rodeio station and viaduct over the Ribeirão dos Macacos on the Don Pedro II Railway in Brazil, 1858.

STATIONS OF THE PAST

External view of the station in the rue Saint-Lazare.

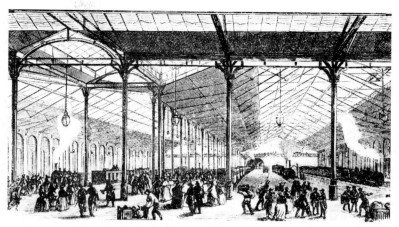

The station concourse of the Rouen, Le Havre, Versailles
and Saint-Germain Railways.

Rouen-Le Havre line was seen in the architecture of its small stations. Here, the Northern Railway company constructed its buildings to a common design but modified each one according to the size of the station.

Small country stations have undergone little change since the early days of the railways. Generally they consist of a central building with accommodation on the first floor to house the station-master and small side annexes for ancillary services.

It was in Britain, particularly after 1851, in other words after the building of Paxton's masterpiece, the Crystal Palace, that the huge glass departure hall started to appear. The departure hall of the old Saint-Lazare station does, however, pre-date these and was one of the very first to be built in this way. We owe it to the science and skill of Eugène Flachat, an engineer whose ideas on both traction and architecture always created the greatest interest. In France, he was the man mainly responsible for the development of the huge metal constructions with their spacious arrival and departure halls. Polonceau, an engineer on the Paris–Orleans railway, also built many such halls in glass and iron. During the Second Empire he constructed the old Orleans station, now the Gare d'Austerlitz. A wonderful example of this style still survives almost unchanged. It is the triple hall at Paddington, the original London terminus of the Great Western Railway, and it was built in 1854 by Brunel. Once again he revealed his amazing far-sightedness, since this station coped with all its traffic needs for

THE GARE SAINT-LAZARE, 1843–1847
Staircase and waiting-room.

50 years, without any change or addition. Only in the twentieth century have there been any extensions to the station. In the early years, and especially in Britain, passengers crossed from one platform to another over a footbridge. Underground passages were not built until a later date. In France, generally speaking, passengers simply walked across the lines, a straightforward but dangerous practice.

The Great Western Railway was the first to build well-designed stations which offered all the facilities the passengers could require. In Temple Meads station, Bristol, for example, as early as 1849 we find the five tracks situated beneath a huge partially-glazed roof, and raised platforms which are on a level with the floor of the coaches.

Generally, passengers in Britain enjoyed the most comfortable conditions of travel. Inside, the stations were glass-covered areas which extended as far as the trains themselves, and, also, outside the station were covered areas where passengers could shelter as they arrived. In France, the first covered area outside a station was at the Gare de l'Est in Paris.

In Belgium, no shelter was provided for passengers for a long time. Similarly no platforms were provided, on the grounds that the carriages were very low-slung. These arrangements may be partly explained by the fact that the passengers on the Belgian railway network consisted more or less of the same people who used the local tram service.

In Germany, stations were often built in an agreeable rustic style which fitted in with the surrounding countryside.

In America, apart from the magnificent stations to be found in the large cities, stations, and particularly small country stations, were very basic, and the early years of the railways saw hardly any improvement to them. Building costs, and irregular and limited traffic, led quite naturally to the building of stations which had no platform and which consisted of a small wooden

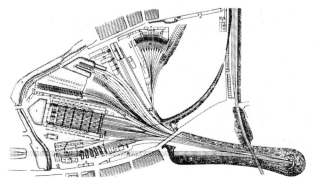

Plan of the Great Northern goods terminus in London, in 1855.

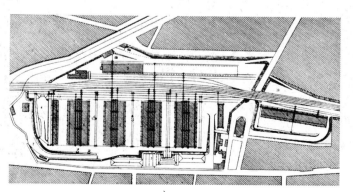

Plan of Bercy goods station on the Lyons Railway, in 1855.

Uintah station (Utah) on the Central Pacific Railroad, in 1869.
A contemporary photograph. (Central Pacific Railroad archive)

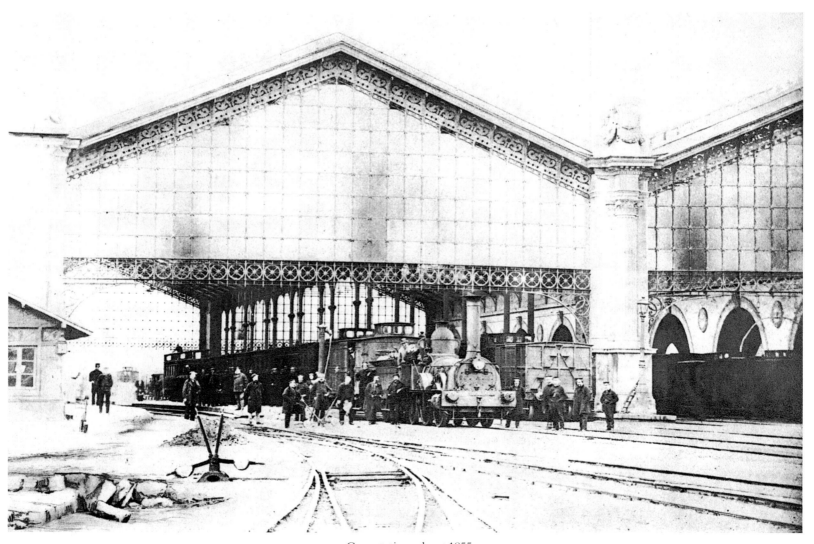

Caen station, about 1855.
A contemporary photograph. (State Railway archive)

OLD STATION PHOTOGRAPHS

The Gare du Midi in Brussels, in 1846.

house to accommodate the station-master, and a shed. Usually the station was manned by only one employee. From the very beginning there were, and still are, unmanned stops without any actual station, simply a small wooden platform and a signal which the occasional traveller can operate himself to stop the train.

When the first railway lines were built, a controversial subject was the location of main stations in large towns. Some people preferred these to be built as near as possible to the town centre. This was the case in Paris for the station for trains to Saint-Germain and Rouen. People had even thought of siting the terminus near the Place de la Madeleine. On the other hand, some people supported the idea of siting stations on the edge of the city. They argued that it would be cheaper, would allow a freer movement of goods, and that passengers could easily reach their destination in the city by using the carriages and cabs which already operated. In London, a central station which would receive all the lines from every network had been planned, but the disadvantages of this system were quickly recognised. Nevertheless, the main-line stations in London are all

Station for the Lyons line in Geneva, about 1856.

located close to the city centre. Very early on, long viaducts were built which allowed the trains to enter the city without disrupting the flow of traffic beneath. In France, in certain large cities, a quite different attitude prevailed, stations being kept well away from town centres. This decision is now bitterly regretted.

Station administrative buildings reveal a number of different arrangements. In Paris, in the Gare de l'Est, the Gare du Nord and the Gare Saint-Lazare, offices were situated at one end of the station. In other stations, for example, in the Gare de Lyon, the offices ran down the side of the station. This arrangement was considered to be the most convenient.

There are some interesting statistics on the main stations in Paris as they were in 1860. The total length of the Gare de l'Est was 1640 feet, of the Gare du Nord 1410 feet, of the Gare Saint-Lazare 1312 feet, of the Gare de Lyon 1181 feet. The length of the arrival and departure hall was in the Gare de l'Est 492 feet, the Gare du Nord 426 feet, the Gare Saint-Lazaire 525 feet, and the Gare de Lyon 492 feet. The total surface area varied from 9 acres at the Gare d'Orleans to 19 acres at the Gare du Nord.

The oldest of the Paris stations are in the Place Denfert and the Place de la Bastille. Saint-Germain station is one of the oldest never to have been modified at all, but it was only built in 1846 and is, therefore, not as old as the Versailles right-bank station. The external architecture of this station, possibly the oldest in France (1839), has not changed at all.

Rouffach: a country station on the Strasbourg-Basle line in 1844.
Lithograph by E. Simon Jr & Th. Muller (*Panorama des Vosges et du Chemin de fer de Strasbourg à Bâle*: M. Armand Boeringer Collection)

The Val-Fleury Viaduct at Meudon, on the Paris-Versailles Left-Bank Railway, about 1855.

End view of the Offenburg Bridge.

Bordeaux Iron Bridge.
Photograph taken in 1860.

Side view of the Offenburg Bridge over the River Kinsig, in 1855.

Willington Dean Viaduct on the Newcastle-North Shields line.

VIADUCTS AND BRIDGES

The first railway-bridge was built in Britain by George Stephenson in 1824, at West Auckland, on the Stockton & Darlington Railway. It was built in rolled- and cast-iron and was not replaced until 1901. The oldest bridge built over a line is George Stephenson's Rainhill Bridge (1829). It is a stone skew bridge. Before starting work on it, Stephenson had a full-size wooden model made.

Wooden viaducts have been in common use in all countries and were still to be found in North and South America until the 1930s. Well-maintained, they gave excellent service. 'Even the heaviest trains can perfectly safely use light wooden bridges and at full speed, providing the different parts are well designed and well assembled.' (A. Perdonnet). The wooden viaduct across the upper reaches of the Tennessee River was 875 feet long and 260 feet high.

The viaduct at Val-Fleury in Meudon is a very fine example of railway architecture. Here, the bottom of the valley was of very soft clay and the engineers were forced to sink foundations down to a chalk layer beneath the clay. As a result: 'The amount of masonry below ground almost equals that above ground, and it proved to be quite a difficult task to lay the foundations for the pillar supports in deep shafts which landslips threatened constantly to fill in'.

The first great cast-iron bridges were Robert Stephenson's Newcastle Bridge, which was 1338 feet long, and Paulin Talabot's Rhone bridge between Tarascon and Beaucaire. Across the Tamar between Plymouth and Saltash, Brunel built the first important bridge in which double tubular arches were used. It was made of riveted plate metal and each of its arches had a span of 455 feet. The first straight tubular bridges were the work of Robert Stephenson. The parts were

rectangular in cross-section and made of plate metal. Such bridges are found across the Conway and the Menai Straits, the latter, the Britannia Bridge, being built in 1850. These two bridges link Holyhead to Anglesey and Anglesey to Wales. Ross built the Victoria Bridge across the St Lawrence River to take the line from New York into Canada. It was nearly 9000 feet long and had 25 arches.

Lattice bridges were frequently used in Germany (at Offenburg, Kehl and Cologne). The lattice bridge at Bordeaux, which is just over 2000 feet long, if one includes its approaches, was built in 1860.

Suspension bridges were used for railways in America, the most famous being the one across the Niagara. It was begun by Roebling in 1852 and opened to traffic in 1856. The single arch was 816 feet long and stood at a height of 242 feet above the river.

The first skew bridge at Rainhill, built in 1829 by George Stephenson.

(Dendy Marshall Collection)

Level-crossing and pedestrian footbridge at Beaumont, in 1846.

(Pierre Lichtenberger Collection)

The Bristol Goods Station, about 1840.
(Great Western Railway Collection)

LUGGAGE AND GOODS

Transportation of inert matter was the principal function of the early railways, which carried material from coal-mines, quarries, and salt-mines. Goods were first carried on the Surrey Iron Railway in 1801. In 1804, the charges were as follows: 3 pence for coal; 2 pence for lime, sand, chalk, bricks, stones, etc; and 3 pence for 'any other goods'.

This function was also, in the minds of the great merchants who took a financial interest in the enterprise, one of the most pressing reasons for the building of the Liverpool & Manchester Railway. Liverpool Station was, therefore, equipped with jiggers and hoists to deal with any goods which might be carried. Waggons could thus be loaded extremely quickly and with a minimum of manpower. As a result, significant savings were made, these being estimated at 6 pence per ton

manually and between 4 and 5 pence per ton using machines. The warehouses built in Liverpool and Manchester by the company, and by the Grand Junction Railway, were valued in 1847 at 7½ million francs. They served lines which ran a total distance of 109 miles. During the same period, the warehouses in Manchester of the Manchester & Leeds Railway could hold 100,000 sacks of flour, 8 sacks weighing a ton. To attract the transport of grain to its line, the company provided free storage for two months. When the Glasgow & Garnkirk Railway opened in Glasgow in 1832, the platforms were built to be at the same height as the floor of the waggons, and tracks were laid along the river banks to enable trucks to unload directly into boats.

In Paris, in 1860, goods stations varied in surface area from 62 acres at the Gare de Lyon to 86 acres at the Gare du Nord. At the time, the covered surface area available was estimated at

between 54 and 215 square feet per ton of goods handled.

From 1830, the traffic of livestock, which until then had always been moved by road or on foot, was seen as an important source of revenue, and special waggons were designed for this purpose.

About 1847, in Britain, there was no charge for luggage, providing it did not exceed between 55 and 100 lbs, depending on the class of journey. Registration was not required, but a label was fixed to each piece of luggage and this was then placed on the roof of the carriage. For greater efficiency on lines north of London, luggage was sorted according to destination and placed on the roof of first-class carriages.

In France, luggage was registered and placed either on top of the carriages or in the guard's van. Travellers were 'asked not to tip the employees since the service is offered free'. In 1846, on the Paris–Rouen line, there was a weight limit of 55 lbs. In Belgium, in 1841, the limit was 44 lbs. Here, as in France, luggage had to be registered, and the charge increased with every additional 22 lbs of luggage.

A special feature of transport at the time was the loading of private coaches onto special waggons. This system enabled people to travel in their own carriage. In France, when the Paris–Orleans line opened, there was a further development in the carrying of private coaches by rail. M. Arnoux, the head of the mail-coach service, decided not to fight the railways any longer but to use them to transport the mail-coaches. In Paris, the body was taken off its underframe, lifted by a crane and lowered on to a waggon, which was then attached to the train. On arrival, the reverse operation took place. Since passengers and luggage remained in the coach no transfer was required and the system reduced to a minimum the loss of luggage and the number of connections missed. The whole operation was carried out in only a few minutes.

Orleans Railway in Paris in 1843: loading the body of a stage-coach on to a truck.

TUNNELS

Road tunnels, built before the railways, were short and narrow and bore no comparison to the tunnels which railway engineers dug for the early lines. The first important tunnels were constructed in France by Marc Seguin and his brothers, between 1826 and 1829, for the Saint-Etienne–Lyons line. These were particularly difficult tunnels because of the nature of the terrain, with its hard rocks, crumbly stone and old mine workings. Seguin wrote: 'The Gier valley tunnel extends approximately 3000 feet and cost about 250,000 francs. Excavation of the Rive-de-Gier Tunnel proved somewhat difficult. A way had to be opened up through old mine shafts. This proved to be extremely expensive and very dangerous for the workmen. The entrance on the Couzon side had to be started three times. The Terrenoire, Rive-de-Gier and Lyons Tunnels are all single track, 16 feet in height and 10 feet wide, built in the shape of an egg to withstand land pressure more effectively.'

The Terrenoire Tunnel was nearly a mile long, and the cost of the tunnels varied from 60 to 240 francs per foot.

Originally, the excavation of the tunnel started with a series of shafts which were sunk a few feet on either side of the tunnel's axis. Then, using pickaxes, the openings were extended to the tunnel's centre and then outwards in both directions. The workmen had only a compass to guide them as they excavated and the inside of the tunnel was lit by lamps. Earth was removed through the shafts and through the tunnel openings. The two common methods of tunnelling were by large section and by divided section.

About 1860, the principal tunnels were the

Liverpool tunnel in 1831.

Nerthe Tunnel between Avignon and Marseilles, which was nearly 3 miles long, the Blaisy Tunnel on the Lyons line, which was 2½ miles long, the Credo Tunnel on the Lyons–Geneva line (nearly 2½ miles long), Rilly Tunnel on the Reims branch-line (2¼ miles long), the Apennines Tunnel between Turin and Genoa (2 miles long), the Hommarting Tunnel on the Paris–Strasbourg line (1¾ miles long), and the Hauenstein Tunnel on the Central Swiss Railway which was 1½ miles long. Blaisy Tunnel, which at the time was considered to be a masterpiece, links the basins of the Seine and the Rhone, through a massif standing 650 feet above the track. Twenty-one shafts 650 feet apart were used in construction and 15 have been retained to provide ventilation. The work required 2,500 workmen and lasted 3 years 4 months. Rolleboise Tunnel on the Paris–Rouen line was 1¾ miles long and was completed in two years. In Britain, tunnels were unusual and never very long, the oldest being the Liverpool Tunnel which was just over 1 mile in length and lit by gas.

For passengers in the early days, tunnels were a fascinating novelty. In 1843, the editor of L'Illustration was invited to the inauguration ceremony of the Paris–Orleans line, and he wrote about the Rolleboise Tunnel: 'The locomotive carries us on to a spot which makes many intrepid souls shiver with fear. We are engulfed in total darkness for a distance of 2 miles. How fast our hearts beat during those 4 minutes. We are suddenly thrust into the unknown. Were we still moving? We thought so, but how could we know? Why had we not said goodbye to all those we loved? How foolish we had been. Why tempt God in this way? He gave us the sun. Why did we scorn that gift? The noise of the panting locomotive, the crash of chains in the darkness, the infernal whistle which

A tunnel on the Bratislava–Trnava line, about 1845. Note the ball signals.
(Ceskoslovensky Zeleznickni)

A 'gallery' built on the Saint-Etienne–Lyons Railway, in 1826.

warns of danger, all combine to inspire the greatest fear, especially when one cannot see. And yet we have emerged from the tunnel. It's wonderful! Was anybody really frightened? In those 4 minutes our hearts experienced so many vivid sensations.'

In the French Parliament, Arago spoke of the twin fears which tunnels inspire. On the one hand, the danger of the engine exploding inside the tunnel, on the other hand, the risks caused by the sudden changes in temperature. Several medical commissions agreed. In some countries public opinion remained for a long time hostile to tunnels for the same reasons, and also out of superstition.

In 1849, the Belgian engineer Mauss boldly proposed excavating the Mont-Cenis Tunnel, an enterprise far ahead of its time. He had visualised the use of mechanical drills which would be driven by a waterfall using a system of cables and pulleys. In fact, taking Colladon's idea, the drills were worked by compressed air provided by a Sommeiller hydraulic compressor. The work, which was begun in 1857, will be described later in the book.

The Terrenoire Tunnel on the Saint-Etienne–Lyons Railway, about 1833.

FIG. 3. — Percement d'un tunnel (méthode par grande section). — Agrandissement de la galerie primitive.

FIG. 4. — Méthode par grande section — Construction de la voûte.

FIG. 5. — Méthode par grande section. — Achèvement de l'excavation et construction des pieds-droits qui doivent supporter la voûte.

FIG. 6. — Percement d'un tunnel (méthode par section divisée). — Ouverture des galeries auxiliaires et construction des pieds-droits.

FIG. 7. — Méthode par section divisée. — Achèvement du ciel de l'excavation.

FIG. 8. — Méthode par section divisée. — Construction de la voûte.

Different systems for excavating a tunnel, about 1860.

From top to bottom and from left to right: The Railway Engineer (France 1843); the Luxembourg Railway (1858); 50th Anniversary of Railways in Paris (1887); Cologne-Mainz (1859); the Law of 11 June 1842 (the largest medal ever struck in France 1842); the Paris Circle Railway (1867); Paris-Saint-Germain (1835); Naples to Nocera and Castellamare (1840); Saint-Etienne–Lyons (1826); the Dutch Railways, (1839). *In the centre*: Brussels-Malines (1835); Liverpool & Manchester (1830); Verviers-Aix-la-Chapelle (1843); the Northern Railway (1846); the Portuguese Eastern Railway (1856). *Bottom row*: Munich-Augsburg (1840); Marseilles-Avignon (1843); Liverpool & Manchester (1830); Picardy and Flanders. (Pierre Lichtenberger Collection)

COMMEMORATIVE RAILWAY MEDALS

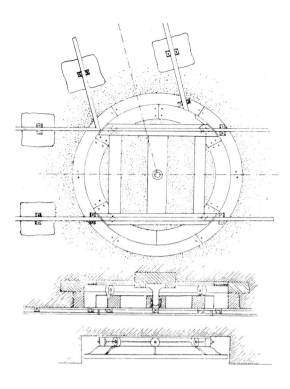

A British turntable in 1830.

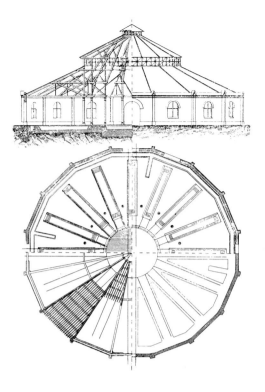

French Eastern Railways engine shed, about 1859.

STATION ACCESSORIES

From the early years, turntables were used, more often for the purpose of changing tracks than to turn waggons round. With the appearance of locomotives, they became far more important since they were then used to enable the locomotive to change direction. Since 1830, there has been little change in their general design, but the small diameter (from 11 to 16 feet) of early turntables influenced considerably the development of locomotives by limiting their overall size. From 1840, trucks were used to move waggons

sideways from one track to another. This was done either by cutting the rails to allow the truck wheels to pass through or by using a truck with hydraulic pistons which raised the axles of the wagon and lifted it across the rails.

Another important device was the water feed-pump. The early ones were made entirely of metal, curved in the shape of a swan's neck, and had no flexibility at all. Later, the process of operating them was simplified by fitting them with a flexible pipe, which meant the whole of the pump no longer had to be turned. In larger stations, the water-tower is also a feature which dates from the beginning of steam-traction. It is

an interesting but little-known fact that it was common practice between 1830 and 1860 to heat the water in these tanks to a temperature of almost 40°C. This was done by using a boiler which burned low-grade fuel and worked a steam-pump which then drove the water to the top of the tower. This reduced the running costs of locomotives and avoided the problems caused by an intake of cold water coming into contact with the walls of the boilers.

Different types of locomotive sheds, some circular, some fan-shaped, were also a feature of railways from earliest times.

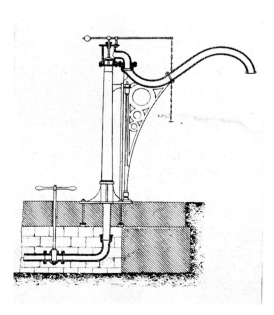

Water-feed pump (1855).

Water-feed pump near Paris (1844):
a decorated plate by Gien.

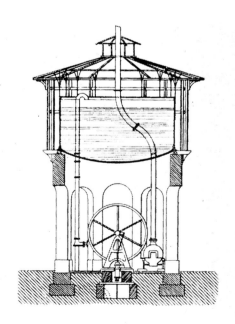

Water-heating tower (1855).

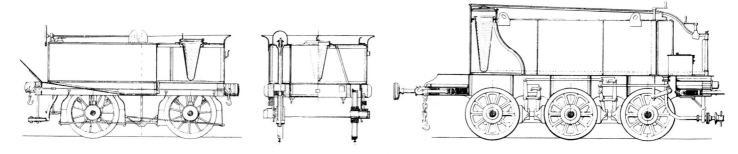

French tenders

Left to right: Side-view and cross-section of a Paris–Rouen tender (1845); section of a Paris–Lyons six-wheel tender (1847).

TENDERS

The first tenders were quite simply small flat wooden waggons for carrying coal. They were fitted at the rear either with a large barrel for storing water or a metal tank.

Like the tenders on the Saint-Etienne–Lyons line, the first American tenders had a covered cab for the driver and the fireman.

The tender as we know it now was originally designed by Robert Stephenson. The first was coupled to the *Northumbrian* in 1830. It was made entirely of metal sheeting and had a horseshoe-shaped water-tank positioned along the sides and at the rear. An opening at the back end of the tender was used to fill it with water. The tender therefore acquired its modern form from the outset. Until about 1860, the underframe was often made of wood, with the sides and the floor always being made of metal. The increase in the speed and power of locomotives meant that tenders had to carry a heavier load, and their size was consequently increased, particularly on express trains which could not take in water at every station. From 1846 onwards, six-wheel tenders, able to carry a very heavy load, were built in Britain and France. When we come to consider braking arrangements, we will see that the considerable weight of the tender, and its position

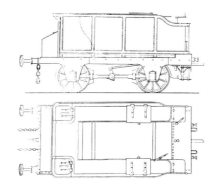

Elevation and plan view of a Strasbourg Railway tender (1847).

(Charles Dollfus Collection)

Model of a Paris–Lyons six-wheel tender (1848).

(Conservatoire des arts et métiers)

close to the driver, resulted in its being used as the main means of stopping the train, a wormgear control being used to press pads against the wheels.

On the large wide-gauge locomotives of the Great Western Railway, tenders were very long and had six wheels. At the back of the tender was a small cab which faced the carriages. In it stood a guard responsible for warning the driver if any emergency arose. It was nicknamed 'The Iron Coffin'.

In the period 1833 to 1840, English tenders, such as those used by Berry engines, could carry 640 gallons of water and nearly half a ton of coal. Twenty years later this capacity had increased to 1100–1300 gallons of water and 2–2¼ tons of coke. This amount of water was sufficient for a journey of 30–40 miles and the amount of coke would last between 120 and 250 miles.

The coupling of tenders required special features because of the pipes which linked the tender to the engine. At first these pipes were made of rubber, but, later, straight brass tubes with a ball-joint were used. Polonceau then replaced these with flexible coiled brass tubes. Finally, rubber was again used but protected by a wire coil. The tender was secured to the engine by a rigid metal bar and buffers, fully screwed down and held in place by a metal plate.

Model of a French Northern Railway Crampton tender (1858).

(Conservatoire des arts et métiers)

Model of a Stephenson tender (1833).

(Conservatoire des arts et métiers)

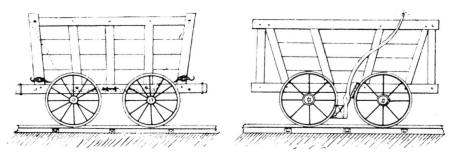

Open third-class carriages on a French train, about 1843.

(Lithograph by Victor Adam: Pierre Lichtenberger Collection)

WAGGONS AND COACHES

Goods waggons were used for a long time before passenger-coaches were introduced. In the middle of the eighteenth century, the coal waggons used in the mines of Newcastle, Leeds and Cumberland were all constructed to a similar design. The body was in the shape of a reversed pyramid. It was solid and easy to maintain. Normally such trucks could carry a load of just over 2 tons and weighed just over 1 ton.

At the end of the eighteenth century, coal-waggons were often coupled and made up into small trains, the coupling being done with chains. Until 1825, the use of locomotives appeared to have had little influence on rolling-stock, except that waggons were strengthened to withstand the damage which the faster and longer trains could cause.

In Germany, coal-waggons were of a more simple design, being a drum-shaped box on a narrow underframe. Instead of wheels, they had small grooved bars which ran along the track. It is highly likely that this model had been used unchanged since the seventeenth century.

In 1803, the Surrey Iron Railway used rectangular waggons which could carry loads of 3 tons and which weighed, when empty, 1 ton.

The first trains on the Stockton & Darlington line were made up of ordinary coal-waggons. Shortly afterwards, thanks to the creative vision of the engineers of the Liverpool & Manchester Railway, the goods waggon made its first appearance. These men had been the first to realise that the railways should not limit themselves to the transportation of raw materials. Their rolling-stock included flat rectangular waggons on which all kinds of goods could be carried and secured under protective covering. There were also open-sided cattle-trucks for cows and two-tiered open-sided waggons for sheep. Waggons for the carriage of goods were never enclosed.

In France, on the Saint-Etienne–Lyons line, goods were carried in coal-waggons and straight-sided rectangular waggons. In 1839, the

Sheet-metal mineral waggon from the Saint-Etienne–Lyons line and two-tub mineral waggon from the Sunderland Railway (1834).

Model of the first passenger-coach on the Stockton & Darlington Railway (1825).

(Science Museum, London)

Mineral waggons from the Stockton & Darlington and Liverpool & Manchester Railways (1834).

Model of a second-class coach on the Bodmin & Wadebridge Railway (1837).

(Science Museum, London)

Montpellier–Cette line was opened, using wag-gons which 'still offer only a choice of two types. There are those used to transport barrels and the platform type for sacks of wheat and salt. Later we intend to build a variety of trucks of different designs which will cater for the needs of com-merce.' This quotation is taken from the leaflet 'Observations on the Montpellier–Cette Rail-way', and shows how these lines were originally considered more as local enterprises.

About 1840, waggons acquired more or less the shape they have today. In France, goods-waggons continued to be built of wood. There is almost no difference between a model of a coal-waggon dated 1855 and to be found in the Conservatoire des arts et métiers, and the trucks which are used at the present time. In England, in 1844, Gooch built closed waggons with an underframe and bodywork made entirely of iron.

On many lines it was forbidden in principle to couple goods-waggons to passenger trains be-cause of the lack of shock-absorber springs.

About 1855, there were many different types of waggons, all determined by the different types of freight. Special waggons were built to transport horses. These were very short, with small-diameter wheels to allow the floor to be closer to the ground. Milk was carried in open-sided two-tier waggons, each of which could hold 200 four-gallon containers. The 'container' system, that is, a system in which boxes or crates were placed on a waggon, was tried on the Liverpool & Manchester Railway but later abandoned. It was used again in France about 1850 to transport horses, being a system very similar to that which operates today on boats.

The history of passenger-coaches begins in 1825 with the opening of the Stockton & Darling-ton Railway. All the guests travelled in coal-waggons, but the train had one passenger-coach based upon the shape of the old stage-coach. This coach was given the name *Experiment*. From 10 October 1825, it ran regularly between the two towns, the charge for a seat being 1 shilling. This was probably the first steam train to have a coach. However, there is some reason to believe that, prior to this, Blenkinsop coupled to his rack locomotives both closed and open passenger-coaches. There is no written evidence for this but various engravings suggest that it was the case.

On the Budweiss–Linz line in Austria, travellers were carried either in open salt trucks or in closed coaches based on the design of the mail-coach. The oldest railway carriage in the world, dating from 1832 and used on this line, is on display in the Technisches Museum in Vienna.

In America, from 1830 onwards, passenger-coaches were built with the chassis of a waggon surmounted by a stage-coach body with seats on the top.

First-class coach on the Liverpool & Manchester Railway (1838).
(*History of the L & MR*: Dendy Marshall)

Private luxury coach from the Dutch Railways, about 1850.
(Railway Museum, Utrecht)

Model of a coach-waggon from the French Northern Railway (1855).
(Conservatoire des arts et métiers)

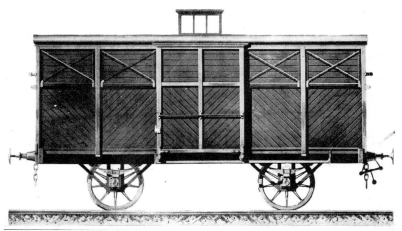

French Western Railways luggage-van, about 1860.

Queen Victoria's carriage in 1844.
(From a drawing by Moyaux)

Queen Victoria receiving King Louis Philippe in the Royal Saloon (1844).
(Pierre Lichtenberger Collection)

Daytime interior of an early Pullman sleeping-car (1869).

It was on the Liverpool & Manchester line that we first find the type of coach still used in the 1930s. From 1830 onwards, first-class coaches were built on a four-wheel sprung chassis. The body was made up of three stage-coach compartments, each of which had bench seats and doors. On the roof was a luggage-rack and a seat for the guard. Sometimes the end compartments were of a smaller size. Each coach was given a particular name and each seat had its own number. Other designs were tried, in particular individual carriages of the mail-coach type.

Second-class passengers travelled in waggons which had bench seats and which sometimes had a door. The back of the seats could be turned to face in the opposite direction. These wagons were fitted with a roof made of a fabric material which gave them the appearance of a tram carriage. In 1831, mixed coaches were tried, the first-class compartments having a second-class compartment on either side.

About 1837, on the small Bodmin & Wadebridge line, there were second-class coaches which consisted of a single body divided into two compartments and having bench seating. The carriage was lit by an oil lamp in the middle of the ceiling and by daylight which entered through the top section of the doors.

Third-class passengers on the Liverpool–Manchester line travelled in open coaches which were sometimes divided into two smaller compartments but often had no seats.

In France, the history of coaches on the Saint-Etienne–Lyons line is of some interest. After a brief period when passengers were carried in coal-waggons, in 1831 the company started building attractive coaches for both first- and second-class passengers. These coaches could run only in one direction, having a platform at the front where the coachman could stand, since, until about 1834, passenger-trains were still pulled uphill by horses and ran downhill by the force of gravity, steam being used only on coal-trains. The second-class coaches had seats on the roof, while third-class coaches were basic and uncovered.

Seguin gave a rather strange description of the need to provide springs in coaches: 'When an engine begins to show signs of wear, when a mechanical body tires, it can only be because a huge expenditure of energy has been involved. This expenditure of energy has to be paid for. Similar considerations apply when a traveller, in a coach with no form of suspension, arrives at his destination exhausted, almost broken. For the passenger to feel this, the horse has had to expend strength and energy. Like the passenger, the coach, when treated in this way, deteriorates quickly and costs much more to maintain. Thus the strength and energy of the horse have been used both to break the limbs of the traveller and to subject the coach to wear and tear. By persuading passengers to sit on straps, and by providing coaches with steel springs, we have found that the coaches last longer, that the passengers are less tired and that the horse's strength and energy are put to a far more profitable use.'

In Roanne, coaches contained three compartments, each of which had three windows, and in Andrézieux the summer carriages resembled

Interconnecting sleeping-cars with triple-decker berths on the Griffin-Atlanta Railroad (Georgia) in 1848.

small tram-coaches.

Although only a small line, the Montpellier–Cette Railway offered passengers a choice of five classes of travel. 'Luxury coaches are based on a model used in Paris and built in the workshops of S. Chaumont. This is our first-class coach. The second-class coach has been built in Montpellier. It has three compartments and can hold 30 passengers, if one includes the seats on the upper deck. Nothing has been spared to make these coaches as comfortable and elegant as the finest horse-drawn carriages. Our two-compartment stage-coaches are built on the lines of the first-class coach but without some of its finer points. Open stage-coach carriages will hold 25 passengers. Our fourth-class coaches have wooden seats and can

carry 30 passengers. Finally, our wagons are only in temporary use. All these coaches have been built by Messrs Servel and Jeanjean, Coach Builders and Locksmiths in Montpellier.'

In Belgium, in 1839, Nicholas Koechlin ordered for the Mulhouse to Thann line a coach of each class to be used as a model by the builder André Koechlin, who then built stage-coaches, open coaches and waggons, the three types representing the three different classes of travel.

About 1840, the Saint-Etienne–Lyons line began to use a much longer type of coach with nine windows. Like American coaches, it had two bogies and access was via the platforms at each end. It is difficult to understand why this interesting development was not imitated elsewhere in Europe and was in fact discontinued.

In 1842, a Royal Coach was built for Queen Victoria who on 13 June 1842 made her first journey by rail on the Great Western Railway between Slough and London. It was in this saloon car that the famous interview with Louis Philippe took place in 1844. Queen Adelaide had her own personal railway-coach as early as 1840, but at that time she was no longer a monarch. Several special trains were built by different networks for Napoleon III. In 1858, a luxury-class coach was built for Pope Pius IX.

German coaches were soon recognisable by their end platforms and by the central gangway running between the bench seats. A fourth class was created which had a bench seat running around the sides of the coach.

The Orleans, Northern, Alsace and Roanne

'Platform carriages' on the Wurttemberg Railway (1867).

railways used open third-class coaches. In 1847, the following comment was made: 'Everybody complains about the third-class coaches on the Orleans and Northern railways. Passengers have no protection from the heat of the sun or from the rain.' Nor, one might add, was there any protection from the smut and the soot unless one bought beforehand at a station the special spectacles designed for third-class passengers and those people travelling on the upper deck.

In Britain, railway companies deliberately tried to discourage third-class travel by refusing to make such travel more comfortable. In 1844, the Cheap Railways Act was passed but it failed to

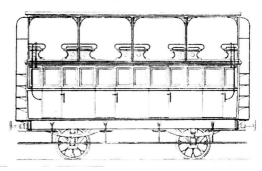

Second-class double-decker coach used on the Paris suburban line, about 1859.

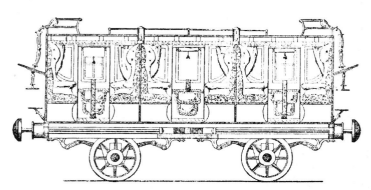

A French first-class carriage (1855).

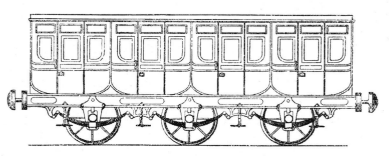

A French second-class coach with six wheels (1855).

improve matters substantially. In France, coaches without windows continued to be used until 1851. In Belgium, railways had proved to be much more popular and a considerable proportion of passengers travelled third class.

In 1855, one of the special features of French coaches involved the use of covered upper decks on the West Paris suburban line and, on the Paris–Lyons line, the provision of lavatories in the guard's van. These could, however, only be used in stations.

Coaches built of metal are much older than many people imagine. In 1836, on the London–Greenwich line, coaches with an iron chassis were used. In 1848, the Great Western built third-class coaches entirely of iron, and in 1848 it ordered a number of these from Stotert and Slaughter in Bristol. These were six-wheeled coaches built to beautiful proportions but spoiled by some unpleasant features. There were no windows in the side walls and passengers could see out only if they stood up to look through a tiny window situated above the doors. The bodywork itself was made of metal plates riveted to corner irons.

American railways were the first to aim to give passengers the levels of comfort required on a long journey. Therefore, about 1840, they built single-class coaches with a central corridor. These coaches changed little in more than a century. The long body rested on two bogies. People entered from the platforms at each end. The seats had adjustable backs which allowed passengers to sit as they wished.

After 1836, on certain lines in America, sleeping berths were in common use. In an 1848 edition of *L'Illustration*, L. Xavier Eyma gave the following description of coaches on the Atlanta to Augusta line: 'These coaches are just like houses. Everything, absolutely everything, which one may need is provided. They are divided into several compartments or bedrooms, some for the use of ladies only, others for the use of men. Each of these bedrooms contains six beds, or rather six berths situated on the sides of the coach on three levels. Until night falls, the two lower berths provide an excellent settee. When it is time to sleep one simply lifts up the back of the settee. When it is in an horizontal position, strong iron hooks operated by an inner mechanism take hold of it and secure it in position. Three perpendicular straps prevent the sleeper from falling out. Ceiling lights illuminate the interior of the room which offers the passenger an attractive and novel spectacle.'

America was the first country to build trains which allowed passengers to walk from one end to the other. Usually their trains also provided a restaurant car, a ladies' car and a car for emancipated black people. Black slaves travelled 'with the luggage in a kind of store at the front of the train where passengers could also smoke'.

In 1858, George M. Pullman decided to improve night travel and tested his ideas at the Chicago & Alton Railroad trials. In 1864, he designed the sleeping-car which carries his name. This is a sleeping-car with beds positioned one above the other and formed from the bench seats, the upper berth dropping down from a section of the ceiling.

Coach interior on the Baltimore & Ohio Railroad, about 1850.

Night time arrangement in a ladies' coach on the Griffin–Atlanta Railroad in 1847.

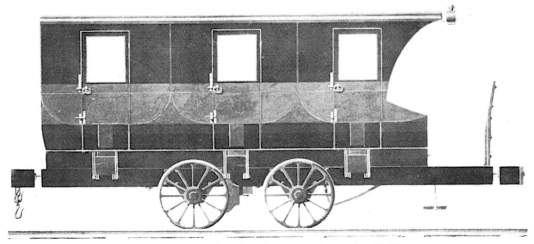

Second-class coach on the Saint-Etienne–Lyons line (1840).

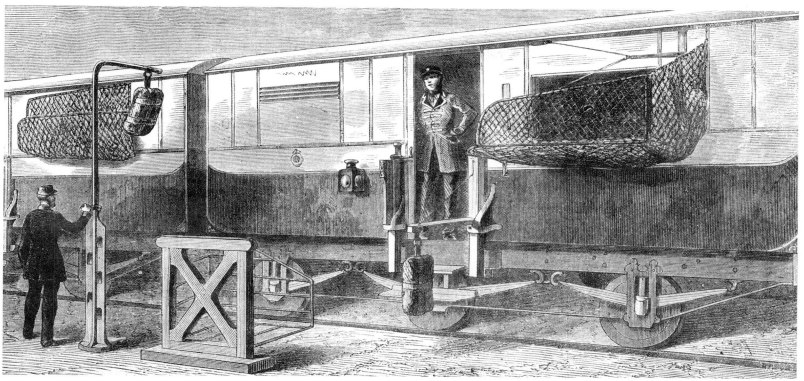

System in Britain for picking up and setting down mail-bags while the train is still travelling (about 1860).

(Ed. de Geoffroy archive)

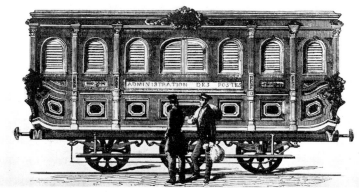

French mail-van in 1848.

Interior of a railway mail-van in 1848.

THE MAIL

The vitally important role which the railways have played in the carrying of mail is not always fully appreciated. One may say that by the 1930s in both Europe and America almost all normal mail was carried by rail. It is, however, strange that this practice, which has proved to be not only essential but also profitable, was not considered to be important in the early years.

In Britain, just prior to 1838, the General Post Office negotiated the carriage of mail with most of the main lines. It paid a charge but also demanded strict conditions in the matter of departure times. A short time before 1840, the Post Office had the Cheltenham mail-coach transported by night train and on the night of 4 February 1840 the first mail-train ran between London and Twyford with some passenger carriages. In 1841, four Post Office coaches were ordered and second-class coaches were modified to carry mail-bags during the day. It was Colonel Maberley, followed by Rowland Hill, Secretary of the Post Office and creator of the 'Penny Post', who initiated mail-transport by rail. In 1855, in England, to speed up the delivery of mail, special mail-trains which did not carry passengers were built.

In France, mail was first carried by train about 1840. The service was well-established by 1848 and excellent Post Office coaches had been built under the supervision of Post Office management. Although the Post Office demanded that mail be carried free, it left the railways free to organise the running time of the trains.

The system of picking up and dropping off mailbags while the train was still moving was devised in Britain about 1840. Time was thus saved, since the train no longer needed to stop at smaller stations.

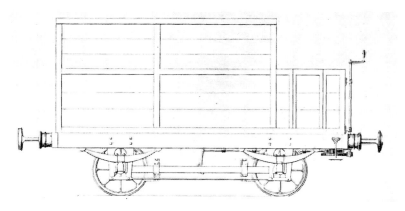

British guard's van with braking platform (1847).

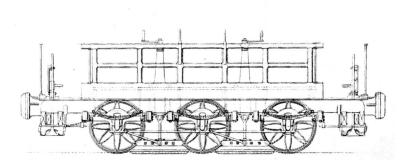

Laignel dual-control brake-van (1850).

BRAKES

Braking is vital to the functioning of any train, and yet brakes remained very basic in spite of their importance being underlined by the death of Huskisson in 1830. At that time, locomotives did not have any brakes, but the wheels of tenders were fitted about that period with a kind of brake-shoe which was operated by a lever. Fortunately, trains were light, and only a few coaches had brakes, these being operated by a guard. A system was invented whereby a heavy weight was released, and as it fell it pulled on a chain which was connected to the brakes. This quickly slowed the train down. However, it required some time to lift the weight back up since the whole system was operated by only one man.

About 1850, Laignel invented his 'braking

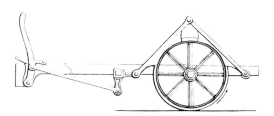

Waggon-brake and lever about 1830.

truck' which was used on some networks. It was a special, very heavy waggon fitted with two wormgear controls which pushed four long pads onto the track.

In 1854, a similar system was used on the Saxony–Bavaria Railway but this was operated by steam, a system which pushed the shoe on to the rail. About 1860, Guerin invented the automatic brake, which was worked by the coach buffers. When the train slowed down, the movement of the buffers, as they were pushed in, activated the brake.

In general, at that time reversed steam was used to slow the train down. This, however, caused soot to be drawn into the cylinders. To prevent this, in 1866 M. de Bergue invented a system of air intake from a special dome instead of from the chimney.

Continuous brakes were first used in America, and it was in America also, in 1856, that Loughbridge took out a patent for a chain brake which controlled all the wheels. The idea was tested but did not prove successful until Westinghouse developed it, using first compressed air, then a vacuum.

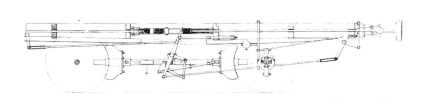

Guérin brake, operated by buffers (1860).

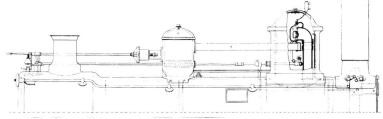

Bergue's cylinder-operated compressed-air brake (1866).

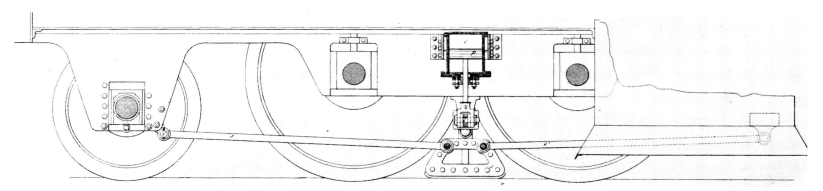

Saxony-Bavaria Railway steam-brake (1854).

Montpellier–Cette Railway letter-heading (1849).

TRANSPORT AND FARES

Railways changed considerably the entire concept of travel, first of all because it made travel cheaper, and second because it made it available to a far greater number of people. Previously most people had never even considered the possibility of travelling any great distance. Commerce and business changed also, since trains were able to carry vast quantities of goods. It is now difficult to imagine what it must have been like for passengers to travel by private horse-drawn coach or by public transport, and especially difficult to imagine the extraordinary complications involved in moving goods by road. Contrary to what many people believed, the 'large, yellow stage-coaches' did not pre-date the railways but came into service at the same time. There was a highly developed system of goods transport by canal and river, water being at the time the only means by which heavy goods, such as wood, hay and building material, could be carried. The 'Railway Revolution', which took 10 years to complete, transformed the nineteenth century.

In America, fares were not controlled and this led to great differences, the charge per passenger-mile varying from 2 cents to 3 cents or even 3½ cents.

In the field of military transport, the first time artillery was transported was in 1842 between Berlin and Potsdam. The railway carried 'a cannon and its horses, trucks and men'.

A comparison with stage-coaches on the question of saving in time and money will explain immediately the success of the railways. In 1834, it took 10 hours and cost on average 12 francs to travel by stage-coach to Liége. In 1839, the same journey by rail took 4 hours and cost on average 5 francs 50. This gave a 60 per cent saving in time and a saving of more than 50 per cent in cost.

The cost of goods carried by rail also proved to be considerably lower than by road and this fact alone caused a great and rapid increase in the use of railways for goods traffic.

Booking-form from the firm of Caillard for a journey by train and stage-coach (1849).

Robert Stevens (1787–1858).

John Stevens (1749–1838).

Pierre Simons (1797–1843).

Von Denis (1804).

THE MEN WHO CREATED THE RAILWAYS

Matthew Murray (1765–1826).

Murray was the first man to build locomotives. He it was who built Blenkinsop's engines, having invented parts of the mechanism, parts in fact which are still in use today. He died in 1826 in Leeds, too soon to be able to participate in the great expansion of that industry which he initiated.

In 1811, Hackworth played an important part in the general management of Wylam's colliery locomotives. In 1824, he collaborated with George Stephenson, and in 1825 was employed as an engineer on the Stockton & Darlington Railway. He worked there for 15 years, sharing the responsibility for the construction of that railway. Finally, he turned to building locomotives himself. He was an intelligent, charming and just man and a great engineer.

In America, John Stevens played an important role in the development of railroads. He had a keen and enquiring mind, and played a vital part in the history of mechanical locomotion both on land and sea. In 1812, he gave to the New York Canal Commission a report on railroads which was to prove prophetic. He then started to put his ideas into practice, and in 1825, in Hoboken, tested a small locomotive. He instigated the building of the Mohawk & Hudson Railroad and lived long enough to see his country totally transformed by this new means of transport.

His son, Robert, even as a child, understood the principles of engineering, met all the great American locomotive-builders and himself became, at an early age, a great engineer. He built the Mohawk & Hudson line, then, later, many other lines and contributed to the development of both traction and track, his most famous invention being the T-rail.

In 1836, Pierre Simons was appointed with his brother-in-law de Ridder to research and supervise the building of the first major network in Belgium. This he did with talent and energy. During his time there, he knew both honour and disgrace, and, embittered, he left Belgium to build railways in Guatemala. Unfortunately, his health had been so ruined by work and disappointment that he died during the Atlantic voyage on 14 May 1843.

Von Denis who was born in 1804 in Bavaria but educated at l'Ecole polytechnique in France, built the first German railway. He built lines from Nuremberg to Furth, from Munich to Augsburg, and from Frankfurt to Mainz and Wiesbaden. Finally, he was made responsible for all railways in Bavaria.

The Great Western Railway had the good fortune to discover a man with a brilliant and creative mind, Saunders, and an engineer with prodigious energy, Brunel, both of whom were 27 years old; and a 20-year-old locomotive-engineer, Daniel Gooch. The number of tools, equipment and machines devised and invented both for ships and railways by Brunel is almost beyond belief. A man of great vision, and completely indifferent to the question of money, he cost the companies he worked for a fortune. He made no money for himself, but he left to those

Paulin Talabot (1799–1855).

Auguste Perdonnet (1801–1867).

Jules Petiet (1813–1871).

Eugène Flachat (1802–1873).

Isambard K. Brunel (1806–1859).

Daniel Gooch (1816–1889).

Thomas R. Crampton (1816–1888).

Wilhelm d'Engerth (1814–1884).

who had had faith in him products and machines of exceptional quality. He alone argued the case for broad gauge. He was right and it must now be regretted that his ideas were not adopted.

Like Brunel, Gooch contributed to the development of the express train. In 1836, he was given responsibility for the construction of broad-gauge locomotives and especially the famous '8-foot single' locomotives. He worked for the Great Western Railway for 51 years, including 27 years as head of the locomotive department and 24 as Chairman.

Thomas Crampton was the other champion of steam. He concerned himself principally with the stability of locomotives and, in 1842, took out the first patent for a locomotive with large driving-wheels placed to the rear of the firebox. But he was not a builder.

Wilhelm d'Engerth, a technical adviser for Austrian railways, was responsible for the development of powerful goods engines. His influence and ideas extended beyond his own country and in particular to France.

Paulin Talabot began by building lines from Alais to Beaucaire and from Avignon to Marseilles. He then became President of the P.L.M. Company. An engineer of vast experience and a formidable businessman, he built railways in Lombardy, Venice, Portugal, Southern Italy and Algeria, and helped develop Mediterranean ship-

Timothy Hackworth (1786–1850).

ping lines, having realised the important of linking them to the railways.

In 1828, Perdonnet and Coste published the first book in French on the railways and, in 1831, Perdonnet devised the first university course to take the railways as its subject. He was the chief engineer of the Versailles Left-Bank Railway and later became head of the Ecole Centrale and a director of the French Eastern Railway Company.

Eugène Flachat was a remarkable locomotive inventor and had a major influence on the use of metal in the construction of stations and bridges. He is known principally for his work on the Paris–Saint-Germain line, where he took his first steps as an engineer and a manager before devoting his amazing energy to the building of many other lines. Flachat was born in 1813 and worked with Talabot on the Alais line in Bulgaria. He became head of the Versailles Left-Bank Railway in 1842 and head of the French Northern network in 1845.

In 1858, Henri Giffard invented the automatic injector which changed the whole technology of water-feed for locomotives.

Walschaerts was an engineer for the Belgian State Railway and, like Giffard, is associated with one essential feature of the railways, in his case steam-distribution, the system which he invented in 1854.

In 1858, Pullman began to look for ways of improving travelling conditions for passengers on night trains and, in 1859, he created the Pullman car with its central gangway and a double row of beds positioned lengthways on to the train. In 1871, many of the luxury trains were fitted with Pullman cars and ran on the great Transcontinental line.

Emile Pereire was a Jewish banker. Pereire, with his brother Isaac, built the Saint-Germain, Northern and Southern Railways.

Henri Giffard (1825–1882).

Emile Walschaerts (1820–1901).

Emile Pereire (1800–1875).

George M. Pullman (1831–1897).

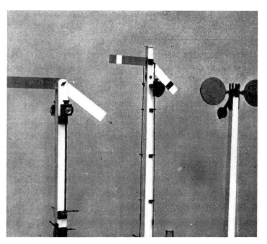

Models from the Science Museum, London of signals used in Britain.
Left to right: flag on the Liverpool & Manchester line, 1834; half-disc on the Grand Junction Railway, 1838; Wood's triple signal on the Liverpool & Manchester line, 1840; London & South Western Railway turning-disc, 1840; ball signal used on the Great Western Railway, 1837; Great Western disc and crossbar signal, 1841; Gregory semaphore signal, 1841; semaphore, 1874; double disc, 1846.

SIGNALS

Originally, railway signals were simply trumpets, flags and lamps, but with the increase in traffic and speed, it became necessary to build fixed signals.

The first fixed signal was installed on the Stockton & Darlington line in 1827. It was a triangular board which pivoted at the top of a post. It carried the word 'Danger' on its face and required trains to stop. The signal was turned on its edge to indicate that the track was clear. In 1834, the Liverpool & Manchester Railway used a small red flag attached to a wooden frame. Face out, it indicated to the train that it should stop, edge on meant that it could pass. In 1840, the London & South Western Railway used a filled-in disc for 'Stop' and an open disc for 'Clear'. The disc was turned by chains and pulleys and controlled both tracks at the same time. The Great Western Railway used a red ball signal. When the ball was in the raised position the train had to stop. This same system was used also in Austria. In 1840, the Great Western introduced a disc and crossbar signal designed by Brunel. This was fixed to a tower 65 feet high and as a result of the increased visibility auxiliary signals were no longer needed. The disc and crossbar were both painted red to make them more visible. The system, however, was confusing, because the red disc meant the track was clear, which was the opposite system to that used by all other companies. Holes were drilled in the face of the signals to reduce wind pressure. In 1840, on the Liverpool–Manchester line, Wood's signal consisted of three squares which could be turned so as to show either two or one to the oncoming train. At night, all these signals were fitted with lanterns which turned with the disc. John Deakin worked for the firm of Stevens and Sons, the first to specialise in the manufacture of signals. About 1848, he invented the fixed lamp with red and green movable windows. He also invented the steel tower for signals and a rod compensator for points.

In 1841, Gregory built the first semaphore signal on the London–Croydon Railway. He was also the first to think of putting the levers for points and signals together in one place on a raised bridge. He invented the stirrup-foot control for signals, a device which was improved by Chambers in 1859. Initially all signals were operated by pointsmen.

' flag indicating track free: Fixed signal   Red flag indicating stop.

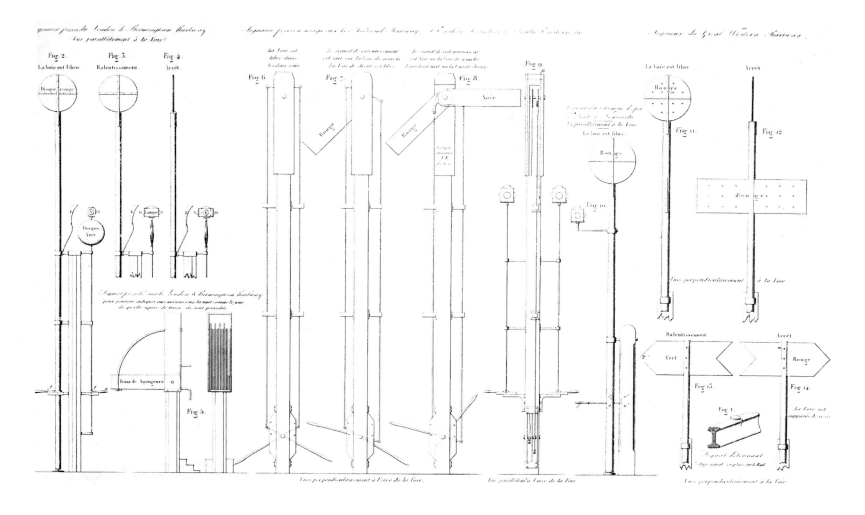

Signals used on railways in Britain in 1847, taken from *Annales des Mines*.

Before 1834, on the Liverpool–Manchester Railway, guards raised their arms when the track was clear, and kept their arms by their side to indicate the train was halted, a system which, certainly to us, seems illogical. Later, all networks adopted the following arm signals: both arms raised meant 'stop', one arm raised indicated 'caution', one arm held out horizontally meant 'the track is clear'.

In 1842, William F. Cooke, a colleague of William Wheatstone, invented the block system and this considerably improved safety on the railways. The system was based on the principle that it was not the time factor separating two trains which mattered, but rather the distance. The block system was first used in 1844 on the Norfolk Railroad in the United States.

In Britain, in 1847, when a train was stopped, an extra safety measure was to send a guard 400 or 500 yards back along the track with a flag or a red light. About 1843, a system of explosives was introduced. This took the form of tins filled with gunpowder and placed on the track in foggy weather. As the locomotive passed over them its wheels detonated the explosive. French railways adopted this device about 1850.

As the railways developed it became the custom to fit a lamp on the front of the engine and to the rear of the last coach. In the very early days, when trains travelled slowly, a metal basket filled with glowing embers was thought to be quite sufficient.

In the period between 1833 and 1839, on the Saint-Etienne–Lyons line, the rules governing the use of signals reveal that whistles were still not in use although it is possible that these rules applied simply to trains without locomotives. 'Article 6 – guards on passenger coaches will have trumpets. They will blow them every minute when the train is passing through a tunnel. They will also blow on them whenever they approach the King's highway or any other path. When they are obliged to stop they will use the bells provided for this eventuality in order to warn any train which

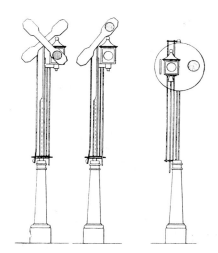

Semaphore and disc used in France (1855).

may approach from behind.

'Article 10 – Guards will also be stationed at each end of the Terrenoire and Rive-de-Gier Tunnels. They will communicate with each other by means of two ropes fitted with a number of bells. When a train wishes to pass through the tunnel the guard will ring the bells, whereupon the guard at the other end of the tunnel will reply in similar fashion. If there is no reply the train will not enter the tunnel.'

From 1850 onwards, networks took the first steps towards standardising their signals.

Explosive used as a signal in fog.

THE TELEGRAPH

The electric telegraph was first used on the railway as a means of sending signals and not telegrams. In 1837, Cooke and Wheatstone took out a patent for the electric telegraph. Wheatstone, a physicist, was the inventor of it. His colleague was more interested in its practical application. Conventional signals were reproduced on a dial by two needles. As they pivoted around the dial their relative positions were noted down. The system was first used in 1837 on the London–Birmingham line between Euston and Camden Town, and the first test took place on 25 July 1837. Cooke and Stephenson were in Camden Town and Wheatstone was alone in an office in Euston. From there he sent a message and received a reply. He wrote: 'I had never experienced such excitement as when alone in that silent room I heard the click of the needles and the words were spelled out'. Shortly after this, the system was used on the Blackwall line and the lines running from Manchester to Leeds, Edinburgh to Glasgow, Norwich to Yarmouth and Dublin to Kingstown.

In 1838, the Great Western Railway tested a Cooke and Wheatstone telegraph between Paddington and West Drayton. This was to be used as both a passenger and track maintenance telegraph. Twenty letters were arranged around a dial which had five needles. When two of the needles met, a particular letter was indicated. The needles were controlled by five separate wires contained in an underground metal conduit pipe. The pipe also contained a return wire. This telegraph aroused keen interest in London, but although it proved useful on the line, the company decided in 1842 to dispense with it. Brunel and Saunders believed the telegraph would improve efficiency by reducing the amount of rolling-stock required. In particular, the company would no longer need the light engines which were often sent against the flow of traffic to check on accidents. This practice was clearly a very dangerous one. They had even hoped that track guards could be provided with a portable version of the telegraph, and that a junction-box would be installed every 400 yards along the track.

Cooke devised a more simple system, consisting of two needles and two overhead wires, and this was installed between Paddington and Slough in 1843. Apart from its use on the railways, this telegraph became instantly popular when it was used to announce within minutes of the event the birth of Queen Victoria's second son, and particularly when it was used in 1845 to inform passengers on a train of the sensational arrest of the murderer Tawell. The Great Western decided, however, that it had no use for this telegraph, unlike most other British companies who made use of it and were perfectly satisfied.

Louis Breguet and Foy* improved the system and a Government subsidy enabled it to be installed on the Paris–Rouen line. Their telegraph had only one needle, which moved round the dial on which the letters of the alphabet were printed. This in fact was the system still in use in the 1930s. On 27 April 1845, the first telegraph message was sent from Paris to Mantes. The Paris–Lille line was equipped with it the following year. From 1852, the French public were able to make use of the railways' electric telegraph service.

In Belgium, the first telegraph was installed on the Antwerp–Brussels line in 1846, and, in Austria, on the Kaiser Ferdinand's Nordbahn in 1847.

Samuel Morse and Vail invented the printing telegraph. The Morse code system is well known. An electro-magnet causes a writing device to press down over short and long periods onto a roll of paper which turns constantly. It was on a Baltimore & Ohio Railroad line between Washington and Baltimore that Morse's telegraph was first used. The original telegraph sent on 24 May 1843 still exists. It is a quotation from the Bible.

In 1867, in France, it was the custom to inform station buffets in advance, by telegraph, how many passengers would require a meal.

Great Western electric telegraph receiver
(1845).

(*L'Illustration*, 24 May 1845)

Receiving a message by Breguet telegraph

(*Le Magasin pittoresque*, 1861)

Electric telegraph wires on the Rouen Railway, in 1845

Laying the golden rivet to celebrate the first Atlantic–Pacific rail link, at Promontory, Utah, 10 May 1869.

(A contemporary photograph: Union Pacific Railroad archive)

THE DEVELOPMENT OF AMERICAN RAILWAYS

Railways were built in America at an extraordinary speed and at an amazingly low cost. In 1833, the South Carolina Railroad, which was 136 miles long, cost only 7,132,000 francs, in other words about 52,000 francs per mile, and that cost includes all materials and equipment. The average cost was between 112,000 and 210,000 francs per mile.

As it expanded, the railway brought life to areas which until then had been completely empty or covered in forest. The railway became a vital and basic element in the development of the United States. Almost all the lines were single-track. Excavation work and tunnels were avoided by engineers who did not hesitate to lay curved track, and build bridges of a size and boldness which are impressive even today. The bridges were often built of wood since it was found in such great quantities in America. Between 1861 and 1865, during the Civil War, the railways played an important role. This was in fact the first time trains had ever been used in a military operation. Armoured trains, the first ever built, were used in battle.

This romantic period also saw other forms of fighting, trains often being attacked by Sioux and other Indians. Such incidents were frequent between 1860 and 1870, and children's books popularised the events. The Indians were in fact not at all frightened by this new means of transport and often travelled by train during the early years of the railways.

A fascinating enterprise was the creation of the Transcontinental link between the Pacific and the Atlantic. Planning was completed in 1855. The three lines involved were the Southern Pacific, the Central Pacific and the Northern Pacific. In 1862, the Union Pacific Railroad Company was formed to link the Pacific to Missouri.

On 22 February 1863, in Sacramento, the Central Pacific Railroad began work. Competition between the two networks was intense, since the speed of progress made would determine the length of line conceded to each company. It turned into a real race. The two lines were to meet on 10 May 1869, at Promontory in Utah, and the event was celebrated by a Western Union telegraph link between New Orleans, New York and Washington. At 2.47 pm the signal was given and a gold rivet was hammered in to join the last two rails. Then, finally, the Central Pacific's *Jupiter* locomotive and the Union Pacific's *119* came together and touched.

Atlanta station in 1864, at the end of the Civil War. Engines in the ruined engine shed.

(Photo: Moore)

Orleans Railway: special train for the Prince-President (1851).

An inspection locomotive, *La Petite*, built by Buddicom at Sotteville (1855).

A contemporary photograph. (Conservatoire des arts et métiers)

OLD LOCOMOTIVE PHOTOGRAPHS

American-type locomotive. W. Mason's engine used on the Baltimore & Ohio R.R. in 1856.

(Baltimore & Ohio Railroad archive)

LOCOMOTIVES BETWEEN 1850 AND 1860

Before concluding this section on the early years of the railways, it may be of interest to review the state of progress of locomotives in the last decade of the period under review. At the time, the three leading countries in locomotive construction were Britain, France, and the United States.

Old illustrations of engines of this period, and even of the preceding period, reveal how the locomotives to some extent by 1847, and completely by 1860, come to resemble both in appearance and mechanical layout engines which operated in the 1930s.

The only exceptions to this were British express locomotives. Amazingly, these retained the general shape and design of the *Patentee* and the *North Star*, that is, the 2–2–2 class with its large-diameter central driving wheels. Famous examples of this class were Wilson's *Jenny Lind* (in 1847), and Ramsbottom's *Lady of the Lake* built in 1859 for the London & North Western Railway. This type was still being built in 1890 when other countries had completely abandoned it.

From 1855, the 2–4–0 class of locomotive, with its two pairs of large, coupled driving-wheels, was being used in France on express trains on the Western and Orleans lines, and in Britain on stopping trains as an alternative to the 0–6–0 goods engine.

For hauling heavy trains, or on mountain lines, it was only in France, Austria and Germany that engineers built engines with more than four coupled wheels, a development of the Engerth system. At this time, Belgian and Dutch locomotives were very similar to British engines, not only in their general lines but also in the ways in which they were built, for example, in the use of brass for the domes, and the design of chimneys.

The first tank engines had been built about 1837 by Forrester, and later developed by Sharp, Roberts and Company. They came to be widely used between 1850 and 1860 on smaller lines and for station shunting. The tender was either incorporated at the rear of the engine or in tanks on either side of the boiler. It retained this shape for almost 50 years. Sometimes the water-tank resembled a saddle covering the top part of the boiler.

A striking feature of all engines of this period, except in North America and Italy, was the absence of a cab for the driver and fireman. The most that existed was a kind of vertical windscreen with two rounded windows. Even the drivers themselves argued that the locomotive could not be driven safely if they had any form of protection.

About 1850, in France and Germany, steel came to be used for moving parts and axles, while Britain continued to use iron. In 1851, in Essen, the first steel wheels were manufactured

Coaches and locomotive of stopping train in Britain, about 1860.

(Photo: Moore)

Ramsbottom's *Lady of the Lake* (1859), modified in 1895 for the London & North Western Railway.

(London & North Western Railway archive)

Tank engine for stopping trains on the London & North Western Railway, built by Francis Trevithick in 1856.

(Photo: Moore)

J.F. Cail's goods locomotive *La Vaux*, built in 1858.

(Charles Dollfus Collection)

at Krupp's.

About 1858, several important changes occurred almost simultaneously in the construction of locomotives. Because of the improvement in the design of grates and the shape of fireboxes, there was a return to the use of coal in the form of the compressed coal brick, coal having been replaced by coke as a locomotive fuel in the period after 1830. The firebox and inner firebox were no longer made solely of brass but sometimes of steel. Finally, within the space of a few years, the Giffard injector totally transformed the question of water-feed and even of the durability of boilers, since the injection of hot water caused no deterioration of the metal. Cylinders were located either on the outside or the inside of the boiler. Similarly, underframes were either outside or inside or a mixture of the two. The counterpoise, invented about 1837 by Sharp and Roberts, was used widely, particularly on the Continent.

Generally, American engines resemble Mason's *William Mason* built in 1856. Unlike in Europe, the driver's cab had become an important feature. After 1860, to pull heavy trains and mountain trains, the United States used coupled six-wheel engines of the 2–6–0 type.

Midland Railway goods locomotive built by Beyer, Peacock in 1858. Note the water-feed pump.

(Photo: Moore)

Locomotive built about 1856 by Beyer, Peacock & Co. for the London, Brighton & South Coast Railway.

(Photo: Moore)

Horse tramway in New York, about 1855.

URBAN TRAMWAYS

The development of a rail system had a decisive influence on town planning, not only because provision had to be made for trains which came from other towns, but also because it led to the development of tramways and underground lines within the city itself.

The first urban tramway was built in 1832 in New York by John Stephenson. It was a horse-drawn line and ran as far as Harlem. It was a four-wheel coach with a harness at each end, thus avoiding having to turn the coach round at the terminus. Passengers sat inside and the driver sat on the roof. It was still operating in 1834, but was withdrawn from service shortly after that date. In 1852, a new tramway ran on Sixth Avenue and, in 1855, four other lines were opened. On these new lines the coaches, with their top deck, double staircase and double harness, were similar to the coaches which operated before the introduction of electricity, since when tramways have been modified and improved continuously. About the same time, trams started to run in Boston and then in New Orleans. An American engineer, George F. Train, imported tramways to Birkenhead, and then in 1861 to London, but the drivers of horse-drawn carriages protested so vehemently that the rails were taken up. A short time later, in 1864, Eastman rebuilt this line.

The first tramway in Paris was built between the Place de la Concorde and Saint-Cloud in 1853 by Loubat. As rails had not been laid in the centre of Paris, when the tram arrived at the Quai de Billy the coach was raised off the ground by means of jacks and the cog wheels were replaced by smooth wheels. The long, well-designed coach, with its open top, has served as a model for all coaches used in Paris up to the introduction of mechanical traction. This 'American Railway', as it was called, was extended as far as Versailles and the Louvre. Another line was opened to Marly. Le Havre and Nantes were quick to build tramway systems, as were Geneva in 1863, Vienna in 1865, and Brussels in 1868.

Steam traction for tramways was first tested in America in 1859 by A.B. Latta, and improved and developed from 1871 onwards by Todd. In 1873, in London, Grantham inaugurated the Victoria–Vauxhall line on which large steam-trams with a top deck and double staircase operated. Steam-trams imported from America by M. Francq first appeared in Paris in 1874.

The first London trams, built by Train in 1861.
(Science Museum, London)

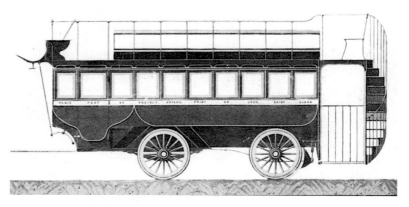

Loubat's *L'Américain*, the first horse tram in Paris (1853).

UNDERGROUND RAILWAYS

The first railway to run within a city – the Metropolitan Railway – was opened in London on 10 January 1863. It was a circular underground line with both standard and broad-gauge track. The chimney of the engines was closed off and steam was exhausted through the water-feed. Initially, the rolling-stock used belonged to the Great Western Railway. A series of shafts and sections where the train ran above ground provided the ventilation required, and allowed the drivers to re-open the damper. Carriages were lit by gas, which was an innovation. The depth below ground of the tube varied from 26 feet to 40 feet. In 1863, the underground carried 9,455,175 passengers, in 1866, 21,273,104, and in 1869, 36,893,791.

The history of the Metropolitan Railway Company of New York is a strange one. Plans were drawn up in 1864 for an underground line to run beneath Broadway, but the work was never started. In 1867, Charles T. Harvey received permission to form the West Side and Yonkers Patent Railway Company, and to test in Greenwich Street an overhead line over a distance of about half a mile. This had already been proposed by John Stevens in about 1830 and by John Randall in 1846. The track was built on a single row of supports between Battery Place and Day Street. Harvey himself was the first to test out a small coach which was hauled by hand along a cable. After a variety of problems, a new company was formed and the line was extended as far as New York Central Station. In 1871, the cables were replaced by traction locomotives, and by 1880 all the elevated lines which now [1935] exist in New York were operating.

A pneumatic railway was built in 1865 by Mr Rammel between London and Sydenham. A fur-lined disc was fitted to the outside of the coach and made contact with the walls of the circular tunnel, in this way forming a piston. This arrangement produced a small amount of low pressure and a large fan was used to create a suction force in the tunnel. For the return journey, the fan drove air down the tunnel and this pushed the coach forward. In 1872, New York's first underground line was based on a similar

Underground train at London's Hampstead Road, and underground scheme (1865).

(*Le Monde illustré*, 28 January 1865)

Baker Street Station on the London Underground (1864).

The London to Sydenham pneumatic railway (1865).

New York's pneumatic underground tube (1872).

Charles T. Harvey's first test of New York's elevated railway in 1867.

(Contemporary photograph: Industrial Museum, New York)

Sectional view of a coach on the New York pneumatic railway (1872).

system – the cylindrical coach acting as a piston.

In Paris, many plans were drawn up for the construction of an underground system. In 1845 *L'Illustration* published M. de Kerizouet's plan to link the Gare du Nord and the Gare de Lyon stations by a railway built under the boulevard, which would carry both passengers and goods. In 1853, Brame and Flachat proposed an undergound railway which would take people and goods to the central market. A similar line was suggested by Baltard, but both plans were rejected as having too limited a use. In 1855, Telle, and then, in 1856, Brame, published plans for an overhead metropolitan railway. Finally, in 1857, Le Hir and Mondot de Lagorce presented a document entitled 'An Underground Railway Public Transport System for Paris'. The system would carry goods and passengers cheaply, and be cheap enough for workers to be able to afford to travel by it, the estimated fare per passenger being only 5 centimes.

Chemin de fer dans l'intérieur de Paris. — Coupe prise sur la rue Amelot et les boulevards.

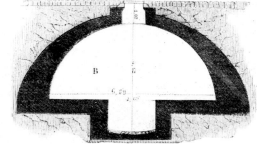

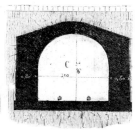

(Chemin de fer dans l'intérieur de Paris. — Galeries existant actuellement sous le sol.)

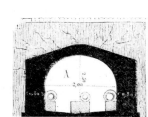

RÉSEAU DE VOIES FERRÉES SOUS PARIS.

(Chemin de fer dans l'intérieur de Paris. — Coupe sur le boulevard des Capucines.)

Le Hir's plan for 'a railway under Paris' (1857).

An early tube system: M. de Kerizouet's plan for an underground railway in Paris, 1845.

| Driver | Mechanic undress uniform | Line Inspector | Dress uniform | Mechanics: in burnons |

| Conductor in burnons | Train inspector | Station supervisor | in greatcoat | Signalmen in summer uniform | in dress uniform |

STAFF UNIFORMS ON THE ST GERMAIN & VERSAILLES LINE

Opening in 1866 of the Enghien to Montmorency Railway, with a
Northern Railway Petiet locomotive.
(*Le Monde illustré*, 14 July 1866)

CHAPTER II

THE GREAT AGE OF THE RAILWAYS

1860–1914

TWO EVENTS CHARACTERISTIC OF THE TIMES

On 27 January 1862, the inauguration of the Rome–Velletri Railway took place. Because of the bad weather, Pope Pius IX could not attend the ceremony. It was his chaplain, the Archbishop Prince of Hohenlohe, who blessed the locomotive and the train. He was surrounded by the prelates of the Apostolic Court and by the musicians of the Sistine Chapel. The French Ambassador and Belgian and Spanish ministers attended the ceremony. Regiments from France and Rome formed the guard of honour. After the blessing, the train set off to the enthusiastic applause of the crowd, and went as far as Velletri, where the representatives of the Pope held a reception. At the banquet which followed, M. de la Bouillerie offered, in the name of the company, a toast to the Pope's health. This first railway in the Papal States was built by a French company.

Another event about the same time which made a great impact was the opening on 6 July 1866 of the Enghien-Montmorency Railway. The reason for the keen interest was the Petiet locomotive, which had been built in Clichy by the Gouin company. The twelve coupled wheels were in two groups of six and gave complete track adhesion. It could, therefore, be used on steep gradients. Such an arrangement ran counter

Inauguration of the Rome-Velletri Railway in 1862. Blessing of the track and the Papal Coach.
(Florange Collection.)

to British thinking in this matter, and it was the subject of heated debate. The underframe supported a water-tank and, above this, a boiler with a Belpaire firebox. The boiler was linked to a steam-tank which contained drying tubes. Above

this was a second tubular body to heat water, which was then pumped into the boiler. The locomotive was in fact so large that the chimney had to be bent backwards to enable it to pass under bridges.

THE 1867 EXHIBITION

No previous exhibition had seen so many locomotives on display. One which particularly attracted attention was an American locomotive, the first to be shown in France. It had four large coupled wheels and four small free wheels, of the type we now describe as a bogie. The wheels were made of cast iron with Krupp steel tyres. The engine, which weighed 28 tons, was easily distinguishable by a strange kind of addition at the front end – a cow-catcher or snow-plough – and by a large bell used to warn people living in towns that a train was approaching. An enormous lantern gave a 'light which was visible at an amazing distance'. What was considered to be an important improvement at the time was the driver's covered cab, since in France the driver still had no protection against the weather. 'The cab is fitted with a bell which is connected to the rest of the train by a cord. The purpose of the bell is to warn the driver of any accident which may occur while the train is in motion.' The tender had a decorative design and ran on two bogies with cast-iron wheels.

However, the star of the exhibition was Petiet's locomotive, the *Titan*, with its ten coupled wheels which guaranteed 'even axle rotation whatever the radius of the curve'.

Another locomotive which attracted a great deal of attention was Verpilleux's, with its driving tender. However, its boiler proved not to have enough power since, on a long steep climb, the train had to stop four times to allow the engine to get up a sufficient head of steam. A Belgian locomotive of the same class, built by Maurice Urban, the chief engineer on the Great Central Railway in Belgium, aroused much in-

The Paris–Orleans Forquenot locomotive and the Northern's Petiet locomotive.

terest, as did the engines built by the Graffenstaden Company for the French Eastern Railway and for the Grand Duchy of Baden. Fairlie and Meyer's four-cylinder tank engines, built especially for mountain lines, were also thought to be particularly interesting.

Typical of these was the coupled ten-wheel tank engine built by M. Forquenot in the Orleans–Ivry Railway workshops. It was intended for use in Cantal, where the track rose continuously over a distance of 11 miles at a gradient of 1 in 33 and contained curves with a radius of 1000 ft. The train was not articulated,

but axle flexibility on the curves was provided by play in the axle-boxes and a special transmission system. The engine weighed 36 tons.

In the coupled eight-wheel locomotive class, that is, engines designed to haul goods trains along gently curving track, the French Northern Railway exhibited an engine from the Fives–Lille line whose long firebox, with its grate and door, had not been seen before, and the Southern–Orleans Railways exhibited Cail engines designed by M. Forquenot. In the coupled six-wheel class, Le Creusot exhibited a very powerful tank engine which could pull up to 700 tons on the flat.

Grant-type American locomotive at the 1867 Exhibition.

Marcinelle & Couillet's Belgian locomotive at the 1867 Exhibition.

Cail built coupled four-wheel engines for the North Belgium Railway Company and Le Creusot built the same class of engine, as well as engines with a single pair of driving-wheels, for the Great Eastern Railway in Britain. Although the British public were indignant at the importing of these French engines, British technical magazines of the time paid tribute to the excellence of French engineering. In fact, however, at the time the British locomotive industry was the most powerful in the world. There were forty railway workshops producing 1,500 engines every year. France had only fourteen workshops producing 1,000 engines per year, Belgium nine which produced 300 per year, Germany, Prussia and Austria, ten each producing 450 engines per year.

At the 1867 exhibition, therefore, Belgium was the most important exhibitor after France in relation to production capacity. Its workshops in Saint-Leonard, Central-Belge, Seraing, Carels, and Couillet had produced exceptional engines. It specialised in building small locomotives to be used in mines, in stations, or on work sites. The station and mine locomotives built in the Couillet workshops in Charleroi had aroused particular interest because of their four coupled wheels, untrue driving-axle, and brakes which operated by the application of brake pads to the rails.

The 1867 exhibition brought fame to the Belgian engineer, Alfred Belpaire. He invented a large boiler grate which allowed cheap fuel to be used in place of coke. The Belpaire boiler became standard equipment on a great number of railway networks. Finally, as far as coaches were concerned, the exhibition revealed a desire by railway companies, not only to offer greater comfort by the provision of wider seats, but also to ensure 'that passengers are not robbed or attacked in a coach as they might be in a wood'.

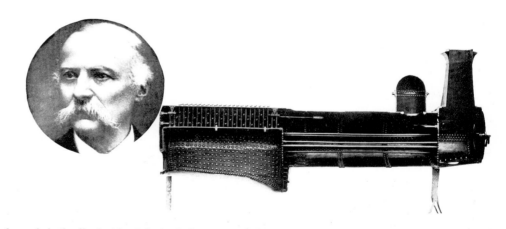

Model of an early boiler fitted with a Belpaire firebox. *(Inset*: Alfred Belpaire, engineer on the Belgian State Railway) (Sociéte nationale des chemins de fer belges)

Double-decker passenger-coaches.

Great Northern Railway locomotive with single pair of driving-wheels, in 1870.

(Sauvage Collection)

Great Eastern Railway locomotive built by Le Creusot in 1865.

(Schneider Company archive)

SOME TYPES OF LOCOMOTIVE BEFORE 1878

Belgian Northern Railway locomotive built by Cail and Fives-Lille in 1867.

A turning-point in the history of the locomotive was reached in 1878. Until then, engines with single pairs of driving-wheels were preferred for express trains, but because of their single axle they were slow to accelerate from rest. The increasing weight of trains required an increase in power. The result was a longer boiler, which increased steam production, and an extra axle either at the front or at the rear to carry the longer boiler.

South African locomotive with two coupled axles, built in 1873.

(South African Railways archive)

Italian locomotive with two coupled driving-axles, built in 1873.

(Italian Communications Ministry)

Spanish locomotive with two coupled axles, built in 1877.

(Madrid-Saragossa-Alicante Company)

A Northern Railway Fives-Lille locomotive with four coupled axles, built in 1867.

Midi-Creusot locomotive with three coupled axles, built in 1872.

(Schneider Company archive)

FRENCH RAILWAYS IN 1870 AND 1871

During the Franco–Prussian war, the railway played an important role in the mobilisation of troops and the evacuation of the injured. In July 1870, *L'Illustration* described the moving scenes at the Gare de l'Est, with soldiers leaving for the war: 'Last Saturday I saw two regiments, the 95th and the 81st, marching along the Boulevard Sebastopol. They were coming from the Barracks in Montrouge and going to the Gare de l'Est. What a sight! There were thousands of people at the windows of the houses. The street was filled with young people and middle-class and working-class people who sang the Marseillaise while the band played. Applause rang out from every side. Hands were shaken. Bunches of flowers were thrown. Cheers were given. At the Gare de l'Est the scene was even more moving, if that is possible. The crowd surrounded groups of soldiers and offered them tobacco and refreshment and shook their hands. How could one not be moved when one saw a young married captain kissing his wife and tiny child goodbye before entering the train. In a corner of the station, a young grenadier was bidding a fond farewell to a whole group of people.'

Departure of troops from the Gare de l'Est in July 1870.

Hospital-train coach for the slightly injured.

Hospital-train coach for the seriously wounded.

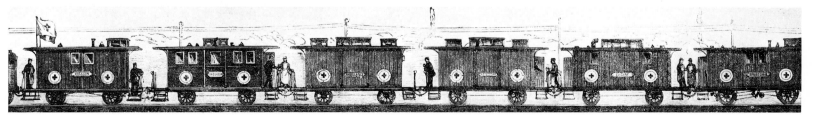

French hospital train in 1870.
(Bibliothèque des arts décoratifs)

The first compound locomotive for use on French main lines, the Northern Company's 701.

(Northern Railway archive)

A train on the Bayonne-Biarritz line in 1873.

(Bayonne-Biarritz company)

THE HISTORY OF COMPOUND ENGINES

With the ever-increasing weight of trains it was necessary to increase the power of locomotives. The first steps taken involved lengthening the boilers to increase their capacity to generate steam and raising their steam pressure to 128 lbs per square inch. There remained, however, the need to improve the effective use of the energy created by steam.

In fact, the operating principle of the alternating steam engine is based on the expansion of steam within a cylinder behind a piston which then moves as a result of the difference in pressure between the steam and the atmosphere. A practical difficulty presents itself immediately: the potential gap between the piston and the wall of the cylinder in which it moves. If the latter is not airtight, leaks occur and there is a corresponding reduction in overall efficiency.

Arthur Woolf had already realised as early as 1803 the importance of dividing the expansion of the steam between two cylinders in such a way that each of them could operate with a 50 per cent reduction in pressure difference. This was the idea that would lead to 'compounding', that is to say steam expansion through a two-phase drop in pressure.

The first practical application of the compound system occurred in the 1860s in naval vessels. It resulted in a reduction of more than 50 per cent in the amount of coal used. By this means the operating range of ships was more than doubled.

The honour of being the first to apply the compound system to the steam locomotive falls to Anatole Mallet. Mallet was one of the first to understand that the efficient use of steam energy during prolonged expansion within a cylinder was inhibited by the condensation which occurs at the beginning of the piston stroke. This takes place when high-pressure steam comes into contact with the cooler surfaces of the piston and the cylinder. Mallet guessed that the most efficient means of combatting this 'cool side effect' was the compound system, which would leave the surfaces of the piston and cylinder relatively less cool by virtue of the fact that expansion is only partial. In 1876, he succeeded for the first time in adapting the compound system to two small locomotives, built by Le Creusot and running on the Bayonne–Biarritz line. The unique feature of this type of engine was its two cylinders of unequal size, and for this reason it acquired the nickname 'the lame one'.

Mallet's example was initially followed outside

Cross-section of the first Bayonne-Biarritz compound locomotive.

The first compound locomotive built in 1876 by Le Creusot for the Bayonne-Biarritz Railway.

(Conservatoire des arts et métiers)

Anatole Mallet (1837–1919),
the inventor of the compound locomotive
and of a class of articulated locomotives.

(Archive of L'Ecole centrale des arts et manufactures)

M. du Bousquet,
chief engineer on the Northern Railway. He ordered
the first compound locomotive for main-line use in France.

(Northern Railway archive)

M. de Glehn,
an administrator with the Alsace mechanical
engineering company. He built the first compound
locomotive for main-line use in France.

(Photo: Alsace mechanical engineering company)

France, in the first instance by Borodine, chief engineer on the South West Railway in Russia. He transformed a locomotive already in use into a 'double expansion' engine. While most engineers were constructing only two-cylinder compound locomotives – particularly in Germany where at least 430 were already operating in 1883 – the English engineer, Webb, who was concerned primarily to increase track adhesion and as a consequence the number of driving-axles, created in 1883 a three-cylinder double expansion engine. The steam, pressurised by the boiler, expanded first of all into two small side cylinders which activated the second driving-axle; its pressure thus having been reduced and, as a result, having 'grown', it needed a larger space to complete its expansion. This it found in the single central cylinder which was much larger in size and which controlled the first driving-axle. As a result, the two driving-axles no longer needed to be coupled. This engine completed the journey from London to Crewe with a 100-ton load at a speed of 50 m.p.h.

Three years later, in 1886, in other words ten years after Mallet's invention, the compound locomotive made its reappearance in France, but this time with four cylinders. The initiative for this belongs to M. de Gleyn, an engineer with a locomotive engineering company in Alsace. He, together with M. du Bousquet, chief engineer with the Northern Railway, built the first four-cylinder compound locomotive to run on a French railway. This engine, the 701, was equipped with two independent driving-axles: one operated by two internal, high-pressure cylinders, the other by two external, low-pressure cylinders situated at the rear of the former.

At about the same time, M. Henry, an engineer with the P.L.M., built the famous C-1 compound locomotive with four cylinders which, in pairs, drove two different axles. This time, however, the two axles were coupled. Not only did M. Henry break with the mistaken tradition which held that coupling increased traction resistance, but he also increased the pressure which the boiler testplate would stand from 156 lbs per square inch to over 200 lbs, an enormous pressure for the time. For this reason, this type of locomotive created a sensation at the 1889 exhibition.

The success of these prototypes was considerable, and in a sense the two engines later merged. Thus, in 1891, the French Northern Railway put into service a compound engine called the 2122 which had a boiler capable of withstanding a pressure of 200 lbs per square inch and two coupled driving-axles of the type found on the P.L.M. C-1. Moreover, in 1892, the P.L.M. modified its C-1 type of engine by fitting a front bogie of the type found on the 701 Northern and changing the outside cylinders to high pressure. In this way, the French compound engine class was created. Engines of this type were then built for the Midi, Western, State, Paris, Orleans and Eastern Railways so that by 1902 the seven great French railway networks employed 1,087 four-cylinder locomotives.

The tests carried out by the Northern Railway were particularly significant. On 25 December 1891, an ordinary train weighing 110 tons and pulled by a 2122 locomotive covered the 81-mile route at an average speed of more than 53 miles per hour. There was a saving of 14 per cent on fuel and a saving of 23 per cent in water. As a result, these trains were able to complete a jour-

French four-cylinder
compound locomotive.

(Les Chemins de fer: Max de Nansouty)

Webb's three-cylinder compound locomotive, with two high-
pressure cylinders and one low-pressure cylinder.

(Nature, 24 March 1883)

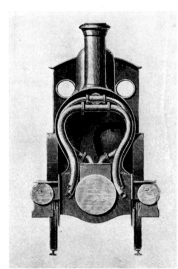

Cross-section of Webb's three-cylinder
compound locomotive.

(Les Chemins de fer: Max de Nansouty)

ney of 150 miles with only one 5-minute water stop.

But trains were becoming heavier, and four years later it was necessary to increase the boiler's grate surface by 12 per cent. Four years after this, it was again increased by 20 per cent. The resulting increase in engine weight required the addition of a fifth axle. A carrying-axle was therefore positioned beneath the firebox, behind the two driving-axles. This led to the building of the famous 4–4–2 'Atlantic compound' class, which attracted so much attention at the 1900 exhibition. The special feature of this engine, with its increased pressure of 227 lbs per square inch, was that the whole of its boiler and its firebox were made of steel plate instead of iron plate. This was the first practical application to a locomotive of a system which had already proved successful in the Navy.

Like the locomotive, the tender also increased in size. It now had water tanks with a capacity of almost 4000 gallons. As a result it was fitted with two articulated bogies.

This 'Atlantic North' class acquired its world-wide reputation on the Paris–Calais line. In 1878, the 'Morning Express' had taken 5 hours 35 minutes to complete the Paris–Calais journey, a distance of 183 miles. In 1908, the same journey was completed in 3 hours 24 minutes. In 1892, a train carrying a load of 155 tons could not travel at more than 40 m.p.h. up a slope with a gradient of 1 in 200. In 1900, the Atlantic North class of locomotive, pulling a train of 180 to 200 tons, could achieve at least 50 m.p.h. up the same gradient.

Similar progress was made on other networks. Between 1878 and 1908, the 220-mile journey between Paris and Nancy showed a time saving of 34 per cent. The Paris–Marseilles journey of 536 miles showed a saving of 20 per cent; other improvements were Paris–Bordeaux (362 miles) 21.5 per cent; Bordeaux–Sete (296 miles) 6.5 per cent; and Paris–Le Havre (142 miles) 41.5 per cent. In other words, there was an average saving overall of nearly 20 per cent. This was achieved principally by the reduction in the consumption of fuel and water, which led in turn to a reduction in the number and length of stops.

To sum up: in 1878, locomotives with a pair of single driving-wheels could pull loads of no more than 100 to 120 tons at an average speed of 37 miles per hour. In 1908, Atlantic engines were pulling 275 tons on two-axle stock, and 300 on stock fitted with bogies, at speeds of 47 and even 50 miles per hour.

It is, therefore, easy to understand the worldwide reputation of this French class of locomotive at the time. As a result, in 1905 the Alsace engineering company received orders for these engines from the Pennsylvania Railroad Company in the United States and the Great Western Railway in Britain. By this time, the British engineer, Webb, had already abandoned his three-cylinder type of engine and had built a four-cylinder type a few years previously called the *France*, which was exhibited at Vincennes in 1900. In Britain, this engine marked a turning-point in the building of the new generation of express locomotives.

Following demands for increased comfort in

The P.L.M. C1 compound locomotive (1889).
(P.L.M. Railway archive)

carriages, toilets, berths, restaurant cars, etc., the deadweight per passenger continued to increase. This meant that Atlantic-class engines carried hardly any more passengers at the speeds of the time than had the old engines with a single pair of driving-wheels in their day. This led to the building of the ten-wheel class (4–6–0), with its third driving-axle and six coupled wheels.

In 1897, for the hilly line running from Beziers to Neussargues, with gradients of 1 in 30, the French Southern Railway required a fast and powerful engine capable of pulling 100 tons. The Alsace company, therefore, built a ten-wheel engine with six coupled wheels and four cylinders, and fitted with a Belpaire steel firebox and a boiler which would take a pressure of up to 200 lbs per square inch. The engine's ability to accelerate from a position of rest was improved by feeding live steam directly into the large cylinders under low pressure, while gases from the small cylinders were fed under high pressure directly into the exhaust pipes. In this way, momentarily, it became a single expansion engine. When the engine went down steep inclines,

a reverse steam device allowed the large cylinders to take in damp steam through the exhaust pipes, and to send it back into the boiler via the small cylinders. The Southern Railway also built a compound-type engine with eight coupled wheels to pull goods trains along the same hilly line.

However, just as compound engines were becoming more popular – in 1912, there were 5,100 in France and 4,500 in Germany – so the system of superheating was also yielding economies. In fact, both Schmidt in Germany in 1898 and Flamme in Belgium in 1901 saw it as a serious rival to the compound engine.

In 1896, Polonceau, working for the Orleans Railway, attempted to avoid the need for compounding by drying the steam as it entered the cylinders, thus improving single expansion. Moreover, a special arrangement allowed the exhaust's steam to mix with the cold water. In this way, the water was heated before it entered the boiler. The success of compounding had created competition.

The 'Atlantic-Nord' compound locomotive which ran on the Paris–Calais Line (1900).
(Northern Railway archive)

Oil-firing tests at Châlons in 1868, in the presence of Emperor Napoleon III.
The reversed engine number is an error by the engraver.

OIL-FIRED LOCOMOTIVES

On 6 September 1868, a train stopped at Châlons station on its way to the military camp at Châlons-sur-Marne. The Emperor Napoleon III alighted from this train and boarded a special locomotive which was coupled to another train. This second locomotive was oil-fired, by means of a device invented by the famous chemist, Henri Sainte-Claire Deville. The Emperor was accompanied by the inventor and by M. Sauvage, the President of the Eastern Railway Company.

The trial took place between Châlons and Mourmelon, and showed a degree of heat control which was impossible with coal, and also an almost total lack of smoke. The mineral oil used was not the volatile oil used for lighting purposes but a viscous substance called 'heavy oil'. At Mourmelon station people were amazed to see the train arrive ahead of time, with the Emperor in general's uniform standing on the tender. The test run did not lead immediately to any further development in the building of locomotives because of the prohibitive cost of heavy oil compared to coal.

In fact, the oil was imported from the Baku Wells near the Caspian Sea. The crude naptha from this region has the appearance of a dark brown liquid. When this is distilled, it first of all yields a highly inflammable benzine, which in the nineteenth century was used only to clean cloth. Then commercial oil and 'sun oil' used for lighting are produced. Finally, there is a heavy liquid residue which has a calorific power greater than coal.

The device invented by Sainte-Claire Deville was developed later by Urquhardt, an engineer working for the Gratzi-Tsaristsin Railway in south-east Russia. The firebox was fitted with brick arches to protect the metal sides. A jet of steam forced air and oil through an injector into the firebox, where the arches' baffle-plates mixed them thoroughly together. The superheated brick arches caused the oil to ignite spontaneously when it came into contact with the air, which was heated at point (A) and then passed along the line indicated by the arrows from the ash box. Some of the flames travelled along the flues (B) towards the bottom of the tubular plate and made contact with it. The oil came via pipe(s) from the tender where it had already been heated by a jet of steam from the boiler. Passing through the coil, the steam returned to the injector feed-pipe (P).

From the driver's cab it was very easy to control combustion by using valve (D) to operate the injector. In this way, excessive fuel consumption was avoided. The oil was filtered both before it entered and after it left the tender. At the bottom of the tender was a tank for the water which is always found in crude oil.

The locomotive was lit by a steamblast from an adjacent boiler. To prevent explosions in the oil vapour which accumulated in the firebox, certain precautions had to be taken. First of all, the firebox was steam-cleaned and then rags soaked in oil were put into it and lit immediately.

An oil-fired locomotive on the South East Russia Railway.
(*Nature*, 18 July 1883)

The P.L.M. 'pointed' locomotive.

(Sauvage Collection)

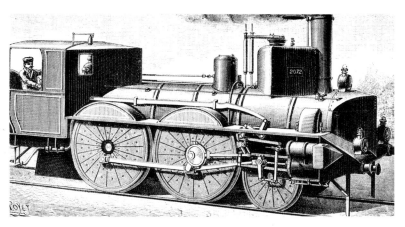

An aerodynamic locomotive, 1887.

(*Nature*, 9 April 1887)

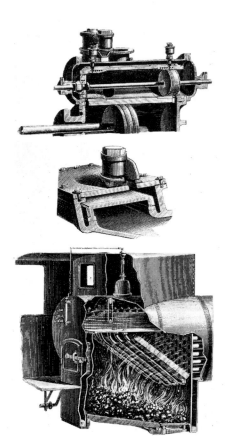

Top: Piston-valve and slide-valve.
Above: Fire-brick shield.

(*Nature*, 9 April 1887)

THE BEGINNING OF AERODYNAMICS

In 1884, M. Ricour, the chief engineer on the French Eastern Railway, had the idea of fitting an air inlet-valve on to the steam intake-pipe. He had found that when the regulator was shut the movement of the pistons drew in ash from the smokebox and this quickly caused wear in those parts which moved against each other. The slide valves were then replaced by piston valves which wear much less quickly, and savings, therefore, were made on repair and maintenance costs.

M. Ricour also placed a firebrick shield in front of the tube plate. This improved combustion because the gases mixed better, and it protected the tube plate from an intake of cold air and from the blasts of heat which came from the firebox.

Apart from these improvements, which produced a 10 per cent saving in fuel, M. Ricour recognised 'that the lack of overall planning in the design of the train caused considerable air resistance'. He therefore fitted the locomotive with a windbreak, and he also filled in the gap between waggons with metal sheeting in order to reduce resistance caused by air turbulence.

In 1894, after tests carried out by M. Desdouits for the Eastern Railway, the windbreak is again found on the P.L.M.'s famous 'pointed' locomotives which had to head north up the Rhone Valley in the face of the Mistral wind.

The value of such a front end was shown particularly on high-speed trains. When Thuile of the Le Creusot Company built his express engine in 1900, he fitted it with a similar device to reduce air resistance. Thuile's engine was remarkable also because the driver's cab was positioned at the front to enable him to have a better view of the track ahead. A few years later the idea was copied by Henschel, a German locomotive-builder, in high-speed trials. The purpose was to enable steam-traction to compete with electric-traction which had just achieved sensational speeds in Germany.

An aerodynamic train, 1887.

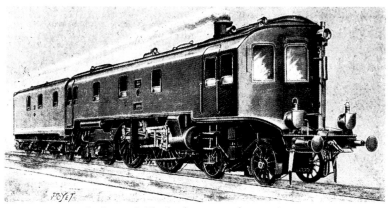

Le Creusot's Thuile-class express locomotive.

(*Nature*, 3 November 1900)

Henschel's locomotive, built to compete with electric traction in 1904.

(*Nature*, 9 July 1905)

THE SEARCH FOR HIGH SPEED BETWEEN 1882 AND 1895

To increase engine speed, large-diameter driving-wheels are needed to avoid increasing to a dangerous level the number of piston strokes and, as a consequence, the number of wheel revolutions. In 1880, in France, wheel diameter reached a record 7 feet. In America, however, it was not possible to exceed 5 feet 10 inches since the lack of track stability forced engineers to maintain a low centre of gravity.

To achieve a speed of 80 m.p.h., M. Fontaine thought of using friction to drive his locomotive. He devised a system in which a slower wheel is driven by the piston and rests not on the rail but on another smaller-diameter wheel. This second wheel is connected to the driving-axle. The system still did not produce enough power, and, in 1886, M. Estrade built a locomotive with six coupled wheels, each having a diameter of 8 feet, and this locomotive achieved a speed of 75 m.p.h. It could, however, run only with stock which had very large wheels so as to reduce resistance. Moreover, the boiler did not produce sufficient steam-power to drive this express.

Speed trials took place in 1889, and shortly afterwards an engine from the Eastern Railway reached a speed of 80 m.p.h. To operate successfully, a locomotive must achieve a balance between steam-production and steam-consumption. M. Flaman, therefore, an engineer with the French

Great Northern Railway express locomotive: a world record-holder in 1895.

(Great Northern Railway archive)

Eastern Railway, invented a boiler with two barrels which were linked to each other. The lower barrel contained horizontal tubes which produced steam, and the upper barrel was filled with water. In 1891, M. Salomon, the chief engineer on the Eastern Railway, installed this boiler in a new type of locomotive with a bogie and four coupled wheels. This engine was able to haul a 200-ton express train between Paris and Châlons at an average speed of 47 m.p.h.

The *Parisienne*, an Estrade-type express locomotive.

Southern Canadian R.R. Fontaine-type friction locomotive, built in 1881.

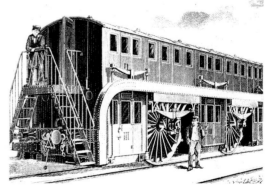

Estrade-type double-decker high-speed coach.

(*Nature*, 3 July 1886)

French Eastern Railway express train pulled by a locomotive fitted with a Flaman boiler (1891).

(Henry Collection)

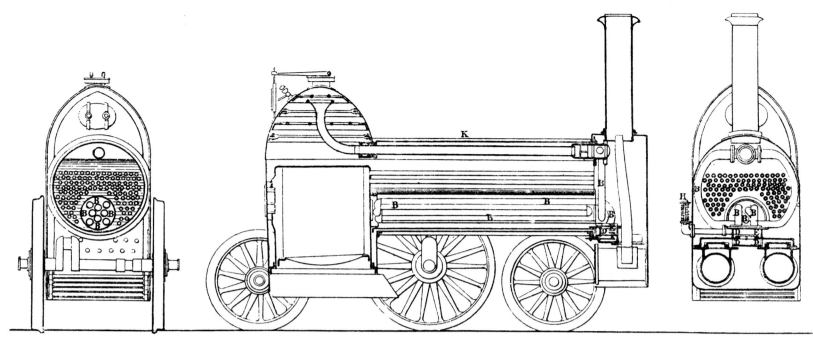

Moncheuil's 1850 patent for a superheater surrounded by smoke-tubes.

SUPERHEATING AND COMPOUNDING

Compounding had played a part in the development of the Atlantic-class locomotive with its two coupled axles. Now, however, on the ten-wheel type locomotive a third driving-axle had been coupled to the two others, and the engine's steam production power no longer matched its adhesion power. Engineers, therefore, turned to superheating, a system invented by Denis Papin. He had noticed a considerable decrease in fuel consumption when on each piston strike he had plunged a red-hot iron into the engine's cylinder. In 1850, Moncheuil, a director of the Montereau-Troyes Railway, proposed a modification to a patent taken out by Quillacq, an engine-builder in Anzin. In the modified system, the steam would go to the cylinders after it had been heated by the firebox's hot gases in the lower part of the boiler barrel.

In 1898, in Germany, Schmidt successfully tested the same idea on the Prussian State Rail-

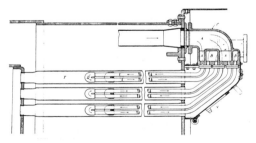

Schmidt superheater inside the smoke-tubes.
(*La Locomotive*: Lamalle and Legein)

way, and in 1901, in Belgium, the system was championed by Flamme. The use of superheated steam did initially cause some problems. Various parts of the engine now had to be airtight, and the grease which was used for lubrication had at first melted under the fierce heat of the steam, but these problems were solved and the steam never rose beyond a temperature of 250°C to 260°C.

From 1901 onwards, the use of superheat was a matter of keen debate between the supporters of superheated, simple expansion and the supporters of double expansion or compounding. In 1910, at the Berne Conference, Belgian engineers supported a return to simple expansion on four-cylinder superheated locomotives. French engineers generally supported compounding in spite of its complicated nature.

The P.L.M. carried out comparative tests on two specific locomotives, both superheated, but one using simple expansion and four independent cylinders, the other having four compound cylinders. A 9 per cent fuel reduction was achieved with the compound system, and, though superheat eventually triumphed, it was only by allying itself to compounding.

If steam is heated when it leaves the boiler, why not heat water before it enters the boiler? The Great Northern Railway tested this idea in 1905 on an old 1883 locomotive, equipping it with a device invented by Halpin and called by him a 'thermic accumulator'. The invention was never a matter of any controversy because everyone agreed that considerable savings were achieved.

Austrian State Railways two-cylinder compound locomotive, fitted with a Schmidt superheater.
(*Nature*, 10 April 1909)

Test by the Great Northern Railway in 1905 of a system for heating feed-water on an 1883 locomotive.
(*Nature*, 29 April 1905)

Le Creusot's four-cylinder compound tank engine with superheater and water-tubes.
(*Nature*, 23 October 1909)

Austrian locomotive fitted with a Brotan water-tube boiler.
(*Nature*, 11 April 1908)

LOCOMOTIVES WITH WATER TUBES IN PLACE OF FIRE TUBES

Locomotives had always been fire-tube locomotives, that is, a number of horizontal tubes ran through the water which was to be vaporised. Inside these tubes were the flames and burning gases which came from the firebox. The tubes, however, were also used as struts between the front plate of the firebox and the front plate of the barrel of the boiler. As a consequence, they freqently suffered from metal fatigue.

Johann Brotan, an engineer on the Austrian State Railway, invented a boiler containing vertical arch tubes containing water instead of horizontal fire-tubes. This type of boiler was easier to build and was used in 1901 in Austria on a goods locomotive which burned lignite. It proved to be very successful.

Some years later the Le Creusot Company built a similar locomotive. It was a four-cylinder compound engine with a superheater in the middle of the boiler. Boiler pressure was raised to 284 lbs per square inch. The locomotive was used to pull mineral and coal trains along Le Creusot's factory sidings. This type of boiler resembles the Du Temple boiler used in the Navy.

Its success led M. du Bousquet, the chief engineer on the Northern Railway, to test it on an Atlantic-class engine, but he modified it first. Above the firebox, where there would be no problems with soot deposits, the boiler contained vertical arch tubes. But in the barrel of the boiler, where soot deposits cannot burn, were the standard horizontal fire-tubes. These allowed the sooty gases to condense and thus prevented an accumulation of soot. Steam-production was excellent, but faults appeared in the fire bricks. In 1908, Du Bousquet fitted an improved version of this boiler to a 4–4–4 class locomotive which weighed 77 tons and pulled trains weighing 280 tons at a speed of 60 m.p.h. up long slopes with a 1 in 200 gradient. In 1911, Du Bousquet's successor, M. Asselin, fitted a water tubular boiler to a 102–ton 4–6–4 Baltic-class engine, and it pulled, without stopping, a 400-ton load over a distance of 112 miles in under two hours.

French Northern Railway's Baltic-class locomotive with water-tubes.
(*Nature*, 2 December 1911)

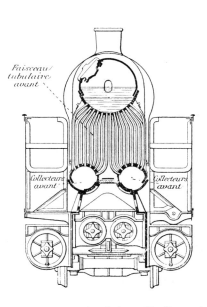

Front cross-sectional view of Le Creusot's water-tube tank-engine.
1909)

Brotan boiler with full-length manifold.
(*Nature*, 23 October 1909)

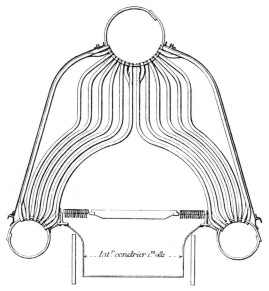

Cross-section of water-tubes on the Northern Railway's Atlantic locomotive.

THE TENDER

The steam locomotive consumes a vast amount of water. After being used in the process of expansion in the cylinders, the water, as steam, is released into the atmosphere. Since this sudden exhaustion causes combustion, by drawing in the hot gases, this in turn vaporises the water which has not yet been used. The result of this process is that the locomotive consumes between seven and nine times more water than coal. There is therefore generally enough coal on the tender of the locomotive to enable the locomotive to return to its depot, but the situation is quite different where water is concerned. If the locomotive had to carry with it all the water it needed for the journey, and could not take on further supplies, it would require an enormous tender and this would increase the train's deadweight considerably.

The rate of water consumption is approximately 1⅓ gallons per square foot of heating surface per hour, and heating surfaces vary in area between 1600 and 2700 square feet. Therefore, an engine with a heating surface of 2600 square feet will consume per hour 3400 gallons of water. For such a locomotive a tender with a capacity of less than 3400 gallons will not be big enough unless it can take on a fresh supply of water after one hour.

The tender's capacity is therefore determined by the distance between water-points and the speed of trains. The distance between water-points is, moreover, determined by the speed of the slowest train on the line. Since good trains generally do not exceed 15 m.p.h., there needs to be a water-point at least every 15 miles. This distance is even further reduced on mountain lines, since the speed of a train climbing certain gradients drops to 10 or 11 m.p.h.

Early versions of tenders carried only about 1000–1750 gallons of water, and between 1 ton and 3 tons of coke. This amount of water limited journey distance to about 30 miles. After 1860, coke was replaced by coal bricks made from tiny pieces of good quality coal. This increased the weight of the tender, which became even heavier as a result of a considerable increase in the amount of water carried. After 1910, tenders carried up to 5200 gallons of water – the P.L.M.'s 'Pacific' even carried 6000 gallons. Often 5 tons and sometimes even 8 tons of coal were carried. Generally, the empty weight of a tender is 10 lbs per gallon of water carried, so a tender with a capacity of 6000 gallons would have an empty weight of 27 tons

and would weigh 54 tons when loaded. The weight of the coal has to be added to this. This means that full tenders weighed almost 60 tons. Two axles were no longer enough. A third axle was added and even a fourth axle, with the tender running on two bogies.

The water tanks were supported by the wooden floor and the chassis. On early tenders, the chassis was made of wood. Later, it was built with two plate-metal frames standing outside the line of the wheels and strengthened by the use of cross-members. Water passed from the tender to the locomotive along a flexible pipe. The fireman's job was made easier when coal was stored in a raised bunker with a floor which sloped down towards its front.

Care has to be taken when coupling the tender to the locomotive. The two vehicles must move freely in curves but at the same time the coupling needs to be sufficiently solid to avoid any sideways play and any sudden forward or backward movement. Usually the locomotive and tender are coupled together by a rigid centre bar or a rigid coupling hook. This makes the operation easier since the hook can be used to compress the buffers. The end of both the bar and the coupling hook is fitted with a pin.

Paris–Orleans tender in 1854, with wooden underframe.

(Paris–Orleans Railway)

Tender with bogies for the 1900 Northern Railway Atlantic compound locomotive. The tender's capacity was such that the Paris–Calais journey time was significantly reduced.

(Northern Railway)

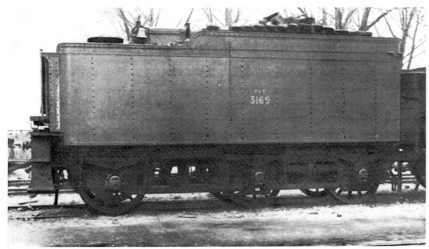

Eastern Railway three-axle tender, built in 1910 in Epernay, which carried nearly 5000 gallons of water and 8 tons of coal.

(Henry Collection)

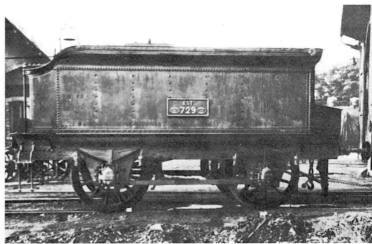

Eastern Railway tender of 1867 which carried 1300 gallons of water and five tons of coal.

(Henry Collection)

Driver in front of his engine.

The locomotive's tachometer is open, showing the roll of paper on which the running speeds are noted.

Repairs to the P.L.M's 'pointed' locomotive.

With its metal spur-shaped projection on the smoke-box door, the locomotive resembles a battleship.

Locomotive depot in Bar-sur-Aube in 1908, on the Paris–Belfort line.

(Henry Collection)

THE LOCOMOTIVE DEPOT

The driver must watch for signals, but the small window protecting him from rain and smoke soon becomes dirty
and he is forced to lean out of his cab.

The fireman's job demands considerable physical effort. For example, during the hour it takes to travel from Paris to Epernay he must move,
almost without respite, between one and one-and-a-half tons of coal.

THE FIREMAN AND THE DRIVER AT WORK

(Photos: Paul Herem)

Jules Claretie eloquently described the role of the driver. *'He is like a pilot on board a ship, the company's fortunes and the passengers' lives are entrusted to him. One second's loss of concentration, one single mistake, and the whole train may be destroyed. As he climbs on board his engine, the station-master gives him written instructions for the safe journey of the train. These must be carried out at the risk of his own life. He is the soldier who fights every day, while other soldiers fight only in times of war.'* Claretie then writes of the fireman. *'The fireman who carries in his hands so many human lives, who night and day in all weathers standing on his engine like a sailor on his ship, like a sentry at his post, casts the coke or coal into the burning furnace, this man, strong and black with grime, who, when the train stops, when the passengers he has brought to their destination descend and run in haste about their business or pleasure or to their loved ones, cleans and tends the engine much as a rider gently rubs down his horse when the race is over.'*

A locomotive at full speed.

One of the sights which await the driver.

The speedometer.

(Photo: Paul Herem)

The engine controls.

(Photo: Paul Herem)

THE TRACK AND THE LOCOMOTIVE

The first train with an outside corridor arrives at Le Tréport.

(Bibliothèque des arts décoratifs)

PASSENGER COACHES ABOUT 1875

In 1873, a train from Amiens arrived at Le Treport. All its coaches had an outside corridor or gallery and aroused a great deal of interest. The gallery coach was the precursor of our modern corridor coach, since the gallery allowed people to go from one compartment to another but only within one coach and via an outside corridor. About the same time, sleeping-cars were fitted with a similar corridor linking the different compartments.

In 1871, a young Belgian engineer, George Nagelmackers, had travelled by train in North America and had been struck by the lack of comfort of European trains compared to American trains. He, therefore, had the idea of building coaches which would contain comfortable beds

An American restaurant-car about 1870.

(La Voie ferrée: Baclé)

and washrooms; these could be coupled on to the express trains which ran between the great European cities. The difficulty he experienced in putting this idea into practice resulted in the formation of the 'Compagnie internationale des wagons-lits'.

Some years later, the first restaurant-car was introduced, the company having decided to serve food to passengers on long journeys. The first luxury train, the 'Orient Express', with both sleeping-cars and restaurant-cars, made its first journey on 1 June 1883 between Paris and Vienna.

The early sleeping-cars consisted of three compartments with a central corridor linking them to one another. In each compartment there were two lower berths and two upper berths. During the daytime, the lower berths were used as bench seats and the upper berths were pushed up to the ceiling of the coach.

A sleeping-car in 1875, with the engineer, Nagelmackers, and Colonel Mann.

(Compagnie internationale des wagons-lit archive)

Coach with an outside corridor, used on the Amiens to Le Tréport line in 1873.

(Bibliothèque des arts décoratifs)

One of the first Orient Express restaurant-cars fitted with bogies, in 1883.

The coach was divided into two saloons, one to hold twelve passengers, the other twenty-four. On luxury trains, the smaller of the two saloons was used as a smoking-car for eight people.

Top: Sleeping-car in 1884.

Left: The compartment at night. *Centre*: The washroom. *Right*: The compartment by day.

Above: Interior of a restaurant-car in 1884.

ROLLING-STOCK OF THE COMPAGNIE INTERNATIONALE DES WAGONS-LITS IN THE 1880s

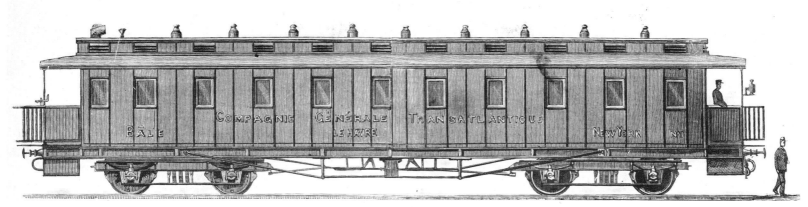

A coach for emigrants belonging to the Compagnie générale transatlantique.

The coaches were used to carry emigrants bound for America from Basle to Le Havre. They came from Switzerland, South Germany, Italy, the Tyrol and Austria.

In 1883, the company carried 35,000 of the 700,000 emigrants who left Europe.

Interior of a C.G.T. coach for emigrants.

There were two kinds of coach; one with 80 seats, the other with 40 seats and a buffet. In the second type of coach, luggage-racks and children's cots were fitted
to the tops of the partitions formed by the backs of the bench seats.

THE C.G.T. EMIGRANTS' TRAIN.

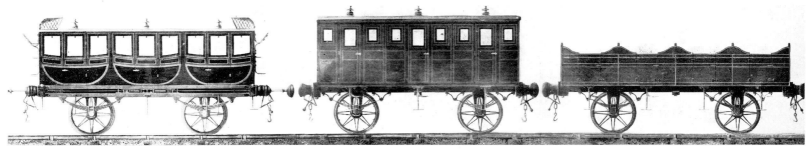

First-class coach in 1840.

Second-class coach in 1840.

(P.O. archive)

Third-class coach in 1840.

Wooden frame of a double-decker coach in 1911 (used on the French Western State suburban line).
The top decks could be open or enclosed. The 72–78 seater coach weighed between 7 and 8 tons.

THE DEVELOPMENT OF
THE PASSENGER COACH

In 1840, first-class coaches resembled in shape the old stage-coaches. Third-class coaches were open, leaving passengers exposed to all kinds of bad weather. By 1854, the passenger-coach had become bigger and heavier. A passenger train with 24 coaches, which was the maximum allowed at the time, weighed on average 185 tons, that is about 8 tons per coach or 4–6 cwt deadweight per passenger. By 1867, the same 24-coach train had increased to 210 tons, that is, an increase of about one ton per coach.

By 1878, the size and weight of coaches had increased yet again. The axles on the new Paris–Orleans coaches were set well apart from one another, and the P.L.M. coaches were built with three axles. The weight of a 24-coach train increased to 255 tons, that is about 10 tons per coach.

In 1883, the average speed of trains barely exceeded 37 miles per hour. The changes in the design of coaches which were intended to improve passenger comfort also had the effect of increasing coach stability. In fact, when the coaches are longer, their stability improves because there is an increase in deadweight. It also

Third-class coach with observation post used on the Paris–Orleans line in 1858.

Norwegian State Railway second-class coach in 1870.

Norwegian State Railway third-class coach in 1875.

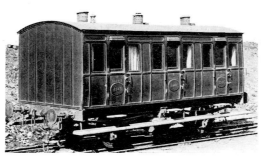

First-class coach in 1854
(3 compartments, 24 seats).

Second-class coach in 1854 (3 compartments, 30 seats).

(P.O. archive)

Third-class coach in 1854
(4 compartments, 40 seats).

Third-class coach with a long wheelbase in 1900.

(P.O. archive)

improves when the coaches are coupled together more firmly. By this time, coaches on express trains weighed 10 to 12 tons and their deadweight had increased to between 5 and 7 cwt per passenger. The distance between axles had reached 20 feet and this contributed again to the coaches' stability. On the other hand, it had now become more difficult for the train to negotiate tighter bends. In America, this problem was solved by the use of bogies, but, in 1883, in France, engineers hesitated to use this device, thinking that such huge coaches would be difficult to manœuvre, particularly on France's smaller turntables.

However, the public continued to demand wider compartments, higher ceilings, washrooms on every train, a restaurant-car, and corridors which would allow passengers to go to the restaurant-car and would give them the greater freedom which they enjoyed on board ships.

In 1889, the P.L.M. put into service coaches with three axles. These were used on day trains between Paris and Marseilles and were to be seen at the exhibition that same year. The coaches retained the features typical of French coaches, in particular a side door in each compartment. This allowed passengers to enter and leave the train quickly without any fear of a crush. The corridor, however, took up the full width of a passenger seat. About this time, bogies began to be used on passenger coaches and the length of coaches increased to 72 feet. All were fitted with doors at each end, and, with 42–48 passengers, they weighed from 35 to 40 tons or 16 cwt per passenger. The deadweight had, therefore, trebled within a period of 25 years, the deadweight being the critical factor where comfort and safety are concerned.

A P.L.M. inter-communicating train put into service in 1889.

(*Nature*, 18 November 1893)

About 1913, passenger-coaches could be divided into two types: British coaches, characterised by separate compartments with side doors, and American coaches, with one long, single compartment incorporating a central corridor and fitted with two or three axles and two bogies. The bogie does not simply allow the train to negotiate a bend at greater speed, but also, because of the larger wheel-base of the coach, it increases the smoothness of the coach's movement as it passes over rail joints. It also prevents sideways movement, and reduces traction resistance by 15 per cent at a speed of approximately 60 m.p.h. However, the deadweight per passenger is greater when the coach is fitted with bogies.

American coaches were, by the nature of their construction, more comfortable for passengers. The reasons why American railway-engineers sought to increase passenger comfort are to be found in the special character of railways in the United States in the early years of their development. In fact, railways existed before roads, and American towns and cities were built alongside the rail tracks, since it was the network of trains which brought men and materials to those cities. In Europe, the opposite was true. The railways linked cities which already existed and which were already accessible by road. In America, therefore, the railway was almost a public highway. Herds of cattle sometimes blocked it, and on certain lines cattle-guards had to be built to protect the line from these animals. Given this situation a train became almost a 'travelling hotel'. It had to be self-sufficient on the long journeys between the towns which were being built at considerable distances from one another.

Third-class coach with end doors and bogies in 1910.

In the illustration on these two pages the coaches are to scale. (P.O. archive)

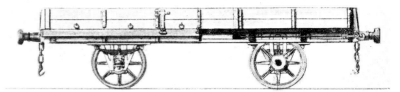

Flat and raised-side platform trucks.

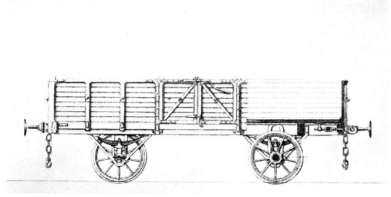

Open waggon with sides.

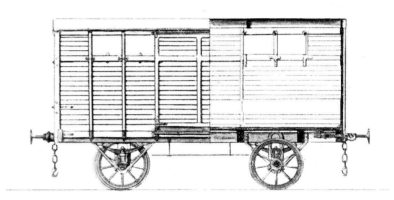

Enclosed waggon with sliding door.

GOOD WAGGONS AND GUARDS' VANS

Though waggons should be built to suit the nature of the goods they carry, if they are too specialised they cannot adapt to the varying needs of this particular service. There are, therefore, generally three types of waggon. First, platform trucks, almost without any sides at all, weighing 4 tons and capable of carrying a load of 10 tons. Second, high-sided open waggons used to transport minerals, stone and coal, weighing 5 tons and able to carry a load of 10 tons, and, third, covered waggons used to carry stock and goods which must not be exposed to the weather. These weighed 5–6 tons and could carry a load of 5–10 tons.

Like most passenger-coaches, waggons were

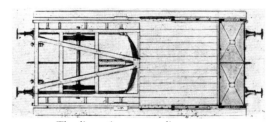

The discontinuous coupling system.
Traction is exerted through the centre bar on the top of the laminated spring in the middle of the underframe, and buffer impact is distributed through the side bars at the ends of the spring.

made of wood, with oak and ash being used for the frame, and pine for the floors and sides. Guards' vans weighed 6–9 tons and could carry up to 5 tons of luggage. They were always

positioned at the front of the train and, quite often, a second one was added at the rear. The guard was always in the van at the front of the train.

There were also special waggons such as coke waggons, slatted-side waggons, tanker-trucks for carrying different types of liquids, and refrigerated trucks used to transport perishable goods.

The standard goods stock is a waggon with a deadweight of 4–6 tons and able to carry a 10-ton load. In the United States, bogie trucks carry loads of up to 30 tons with a deadweight of 12–15 tons, but when wood was replaced by steel the deadweight as a proportion of the load was reduced. This led to the building of waggons capable of carrying 40 tons and with a deadweight of 15 tons. As a consequence, trains and, of course, sidings became shorter.

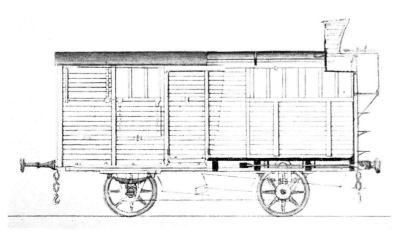

Enclosed waggon fitted with braking-post.

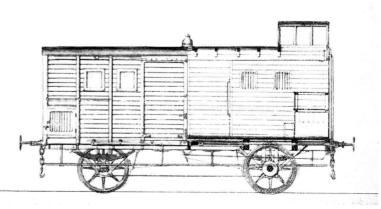

Guard's van with look-out point.

The wooden frame of a French mail-coach in 1900.

MAIL COACHES

The Postal Service had considerable importance in a country as huge as the United States, especially since the railway was, in its early years, the only public highway to link developing towns with the rest of the country. The light track, however, which had been laid in some haste throughout the New World, limited the speed of trains and increased journey time. Therefore, to save time and to avoid express trains having to stop when no passenger wished to get off, an automatic system was devised which allowed mailbags to be taken on the train and dropped off while the train was still moving.

Although American track was not particularly strong, some drivers drove at dangerously high speeds. Moreover, trains were often attacked by bandits. In 1895, therefore, the American Postal Service had mail-coaches built which resembled armoured fortresses. They were called Burglar- and Collision-Proof Mails. These coaches, which first ran on the Erie railroad between New York and Chicago, were designed by M.E.W. Grieves, the head of rolling-stock on the Baltimore & Ohio Railroad. To reduce the risk of theft, and avoid unwanted visitors, there was no central corridor communicating with the rest of the train. The sides of the coach consisted of steel plates which were riveted and bolted to steel girders.

The mail in 1875 in the United States.
Without stopping, the mail-coach takes on a bag of mail.
(*L'Illustration*, 30 October 1875)

Each end of the side frames which supported the metal structure rested on two- or three-axle bogies. The steel top of the coach was fitted with windows which allowed light to enter. At night, the coach was lit by oil-lamps and lamps running off compressed gas. At one end of the coach were beds arranged like berths on a ship. If the coach was derailed, or if it was attacked by thieves, the postal workers inside were well protected by the extremely solid and rigid structure.

In Europe, it was quite different. Mail-coaches, like all coaches, were still made of wood. The railway company was responsible for the maintenance of the underframe while the Post Office was responsible for the maintenance of the coaches' bodywork. Mail-coaches of this type weighed slightly over 7 tons.

However, some years before the First World War, to improve levels of comfort and general working conditions for its railway staff, the Post Office built two-axle mail-coaches which were 46 feet long and weighed 17 tons when empty, with an operating weight of 22 tons. It even built two-bogie mail-coaches which were 59 feet long. They were still, however, made of wood, and this led postal workers to demand that the coaches be strengthened, since they were frequently badly injured when the train was involved in an accident.

A French mail-coach in 1880.

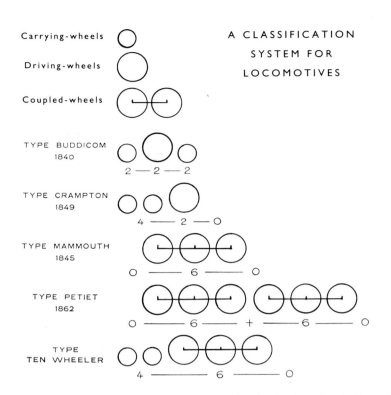

Carrying-wheels

Driving-wheels

Coupled-wheels

TYPE BUDDICOM
1840
2 — 2 — 2

TYPE CRAMPTON
1849
4 — 2 — 0

TYPE MAMMOUTH
1845
0 — 6 — 0

TYPE PETIET
1862
0 — 6 — + — 6 — 0

TYPE
TEN WHEELER
4 — 6 — 0

A CLASSIFICATION
SYSTEM FOR
LOCOMOTIVES

Whyte's classification system which originated in America and was based on the number of driving-and carrying-wheels. The system can be based on axles rather than wheels, in which case the wheel number is divided by two.

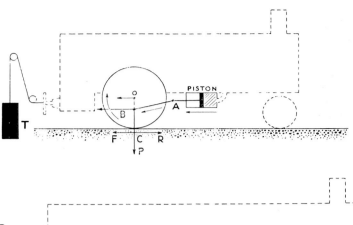

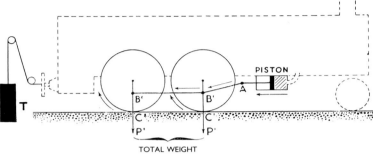

Adhesion.

To ensure that the driving-wheel does not slip, the motor force (F) must be smaller than the friction (R) of the wheel against the rail. By increasing the weight (P), friction (R) is also increased. If (P) is too heavy for the rail, two driving-wheels are used and this distributes the driving force between the two wheels.

TRACK ADHESION AND THE COUPLING OF DRIVING WHEELS

Three different types of power confront each other in a locomotive: motor-power, which is produced by steam-pressure; the train's resistance to movement; and adhesion, which is the vital factor if motor-power is to overcome resistance. The thrust which steam imparts to the piston is transmitted to the rim of the wheel by a 'tangential' effort; this is proportionate to the speed of the piston and inversely proportionate to the wheel's diameter. In other words, the same thrust will cause a large driving-wheel to transmit to the wheel's rim less energy than would a small driving-wheel. For this reason, goods locomotives, which need to be more powerful, have

smaller wheels. However, what the engine gains in power it loses in speed.

The effort (F) made by the rim of the driving wheel as it turns is opposed by the friction (R) of the wheel as it brings the weight (P) down on to the rail. The heavier the wheel, the less smooth the contact made and the greater the friction. If this friction is greater than the effort (F) at the rim, the wheel will start to turn in spite of the train's mass which resists this forward movement. If this friction or adhesion is not as great as the rim's effort relative to the train's mass, the wheel will 'skid' and the train will not move.

To improve adhesion, it is possible to increase the roughness of the surfaces which come into contact with one another. One means of increasing adhesion was to scatter sand along the rail in front of the driving-wheel.

Another was to increase weight (P) but weight

is limited by the rail's strength and the track's resistance. Before the First World War, the axle-load limit varied from 13 to 18 tons. In order not to exceed this limit, engineers were forced to increase the number of driving-wheels and couple them together so that the front driving-axle's spin resistance was increased by that of the second driving-axle and so on and so forth.

As a means of classifying locomotives, a very simple system was devised, based on the number of driving-wheels and number of carrying-wheels. The first number corresponds to the number of carrying-wheels at the front of the engine, the second number to the number of coupled driving-wheels, and the third number to the number of carrying-wheels at the rear. Thus the 'Pacific' type engine is classified as 4–6–2. An articulated locomotive is considered as two locomotives joined together, so the 'Mallet'-type locomotive with its two pairs of four coupled wheels giving increased adhesion is represented by 0–4–0 + 0–4–0.

If the steam's thrust is transmitted to the driving-wheels by rods and cranks, the system used since 1860 to distribute this thrust to the piston has been Walschaerts' valve gear, Walschaerts being the sometime head of the Belgian State Railway and the inventor of the system. Stephenson's link motion requires two eccentrics per cylinder, that is, two eccentric circles which move one within the other. A two-cylinder locomotive will therefore have four eccentrics. These create considerable friction which causes wear and, in particular, loss of engine power. Walschaerts' valve gear, on the other hand, requires only one eccentric per cylinder and therefore wear is reduced.

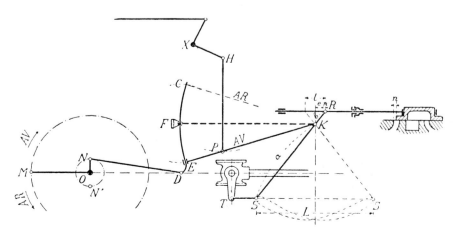

Walschaert's valve-gear, which replaced Stephenson's link motion.

American-type in 1899.

(Paris–Orleans company)

Atlantic classs in 1903.

(Paris–Orleans company)

THE DEVELOPMENT OF THE EXPRESS

For a long time, engineers hesitated to couple wheels on passenger locomotives because they believed the turning speed of the wheels was unsuited to coupling.

The Paris–Orleans line was one of the first to couple wheels on passenger trains, and in 1860 it built the 2–4–0 type. Such engines were still being used in 1914 on secondary lines to pull light passenger trains. Sometimes their firebox overhangs behind two coupled-axles, sometimes it is between them or above the rear driving-axle.

A variation on this type is the 0–4–2, with its carrying-axle at the rear instead of at the front, but all these types suffer from a weak wheelbase and, therefore, poor stability at high speed. The firebox of the 2–4–0 type was therefore lengthened, and a carrying-axle added at the rear, and this led to the creation of the 'Columbia' class 2–4–2 engine. One of these was the famous locomotive *Forquenot*, Forquenot being the inventor and an engineer working for the Paris–Orleans Company. It was a simple expansion locomotive weighing 47 tons, with an adhesion weight of 28 tons, and it ran successfully from 1875 to 1900 on a passenger line.

Because stability was still not adequate, a second carrying-axle was added, not at the rear

Pacific class in 1908.

(Paris–Orleans company)

Express locomotive with coupled axles in 1860.

(Paris–Orleans company)

but at the front, and on a bogie. This was the 'American'-type 4–4–0 (the 'Grant' locomotive at the 1867 exhibition). It was tested first of all with a compound engine, with two, and later four, cylinders and later still with superheat. The P.L.M.'s famous 'windbreak' locomotive and Flaman's last Eastern Railway locomotive also belonged to this class.

But as trains became heavier, more power was needed and more steam had to be produced. Therefore more and bigger fire-tubes were needed, and the grate area had to be increased, since the amount of coal burned is proportionate to the amount of steam which has to be produced. This led to an increase in the weight and size of the boiler, more in terms of its length than its height or width, the latter being particularly limited by the gauge of the track. Later, a fifth axle had to be added at the rear and the 4–4–0 class became the 4–4–2 class, known as the 'Atlantic' because it first ran on the Philadelphia–Atlantic City line.

But the 'Atlantic', with its two driving-axles, experienced the same problems as had the single driving-axle 'Crampton' before it, that is, its adhesion weight was insufficient, given the power of the boiler, and the axle-weight limit prevented an increase in power. So the rear carrying-axle was coupled to the two middle driving-axles to create the 4–6–0 'Ten-Wheel' class which could pull both faster goods trains and heavy express trains. It had a four-cylinder compound engine and was used on all the French networks. The search for greater power continued and a sixth carrying-axle was added at the rear of the 4–6–0 class, and, in 1902, on the Missouri–Pacific Railroad in the United States, the famous 4–6–2 'Pacific' class ran for the first time.

Later, the 4–6–4 'Baltic' class was built when the sixth carrying-axle at the rear was replaced by a bogie. It was first introduced on the Northern Railway in France.

'Ten-wheel' type in 1907.

(Swiss Federal Railways)

THE DEVELOPMENT OF GOODS LOCOMOTIVES

For a long time the most common type of goods locomotive was the 0–6–0 type built by the Le Creusot Company in 1867. However, in this engine the firebox and cylinders overhung, and this was dangerous at speed. The engine had also become too heavy to be carried by only three axles and so, to increase power, a carrying-axle was added at the rear to give the 0–6–2 class and, in some cases, a Bissel axle was added at the front instead to create the 2–6–0 'Mogul' class, this being the name of the first American locomotive built in this way. In 1900, in France, the Southern Railway modified old engines to build this class which hauled fast goods trains and heavy express trains with equal success.

But a fourth driving-axle was needed for heavy goods trains. The 0–8–0 'Cail-Fives-Lille' class which had been seen in the 1867 exhibition was succeeded by the famous 2–8–0 'Consolidation' class, with an extra carrying-axle. In 1902, this locomotive operated on the Southern Railway in France and at the time was the heaviest locomotive in operation. It was particularly suitable for use on the hilly line between Beziers and Neussargues. In 1903, the Paris–Orleans Railway built a locomotive of this class capable of pulling up to 1,400 tons on the flat and 750 tons up a slope with a gradient of 1 in 100. In the United States, companies which had used the 4–8–0 'Twelve-Wheel' class returned to the 2–8–0 'Consolidation' class, since it allowed adhesion weight to be a greater fraction of total weight.

An extra rear carrying-axle was added to the 'Consolidation' class locomotive, and this led to the creation of the 2–8–2 'Mikado' class, named after an engine first built for Japan. This type impressed many people by the smoothness of its movement both in forward and reverse drive.

In the United States, between 1900 and 1903, the 0–10–0 class with its five driving-axles and maximum adhesion was replaced on the Atchison, Topeka and Sante Fe Railroad by the 2–10–0 'Decapod' class and the 2–10–2 'Sante Fe' class. These engines ran on particularly steep track in the Rocky Mountains. In 1905, the Sante Fe weighed up to 130 tons with an adhesion weight of 106 tons. But the normal weight of American goods trains was between 1,800 and 2,000 tons, and the 90- to 100-ton Consolidation-class engines, with an adhesion weight of 80–90 tons, were generally adequate.

The 'Decapod' type was also used in Europe. The Belgian type 'Flamme' (from the name of its builder, a famous engineer on the Belgian State Railway) was particularly well known and ran from 1909 on the hilly lines of Luxembourg. It was the most powerful goods engine operating on the Continent. It had a four-cylinder, simple expansion, superheated engine, and a steam-valve gear.

Illinois Central Railroad 'Mikado'-class, about 1900.

(Die Eisenbahn Imbild)

Belgian State Railway's 'Decapod Flamme'-class (1908).

(*La Locomotive*: Lamale and Legein)

The Paris–Orleans 85–ton 'Decapod' class (1908).

(Paris–Orleans company)

Baltimore & Ohio R.R. 'Mogul'-class in 1875.

French Southern Railway 'Consolidation' class in 1902.

(*Nature*, 24 May 1902)

THE DEVELOPMENT OF RAILWAYS IN EUROPE

A map of 1765 reveals how people travelled from Paris to different towns in France. The map shows routes radiating out from the capital and foreshadows what would be the network of railways a century later around Paris. In 1765, by various means of transport – carriage, stage-coach, mail-coach – it required 12 days to travel to Marseilles and 16 to travel to Toulouse. By 1814, travelling by mail-coach, Marseilles was reached in 112 hours (instead of 288) and Toulouse in 104 hours (instead of 384). In 1834, the same mail-coach service took only 80 and 70 hours respectively. It is true that by this time the railway had been established, but only in the region round Saint-Etienne. It was not until almost 22 years later, in 1846, that Paris was linked to Belgium and the Touraine. The rest of France had only isolated sections of track.

Meanwhile, other countries whose first railway had been built long after the first railway in France had well-developed networks. Belgium was already aiming to link up with Germany by rail, and Prussia itself had a well-established rail network. In fact, Belgium aimed to link up with Germany before France had realised the importance of building railways up to its borders.

In a fascinating article published in a geographical review in September 1931, M. L.M. Jouffroy wrote of the Belgian railways: 'The impression is that some force, superior to anything we have, planned a complete rail network and persuaded a country of under 30,000 square kilometres [11,500 square miles] and with fewer than 4 million inhabitants to spend nearly 150 million francs, that is a sum of money one third greater than the annual State budget. By 1843, Belgium had already passed the stage of rail development that France would reach only ten years later. It already had 560 kilometres [350 miles] of track whereas France only had less than 600 kilometres [372 miles].'

Belgium had realised it could link Ostend and Antwerp with Germany, by-passing Rotterdam and the Rhine corridor. Moreover, in Germany it would link up with lines already taking traffic towards the Adriatic and the Black Sea.

In fact, the German states, in spite of their independence from one another, seemed to have realised instinctively the need to unite, and they were already in the process of building a remarkable network linking Aix-la-Chapelle and Cilli along the route to Trieste. Navigable rivers in Germany in general ran from north to south. They were then linked by the main lines of the German railway network which cut across them latitudinally, in this way extending the lines from Belgium. In the same way, Belgium's main lines had cut across the Meuse, Escaut and Lys waterways. Belgium and Germany had, therefore, already managed to co-ordinate waterways and rail networks.

How would France react to this situation? It was, of course, at the very centre of two great movements of international traffic from the North Sea to the Mediterranean and from Central

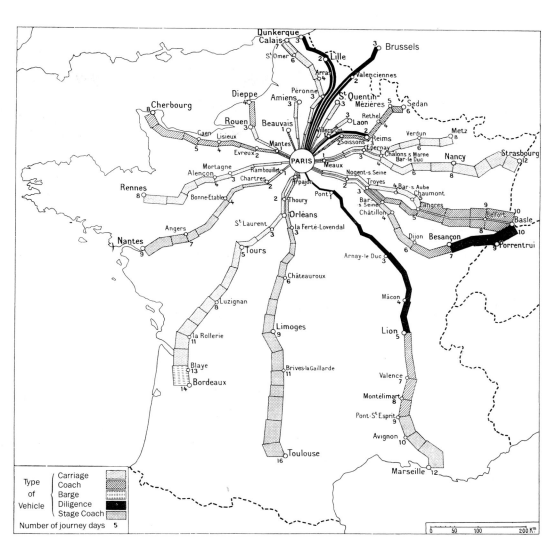

Travelling from Paris to main towns of France in 1765.
Taken from *A Traveller's Guide* by Lord Michel, the Royal Geographer at the Observatory.
The figures indicate the number of days travelled.

Europe to the Atlantic Ocean. Its only waterways were either of variable depth, like the Rhône, the Loire, and the Moselle, or winding and difficult to navigate like the Seine and the Marne. The logical answer, it seemed to Jouffroy, was to build a line from Boulogne to Lyons, linking, via Laon, the manufacturing, mining and metal-producing industries in Reims, Saint-Didier and Chatillon-sur-Seine. It would then be extended to Marseilles, and a second line of communication from Strasbourg to Châlons-sur-Marne would link up with the first. These lines would have the further advantage of integrating with the natural waterways. A further logical step would be to build a line from Amiens to Le Havre, which would allow English cotton and Scottish and South American wool to be carried to Central Europe. Such a plan would have led to the building of the Northern, Eastern and Mediterranean railways long before 1848. They were, of course, not built until much later.

The French railways developed without any overall plan. It was, in fact, almost as if pleasure was taken in building lines to compete with

transport systems already in existence. Thus the Rouen line ran parallel with the Seine. The Northern line to Belgium ran parallel with the navigable waterways linking the Oise, the Meuse and the Escaut. The Lyons line ran parallel to the Burgundy Canal which had only just been completed. Similarly, with the centralised system of roads which radiated out from Paris, instead of co-ordinating with it, railways simply tried to imitate it and so railway lines too radiated out from the capital. The idea of linking up with railways in other countries did not seem to occur at the time to people who seemed too preoccupied with the political dreams of 1848. As a result, trains from Le Havre to Central Europe were diverted via Antwerp and, in 1850, Trieste became a more important port than Marseilles since there was no line for more than 300 miles between Tonnerre and Avignon. Moreover, Jouffroy points out that the famous 'India Mail' no longer came through France with the result that, in January 1851, 'English newspapers published news from India two days before letters sent to France arrive in Paris. Via Trieste the journey is

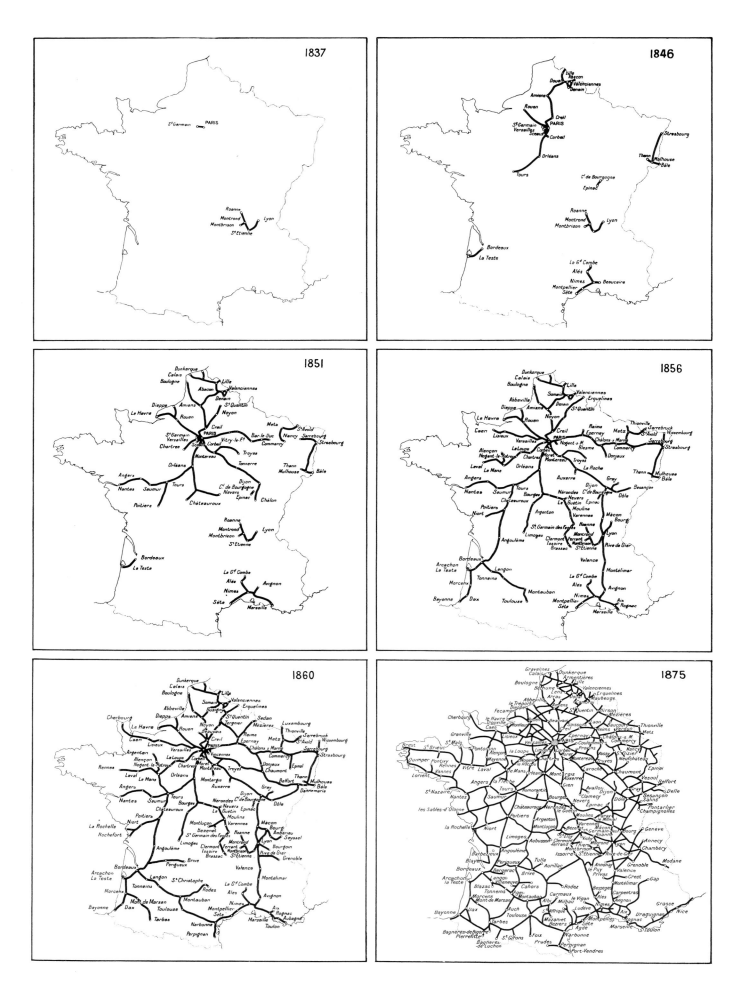

THE DIFFERENT STAGES IN THE
DEVELOPMENT OF THE FRENCH RAILWAYS.

now 40 hours shorter than via Marseilles.'

From 1851 onwards, because of its rail technology, France started to catch up. Train speeds in France became comparable with the fastest in Britain and, by September 1855, the French rail system was co-ordinated and well developed around the capital. Every major provincial town was linked by rail, apart from Toulouse, which had to wait until the following year for a line to Bordeaux, and Brest, which had to wait until 1866. Other towns, however, such as Toulon, Grenoble, Cherbourg and Rennes were not part of the rail network. Only one section was missing from the Paris–Marseilles line and that was the section through Lyons. Since the Fourvière Tunnel had not yet been built, the link by coach from La Guillotière to Vaise delayed the journey by two hours. Stage-coach services were still frequent and there were far fewer railway stations than there were to be 50 years later, mainly because there was no public demand for them.

In Britain, railways continued to develop and it had already been realised that the railways could be used as a means of maintaining power in the colonies. British colonies were the first to have a rail network. The British very quickly perceived the strategic importance of a line in Africa that could link South Africa and Egypt. Such a line would be as important as the Canadian Pacific Railway which ran across territory in North America which was entirely British. It stretched from the Atlantic to the Pacific and would be the safest, fastest and shortest route to connect with Australia, the Far East and even India, if Suez was for some reason cut off.

In 1848, these geopolitical views did not appear to be a matter of concern to the French. This had already resulted in a considerable delay in the development of railways in France, and the same attitude surfaced again when railways came to be considered as an instrument of political policy. The result was the rapid development of local lines which ran from village to village, almost from door to door. This was a far cry from the incomparable means 'of long-distance, large-scale linear transport' as originally conceived.

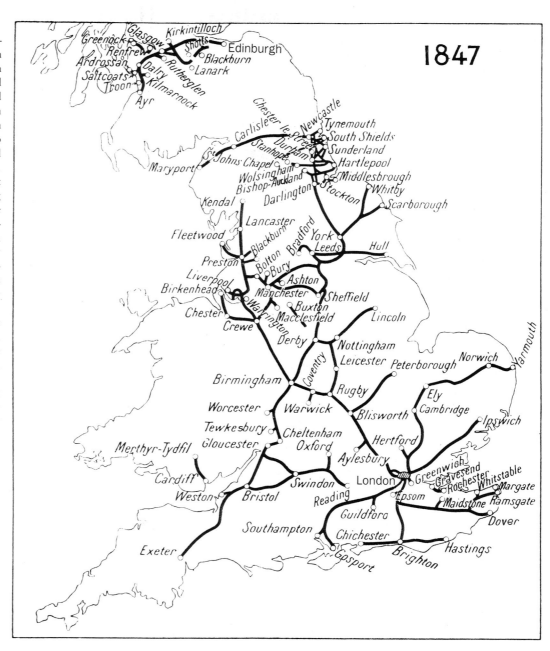

Railway development in Britain in 1847.

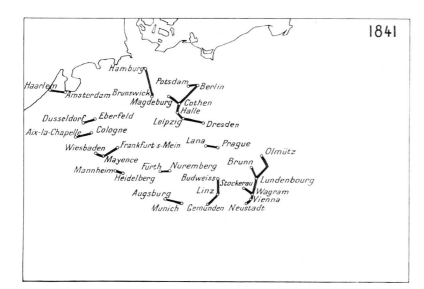

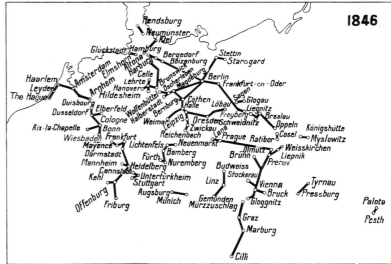

Two stages in railway development in Germany (1841 and 1846).

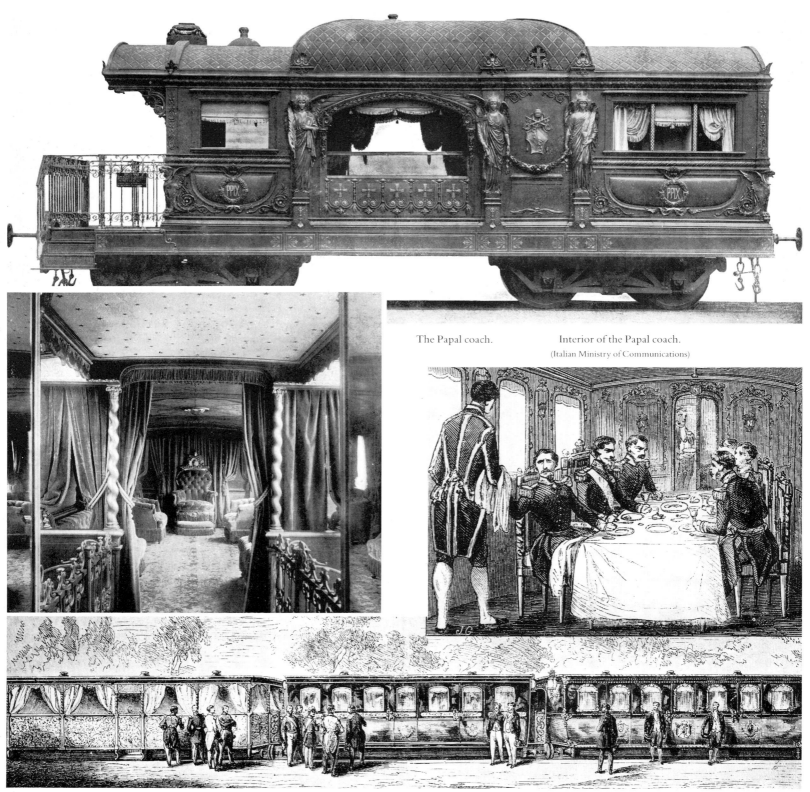

The Papal coach.   Interior of the Papal coach.
(Italian Ministry of Communications)

Three coaches of the French Imperial train.

SPECIAL ROYAL COACHES

Before the coming of railways, monarchs travelled in luxury carriages. It was natural that, as the railways developed, special coaches should be built to provide a similar level of comfort.

In 1863, for example, the Pope had a special coach provided in which he could travel within the Papal States. It was built for him by French engineers working on the Rome–Velletri railway.

During the same period, Emperor Napoleon III travelled in a special train built by the Eastern Railway. It consisted of nine inter-communicating coaches: a luggage truck, two first-class coaches for the Emperor, a dining-car, a promenade-carriage, a saloon and smoking-car, a sleeping-car, and, for the Empress's female staff, a first-class coach and a luggage truck. The coaches were painted on the outside in green and gold. The panels of the saloon-car's doors were emblazoned with the Emperor's arms. Every detail, the door-handles, the bronze lamp-fittings, the gold paintwork, helped to create a feeling of opulence and elegance. Passengers entered the train by climbing the steps which led to the balcony on the promenade-carriage or via steps which led to the saloon-car.

In 1892, the President of the Republic's double coach was less luxurious. It had two saloon-cars, and these also had been built by the Eastern Railway.

THE DEVELOPMENT OF THE TANK ENGINE

As we have seen, locomotives need to carry much more water than coal and often have to stop to take on water. To avoid this, the locomotive must pull a heavy tender which increases considerably the train's deadweight and reduces by a corresponding amount the profits it can make. Engineers, therefore, built locomotives capable of carrying their own supply of water, to be used particularly on short journeys and to haul heavy trains which already had sufficient deadweight. The load would be carried by the driving-wheels and this would increase the engine's track adhesion. This new locomotive was the tank engine. It was used on suburban lines, for shunting at stations, and to pull goods trains on hilly lines where frequent stops were normally required to take on further supplies of water. Without its tender, the locomotive is shorter, more compact and better-suited to manœuvring within stations. It can be more easily operated in forward and reverse drive and is, therefore, particularly appropriate for use on commuter lines.

The older tank engines often had two coupled axles and one, two or more carrying-axles. On the French Northern Railway a 4–4–4 type, with two bogies and two pairs of driving-wheels, used to operate. However, it was not long before it became necessary to fit three driving-axles and among older models of this type still operating successfully in 1914 was one for the French Western Railway. The same idea produced a Swedish tank locomotive with three coupled axles and maximum adhesion. The water-tanks were on the side of the engine, as on the 4–6–0 type locomotive which was used from 1902 on passenger trains on the Paris Inner Circle line. This engine was built by Du Bousquet, the chief engineer on the Northern Railway, and it proved particularly efficient, since the increased adhesion arising from the weight of the coal and water allowed the engine to cope very well with the frequent stops and starts. A particular feature of this engine was the tandem compounding arrangement, with the cylinders positioned one behind the other.

A short time later, the Western Railway's 2–6–2 class was particularly popular, as was the Eastern, Northern and P.L.M. Railways' 4–6–4, with its two bogies and three driving-axles. The 2–6–2 had a water-tank capacity of 1500 gallons and

Great Eastern Railway ten-coupled tank engine (1903).

(Sauvage Collection)

State Railway 'Mikado'-class tank engine (1912).

(State Railway)

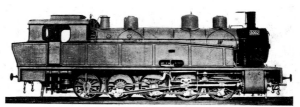

French Southern Railway maximum adhesion ten-coupled tank engine (1909).

(Cail Company)

coal-bunker capacity of 2½ tons. The 4–6–4 engine carried 1900 gallons of water and 3 tons of coal.

To compete with electric tramways, the Great Eastern Railway in Britain built a maximum adhesion 0–10–0-type engine. On suburban lines, it was able to offer faster trains because of its increased acceleration. With a train of 315 tons, carrying 1200 passengers, it reached a speed of 30 m.p.h. in only 30 seconds.

About 1909, the Cail Company built another maximum adhesion 'Ten-Coupler' type tank en-

gine for the French Southern Railway Company, to be used on its hilly lines and to haul goods trains. About 1905, the State Railway built the 2–8–2 'Mikado' class for its particularly busy suburban lines. It was hugely successful on all the networks and was even used to pull express trains. The symmetry of its driving- and carrying-axles gave this engine stability in both forward and reverse drive. An example of a four-coupled tank engine was the 4–8–0 French Southern Railway class, with its front bogies and superheated steam.

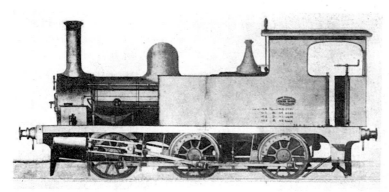

Swedish tank engine (1875).

(Swedish Private Railways)

Tandem compound locomotive on the Paris Circle line (1902).

(*Nature*, 31 January 1903)

The biggest locomotive in the world in 1913 – the Atchison, Topeka & Santa Fé R.R.'s Mallet-system locomotive.
(*Nature*, 18 January 1913)

THE DEVELOPMENT OF THE ARTICULATED LOCOMOTIVE

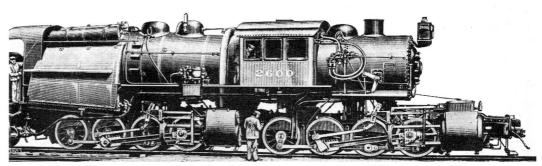

Erie Railroad Mallet-system giant locomotive (1908).
(*Nature*, 21 December 1907).

To increase traction power and, as a consequence, adhesion, engineers were forced to increase the number of driving-axles, but the increase in length of the rigid wheelbase and axle-systems proved a problem on curved tracks. In mountainous areas, these curves are particularly sharp and the gradients demand a high level of adhesion. To reconcile this need for adhesion and flexibility, the axles were divided into two groups which acted independently from each other on curves. This gives what is described as an articulated locomotive. The two groups of driving-wheels are driven independently, using a separate two-cylinder system for each set of wheels. This arrangement also offers the advantage of being more suited to the compound engine, since one cylinder-system can be high-pressure and the other low-pressure.

For the Bolivian railways, the Yorkshire Engine Company in Sheffield built the 'Fairlie'-type locomotive, in which two Belpaire-type boilers were positioned back to back on the same chassis. Mallet, the inventor of compound engines, found another solution, with the two articulated sections supporting a single boiler. The high-pressure cylinder-system was built onto the engine's underframe in the usual way. The low-pressure set of cylinders pivoted in the centre of the locomotive, low-pressure being chosen for the articulated group of driving-axles since the movement of steam between the boiler and this group requires an articulated joint which it is easier to make airtight when low-pressure rather than high-pressure steam is used. Mallet's articulated system was widely used on tank locomotives. It was first used on the 1889 exhibition railway on a 'Deauville'-class engine with a 60 centimetre (1 ft 11½ in) gauge track.

In 1905, Du Bousquet, the chief engineer with the Northern Railway, was inspired by the 'Mallet' system to build a 0–6–2 + 2–6–0 compound tank locomotive which was used to pull 950-ton coal trains up steep gradients on the lines from Valenciennes to Hirson via Avesnes and from Busigny to Hirson. The older locomotives with three coupled axles could not pull loads of more than 490–600 tons.

From 1906 to 1913, increasingly powerful engines equipped with the 'Mallet' system began to run in the United States, first on the Baltimore & Ohio Railroad, hauling trains weighing almost 3,000 tons, then on the Erie Railroad where a gigantic maximum-adhesion locomotive was capable of pulling up to 10,000 tons at 10 m.p.h., and finally on the Atchison, Topeka and Sante Fé Railroad. Their 2–10–0 + 0–10–2 weighed 279 tons, 382 with its tender, and its huge oil-fired engine was capable of 2,500 h.p.

Bolivian Fairlie locomotive (1907).
(Bibliothèque des art décoratifs)

Eastern Railway Mallet-system locomotive (1908).
(Sauvage Collection)

Du Bousquet's Northern Railway Mallet-system locomotive (1905).
(Northern Railway)

METAL USED FOR THE FIRST TIME IN THE BUILDING OF ROLLING-STOCK

In 1905, railways found themselves having to face the problem of how to lighten their rolling-stock, their goods-waggons and passenger-coaches. They looked for a way to reduce deadweight, and it immediately became apparent that this could be achieved by replacing wood with steel.

American railroads did not hesitate to build goods waggons entirely of steel. Passenger-stock was not such a straightforward matter. Metal was certainly lighter, and no less comfortable, but passengers were demanding more and more comfort and this meant additional weight, whether it was a question of providing more room or the benefits of new heating, lighting and ventilation systems, etc. As a consequence, it was not necessarily certain that, expressed as weight per passenger seat, a steel coach would be lighter than a wooden coach. In 1907, in the United States, trains already had a deadweight of nearly 1 ton per passenger seat, and the seats were not always occupied. To replace wood with metal would not automatically bring about any substantial reduction in weight.

There was, however, one overriding argument in support of metal and that was the question of safety. In the United States, derailments and collisions were relatively frequent, since railway construction work had not been carried out as meticulously as in Europe. In accidents, wood fragments, and it is the pieces of broken wood which cause the most serious injuries. By contrast, metal tends simply to bend and twist.

Moreover, accidents often resulted in fires. When electric trains, which were in their infancy, had been derailed, fires had sometimes broken out following a short circuit. In August 1903, people had been stunned by the disaster on the Paris Metro when many passengers had been asphyxiated by smoke from the burning coaches. A similar accident occurred in 1906 on the New York Subway. Electricity had caused a fire in a derailed coach and yet the coach behind, made completely of steel, suffered very little damage.

The New York Subway therefore decided to

The result of coaches being built without sufficient strength is seen here in this accident at West Hampstead on 26 October 1907.
(*Nature*, 21 December 1907)

build its trains entirely of metal. The framework of the coaches was made up of strong lengths of steel. The window-frames were also made of steel. The floor consisted of sheets of corrugated iron covered in a flame-resistant layer of cement and hardwood. In turn, this was covered simply by thin strips of wood which reduced considerably the risk of fire. The roof was also made of

metal and it had a non-flammable wood-base composition applied to it.

At the 1905 Liège exhibition, the French State railways displayed a coach built by Dyle and Bacalan. It was made largely of steel and, as a result, the deadweight per passenger seat had been reduced to 1433 lbs which compared with almost 1900 lbs on Belgian railways.

The metal frame of the New York Rapid Transit Subway's first steel coaches (1906).
(*Nature*, 26 May 1906)

Two examples of damage suffered in a collision. *Left*, a metal Pullman car (1906); *right*, a wooden coach.
(*Nature*, 26 May 1906)

Only the tender is left of the locomotive which exploded in the Gare Saint-Lazare.
(*Génie civil*, 17 December 1904)

ACCIDENTS

On 6 September 1881, a signalling mistake in Maisons-Alfort resulted in an express train colliding at full speed with a stationary train in Charenton station. The impact reduced the passenger-coaches to tiny fragments.

The frailty and vulnerability of these wooden-coaches had already been apparent in the accident near Arras on 20 February 1864, when an express train, fortunately not at full speed, collided with a goods train as a result of a points error. In spite of the relatively low speed some waggons were destroyed completely and the ground was covered in debris.

Another kind of accident, but not as frequent, involved exploding boilers. On 24 December 1888, an elderly locomotive which had been in service for 34 years was pulling a passenger train as a speed of 30 m.p.h. on the Cincinnati–Baltimore line when suddenly it exploded. The noise was heard five miles away. By an amazing miracle the driver and the fireman were not even injured though covered in soot and debris.

A similar explosion occurred at about 10.45 am on 4 July 1904 in the Gare Saint-Lazare. Pieces of metal showered on to neighbouring blocks of flats near the Pont de L'Europe. Once again the driver and the fireman, who had just left their cab, escaped without injury.

Another extraordinary incident occurred in the Gare Montparnasse on 22 October 1895. The Granville train, consisting of a locomotive, two luggage trucks, a mail-coach, six passenger-coaches, and a guard's van, entered the station faster than was usual because the brakes had failed to operate. It passed straight through the buffers, mounted the platform, destroyed the station wall, and fell into the square below, crushing the kiosk.

Two trains collide on the Northern line near Arras.
Although the engines did not mount each other, the track was strewn with debris. (*L'Illustration*, 20 February 1864)

THE CHARENTON DISASTER ON THE LYONS RAILWAY
(6 September 1881).

A sketch made by M. Gaidraw two hours after the collison. The wooden coaches were totally destroyed, while the metal engine was almost undamaged.

The result of a locomotive explosion in the United States.
(*Nature*, 23 February 1889)

THE COMPRESSED AIR BRAKE

A braking accident: the front of the Gare Montparnasse destroyed by a runaway train, 22 October 1895.
The only victim was the woman selling newspapers in the kiosk which was crushed by the locomotive. (*Nature*, 9 November 1895)

Brakes operate in such a simple way that it is difficult to explain the Montparnasse accident. In fact, an air pump compresses air in a main tank beneath the locomotive. By means of a valve, the driver sends this air along a pipe to an auxiliary tank beneath each coach. This tank connects with a brake cylinder and with the pipe through a triple valve. In the brake cylinder, two pistons push the brake blocks against the two pairs of wheels. As long as the compressed air pressure is maintained in the main pipe, the brakes do not operate. If the driver turns the valve to a certain angle, it releases a certain amount of air from the main pipe. The reduced pressure activates the triple valve, and some of the compressed air in the auxiliary tank under each coach enters the brake cylinders. The pistons are than pushed forward and the brakes operate. The same would happen if the coupling fractured and pressure was reduced in the main pipe.

To release the brake, the driver sends compressed air along the main pipe. The triple valve then blocks off the pipe running from the auxiliary tank to the brake cylinder. This causes the brake cylinder to release air and the auxiliary tank is recharged.

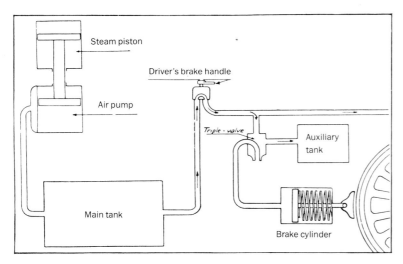

The triple valve allows the auxiliary reservoir to fill with compressed air and the brake-cylinder to be discharged.

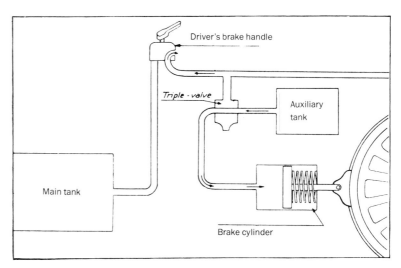

The triple valve allows the auxiliary reservoir to send compressed air to the brake-cylinder.

THE PRINCIPLES OF THE WESTINGHOUSE BRAKE SYSTEM

(State Railway archive)

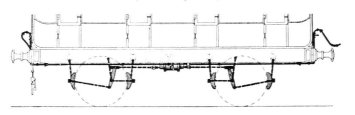

The main pipe, the auxiliary reservoir and the brake-cylinder beneath each coach.

LIGHTING ON PASSENGER COACHES

For many years, the oil used to light passenger coaches was 'vegetable oil'. The old lamps with their flat burners gave out a smoky and flickering light. Oil sometimes dripped from them and fell on to passengers' clothes. The Northern Railway improved matters by installing lamps with round burners and long wicks. They had a cylindrical glass shade and a nickel-plated steel reflector which cast light into every corner of the compartment.

Gas-lighting was used first of all in Germany, Britain, Belgium and Italy, and then, later on, in France. The most common system was the Pintsch system. Each coach was fitted with a tank of coal gas or mineral oil gas. The gas entered the tank at a pressure of 284 lbs pen square inch. In the tank it expanded as pressure fell from 200 to 100 lbs per square inch and, during use, a regulator compensated for the fall in pressure which resulted from consumption. Each lamp was fitted with a shade which could be used to dim the light given off. Later, incandescent gas-lighting was developed and came to rival electric-lighting systems.

In 1895, the P.L.M. company tested pure acetylene gas compressed to 140 lbs per square inch. However, it proved to be dangerous and the company settled for a mixture of acetylene and coal gas with a pressure of 100 lbs.

About 1910, gas-lighting was the most common form of lighting in France, particularly on the Southern, Eastern and P.L.M. Railways. On

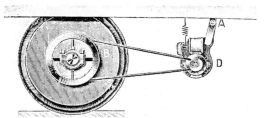

Lighting by compressed gas.
Above: Recharging reservoir (A) (*Nature*, 13 August 1910)
Below: the coach lighter.

the State Railway, gas was used only for local trains whereas the Paris–Orleans Railway used oil-lamps on its local trains. All express trains on the Northern, State and Paris–Orleans Railways were lit by electricity.

It was the Auer incandescent mantle which delayed the introduction of electric-lighting. However, the question of passenger safety and the possibility of fire following accidents contributed greatly to the development of electric-lighting on trains. Following the accident at Grantham on the Great Northern Railway on 7 November 1906, an official from the Board of Trade pointed out in his report that one of the coaches had been destroyed by a fire caused by a gas explosion in the tank beneath the underframe. The report seemed to suggest that it would be preferable to use electricity.

From 1882 to 1893, on the French Northern Railway, the Sceaux line, the Jura-Simplon line, on mail-coaches in Germany and in Austria and Italy, lighting by means of storage-batteries was tested. However, because of the weight of the batteries (1100–1300 lbs) and the constant need to recharge them, gas was preferred. About 1900, electricity was tried again. This time it was produced by generators with one or two small dynamos per coach or a single dynamo for the whole train. This was placed either in the front guard's van or on the locomotive itself. When it was on the locomotive, it was unable to maintain the current during stops, and a small storage battery was required.

Lighting by means of a generator in the guard's van and a dynamo driven by the axle was installed on the Paris–Orleans Railway, the Paris Circle Line and in both Russia and the United States. Generally, however, companies preferred independent lighting for each coach (such as the Stone system in England), since this enabled carriages to be added to the train or taken off midway through the journey.

Since electric-lighting systems are heavier than gas and almost twice as expensive, it was the question of safety which settled the matter.

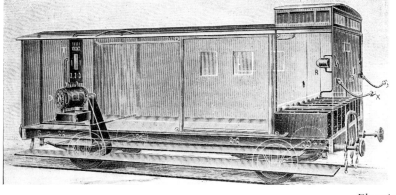

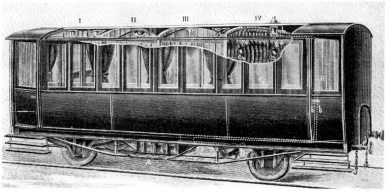

Electric lighting.

Top: Stone's device for individual lighting mounted beneath each coach. (*Nature*, 7 April 1906)

Left: A central lighting system on a leading guard's van on the Paris Circle line. *Right*: Individual coach lighting.

(*Nature*, 3 August 1912)

HEATING IN PASSENGER COACHES

For a long time the heating system consisted of placing two flat, long, hot-water containers in each compartment. This was thought to be the most efficient means of heating, given the internal layout of the coaches, divided as they were into three separate compartments. Because the compartments were narrow and separate, the hot-water containers gave out sufficient heat.

After use, they were not emptied but simply passed by means of a noria conveyor through a vat of boiling water, an operation which delayed the train for only five minutes. A quicker system was to heat the water inside the containers by a high-pressure jet of steam. However, both systems required special equipment and could be operated only in reasonably large stations. Moreover, such systems proved to be inadequate in severe winters.

Some railways tested containers filled with sodium acetate since this has the property of maintaining a temperature of approximately 55°C for several hours, at which point it starts to crystallise. In Germany, containers filled with hot sand had been tested but were not successful.

The Belgian State Railway experimented with foot-warmers, which had a double casing. A red-hot steel bar was placed between the two walls and its heat passed into a padding of mineral wool inside the double casing, mineral wool being a poor conductor of heat. However, with use, the material disintegrated and was no longer efficient. Passengers sometimes burned their feet

Putting foot-warmers beneath the feet of passengers.

on the device and it lost its heat too quickly.

In Germany, foot-warmers were placed under seats or beneath passengers' feet. They contained a specially manufactured chemical in the shape of a slow-burning coal brick. However, it proved difficult to prevent the fumes which were given off from entering the compartment. The French Northern Railway, therefore, devised a system which involved the use of both water-filled and coal brick-filled foot-warmers. Heated by the coal-brick containers, the water-filled foot-warmers were placed in the compartments. In this way, passengers were no longer bothered by fumes from the coalbricks since these were placed at some distance from the compartments.

In countries which experienced periods of intense cold, such as Germany, Sweden, Switzerland and the United States, stoves were preferred for a long time. With this system, a firebox was placed beneath each coach. The air circulating inside the firebox was heated and then distributed through the stoves in each compartment.

In France, during the bitterly cold winter of 1891, some trains without any heating system at all still operated and this provoked violent protests from the public to such an extent that carriage-heating became a matter of urgent concern. The Eastern Company was the first to develop the thermo-siphon. Beneath each coach, a double firebox filled with coal heated a water-filled container. This water passed along a pipe and then entered the radiator placed in each compartment. This system was used on certain types of coach on the Eastern, Western and P.L.M Railways, but variations did occur from

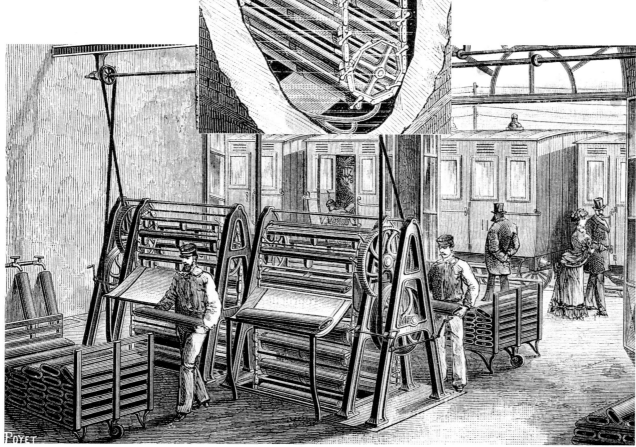

Above: The foot-warmer noria.
Below: Eastern Railway machine for heating feet-warmers.

(*Nature*, 3 January 1885)

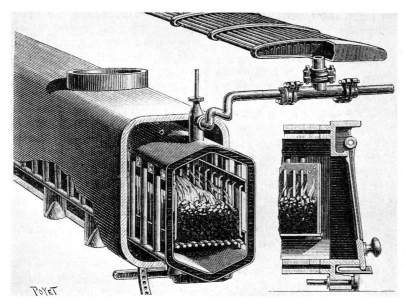

Heater in position beneath the underframe.
(*Nature*, 14 February 1891)

Heater used in a coach.
(*Nature*, 14 February 1891)

company to company. The fuel used in the system was either anthracite or peat coal.

The thermo-siphon system was also used in Belgium, but not as an independent system serving only one coach. As the heated water left the tender, it was driven by a steam-injector along heating pipes which ran the full length of the train. After being distributed to the various radiators, the water returned to the locomotive and was reheated. Under this system, the coaches' water pipes were linked by flexible connections.

From 1900, the heating system in general use was steam heating. Steam was taken from the locomotive and then passed through a valve which reduced its pressure. It was then directed along a central pipe which ran from one end of the train to the other. The steam was distributed to each compartment by a special system of piping. The coaches were linked by a flexible pipe fitted with an automatic safety-valve which remained open when the system was not working so that any condensed water could be released. The valve closed automatically when the pressure rose above 7 lbs per square inch. The problem was that the further away the compartment was from the locomotive, the less efficiently the system

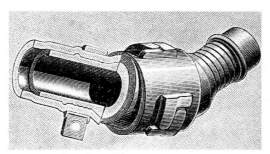

Coupling of the main pipe in the continuous steam- and air-heating system.
(*Nature*, 1 June 1895)

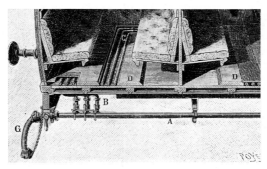

Pipe layout in the continuous heating system.
(*Nature*, 1 June 1895)

worked. And so, on the Prussian State Railway, a heating-van was positioned in the middle of the train to heat coaches at the rear. When operating such a system, the locomotive consumed 4½ lbs of coal per coach per hour.

Certain variations were to be found on French railways. Sometimes the radiators were steam radiators, sometimes they were a mixture of steam and compressed air. Sometimes in each compartment a non-freezing liquid was heated by steam from the locomotive. Sometimes in each compartment water was heated and then distributed under the pressure of steam from the locomotive.

About 1910, on the Valteline line in Italy and the St Moritz line in Switzerland, a system using an electric current was tested. A series of resistors slowed the current down and this generated heat.

Generally speaking, the problem of heating passenger compartments was one of the most difficult to solve. The public failed to understand the technical complications involved and thought it was being ignored. As for cartoonists, they found in this subject a rich vein of material which they exploited, of course, at the expense of the railway companies.

Steam-heated thermosiphon.
(*Nature*, 28 January 1899)

A dangerous position when coupling waggons.
(Photo: Northern Railway)

The correct position when coupling waggons.
(Photo: Northern Railway)

Coupling waggons.
The coupling-screw and hook are joined together.
(Photo: Dutch Railways)

BUFFING GEARS AND COUPLING SYSTEMS

A train is like an enormous accordion. When it sets off it becomes longer and when it slows down it becomes shorter. Devices must therefore be fitted to enable the train to cope with these moments of traction and impact.

Generally, along the axis of the underframe and running parallel to the rails, there is a draw-bar. This is attached to the top of a laminated spring in the middle of the underframe. The other end of the draw-bar is fitted with a draw-pin and a coupling-screw.

The two buffers, which are on each side of the draw-pin and the coupling-screw, are extended longitudinally by impact bars. These run parallel to the draw-bar and connect to each end of the laminated spring. The same spring is used for both traction and impact. Each half of the waggon has its own spring, the two springs being separated by a transverse bar which they bear against on impact. This is discontinuous coupling.

Continuous coupling is used principally on goods trains. Here the buffing gears and coupling systems at each end of the waggon do not work independently. The draw-bar runs the whole length of the waggon and is fitted at each end with hooks which couple onto the other waggons. This coupling-bar runs through a volute spring compressed by two metal plates. The ends of these plates take the impact of the buffers.

Passenger-coaches are coupled by tightening the coupling-screw, using its lever, until the buffers are sufficiently compressed to absorb shocks and any rocking movement. Goods waggons however are coupled 'loosely' to reduce traction effort when the locomotive sets off, since it would be unable to pull from rest a train of heavy waggons coupled tightly together.

In America, since 1893, the system of automatic coupling has been used universally. This involves a single central buffer linked to the underframe by a single spiral spring which is used therefore for both impact and traction.

When the two coaches to be coupled are pushed together the two buffer-knuckles lock and are held in position by a guard. They can be uncoupled by simply withdrawing the pin which keeps the guard in a closed position.

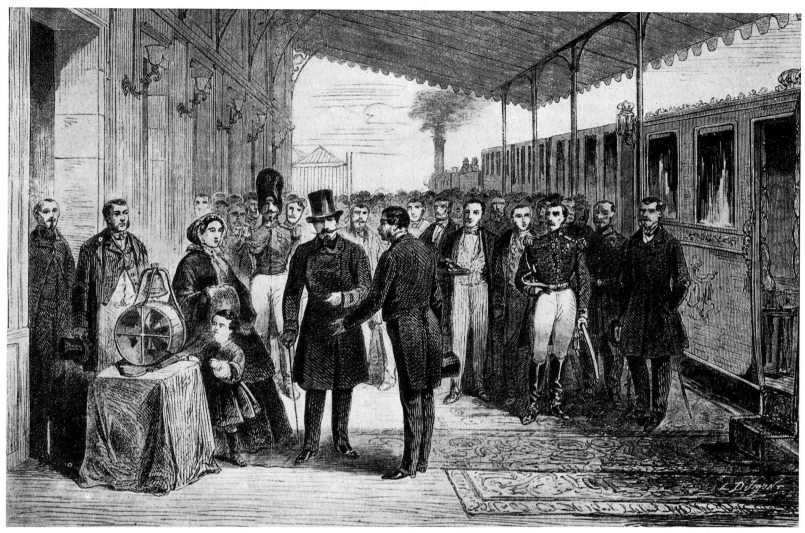

Before the train leaves Compiègne, Emperor Napoleon III inspects the Bazin alarm signal.

PASSENGER ALARM SIGNALS

The murder of passengers on moving trains has often raised the question of providing alarm-signals in each compartment so that passengers can contact the guard. On 6 December 1860, President Poinsot was murdered in a first-class carriage on the Eastern Railway, and a few weeks later Dr Heppe was robbed and killed. As a result, various alarm-systems were invented. Therefore, when Emperor Napoleon III with the Empress and their young son left Compiègne, he was able to inspect a Bazin alarm-system which would enable him to contact the policeman on the train by means of a bell. The passenger in distress pulls a cord inside the compartment. This releases a rod fitted with six blades from a horizontal drum placed on the roof of the coach. The movement of air turns the blades which operates a lever fitted with a hammer which strikes against a bell.

The system, however, was not successful and in 1863 and 1879 commissions were set up by the French Minister of Public Works to study the problem.

Since 1866, French companies have used the Prud'Homme Electronic Inter-Communication system. Each wall separating compartments from one another is fitted with a small triangular window which allows passengers to see into the next compartment. It was thought that this system would frighten off any thief or murderer. The problem was, however, that if it did not how could help be given to the victim. In 1886, the Northern Railway fitted into the compartment

The Northern Railway's alarm signal inside the triangular window which must first be broken.

(*Nature*, 28 February 1886)

dividing-walls a double-glass triangular window. Between the two glass windows was a ring fastened to a chain. When the glass was broken the passenger would pull the ring and this worked a rod which protruded on each side of the coach. On each end of the rod was a white V signal which moved from a vertical to a horizontal position when the system was operated. At the same time, the rod completed an electric circuit and a bell rang in the guard's van. The position of the white signal allowed the policeman to locate immediately the compartment where the alarm had been set off.

It was the Western Railway which invented the system that all railways eventually adopted. This consisted of using the compressed air from the Westinghouse system brake-pipe which runs beneath every coach. When the passenger pulls a ring inside the compartment, compressed air is released. This operates a whistle on the roof of the coach and another whistle on the locomotive. At the same time, the train slows down automatically since the reduced pressure in the brake-pipe causes the brakes to operate.

In spite of all the systems tested, the main problem remained, namely, that the lack of a central corridor prevented the policeman reaching the scene of the crime. This problem was solved when through compartments were built.

Manufacturing wheels in the Arbel, Desflassieux Brothers & Peillion workshops in the Loire.
Large clamps mounted on a truck carry the incandescent wheel from the furnace to the power hammer mould.

RAILWAY WHEELS

The railway wheel consists of a main body locked onto the axle, and a flanged tyre running round the outside rim. Early wheels were made of cast iron but in frosty conditions they proved to be brittle. Rolled iron was then used and finally steel.

In the Arbel process shown here, the hub, the spokes and the rim of a wheel were manufactured separately and then secured to each other by wire. This was then placed in a furnace and when it

Petin and Gaudet stand at the 1867 Exhibition, showing axles and wheels.

became incandescent it was placed in the press and a power-hammer welded the different parts together. It was heated a second time and then hammered once again. Finally, the wheel was taken from the press and the rough edges were removed. In fact, a locomotive-wheel, weighing between half a ton and one ton and with a diameter of about 5½ feet is struck much as one strikes a coin. In 1862, the Arbel factory turned out 12,000 waggon-wheels and 1,500 tender- and locomotive-wheels. Tender-wheels weighed between 400 and 500 lbs each, waggon-wheels between 200 and 250 lbs each.

About 1900, it was realised that spoked wheels on express trains produced a powerful air movement which created clouds of dust. This dust eventually got into the spindle boxes and caused overheating. Thereafter, solid wheels were used, particularly on passenger-coaches.

In Britain and Germany, companies often used wheels whose centre was made up of teak sections. These were compressed between the hub and the tyre and reinforced by iron rings. The Pullman Company even used wheels whose centre was made of paper compressed by a pressure of between 500 and 600 tons. The aim in using wheels made of wood and compressed paper was to provide a smoother ride and to reduce noise levels. It was also claimed that such wheels slowed down tyre wear. On the other hand, it was found that Westinghouse brakes operated less efficiently on them.

The rim of a railway wheel is fitted with a tyre which comes into contact with the rail and which keeps the wheel on the track by means of its flanged edge. Initially, tyres were made of iron, but this was soon replaced by steel which was more durable. To ensure that the tyre does not leave the rim, its internal diameter is slightly smaller than the rim's external diameter. The tyre is expanded under heat and fitted onto the rim. It then cools and the difference in the two diameters causes the tyre to sit tightly around the rim. The wheels are than fitted onto the axle hubs by hydraulic press at a pressure of between 30 and 40 tons.

RAIL CARS

This was the term used about 1897 to describe vehicles which, thanks to the Serpollet steam-boiler, had both a driving and carrying capacity. The Serpollet was a water-tube boiler with instant steam generation and was relatively light in relation to its power. It had been intended for use on a tricycle, but in 1891 the inventor used it in a four-seater coach. In 1894, it was tested on steam-trams and, in 1897, on the P.L.M. Railway, where it pulled light trains and luggage vans.

At about the same time, the Northern Company used a separate mail railcar between Creil and Beauvais to pull two mail vans and sometimes two guard's vans and a waggon laden with seafood.

In 1900, the International Railways Congress, meeting in Paris, expressed the following view: 'On railway lines the use of railcars has up till now been fairly limited but it appears that we ought to continue to develop them in order to ascertain what use they may be put to, not only on lines where there is little traffic but even on busier lines'.

In 1903, the Paris–Orleans Railway gave a trial run between La Fleche and Salle to a Purrey car which was similar to one running on the London & South Western Railway in Britain. In 1904, on its short-distance and less busy lines, the State Railway put into service a steam railcar 'which would replace an expensive train with its locomotive, its tender, its leading and trailing guard's vans and would allow the company to make a

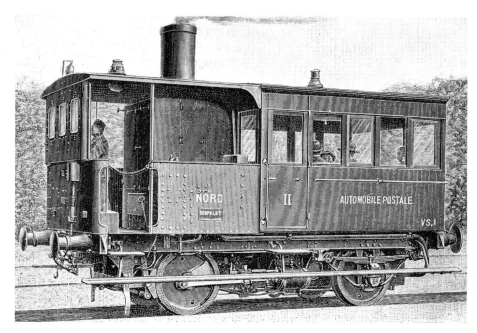

Northern Railway's rail-car with a Serpollet boiler.
(*Nature*, 7 August 1897)

A gasoline-driven American railcar.

State Railway's steam-railcar.

considerable saving. The benefit to passengers will be considerable since it is hoped that a much more frequent service can operate.' Two similar cars ran between Ales and L'Ardoise.

Railways in Britain were probably the first to try to replace steam by oil-engines. These did not, however, have the flexibility of steam, and solutions still had to be found to the problems of starting the engine and of transmitting power to the driving-wheels. In 1907, a petro-electric railcar was invented and, in 1911, the Americans tested a gasoline railcar between Kansas and Colorado, nicknamed the 'Torpedo' because of its shape.

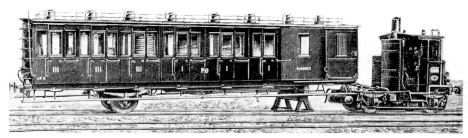
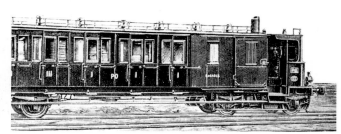

A Paris–Orleans railcar with a Purrey boiler in operation, and dismantled.
(*Nature*, 25 August 1906)

RAILWAY TRACK

The cuttings, embankments, bridges and tunnels are what might be described as the infrastructure of a line, the super-structure being the two parallel rails themselves, made of iron or steel and resting on wooden or metal sleepers. These sleepers stand in a layer of gravel which is termed 'ballast'. The rails are joined end to end by fish-plates which are fixed in position by pins. The rails are also fastened to the sleepers by special screw spikes. Sometimes, as in the case of footrails, the rails are attached directly, and sometimes indirectly, as with single-headed rails. In the latter case, chairs are needed. The rail slots into these and is held in position by wooden wedges driven in under power.

Whether the rail is a Vignole rail (from the name of the English engineer who brought it to Europe from America about 1836), or whether it is a bull-headed rail, it is based on the shape of a double T. The footrail rests directly on the sleeper. It is, therefore, more economical, since it dispenses with the chairs needed for the bull-headed rail. However, the chair-type rail can be replaced more quickly, since it has no screw spike which must be unfastened. Initially, bull-headed rails were symmetrical in cross-section. They could then be turned over when the upper surface had worn. However, this practice disappeared when longer lasting steel replaced iron, and the

heavy section bull-headed rail was invented. In any case, the chairs left marks on the rail, and when the rail was turned over its rough surface created problems for the trains which ran along it.

From 1872, as a result of the increasing use of steel, rail consumption decreased considerably in spite of the continuing development of the railways. The steel rail proved to be eight to nine times more durable than iron.

The chair-rail was used widely in Britain, whereas, in France, the Eastern, Northern and P.L.M. companies preferred the Vignole rail, and the Southern, Paris–Orleans and Western Railways tended to use the bull-headed rail.

Initially, rails had been nearly 20 feet in length. Gradually, however, they were made longer in an attempt to reduce the number of joints, since these were the principal factor in creating a rough or smooth ride. Rail length increased from 26 to 33 to 40 to 49 to 59 feet and even 78 feet on the main P.L.M. lines in about 1900. Their weight also increased from 20–27 lbs per foot up to 33 lbs per foot. The Belgian State Railway even used a rail called the 'Goliath' weighing 35 lbs per foot, which was a record at the time. The increase in rail weight was a necessary consequence of the continued increase in weight and speed of trains.

Whatever the type of rail employed, an 'overhanging' joint was generally used; the rails were joined together between two sleepers using two fish-plates, one on each side of the rail. To increase the strength of these plates, they were manufactured in the shape of a corner-iron, and the lower section was positioned beneath the rail in such a way as to fit round the lower edge. A rail of this type was used on the P.L.M. Railway. Generally, sleepers are made of oak, ash or pine,

Foot-rail and Vignole-rail.
(*Les chemins de fer*: Max de Nansouty)

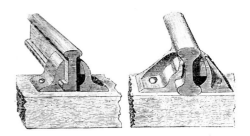

Single-headed and double-headed rails.
(*Les chemins de fer*: Max de Nansouty)

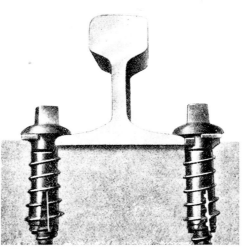

Expandable screw used on Vignole track where sleepers have been damaged by screw spikes, thus allowing the sleeper to continue to be used.
(*Nature*, 5 October 1912)

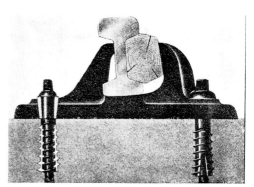

Expandable screw used on chair track, when sleepers have suffered damage from screw spike. In this way the sleepers can continue to be used.
(*Nature*, 5 October 1912)

Rail consumption in France from 1869 to 1887.
(Ministry of Public Works Statistical Records 1888)

STEEL

IRON

An unnecessary and dangerous bend in the track at Illiers station between Chartres and Thouars.

oak being preferred in France. For longer use, they are impregnated with creosote or zince chloride. From 1881, metal sleepers started to be used but they were not generally popular since, unlike wooden ones, they never settled to become an integral part of the track.

Ballast is used to protect the track and to act as a kind of mattress, reducing shock and distributing pressure. It must also allow rainwater to filter through quickly in order that the track remains dry. Crushed stones may be used or sand containing flint, crushed brick, clinker, even cinders. Ballast must be free from chalky matter or clay which create dust in summer and mud in winter.

About 1900, tracks were strengthened by laying sleepers closer together in such a way that the fish-plating rested on three successive sleepers. However, compared to the 'overhanging' system this gave a more rigid track.

In America, track formation is much wider than in Europe, even though rails are the same distance apart, namely the standard gauge of 4 feet 8½ inches. As a result, American passengers enjoyed a far smoother ride.

On curves, it is essential to raise the outer rail in such a way as to cancel the effect of centrifugal force which would tend to cause trains to be derailed when negotiating curves. It is also vital to avoid unnecessary curves in the track.

On very steep curves, rails are laid slightly further apart to reduce flange friction on the rails. Such friction causes a screeching noise which passengers find unpleasant.

A level-crossing guard of the past.

159

Clearing snow from the track at Montargis.

Protection from snow in the Sierra Nevada,
on the Central Pacific Railroad about 1880.
(Bibliothèque des arts décoratifs)

Track protected in Switzerland from avalanche by small dry stone walls and the planting of larch trees (1914).
At the bottom of the picture, the line is protected on the bend by a wooden gallery.
(Bernina Railways Collection)

THE FIGHT AGAINST SNOW

TRACK INSPECTION AND PROTECTION FROM SNOW

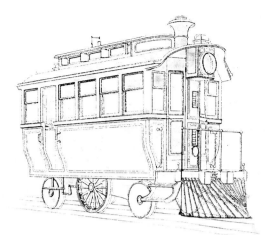

An inspection locomotive car on the Philadelphia–Reading Railroad.
(1867 Exhibition Records)

A railway track must constantly be inspected. Each area is supervised by a plate-layer who walks along the track looking out for the slightest fault, for any screw spike or bolt which has worked loose, for any wedge which needs to be driven back into the chair, etc. If he sees a rail which is split or broken he has everything he needs: flags, explosives, horn to slow down or stop any train which may arrive. This constant checking enables the track to be maintained efficiently. The work is done by teams under the supervision of a foreman, the main tasks being cleaning, packing, track adjustment, renewing ballast, replacing rails, sleepers and accessories.

Generally the work is carried out in this way. The team works its way along the section effecting all necessary repairs. When it arrives at the end of the section, it goes back to the beginning and starts again. A different system involves sending a team to those parts of the track where emergency work is known to be required.

Track maintenance staff may have to travel quickly to a point in their area, making use of lightweight inspection cars. The United States was the first country to use these fast lightweight cars because in America, especially in the early years of the railways, enormous distances often had to be covered between stations. The use of

Car used to inspect track on Michigan, Port Huron-Grand Rapids, and Saint-Louis R.R. in Chicago.
(*Nature*, 25 November 1882)

steam-driven inspection cars was also widespread there.

An obstacle which engine-drivers particularly feared was snow. During the terrible winter of 1879–80, for almost a week, large sections of French lines were blocked by snow and manual labour had to be used, since snowploughs did not exist.

Snow is even more threatening on high-altitude mountain lines where avalanches can cause whole sections of track to disappear. Where the Central Pacific Railroad crosses the Sierra Nevada, tracks have had to be covered with tunnels several miles long, made up of sections of wood which fit tightly together. Such tunnels also offer protection from falling rocks.

In Switzerland, to protect tracks which lie at the bottom of steep rocky slopes, small dry walls were built which offer a barrier against falling rocks and snow. Where slopes consist of pasture land, rows of larch trees are planted in such a way that the track is protected almost totally from any avalance which might occur.

Where the snow is only a few inches deep it is easily removed by attaching a metal faceplate to the front end of the locomotive, creating in this way a kind of snowplough. This system has the disadvantage of simply moving the snow from one track to the other. When the snow is 3 or 4 feet deep, turbines have to be used. A vertical wheel with paddles set at an angle and fitted to the front of a special waggon is pushed by a locomotive. The wheel is driven by a powerful engine, and a strong fan enables the snow to be deposited some considerable distance from the track.

Track inspection steam-car used on the Missouri, Kansas and Texas R.R.
(*Nature*, 12 January 1896)

A Swedish manually-operated track car.
(Swedish Private Railway archive)

A passenger train in a snow storm in Norway.
(Norwegian State Railway archive)

A rotating snow plough in the Bernese Alps.
(Swiss Railway archive)

TRAINS IN THE SNOW

POINTS' AND SIGNAL BOXES

To begin with, changing points and signals was always done 'on the spot'. Before changing points, the pointsman would run and set the signal so that it did not conflict with the direction the train was to take. This led to the idea of linking points and signals so that the two could never contradict one another. In 1856, M. Vignier, a pointsman working on the Western Railway, devised a system in which the points and signal-levers were positioned close together. A block of wood was placed between the levers so that one could not be changed if the other had already been moved to the correct position. The system was designed to improve safety by removing the possibility of human error. This system of 'reciprocal locking' is termed 'interlocking'. At the same time, signals and points controls were concentrated in the same box. By 1878, therefore, points and signals were remote controlled. However, with the rapid increase in traffic flow, the Vignier signal-box soon proved to be inadequate. Moreover, the pointsman could see only the levers, and was unable to go and check on the track the position of the points and the signals. He needed equipment which would show him clearly that the signals had operated correctly, and which would set the signal at 'Stop' if a problem occurred.

In 1880, the Saxby and Farmer signal-box was fitted with a much greater number of levers. Interlocking involved a grill which pivoted round a horizontal axis and moved against scotch blocks. Thus it was possible to interlock simply by pushing the spring handle at the end of the lever, but it was not possible to reverse the process until the lever had completed its full stroke. Control of the operation was carried out mechanically by inserting movable bolts into the corresponding holes on the points frame and locking them in place. If contact was not made, the pointsman could not move the lever which controlled the bolts. About 1882, Lartigue invented an electric control which caused a bell to ring when the points remained open.

The increase in traffic led to a corresponding increase in the number of points and signal levers, and in large stations signal-boxes often required several signalmen to operate the 150 or 200 levers grouped together. Moreover, operating a single lever required a physical effort of some 100 lbs and one train alone could require between 10 and 20 lever changes. It is, therefore, easy to see how demanding and exhausting a job it was. As a result, in 1898 M. Moutier, the chief engineer on the Northern Railway, created a new system. One lever would replace all those which interlocked when a train took a particular route. This led to the idea of a 'route lever'. One single lever in one single movement would operate all the points and signals along the route the train would take, and at the same time prevent any possibility of anybody allowing another train to pass along the same route.

This concentration of remote control was made possible by the use of fluid substances such as compressed water and air (Aster's hydro-pneumatic system) and electricity (Thomson-Houston's electro-dynamic system). Fluid has the further advantage of giving 'total control', in that it is the switch blade itself which, once it is in position, controls the fluid which will change the corresponding signal.

Electrodynamic signal-box at Villeneuve-Saint-George (1913).

The electricity is sometimes used simply to transmit the signalman's decision, since it does no more than activate the water

or compressed-air control valves of the points motors.

(P.L.M. Railway)

Western Railway pointsman operating a Vignier-lever in the open air.

Western Railway pointsman operating a Saxby lever inside a points-box.

Old signal box on Western Railway. This operated points and signals.

CENTRALISATION OF POINTS AND SIGNALS LEVERS

Interior of an old Vignier signal-box at Moret.
(P.L.M. Railway)

Interior of the Saxby signal-box which replaced the one above.
(P.L.M. Railway)

INTERIORS OF CENTRALISED SIGNAL BOXES

THE MOVEMENT OF TRAINS WITHIN A STATION

Inside a station, safety is not just a matter of protecting trains which have stopped there from trains which are passing through. Trains need protection also from those trains which are being shunted from one place to another and engines which are shunting other stock need protection from one another.

In some large stations, trains which had stopped were sometimes protected from trains which might arrive by an arrangement which consisted of blocking off all the main lines in a particular section.

Since small and medium-size stations are normally situated at the end of a block section, they are protected by the semaphore signal at the entrance to the section. However, a train stopped in a station must not be allowed to hold up the movement of other trains for a long period of time. It is generally agreed that a train within a station's limits is adequately protected by the station's special signals, for example, the red disc or the red and white checkboard. It is therefore possible to unblock the station section and allow trains to advance as far as the special signals, where they must wait until the station is clear.

To protect trains which are stopped in a station from moving trains and moving trains from one another, the system of interlocking signals with their corresponding points is used. In principle, interlocking is always reciprocal. If a lever interlocks, that is, prevents another lever from being moved, the second lever interlocks with the first; that is, it prevents it from returning to its normal position. Such a system allows trains to move safely about within the station area.

But in smaller stations, where there is far less traffic movement, this system of interlocking with its large number of levers concentrated within a signal-box is not required. Instead, Boure locks are used since they are very cheap to install.

To picture what a Boure lock is like, one has simply to imagine a lock sawn in two along its length. One of the halves is then secured to the ground by a chain and the other half is attached to the lever of the signal or the point which is to interlock with it. When the lever is immobilised the two parts of the lock are fastened together. To move the lever, the key is required. This separates the two halves of the lock and releases the lever.

A Boure lock used on the
State Western Railway in 1911.

The key, however, cannot be removed from one of the two halves except by joining the two halves together, in other words by once again immobilising the lever. Moreover, the key is kept in the station-master's office in a central locking system. The system is built in such a way that the key can be released only if all the other keys of those points and signals whose movements are incompatible with the movement one wishes to make are in position.

Often a lock is made to fit a particular point and its key is attached to the signal lever. The key can be removed only if the signal indicates that the track is not clear and the points' key can be removed only if the points have returned to their normal position.

The disadvantage of this system is that it requires the signalman to be constantly on the move; therefore, when the points are some distance from the disc levers, a system of electrically-operated remote-controlled locks is used for the reciprocal interlocking of points and signals. It operates in this way: signal box (A), controlling, for example, a set of points, is linked electrically to signal box (B) controlling the corresponding disc. (B)'s lever is fitted with a Boure lock and interlocks electrically and reciprocally with (A)'s lever. The key for the points controlled by (A) can be removed only with the permission of (B). However, signal-box (B) cannot move the lever, that is, give the permission requested, until it has opened the locks on the levers. To do this it must remove the keys from a safety device which has been immobilised. The two signal-boxes can only communicate by a system of bells.

Movement of trains within a station is not limited to trains passing from one track to another by means of points. This type of movement can in fact be avoided completely in the case of single waggons by using a travelling platform to transport the vehicle. This system had been adopted in large stations by 1900, as soon as electric energy was available, since the electric motor, being small, light and easily manoeuvrable, is particularly suited to such work. The platform's rails cut across several tracks and this means that the corresponding signals have to be closed while the manoeuvre takes place. The platform is also fitted with an electric capstan which can be used to haul waggons when it is not required to transport them from one track to another.

Waggons have in fact been pulled by capstans in Britain since about 1870. In France, the same task was carried out by horses, and many people can still remember seeing in certain stations a huge cart-horse led by a teamster dragging heavy chains which would be used to harness it to the waggon it was to pull. But in 1880, at La Chapelle station, the Northern Company abandoned this system and decided to use a hydraulic capstan until such time as electricity was available, some nine years later.

An electric shunting truck in the Gare Montparnasse.
(*Nature*, 9 September 1905)

Using a hydraulic capstan to haul waggons at La Chapelle station.
(*Nature*, 20 December 1884)

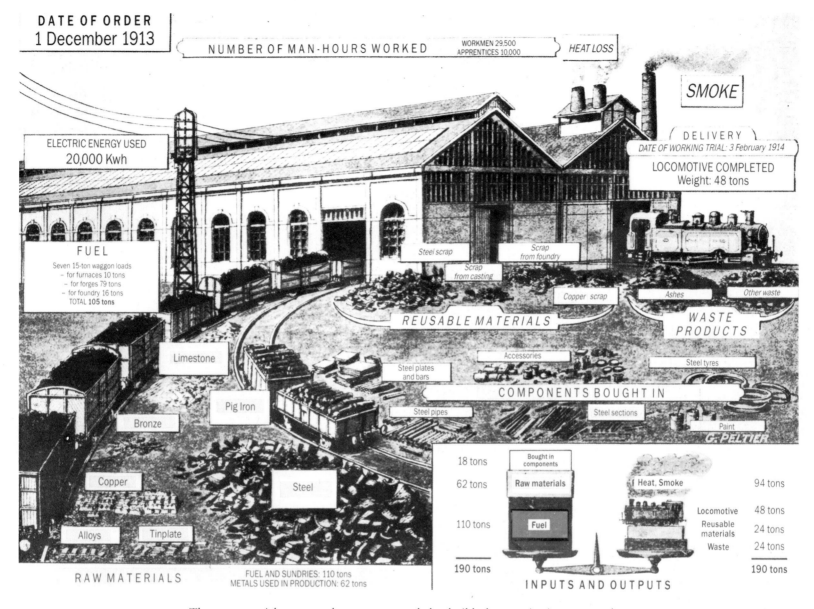

DATE OF ORDER
1 December 1913

NUMBER OF MAN-HOURS WORKED — WORKMEN 29,500 APPRENTICES 10,000 — HEAT LOSS

SMOKE

ELECTRIC ENERGY USED
20,000 Kwh

DELIVERY
DATE OF WORKING TRIAL: 3 February 1914
LOCOMOTIVE COMPLETED
Weight: 48 tons

FUEL
Seven 15-ton waggon loads
– for furnaces 10 tons
– for forges 79 tons
– for foundry 16 tons
TOTAL **105 tons**

Steel scrap   Scrap from foundry
Scrap from casting

REUSABLE MATERIALS

Copper scrap   Ashes   Other waste

WASTE PRODUCTS

Limestone

Accessories   Steel tyres

Steel plates and bars

Pig Iron

COMPONENTS BOUGHT IN

Bronze   Steel pipes   Steel sections   Paint

G. PELTIER

Copper   Steel

18 tons
62 tons
Bought in components
Raw materials
Heat, Smoke   94 tons
Locomotive   48 tons
110 tons
Fuel
Reusable materials   24 tons
Waste   24 tons

190 tons

Alloys   Tinplate

RAW MATERIALS   FUEL AND SUNDRIES: 110 tons   190 tons
METALS USED IN PRODUCTION: 62 tons   INPUTS AND OUTPUTS

The raw materials, parts and manpower needed to build a locomotive in two months.

LOCOMOTIVE CONSTRUCTION

A steam locomotive contains a huge number of different parts, and many workers are involved in the building of it. The illustration above details the materials required. On the left: coal, swarf, iron, etc are piled up ready to be taken into the factory where they will be handled by hundreds of workers who will transform these raw materials into engine parts which will then be assembled. A locomotive with a non-operating weight of 48 tons requires fuel and a variety of metals whose total weight will be 190 tons, that is, almost four times its finished weight.

At a lecture given on 26 January 1906, M. Le Chatelier, the President of the Cail company, revealed that when a locomotive was built there were 564 sheets of plans, 13,786 parts excluding all the rivets required, and that 2,942 of these parts were different.

Building just one locomotive, costing at the

Putting wheels on a Pacific locomotive in the Western Company's workshops at Sotteville (1907)
(Sauvage Collection)

time 100,000 francs, was a task of enormous magnitude, since it involved the drawing up of almost 500 plans, writing to the hundreds of suppliers, making sure that they delivered on time and manufacturing all the tools and equipment necessary. This meant that if a locomotive was to be a commercially viable proposition an order for at least 15 to 20 needed to be taken.

This number of locomotives would have a total finished weight of approximately 1,000 tons.

To build locomotives on this scale 5,000 tons of coal, 5,000 tons of iron ore and 150 tons of brass are needed.

The extraction of the coal and ore, the metallurgical process, the manufacturing of the parts, the assembling of these parts, the painting, testing, transporting of raw materials and of the locomotive, all of this meant employing and paying approximately 1,000 workers for approximately one year.

Twenty-five per cent of these workers were mine or metal workers, fifty per cent were in the engineering industry, and the rest worked in transport and a variety of smaller industries.

The main station in Danzig in 1890.
(Bibliothèque des arts décoratifs)

Arrival and departure hall at the Anhalt station in Berlin about 1880.
(Bibliothèque des arts décoratifs)

TWO DIFFERENT TYPES OF OLD GERMAN STATIONS

Top: Swiss Federal railway station in Basle, built about 1904.
(Swiss Federal Railway archive)
Above: Baden station in Basle, built in 1914.
(*Génie Civil*, 15 December 1914)

SOME FAMOUS STATIONS

It is not possible to review here all the great stations built before the war. We shall simply consider the most typical of them.

Basle is an important centre of international rail traffic, since most of the lines which finish there are main lines from France, Germany, Austria (via Constance and Zurich) and Italy (via the Simplon and Lotschberg Tunnels). For this reason it has been called the turntable of Central Europe. It is not surprising, therefore, that the first great Swiss station was built in Basle. About 1904, the Swiss Federal Railway carried out

Rome Central station, built about 1874.
(Bibliothèque des arts décoratifs)

reconstruction work to cope with the increase in traffic.

Basle has another station called the Baden station, and this is where trains from Freiburg and Constance via Lörrach and Waldshut arrive. The two stations are linked by two lines which cross the Rhine, one upstream from the town, the other downstream. The Baden station was rebuilt in 1914, and is remarkable for its huge belltower which dwarfs the roof.

Italian stations are distinguished by the delicacy of their architecture. Since 1905, most Italian lines have been state-owned, and their capacity to handle goods and passenger trains was developed from the same date but never kept pace with the increase in traffic. Thus between 1906 and 1910 track length increased by 37 per cent and shed capacity by 25 per cent whereas traffic increased by 40 per cent. Following the earthquake in December 1908, station costs on the Sicilian and Calabrian lines were particularly high. These were met by government grants given specifically for the repairs to buildings and lines.

After completion of the Rome–Naples line, Naples main station was extended shortly before the First World War. Until then, rail links between the two cities had been unsatisfactory and not suitable for express trains. Trains arrived at Naples Central station after passing through a tunnel built on soil which was excavated from extinct volcanoes. The Rome–Naples line was linked to the Central station by a tunnel which

Antwerp Central station in 1910.
(Belgian State Railways)

Ostend station in 1910.
(Belgian State Railways)

BELGIAN STATIONS BEFORE 1914

The façade of the Anhalt station, Berlin, built in 1879.
(Bibliothèque des arts décoratifs)

was 30 feet below the station. This was extended along both sides to house passenger facilities and luggage offices for passengers from the Rome–Naples line. The station's tracks are all double and the principal routes are separate from one another. One mile from Naples they diverge, some going inland to Rome and Foggia, others to Salerno and the sea.

The width of a station is determined by the number of lines and platforms and the size of the station buildings. Its length depends on the trains

which will use it, but it must at the very least be able to take a 24-waggon train, in other words it must be at least 650–800 feet long. In Germany, where trains are even longer, the minimum length must be nearly 1000 feet.

In Germany, most lines are state-owned, and, in 1880, the State began completely to reorganise its railways, in particular ensuring that stations were as close as possible to the city centre. An important feature of this reconstruction work was the replacing of various small stations, scattered

throughout the city, by a central station. In most cases this was built as a through station.

Architecturally, German stations have two main types of frontage. Sometimes they are neo-Gothic constructions; sometimes they are modern buildings with tall bay windows and a grand and imposing appearance. Examples of the latter type are Frankfurt, Dresden and the Anhalt station in Berlin. These stations all have arched roofs which impress by their size and lightness. The arrival and departure halls, like the one in Cologne

An old German station, Saxony-Bavaria Railway's Leipzig station in 1842.
(Bibliothèque des arts décoratifs)

Euston station about 1910.

Waterloo station about 1900.

TWO LONDON STATIONS

Union station, Washington, one of the largest stations of the time, with 32 covered tracks (1907).
Opposite the station is the monument commemorating the discovery of America by Christopher Columbus. (Photo: Underwood and Underwood)

which is 80 feet high, 210 feet wide and 840 feet long, are spacious and well-ventilated. Another feature typical of these stations is the width of the platforms, which are build with sufficient room to accommodate waiting-rooms, buffets, washrooms, toilets, etc. Junction stations are built with double-length platforms which mean that one track can be used for several trains at the same time.

In Britain, station platforms are invariably higher than the track and overhead passageways take passengers from one platform to another.

Junction stations often have double-length platforms, examples being York and Crewe. In terminus stations, the main building is at the end of the platform facing the tracks, with the various services such as waiting-rooms and ticket-offices located side by side. Luggage-offices and facilities are not thought important, and so the entrance-hall often leads directly to departure platforms in order that passengers can proceed easily from their car to the train. Between the platforms there are generally two tracks, sometimes three, the middle one being used for rolling-stock waiting

to be brought into service.

Initially, American stations were quite basic. Slowly, however, as railways developed, facilities improved throughout the United States. The best facilities are found generally in terminus stations. Until 1910, South Boston station was the largest in the world. It was built on two levels, accommodating 28 tracks at ground level and 4 below ground level, and 19 platforms. It was completed in 1899, and was bigger than Saint Louis Union station which itself was only slightly larger than the Gare Saint-Lazare completed in 1896. In 1900,

Pennsylvania R.R.'s Broad Street station in Philadelphia (1910).
Opened on 5 December 1881, this station was at the time the largest station in the world, with eight tracks beneath two arched roofs. (Pennsylvania R.R. archive)

Chicago & North Western R.R.'s old Chicago station.
This was replaced in 1910 by the station which is still there [1935].
(Photo: Underwood News)

Maastricht station in 1912.
(Dutch Railways)

Waiting-room in Maastricht Station.
(Dutch Railways)

A DUTCH STATION BEFORE THE 1914–18 WAR

a total of 50 million passengers, transported by the New York, New Haven and Hartford, Old Colony, New England, and Boston and Albany Railroad Companies, passed through Boston station. Every day a total of 2,000–3,000 trains used this station. Ground level was reserved for main-line trains, the lower floor for suburban trains. The arrival and departure hall, with 28 lines, is more than 560 feet wide and 600 feet long.

Granite and dark brick were used to give Boston station an attractive appearance. Because the site had been reclaimed from the sea, the foundations of the station front (nearly 2000 feet wide) required a vast amount of work. Thirty-thousand pillars had to be sunk into the ground to provide a solid base and the underground section had to be enclosed in a kind of waterproof cofferdam. The floor was built on an impermeable base with its own drainage system.

In 1910, New York's Pennsylvania station

Huelva station on the Seville Railway (Spain) in 1880.
(Bibliothèque des arts décoratifs)

East station in Budapest (Royal Hungarian State Railway).
(Hungarian State Railway Collection)

Varna station, Bulgaria.
(Bulgarian Railway archive)

became the largest in the world when the Pennsylvania Railroad and the Long Island Railroad were linked together in the heart of New York. In the past, passengers had had to take the ferry-boat across the Hudson and East Rivers to reach the two stations. Then tunnels were built beneath the two rivers and the result was this magnificent station in the heart of New York, built in such a style that passengers immediately feel themselves to be not only at a main-line terminus, but also a gateway to a great city. The impressive Doric station front is over 400 feet wide and leads to an entrance hall which is almost as high as the knave in Cologne Cathedral. A wide corridor with stairs and lifts lead to the underground platforms used by 1,000 trains per day. The station is built between the two tunnels which take passengers beneath the rivers.

However, in 1913, New York's Grand Central station became the largest in the world. Like Cologne's Central Station, and Paris's Gare Saint-Lazare, it has approximately 3½ miles of track. On the other hand, the Gare Saint-Lazare has 16 platforms, 14 of which are double, whereas Cologne has only 9. Boston Station has 15 miles of track and 19 platforms. Pennsylvania station has 16 miles of track and 11 platforms and Grand Central has no less than 33 miles of track and 30 platforms. The track is on two levels, 42 at ground level, which are used by main-line trains, and 26 below ground for suburban trains. The vast network of lines is controlled by one central signal-box divided into two areas with 420 and 362 levers respectively. The central section of the huge station front is built in the shape of a half-Doric, half-Renaissance, triumphal arch. The interior shows architectural influences from buildings as diverse as museums, theatres, music hall, banks and commercial stores. Its most striking feature is the Central Hall with its starred ceiling.

This station was built as a result of the extraordinary increase in traffic which followed the replacement of steam traction by electric traction on New York's suburban lines. Even while construction work took place, a full passenger service was maintained.

THE GARE DU NORD

Continuous increases in railway traffic forced large stations to expand from time to time. The Gare du Nord in Paris had already undergone a major change in 1864, but in 1884, in spite of its being seen at the time as a station of some considerable size, it had to expand once again. Its area remained the same, but the number of lines increased to thirteen as a consequence of the development of its suburban services. This made it, after the Gare Saint-Lazare, the most important station in France as far as suburban traffic was concerned.

In 1889, as this traffic increased, more platforms had to be built and a vast amount of reconstruction work was carried out. The waiting-room near the departure-hall (to the left as one faces the front of the station), and various parcel offices on the right of the arrival-hall, were

Front of the Gare du Nord in August 1914.
(Northern Railway archive)

Interior view of the station about 1860.
(Northern Railway archive)

Entrance to the station.
(Northern Railway archive)

Gare du Nord about 1860.
(Northern Railway archive)

demolished to create space for the extra platforms, eighteen in all. These were then divided into four distinct groups: Platforms 1–5 were for trains going in the direction of Chantilly. Platforms 6–9 were for the Pointoise line and branch lines, 10–13 were for the Soissons line, 10–16 for main-line arrivals and 17 and 18 were for the 'tram-trains' which ran every 15 minutes to Saint-Denis and Saint-Ouen-les-Docks.

This work in 1889 introduced a number of improvements inside the station which made the movement of trains much easier. There were electric capstans to haul waggons and better signal-boxes and points-boxes. Moreover, the parcels services which had been next to the arrival-hall were moved next to the station's administrative offices on the Faubourg-Saint-Denis near the Boulevard de la Chapelle. In 1892, a proposal was made to link the station to the underground network which was then being planned.

THE P.L.M. STATION

As with the other stations in Paris, the advent of the 1900 exhibition and the increase in passenger traffic meant that the Gare de Lyon also had to be enlarged. In 1880, 1,630,000 departures had been recorded. In 1896 the figure was 3,259,000 and yet, because it was some distance from the city centre, the Gare de Lyon did not have a great deal of suburban traffic. Up to 1896, no changes had been made there, whereas reconstruction work had already taken place twice at the Gare Saint-Lazare and the Gare du Nord. A two-storey station was envisaged at first, but the handling of vast amounts of luggage at certain times of the

View from the rue de Chalon of the Gare de Lyon in Paris in 1895.

year would have created problems, and so the plan for a single-storey building was accepted. The two sloping access roads for passengers arriving at and leaving the station were retained, but instead of leading into the two yards to the right and left of the station building, they con-

verged in an area in front of the station. Pedestrians had easy access to this area up a wide flight of steps. The rue de Bercy was moved, and this increased the size of the right-hand area of the station. Four more platforms were added taking the number to seven. The main-line ticket offices ran down one side of a large waiting-room on the left of the station near the cour de Chalon. A smaller room which looked out on to the cour Diderot was built for suburban passengers. The luggage-registration office was between these two rooms. Main-line passengers would leave the station through a covered area on the right-hand side and would also collect luggage there. Suburban passengers would leave the station through the cour Diderot.

Top: Gare de Lyon seen from Boulevard Diderot in 1895.
Above: Gare de Lyon seen from Boulevard Diderot in 1901.

On the left: Luggage services at the corner of the rue de Saint-Petersbourg, (now rue de Pétrograd and rue Mosnier (now rue de Berne).

BIRD'S EYE VIEW OF CONSTRUCTION WC

On the right: Ticket offices and administration block in rue de Rome.

THE GARE SAINT-LAZARE IN 1886

179

Manufacturing postal balloons
in the workshops at the Gare d'Austerlitz
during the Franco-Prussian War.

THE STATION FOR THE ORLEANS RAILWAY

In 1862, the Orleans Railway spent 18,000,000 francs on the reconstruction of its terminal in place Valhubert. On 16 September 1870, during the Franco-Prussian War, a reconnaissance mission, carried out on locomotives, discovered that the enemy had cut the line near Juvisy. The capital was therefore isolated. As a result, the goods halls were transformed into mills where locomotives were used as stationary engines to turn the mill-wheels. While still carrying out their railway duties, rail workers formed a National Guard Battalion to defend France. During the siege, Paris communicated with the rest of France by balloons, and the Gare d'Austerlitz was transformed into a huge workshop where these balloons were manufactured.

As time passed, and rail traffic continued to increase, it soon became apparent that the Gare d'Austerlitz was much less used than other stations in Paris. On 21 October 1896, a reporter on

Cross-sectional view of the station for the Orleans Railway on the quai d'Orsay during its construction in 1898. Steam trains can be seen here but electric traction was eventually preferred.
(*Nature*, 1 October 1898)

L'Illustration wrote: 'There is no doubt that if the terminal is built in the centre of Paris, Parisians will rush to build houses in the Orléans suburb even though they have ignored its station because of its distance from the city centre. It is, of course, also true that those people who have to travel to Orleans, Tours, Bordeaux, Toulouse, or Spain are not pleased to have to make first of all a journey taking three quarters of an hour in an open carriage along one of the worse roads in the capital. In fact, the situation has become so bad that the Gare du Nord is now running luxury trains on the Paris–Orleans line. Finally, if the Gare d'Orsay is built it is likely that it will be connected to the Gare des Invalides and the Exhibition.' In the light of such comments it was not difficult to foresee what would happen.

The Treasury building was demolished leaving a large area of land empty. The Orleans Railway immediately contacted the Government with a view to buying the site, together with nearby land, at the time occupied by a military barracks. It was encouraged to do this by the fact that the extension of the Sceaux line had increased its passenger traffic by 40 per cent. Negotiations were completed in December 1897 and in the space of two and a half years two and a half miles of track were laid in the heart of Paris. The two centre lines of the Gare Valhubert's seven lines were chosen to run beneath the nearby square along a downward slope with a gradient of 1 in 90. These lines ran alongside the Seine and were on a level with the river. The slightest rise in the level of the Seine would, therefore, have caused flooding if the engineers had not thought to build a waterproof concrete base; even this, however, proved to be inadequate.

Orleans Railway station in place Valhubert, about 1865.
(Florange Collection)

STONE BRIDGES AND VIADUCTS

The oldest stone railway-bridges and viaducts in France are the Meudon Viaduct on the Versailles–Paris left-bank line; Nogent bridge above the Marne which, including its approach viaducts, is 765 yards long; Morlaix Viaduct, with its two levels of arches in the classical style on the Paris–Brest line; and Chaumont Viaduct, which is 650 yards long and 160 feet high. Amazingly, it was built in less than a year, the men working through the night by means of electric light. The Auteuil Viaduct bridge over the Seine should also be mentioned. This is part of the Paris Circle Line and spans 620 feet across the river with a total length of 1640 yards.

In many ways, stone constructions are better than metal, since, providing quality materials, such as good mortar and stones, are used, they last almost indefinitely. Laying track is also more straightforward on stone rather than iron. If the train is derailed, stone is in itself less dangerous and offers the further advantage of requiring little maintenance. On the other hand, stone foundations have a tendency to settle and this can damage the bridge or the viaduct. Generally, however, in such matters, it is the size of the undertaking which is the main factor. If the bridge or viaduct is small, it can be built on less solid ground since the foundations can be built onto a raft in such a way that the piers are linked together and form an almost solid block. Where the bridge or viaduct is to be a large one, however, the piers must be built onto solid foundations which will withstand anything.

There are three types of river-bed which the bridge builder will encounter. In some cases, the river-bed is made of hard rock and can bear heavy loads without any chance of erosion. Frequently, the river-bed consists of gravel, pebbles, sand, compacted clay or tuff. Again, such ground cannot be compressed further and will carry heavy loads. There is, however, a possibility that it may shift. Basically, if the land is peat or mud, it can be eroded and will not support a heavy load. In such cases, the foundations have to be sunk down until they reach a solid base. Where this method proves impractical, compressible soil can still be built on. This is done by increasing the surface size of the base so that the pressure the soil must withstand is reduced.

Chaumont Viaduct, one of the oldest French viaducts.
From Weismann's original model. (Eastern Railway Collection)

When a viaduct is to be more than 150–160 feet high, it is normal to build it on two levels to avoid any possibility of the piers buckling. On such viaducts, the upper and lower levels are generally built in the proportion of 3 to 2 in order that the overall effect should be pleasing to the eye.

The feature of Chaumont Viaduct is that it is built on three levels. Goltzch Viaduct on the Leipzig–Bavaria line is 260 feet high and built on four levels.

Construction methods for different types of bridge.

Fades Viaduct across the Soule in the Puy-de-Dôme (1901–1909).
(Cail archive)

STRAIGHT GIRDER METAL BRIDGES AND VIADUCTS

In the United States, engineers built bridges which their European counterparts would not have dared to attempt. One of the most remark-

Bridge across the Yssel at Zwolle, built in 1863. (Dutch Railways archive)

able, with respect to its length and mode of construction, is the Pennsylvania Railroad Poughkeepsie Bridge across the Hudson. It is 1700 yards long and has five 520 feet spans. Even its piers are made of metal.

In France, a similar enterprise was the Fades Viaduct built between 1901 and 1909 by Cail. This is one of the highest constructions in the

world, since the railway line is 435 feet above the Sioule Valley, between Saint-Eloi and Volvic in the Puy-de-Dôme. Scaffolding was used to erect the two end spans, but the central span was constructed by a daring process in which the piers were used as intermediary supports for iron roller bars. As each span was assembled, it was pushed out over the bars from the platform around the pier. This operation was conducted simultaneously from each of the two end piers, and the two sections of the central span eventually met in space.

Another way of constructing straight-girder metal roadways is the 'overhanging' system, used to great effect by Eiffel on the railway viaduct between Saigon and Mytho in Indo–China. In this system, bolts secure each section to the previous section. Two sections are then riveted together, and the new 'overhanging' section then has another 'overhanging' section secured to it in the same way. The roadway, advances slowly 'in space' until it reaches a pier. Since it tends to sag under its own weight, jacks are used to raise it up, and it is then secured to the pier. Sometimes this kind of bridge is built from both sides and the two sections meet in the middle without any intermediate support.

Straight-girder bridges are generally made using long parallel lattice-side sections which support the central roadway, either at the top, as in the case of Fades Viaduct, or at the bottom, as in the Dutch bridge illustrated here. Bridges sometimes resemble a square lattice-work cage. This is the style of the Embabeh Bridge built by the French company Dayde across the Nile near Cairo.

Searching for the remains of the train, 29 December 1879.

METAL BRIDGES WHICH COLLAPSED

The Tay straight-girder bridge linking Dundee and Edinburgh was considered in 1879 to be a marvel of engineering. On 28 December that same year, a severe storm occurred and at 7.30 pm as the Edinburgh train crossed it, the bridge collapsed. The whole train sank beneath the water, with all its passengers and crew. This bridge was 1¾ miles long and had 85 spans, 11 of which were each 242 feet long. These were the spans which gave way under the combined weight of the train and the force of the storm. People reacted with disbelief to the horrifying news. A steamboat reached the scene of the tragedy with great difficulty because of the dreadful weather and by the light of the moon it could be seen that more than 1000 yards of the bridge's length had broken away.

It was difficult to ascertain the exact causes of this catastrophe. Sometime before, it had been observed that the bridge shook when trains passed over it. The men painting the supports at the time had even been forced to hold on to their tins of paint. A Commission of Enquiry found that one of the causes must have been the combination of the extraordinary power of the side wind and the bridge's tendency to oscillate. In 1888, the bridge was rebuilt.

American railway bridges frequently collapsed, having in many cases been built with far too much haste. Between 1877 and 1887, 251 such incidents occurred in the United States, caused by structural defects, overloading, collisions, etc. Construction methods were therefore changed completely and 'articulated' bridges were replaced by 'riveted' bridges.

In 1891, the collapse occurred of the Moenchenstein Bridge near Basle. A train carrying 600 passengers caused the bridge to break, and large sections of the train were literally crushed as they fell into the waters of the Boise. Of the passengers, 110 were killed and 150 injured. The bridge had been built in 1872 for local trains with a maximum speed of 18 m.p.h., but it had begun to be used by the Calais and Paris expresses which had started to travel via Belfort rather than Mulhouse. These trains, travelling at over 40 m.p.h., must have been the cause of the disaster.

The Moenchenstein disaster near Basle involved more than 100 victims.

Lift-arch bridge over the Blue Nile at Khartoum (1909).
(Photo: Cleveland Bridge and Engineering Co. Ltd.)

Raised bridge over the Koningshaven in Rotterdam.
A bascule bridge can be seen in the background. (Dutch Railways archive)

PARABOLIC SPAN BRIDGES

As bridge spans became longer, engineers found that a straight span did not have sufficient strength to carry the bridge. Therefore, the top plate of the parallel side beams was built in a parabolic shape since, to use an engineering term, such a shape gives a solid of uniform strength. Whereas on a straight-span bridge, the centre girder is normally the weakest, on a parabolic span it becomes the longest and as a consequence has the greatest strength.

Sometimes rail bridges across rivers have to include a movable span so that ships may pass underneath. The three types of movable span are lift, raised and swing. As on a canal lock the operation may be carried out manually, hydraulically or electrically.

Caronte swing-bridge between Lake Berre and the Gulf of Fos over the Marseilles-Rhône Canal. Completed in 1916.
(Schneider Company archive)

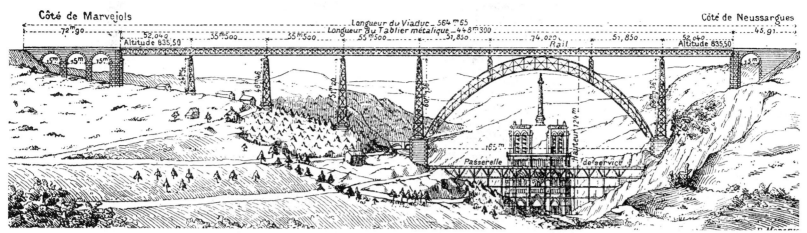

The Garabit Viaduct in Cantal over the Marvejols–Neussargues line.
(*Nature*, 24 February 1883)

ARCHED METAL BRIDGES AND VIADUCTS

When a bridge has to be built across a wide, deep valley or river estuary along which ships pass, the arch method of construction is used. The first practical application of this was by Eiffel when he built the great Douro Bridge in Oporto and, later, it was adapted for the construction of the famous Garabit Viaduct.

The height of the arch gradually increases and when completed it has the shape of a crescent. On the Garabit Viaduct across the Truyère Valley, the arch is 400 feet high.

The Viaur Viaduct, with its three hinge-joints, has a central arch spanning a distance of 720 feet and reaching a height of 377 feet. It consists of two symmetrical sections which butt together at a hinge-joint and which stand on two stone piers to which they are secured by two further hinge-joints.

Testing the Garabit Viaduct with a 405-ton train, in April 1888.
(*Nature*, 17 November 1888)

Viaur Viaduct over the Carmaux–Rodez line. (Batignolles company photograph)

Road and railway bridge over the River Po, at Mezzano Corti.

The road and railway are one above the other, with the railway underneath. The entrance to the road bridge is at right angles to the main bridge.

The viaduct at Fribourg, in Switzerland.

(Engraving by Rasfi Schulbhetz, *Illustrirte Zeiltung*, 1862. Federal Swiss Railways)

TWO EARLY RAILWAY BRIDGES

CANTILEVER BRIDGES

The bridge across the mouth of the River Forth, slightly to the north of Edinburgh, created particular problems for engineers in 1883. The distance was over 1500 yards with a small island in the middle. However, on both sides of the island the river was nearly 200 feet deep which made it impossible to sink a pier support on to the river bed. The only solution was a single 1700 feet span across each of the two halves of the river. This led to the invention of the cantilever bridge.

Three tall 360 feet towers act as piers, and support corbelled metal sections which balance each other perfectly and project out across each side of the river. Since they do not quite meet, a small centre span is added and links each of the cantilever sections. The total weight of the metal part of each span is more than 15,000 tons and the maximum load it can carry is not greater than 5 per cent of its weight, which would allow two goods trains with a total weight of 800 tons to cross it simultaneously. The engineers, benefiting from the experience of the Tay Bridge disaster, took all necessary precautions when building the Forth Bridge. During construction, wind strength tests were carried out and a wind pressure of 20 lbs per square foot on the surface of the bridge was allowed for. In the calculations for the Tay Bridge, allowance had only been made for a pressure of 9 lbs. Work began on the Forth Bridge in 1883, and was completed in 1890, and in 1906 it was still the largest bridge in the world.

Engineers met a similar problem in Canada, when faced with the construction of a bridge across the St Lawrence River at a point 5½ miles upstream from Quebec. The bridge was to carry trains from the Great Northern Railway, the Quebec and St John Railway, the Canadian Pacific Railway, the Grand Trunk Railway and the Quebec Central Railway. The span would need to be 1800 feet whereas for the Forth Bridge it had been 1700 feet. The central suspension span which linked the two ends was to be 672 feet long and 130 feet high. The bridge would carry two railway tracks, two tramways, two carriage-ways and two corbelled footpaths. On the evening of

Construction of the cantilevered Forth Bridge in Scotland, April 1887.
(*Nature*, 30 July 1887)

The Forth Bridge at a more advanced stage.

13 August 1907, a tremendous explosion occurred and the bridge partially collapsed, killing 75 men. A weak section had been compressed beyond its limit by the weight of the structure and had buckled. In 1912, after a long enquiry, work restarted with some modifications. The corbelled girders and the intermediate span girders were to be built in nickel steel. The bridge would carry only two rail tracks and two pedestrian passageways which would lighten the superstructure. On 11 September 1916, the centre span was brought by barge, a dangerous operation given the currents and tides of the river, and just as it was being raised into position it fell from a height of 36 feet into the river, and sank to a depth of 230 feet. Later, the bridge was finally completed.

The Forth Bridge seen from South Queensferry. (*L'Etat notre réseau*)

VIADUCTS NEAR WASSEN ON THE SAINT-GOTHARD LINE

The fast-flowing Reuss is crossed three times by the line, with the two tunnels of Leggistein and Waltinger, in
between the bridges, being in the form of a spiral.

(Engraving by J. Nibrikes, *Illustrirte Zeitung*, 1882. Swiss Federal Railway archive)

Manoeuvring the struts on the Faux Nam Ti viaduct.
Left: First phase at 8.00 am. *Right*: Second phase at 10.00 am. *Below*: Keying together at 11.00 am.

The Faux Nam Ti viaduct.

(Batignolles construction company)

RAILWAY ENGINEERING FEATS

An exceptionally bold engineering achievement was the building of a bridge across a steep-sided gorge, 230 feet wide and 328 feet deep, to carry a railway-line from Lao Kay, a town on the border of Indo-China, to Yunnan Sen, the capital of the Chinese province of Yunnan. This bridge across the Faux Nam Ti River was an arch-bridge with three hinge-joints. The arch consisted of two triangular struts which rested at their bottom end on a hinge-joint on the rock face. At the top end, they butted into a hinge-joint at the key of the bridge. Above the arch, the straight roadway was supported by two intermediate pylons and at each end by the walls of the gorge itself. The arch was swung into position in one morning, using winches positioned in the upper part of the ravine and joined to the struts by chain hoists. Work began on 11 March 1908 and was completed on 30 November in the same year. The Lao Kay–Yunnan Sen line was opened on 1 January 1910.

Another special construction is the viaduct which carries the Cerdagne line in the Pyrenees across the Cassagne gorge between Villefranche and Bourg-Madame. The ravine is 836 feet across and the line runs 260 feet above the river. The bridge has three spans, two being side spans 128 feet in length, and the third being the large central span which is just over 500 feet long. It resembles an ordinary suspension bridge supported on stone piers with an average height of 100 feet from the foot of the gorge. Metal pylons 95 feet in height stand on the piers. The bracing wires run from the top of the pylons to the central span and to the two side spans. On an ordinary suspension bridge, the roadway is secured to a cable which runs from the top of the pylons, and its lowest point is in the middle of the span. Although the

Cassagne Viaduct has a cable which runs to the roadway, the cable is attached to the base, not to the top of the pylon, and the middle of the roadway is its highest point since the bracing wires which come from the top of the pylons are secured there. With such a system the central span remains rigid. It was tested in October 1909 using a train made up of six electric cars and weighing 192 tons. The maximum sag at the middle point of the central span did not exceed one thousandth of the total span, which is the amount permitted on rigid metal bridges. This ingenious method of construction was devised by Commandant Gisclard. Such a viaduct was particularly remarkable because the suspension bridge had been abandoned following a series of accidents.

The famous railway suspension bridge across the Niagara Falls, which had been built between 1848 and 1855 with a span of 800 feet and a height of 240 feet above the Falls, was replaced in 1897 by a large metal arch-bridge on two levels, the top one for trains and the lower one for pedestrians, cars and trams.

In 1883, the Niagara Suspension Bridge's world record for length of span was broken by the famous Brooklyn Bridge across the East River in New York. This famous bridge is not in fact a railway-bridge but was built for two tramways. The engineer was Washington Roebling, the son of John Roebling, who in 1866 built the Cincinnati Suspension Bridge across the Ohio River with a span of 1056 feet. In the building of Brooklyn Bridge the main problem to be overcome was the building of the foundations of the two piers. This was done by putting metal drums which were open at one end into the water. Compressed air was then used to expel the water from the open end of the drum. The men were able to work inside this area of compressed air, entering and leaving it via a chamber from which pipes linked alternatively with the outside air and with the compressed air in the drum. When solid rock was reached the drum was filled with hyd-

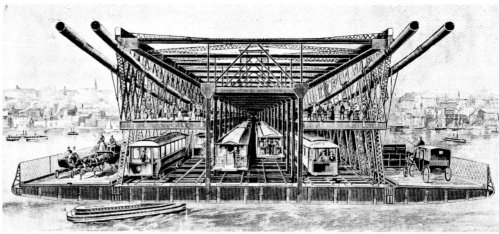

Cross-sectional view of Brooklyn Suspension Bridge.
(*Nature*, 26 March 1904)

Grand Central Pacific train ferry at the mouth of the Sacramento in California (1881).
(*Les Voies ferrées:* Baclé)

Train ferry carrying a complete train.
(*Les Voies ferrées:* Baclé)

raulic cement and set on the rock. The piers were then built onto this. They stand 275 feet high above the river and carry the four cables, each being 15 inches in diameter and weighing 11½ tons. The cables run for a length of 3450 feet and support a roadway 85 feet wide, which has rail tracks, carriageways, and two pedestrian footways.

When it is not possible to construct a fixed bridge across a river or waterway, train ferries are used. This was the system on the Firth of Forth and the Firth of Tay while reconstruction work on the collapsed bridge was being carried out. Since the level of the water may rise and fall, special systems have to be devised to allow rail-waggons to run from the track onto the boats. In the United States, in 1880, a huge ferry-boat, capable of carrying a complete train and its locomotive, was built. This was the *Solano* which ran at the mouth of the River Sacramento in Carquiniez Bay in California. It was worked by two driving-wheels producing 2,000 h.p. It was 420 feet long and weighed 3,600 tons. Its four sets of track allowed it to carry 48 goods-waggons, or 24 passenger-coaches and their locomotives.

The first train to arrive from Italy through the Mont Cenis Tunnel. There was an inauguration banquet for the guests.
(*Le Monde illustré*, 23 September 1871)

The first locomotive to pass through the Mont Cenis Tunnel, at the intersection of the main tunnel and the link tunnel.

TUNNELS

In 1857, the Sardinian Government decided that a tunnel 7½ miles long should be dug between Modane and Bardonneche (the Mont Cenis Tunnel), to attract much of the international traffic which went from Britain and France to Italy and the East. A solemn inauguration ceremony attended by King Victor-Emmanuel and Prince Napoleon took place, and the work was completed thirteen years later, at the end of 1870. The length of time required to build it gives some indication of the difficulties the engineers had to overcome. These problems brought fame to M. Colladon, a physicist living in Geneva. He was the first to see how compressed air could be used to drive drills and at the same time ventilate tunnels. This process was developed even further by Sommeillier, the Italian engineer. Drilling caused the temperature to rise as the tunnel went deeper into the ground and a temperature of almost 30°C was recorded in the final 500 yards of the centre section. The workers were beginning to suffer from anaemia, but fortunately the galleries were linked in time and this brought fresh air into the tunnel.

In 1872, about two years after the Mont Cenis Tunnel was completed, work began on the Saint-Gothard Tunnel which was to link Germany and Italy. It was just over 9 miles long and was built

Stonework and track in the middle of the Simplon Tunnel,
by the light of a lighting-waggon.

The hot-water spring which suddenly flooded through the
south side of the Simplon Tunnel.

by a Frenchman, Louis Favre, who was able to benefit from his experience in digging the Mont Cenis Tunnel. Compressed-air drills had improved and dynamite had replaced gunpowder.

However, the temperature rose to 35°C and even the strongest of the workers were not able to work more than two days in three even though the working day had been reduced to five hours.

The main feature of the Saint-Gothard series of tunnels, which are 9 miles long, is the spiral shape of seven out of the thirteen. The line rises up the sides of different valleys and eventually reaches the main tunnel at the top. As the valleys get higher, they follow each other in quick succession, with the result that there is no room for the train to turn and it has to cross over a bridge or viaduct to the opposite side of the valley. There it enters a tunnel which rises and turns to emerge at a higher point still. From there, the train crosses another bridge or viaduct and re-enters the hillside it has just left.

Faced with this question of access to the Saint-Gothard Tunnel, engineers divided into two camps; those who supported the idea of a high-level tunnel, and those who preferred a tunnel at a much lower level. Mont Cenis and Saint-Gothard are both high-level tunnels whereas the Simplon Tunnel is low-level. To reduce as much as possible the amount of excavation required, the line is built at as high a point as possible, which made the engineering work extremely expensive. The

Lighting-waggon used to inspect the Simplon Tunnel.

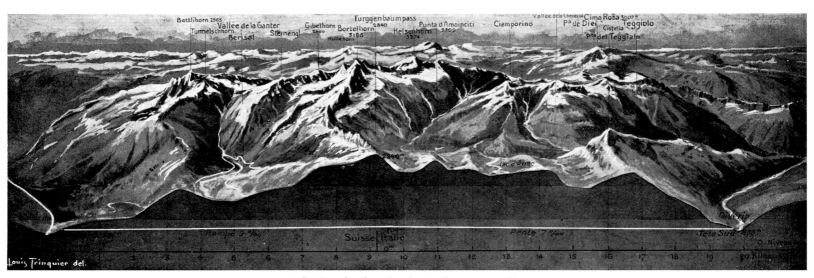

The Simplon low-level tunnel seen in profile.

low-level tunnel does not face the same problems, but is much longer. For example, Mont Cenis Tunnel and the Saint-Gothard Tunnel are 7½ and 9 miles long respectively whereas the Simplon Tunnel is almost 12½ miles in length.

Since the mountains above the Simplon Tunnel are higher and it is only 220 feet above sea-level, temperatures inside the tunnel were much greater. Work began in 1898, but soon came up against a difficult problem. In the middle of the tunnel, the temperature of the rock was 55°C. Air temperature varied between 27°C and 33°C. Not only was ventilation urgently required, but cold water had to be used to cool the air. A second problem which almost put an end to the enterprise was a sudden flood of water entering the tunnel at a rate of nearly 4000 feet per second from a lake higher up.

The tunnel was not completed until 1905, having taken 6½ years to build. On average, 28 feet of tunnel had been excavated every day. It proved, however, to be extremely important for French commerce and industry, since the Paris–Milan line now ran via Dijon, Pontarlier, Vallorbe and Lausanne, a distance of 525 miles instead of via Saint-Amour and the Mont Cenis Tunnel, a distance of 575 miles or via Belfort and the Saint-Gothard Tunnel, 857 miles.

Another important rail tunnel was the Arlberg in Austria, between Innsbruck and the Swiss border. After the Simplon, Saint-Gothard, and Mont Cenis Tunnels it was at the time the longest in the world, measuring 6¼ miles. An important feature is that it runs in a straight line. Work began in June 1880 and was completed November 1883, at an average of just under 2 miles per year.

The Simplon Tunnel led logically to the digging of a tunnel through the Lotschberg. This would shorten the Paris–Milan journey to a distance of 519 miles with the line passing through Pontarlier and Berne. It would also establish a

direct link between Basle, Berne and Italy, much more direct in fact than via the Saint-Gothard. In 1906, a French company began the enterprise. It is built at nearly 4000 feet above sea-level, and has access tracks with a gradient of up to 1 in 37.

In the early years of the century, electric traction had been tested and had proved itself to be cheap and particularly suited to mountainous regions. It had the further advantage of overcoming the problem of ventilation in long tunnels like the Simplon, whereas the steam locomotive simply increased this problem through its emission of waste gas.

On 24 July 1908, during excavation work on the Lotschberg Tunnel, a disaster occurred nearly 600 feet below the bottom of the Gastern Valley along which flows the river Kander. In spite of the distance between the tunnel and the river-bed, the river suddenly burst into the gallery, blocking it with sand over a distance of 1300 yards. It destroyed six months' work and caused the deaths of 25 workers. This particular working was abandoned, and the tunnel, instead of being straight, turned towards the east, a detour of 875 yards which made the tunnel's total length 9 miles. In spite of this unexpected curve, it met up with the other two galleries ahead of schedule on 31 March 1911. The work had taken 4 years 5 months at an average rate of progress of 30 feet per day. Powerful compressed-air drills and hammer-drills had been used. Train traction had also been by compressed air and, as it expanded, this air improved ventilation in the tunnel. Temperature did not exceed 33°C and was efficiently reduced by spraying cold water (emulsified by compressed air) on to the hot rocks.

The access slopes were climbed by electric traction, using single-phase 1500-volt current from overhead cables. The electric locomotives produced 200 h.p. and could pull 310 tons up a gradient of 1 in 37 at a speed of 25 m.p.h.

The Lotschberg Valley.
The Lotschberg Tunnel is a high-level tunnel. Steep gradient tracks were needed to reach it.

The bottom of Gastern Valley, 590 feet above the tunnel.
The broken lines indicate the line of the tunnel and the point at which the River Kander burst into the gallery.

The rack railway which climbs Mount Pilate.

The Lochers system is employed, and some gradients are 1 in 2.

(Drawing by J. Nibriker in the *Illustrirte Zeitung*, 15 June 1889. Swiss Federal Railway archive)

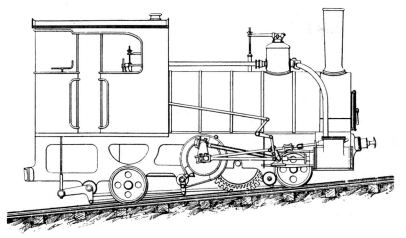

Arth-Righi locomotive with horizontal boiler for the Lake Zug to Righi
line. This could run only on a rack railway.
The wheels without connecting rods are carrying-wheels (1874).
(*Industrial Review*, 11 July 1877)

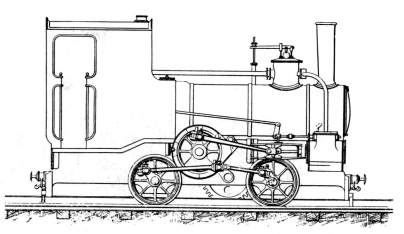

Mixed-line locomotive running from Wasseralfingen to Wurttemberg.
As the rods on the driving-wheels show, this engine could operate on both rack and
adhesion railways (1876).
(*Industrial Review*, 11 July 1877)

RACK RAILWAYS

When gradients begin to climb more steeply, track adhesion is inadequate on smooth rails, both because traction resistance increases and because adhesion is reduced as the driving-wheels exert pressure on the rails. Thus, on a gradient of 1 in 24, the load the locomotive·can pull is equal to only double the locomotive's adhesion weight. On a gradient of 1 in 16, the locomotive can only pull its own weight. By increasing the number of driving-wheels, in other words by coupling as many axles as possible, the problem is solved only temporarily since it recurs as the gradient becomes steeper. To help solve the problem, there was a return to the ideas of Blenkinsop, who worked as an engineer in the Middleton mines in 1811. There he built a locomotive with a cog-wheel beneath the boiler which engaged with a central rack between the rails. It was becoming increasingly important to build railways up very steep slopes in mountainous areas, both to develop the rail network as widely as possible and to reduce initial expenditure and increase capital return. The Swiss funicular railways on the Righi and Pilatus Mountains were built for the first reason and the railway across the Andes for the second. The latter climbs gradients of 1 in 12; construction work was started in 1913 to link the Atlantic and the Pacific.

In a patent dated 12 March 1862, Nicolas Riggenbach, a Swiss engineer, described a rack system as 'a new track and locomotive system which will enable trains to cross mountains'. In 1866, he suggested using his system on the very difficult Saint-Gothard line. In 1868, in the United States, Sylvestre Marsch built the rack railway on Washington Mountain in New Hampshire up an average gradient of 1 in 4 and a maximum gradient of 1 in 3. The rack was a kind of ladder in the middle of the track, with rounded rungs which acted as cogs.

In 1870, in Vitznau Righi, the first rack railway in Europe was completed. It was of the Riggenbach type. The same year saw the inauguration in Ostermundigen near Berne of the first mixed railway, that is, a track where both adhesion and

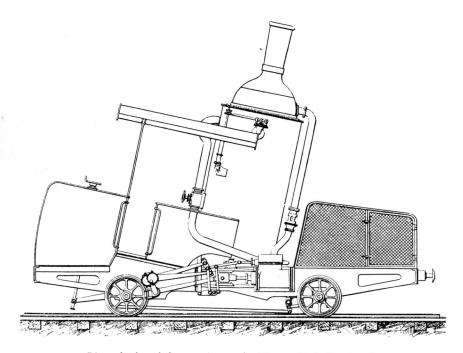

Riggenbach rack-locomotive on the Vitznau-Righi line (1870).
This could run only on a rack railway.
On upward slopes, the boiler is in a vertical position to reduce water movement.
(*Industrial Review*, 11 July 1877)

THE RACK RAILWAY FROM LAKE LUCERNE TO THE RIGHI (at an altitude of 5741 feet) BUILT IN 1870.

Top left: rack locomotive; *top right*: terminus at Vitznau; *bottom left*: track; *bottom right*: bridge and northern entrance to the tunnel.

(*Illustrirte Zeitung*, 16 September 1871. Swiss Federal Railway archive)

rack systems are used. On the Righi railway, the rungs of the ladder which acted between the rails as a rack, had a trapezoidal cross-section to prevent them turning round when the locomotive's cog-wheel engaged with them. The cogs are made so that if wear does occur the system will continue to operate efficiently. The Riggenbach locomotive used in Righi had two axles. In the middle of each was a cog-wheel which engaged with the rack. The cylinders drove an auxiliary shaft fitted with two cog-wheels. These engaged with two other wheels on the lower axle which also carried the rack wheel. This was, therefore, the driving-axle. The auxiliary shaft was fitted with an air-brake drum with water injection, which had the same effect as reversed steam when the locomotive descended a gradient. It was for the invention of this type of brake that Riggenbach was awarded the Montyon mechanical engineering prize in 1885 at the Academy of Sciences. The locomotive had a vertical boiler. As a result, there was little fluctuation in the waterlevel and, even on slopes, water covered the top of the firebox.

Mixed locomotive on 1 in 9 gradient, above Gletsch on the Furka-Oberalps line (1913).

(Swiss Federal Railway archive)

This engine was used only on rack railways. However, where there are mixed lines – track with both adhesion sections and rack sections – locomotives had to be built which could operate both systems and change from one to the other without stopping. Riggenbach therefore decided to use the engine's carrying-wheels to improve traction. Their adhesion, he argued, could reduce the demands made on the rack. The boiler in this type of engine is horizontal not vertical. There are three axles – the two axles of the adhesion wheels and, between them, the cog-wheel axle. The auxiliary shaft was driven by the pistons and engaged with the cog-wheel shaft which was fitted at each end with cranks and rods. These drove the adhesion wheels. As a result, the cogwheel turned during the whole of the journey, but not of course engaging where the section of track were of the adhesion type. On the rack sections, traction was both by adhesion and by the cog-wheel engaging with the rack. At Langres in France, in 1887, the rack railway operated in this way. When the track's system changes, the locomotive is able to pass from the smooth

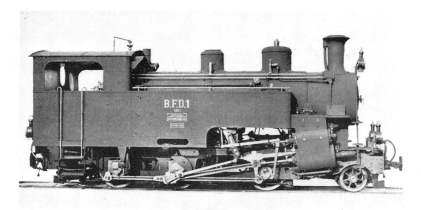

Four-cylinder compound locomotive with Abt rack system and adhesion, from the Furka line (1913).
(Swiss Federal Railway archive)

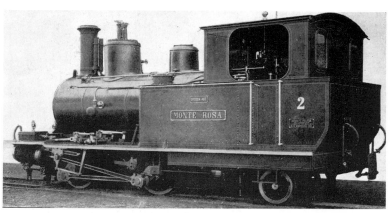

Twin-cylinder mixed locomotive for the Abt rack railway from Viege to Zermatt (1890).
(Swiss Federal Railway archive)

section of rail and engage immediately with the rack without having to stop. This is made possible by fitting a kind of sprung, articulated jaw to the end of the rack. It opens gradually and engages with the cog-wheel. This railway links the station and the town of Langres, which is on a plateau 430 feet above the station.

Some powerful locomotives are fitted with both systems, but these operate independently from each other. A former colleague of Riggenbach, the Swiss engineer Abt from Lucerne, invented a two- or three-blade rack to replace the older system. The blades have teeth and are set next to each other in such a way that each set of teeth is out of alignment with the next. The blades form a single rack which is positioned between the rails. They engage with an identical number of driving cog-wheels, which are set side by side like the blades, each cog-wheel engaging with its own rack. Under this system, propulsion is smoother, faster and more powerful. In a two-blade rack, the teeth on the first blade are positioned next to the gaps on the second blade. In a three-blade rack, the teeth on each blade are out of alignment, by one third of the length of a cog, with the teeth on the next blade. Three-blade racks are used on lines where the curves have a minimum radius of 800–1000 feet and where the gradients are steep. Two-blade racks are used on narrow-gauge track with less pronounced curves. The first practical application of Abt's system was in 1885, on the standard-gauge track on the Blankenburg to Tanne Railway.

Strub's track is in some ways similar to Abt's system, but the teeth are cut out of a Vignole rail set on a raised foot and not out of the blades. This system was first used in 1899 on the Jungfrau Railway. In 1912, this was the highest rack railway in Europe.

Locher's rack is more like Fell and Hanscotte's centre-rail system. In 1886, it was fitted to the railway on Pilatus Mountain where there are slopes with a gradient of 1 in 2. However, the cog-wheel often slips out of the rack, and to prevent this Colonel Locher invented a system in which the teeth and the cog-wheel were on a horizontal rather than a vertical plane, the two horizontal cog-wheels engaging with two horizontal racks set back to back.

Two-cylinder Locher rack locomotive for the Mount Pilate line (1886).
(Swiss Federal Railway archive)

Cog-wheel control mechanism in the Riggenbach system.
(From a model in the Science Museum, London)

CENTRE-RAIL TRACK

Traction on steep gradients using a centre rail for extra adhesion was first tested in 1830 by Vignole and Ericksson on the Panama Railway, and again in 1847 on a mine railway in Pennsylvania. In 1863, Fell, a British engineer, used it on the Cromfort Railway in the High Peak area of Derbyshire and, in 1865, in a more sophisticated form on Mont Cenis, while the tunnel was being built. The train had to climb from Lans-le-Bourg in France to the top of the mountain, which was at an altitude of nearly 6000 feet. It was a distance of 1¼ miles and the line rose nearly 500 feet, with gradients of 1 in 12. The locomotive, which had already been tested in Derbyshire, climbed the gradient at an average speed of 8 m.p.h., pulling three waggons with a total weight of 16 tons. An improved version of the same locomotive com-

Centre-rail railway built in 1866 on Mount Cenis while the tunnel was being constructed.
(*Les Merveilles de la science:* Louis Figuier)

Fell locomotive mechanism, with horizontal driving-wheels which grip the centre rail.
(Model from the Science Museum, London)

pleted the journey pulling five waggons, with a total weight of 42 tons at an average speed of nearly 7 m.p.h. With only three waggons, and a total weight of 33 tons, it climbed at more than 8 m.p.h. On the descent, speed was limited to 6 m.p.h.

However, the system lacked flexibility and had difficulty in negotiating curves. Sometimes, the wheels, having slipped, would suddenly adhere, and this frequently caused connecting-rods to break. These problems, combined with the success of Riggenbach's rack system, caused the centre rail system to be abandoned.

However, much later, in 1904, M. Hanscotte, an engineer with Fives-Lille, invented another centre-rail system. In Fell's locomotive, the horizontal wheels which adhered to the centre-rail were inside the engine's wheelbase. This created inflexibility. Hanscotte made the horizontal-wheel mechanism independent of the chassis, by positioning the wheels outside the wheelbase at each end of the underframe, in front of the leading

driving-axle and behind the third. This reduced the horizontal wheels' resistance to the centre rail as its position changed in relations to the track. Moreover, there was sufficient pressure to maintain adhesion to the centre rail, the horizontal pressure changing with the slope of the track. As the incline changed, the horizontal adhesion wheels moved towards and away from the centre rail by means of a compressed-air return mechanism in which a suspended weight activated the air admission-valve.

This type of locomotive was first tested in 1904, and again in 1905, on the La Bourboule electric tram line, and in Switzerland on the Brigue Railway from La Furka to Dissentis. But the fame of the Hanscotte locomotive was only properly established in 1907 when it was used on the Clermont-Ferrand to Puy-de-Dôme Railway. On 17 April 1917, five such engines weighing 31 tons were requisitioned for use during the war, to haul heavy artillery up the steep gradients in the Vosges mountains.

Fell's centre-rail locomotive (1867).
The horizontal wheels with centre-rail adhesion are between the two axles inside the wheelbase.
(*Les Merveilles de la science:* Louis Figuier)

Hanscotte's locomotive for the Puy de Dôme (1907).
The horizontal wheels for centre-rail adhesion are at the two ends of the underframe, outside the end axles.
(*Nature,* 16 March 1907)

CABLE-CARS, MONORAILS AND FUNICULAR RAILWAYS

The funicular system appears to have existed for many years. In *Le Diverse et Artificiose Machine del Capitano Agostino Ramelli*, there is an example from 1588 of horse-power replacing manpower to pull a loaded truck up a steep incline. This is the operating principle of the funicular railway.

When the problem of rail traction in mountainous regions first presented itself this system was pressed into service, particularly on steep slopes. In 1879, a funicular railway was built up Mount Vesuvius, where there are gradients of 1 in 2. The track consisted of longitudinal frames on which a single rail guided the trucks up the gradient. The upward and downward tracks ran parallel to each other. The beams were made of oak and strengthened by sleepers which acted as stays. The stationary engines at the bottom of the hill had two 45 h.p. steam engines. In 1901, this funicular railway was modernised and electrified.

In 1879, the funicular system was fitted with a

Ascending and descending train on the Vesuvius Railway. The guard's sole task is to apply the brake if the cable fractures.
(*Nature*, 7 August 1880)

rack when the Giessbach funicular was built in Switzerland on Lake Brienz. Motive-power was provided by the weight of the water which was taken on by the car just before its descent. The combined weight of water and car pulled the other car up the slope by a double-acting traction cable. The Riggenbach-type rack acts as a guide and is also a powerful braking device. In an emergency it can be used to move the cars manually. Some short time later, the Territet-Glion funicular was built to the same design.

In 1883, the engineer Thomas Agudio built an unusual funicular some miles from Turin, at Superga. It has a special locomotor with driving-wheels turned by an endless cable. The cable runs the full length of the track, a distance of nearly 3500 yards in both directions. The cable is driven by two stationary steam engines. The track consists of two ordinary rails and a double-cog-wheel centre-rail, which Agudio called the spinal column of his system. On the locomotor, the cable winds round the grooves of the two large left-hand pulleys. The movement of these pulleys is transmitted by wheels and gears to a pair of horizontal cog-wheels which engage with the cogs on the centre-rail.

The Vesuvius Railway in 1880.
(*Nature*, 7 August 1880)

The Superga Railway, near Turin in Italy.
(*Nature*, 15 November 1884)

Agudio's locomotive on the Superga Railway.
(*Nature*, 15 November 1884)

Agostini Ramelli's device for hauling trucks (1558).

(*Le Magasin pittoresque*, 1847)

Top: Seventeenth-century drawing by Faust Wranczi of the 'overhead ferry'.

(*Le Magasin pittoresque*, 1850)

Above: An early cable-car.

Another funicular-type system was used in 1878 by Handyside, on a slope at Hopton in Britain. When the slope is too steep, the locomotive leaves the train at the bottom of the hill and, as it climbs, it unwinds a cable attached to the leading waggon. When the full length of the cable has been let out, the engine stops, is clamped to the track by brakes which grip the two side-faces of the rails, and hauls up the train by means of a winch at the rear of the engine.

Cable-cars have also existed for a long time, if we are to believe Faust Wranczi's seventeenth-century engraving of the 'overhead ferry'. The system was first used about 1860 in the United States, in the Pennsylvania and Vermont quarries. It carried loads weighing up to about 4 tons. Since then it has been used increasingly by industry and, in 1909, the largest cable-car system in the world was built in the copper-mines of Famatina in Argentina, at the summit of the Andes close to

the border with Chile. Here, mules capable of carrying a mere 4000 tons of ore per year were replaced by cable-cars. As the crow flies the distance involved was only 22 miles, but the track itself rose nearly 12,000 feet. A stationary cable was used to guide the waggons, which carried loads of half-a-ton and followed each other at intervals of 300 feet. A second cable was used for traction. The system was capable of transporting 40 tons per year.

The Monts d'Enfer cable-car near Ebensée in Salz Kammergut, Austria (1912).

(Photo: Franz Walden Wien O.V.B.)

The Brennan monorail, tested for the first time in Britain in July 1907.

Overhead passenger railway, operating from Morand bridge to Tête-d'Or park, built for the 1872 Lyons exhibition.

Mention must also be made of the suspension railway, built in 1911 on the Aiguille du Midi, which carries tourists up the mountain side near Mont-Blanc. The first section from Chamonix is 2000 yards long and reaches a height of 2500 feet. The second section climbs a further 2500 feet and is 1300 yards long. Three cables are used: the first guides the cars' bogies, which can carry up to 24 passengers with a total weight of 4 tons; the second cable is the traction cable, and hauls the cars by means of an electric engine; the third cable is used for braking.

The monorail originated in Lyons in France. Its inventor was M. Duchamp. He built it for the Lyons 1872 exhibition and it ran for a distance of 1200 yards. The car, consisting of two symmetrical parts which ran on each side of the centre-rail, is driven by an endless cable.

About 1880, the same idea was developed by Lartigue for use in industry, and it functioned very successfully on the Esparto farms on the high plains of South Oran in Algeria. In 1887, the same system, with some modifications, was used in passenger service on the west coast of Ireland to link Listowel and Bullybunnion, a distance of just over 9 miles. The coaches run along a centre-rail. Two side-rails are fixed to the raised centre-rail to support the coaches in the event of one side becoming heavier than the other. Traction is provided by the train's engine, the locomotive consisting of two identical engines which balance each other on each side of the rail. Each has its own boiler, firebox and chimney.

The electric-traction suspension railway which was installed in 1899 between Barmen and Elberfeld along the river Wupper is a single-rail system. The coaches can hold 50 passengers, 30 seated and 20 standing. The track runs for a distance of 8 miles, 6 of which are above the river. An automatic block-system operates, with trains running at two-minute intervals.

The principle of the gyroscope, a typical example of which is the child's top which remains upright as it spins, is well known. In 1907 a British engineer, Louis Brennan, invented the monorail, with a 22-ton waggon which maintains its balance by means of its rotating gyroscopes. Like the vehicle itself, these are driven by two oil-fired engines using dynamos. The system was tested in Germany in 1909 by Scherl, but was not developed.

Lartigue-type monorail, operating from Bullybunnion to Listowel, opened in 1887.
(*Nature*, 27 December 1902)

Elberfeld suspension railway, with part of the line above the River Wupper.
(*Le Génie civil*, 10 March 1900)

Port Arthur in Canada. The first train to link the Atlantic and the Pacific (30 June 1886).

At the time it was a single-track line belonging to an individual not a company. (Photo: Francis Dickie)

Lord Strathcona lays the golden rivet to join the two sections of the Transcontinental railway (7 November 1885).

(Photo: Francis Dickie)

UNUSUAL AND EXOTIC RAILWAYS

Early Canadian and American railways were built near lakes and rivers. Later they were extended as far as the great seaports.

The first line to be built was the Grand Trunk Railroad in 1851. It followed the St Lawrence from Montreal and the north of Lake Ontario to Toronto. In 1856 it reached Detroit. When the Victoria Bridge (3000 yards long) was built over the St Lawrence at Montreal, this line linked up with lines in the United States. Later, a parallel line was built by the Great Western Railroad, again from Toronto to Detroit but via Niagara and London. Then, from 1867 onwards, the so-called inter-colonial lines were built from Toronto to Halifax in Nova Scotia, and a further two narrow-gauge lines were begun, to run from Toronto to Lake Huron and Lake Nipissing.

To compete with the Grand Trunk and Great Western Railroads, which had joined forces, a third company, the Credit Company, was formed with grants from town councils. Another line was built from Toronto to Detroit, this time from Saint Thomas where it met the Southern Canada Company line. This new line saw the construction of some remarkable wooden bridges and viaducts, typical of those built by North American engineers, who hardly ever used stone, on grounds of time and cost.

On 29 June 1880, Sir John MacDonald launched his project to link the Atlantic and the unknown and almost uninhabited Pacific coast. On 7 November 1885, in Craigellachie, a tiny village in the mountains of British Colombia, the last rivet was driven home and the two oceans were joined by a line 2800 miles long. From Quebec, the line goes first of all to Ottawa along the St Lawrence, then, turning west, it crosses 400 miles of land which, in 1895, was still wild and uncultivated and inhabited only by Indians. It then reaches Winnipeg, an important rail centre. From there, some lines run south to the United States, others run north to Hudson Bay. It crosses the Rocky Mountains and, from its highest point at Mount Stephen, at an altitude of nearly 6000 feet, it descends to the Pacific Coast, arriving at Vancouver via Mission Junction, where it links with the Washington State line. One feature of the line is that it needs constant protection from herds of cattle, from snow and from cold, temperatures varying from 35°C to −45°C.

Building a line across the Rocky Mountains had always been an ambition of American railroad engineers. In 1889, a new line crossed them, near Silverton in Colorado. At its highest point, not far short of 13,000 feet, it passes Lake Argent, famous for its precious minerals. Here donkeys had to be used to transport the rails. The line was to link the town of Ouray, a terminus on a branch of the Denver and Rio Grande Railroad, and Silverton, another terminus belonging to the same company. It had to cross over high mountains and through deep valleys and gorges, with granite walls rising vertically nearly 3000 feet above the track. One of these is Arkansas Gorge, nearly 7 miles long, 40 feet wide at the bottom and only 70 feet wide at the top. A torrent roars along the bottom of this gorge, and a kind of suspension bridge had to be built along its sides from one end to the other 160 feet above the torrent. In another granite canyon called Black Gorge, which is 1300 feet deep, a 200 foot-high embankment had to be built above the level of the water to enable the train to pass through. In places, as it climbs, the train almost touches the sides of the narrow gorge.

American railroads not only tamed the most inaccessible mountains but even seas and glaciers. In 1908, the Florida East Coast Railroad began the construction of a line between Florida and the Caribbean across the coral reefs. This line, which had finished at Miami, was extended as far as Key West. The track crosses the open sea by means of bridges, dykes and viaducts. Of the 155 miles of track, 75 miles run across water. Swing-bridges were built to allow pleasure-boats and fishing-boats to pass beneath. Journey time to Havana was reduced considerably by this railroad.

In 1909, in Alaska, the American railroads were confronted by the Allen glacier, 5½ miles of solid ice. The covering of ice was first of all dynamited and then the track was built on a kind of shield made of morainic ballast. However, it had constantly to be repaired, and trains were unable to run along it at any speed.

This blind faith in railroads had already caused various Americans to conceive some extraordinary projects. About 1880, a Captain Eads had designed a system for putting boats on railroad lines and using locomotives to pull them across the Tehuan Isthmus from the Gulf of Mexico to the Pacific. He claimed that this would be more economical than a canal. In fact, in 1894, a line was built across the Isthmus, and the distance between European ports and American ports on the Pacific coast was reduced by about 1400 miles.

A line through one of the gorges in Colorado.
The Denver & Rio Grande R.R. (1889).
(Bibliothèque des arts décoratifs)

However, passengers had to transfer twice at the ports of Coatzacoalcos and Salina Cruz.

Another daring exploit was the building of a railway across the Andes in South America. This chain of mountains had always been virtually inaccessible, with passes at more than 16,000 feet and a steep drop down to the Pacific. Although there were coal seams about 18 miles from Lima, the capital of Peru, Peruvians had had to import from Britain since they had no means of transporting their own coal. In 1870, therefore, construction started on a railway-line between Callao, the port of Lima, and La Oroya on the other side of the Andes, 136 miles from Callao and lying at an altitude of 12,000 feet. From Callao the train climbs for 50 miles and then, at a height of

6000 feet, crosses a magnificent metal viaduct 250 feet high and with a span of 575 feet. Further along the line is a second viaduct, built by Eiffel. The train continues to climb until it reaches its highest point at just over 15,000 feet, after an uphill journey of 100 miles. From there, via a 1200-yard long tunnel, the track emerges on to the opposite slope, and the train descends to La Oroya. Altogether there are 30 tunnels on the line, but with a total length of only 3 miles since they are all high-level tunnels. There are also 30 bridges and viaducts. This line first operated in 1875.

About 1892, two other lines were built across the Andes, one from Mollendo, a port on the Pacific Coast of Peru, to Punho, a port on Lake

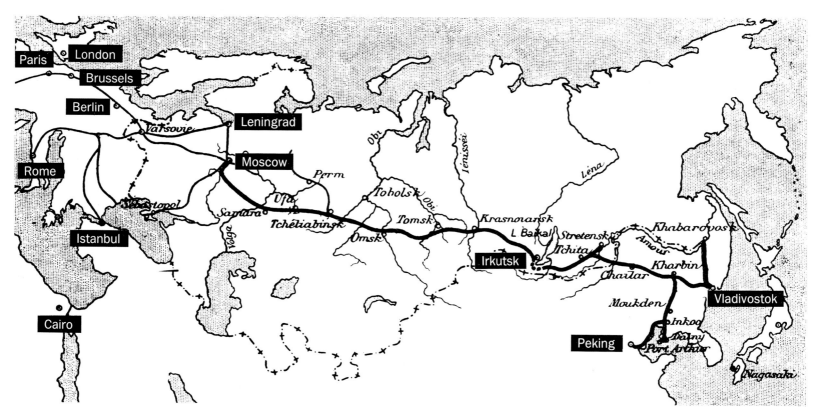

The Trans-Siberian railway (about 1903).
(*Nature*, 30 April 1904)

Titicaca, with a highest point of over 15,000 feet, the other from the Chilean port of Antofagasta across the Atacama Desert to Uyuni. This line climbs to a height of over 13,000 feet. At this altitude, both lines cross the Bolivian high plateau where they face problems of extreme cold, and air with a low oxygen-content which causes mountain sickness among passengers and railway personnel. The journey must, therefore, be spread over several days, with passengers staying overnight in hotels so that they may become accustomed to the high altitudes.

Finally, there is the strange line from Valparaiso to Mendoza, which is the only one completely to cross the Andes and link the Pacific to the Atlantic. In 1893, trains ran only on the sections from Valparaiso to Santo Rosa de los Andes at the foot of the mountains, and from Mendoza to Buenos Aires. The central section across the mountains was still being built. Because of the difficulty of the undertaking, it remained unfinished for a long time, and passengers had to make the dangerous journey from one section to another by donkey. On 2 April 1910, the first train ran from Argentina to Chile, passing through a tunnel more than 3200 yards long at an altitude of more than 10,000 feet, beneath Mount Cumbra. In this mountainous region, the track is only 1 metre wide, whereas nearer to Valparaiso and Buenos Aires it is 1 metre 65 centimetres wide. The total length of the railway is 884 miles, 190 of which are in Chile. From Europe, this was,

in the 1930s, the most direct route to Chile and to other countries on the Pacific Coast of South America. The journey from Buenos Aires to Valparaiso took only 36 hours, while the voyage through the Magellan Strait took ten days.

In Japan, a single-track railway, 1 metre 67 centimetres wide, was built in 1872 between Tokyo and Yokohama and, in 1878, in China, the port of Woo Sung was linked to Shanghai by rail. This first Chinese railway encountered the problem of hostility from local people who regarded the locomotive, the 'fire dragon', as an abominable creature from hell. As a result, the line from Shanghai to Tientsin was not built until about 1890.

In India, however, the building of railways presented no such problems. In 1877, there were already more than 6000 miles of track and by 1892 more than 13,000 miles.

At the same time, the Russians proved to be bold railway pioneers when they built their Trans-Caspian and Trans-Siberian railways, the first of which proved particularly difficult. None of the materials required was readily available, and wood, iron and even water had to be transported. General Annenkof, who was in overall charge, built a barracks train made from enormous double-decker waggons. Between Merv and Tchardjoni, the track had to be built across constantly shifting dunes which were sometimes 200 feet high, and a mixture of clay and sea-water was used to stabilise the ground. The line was originally a military one, with observation towers every 8 miles and mounted soldiers patrolling each section of the line. The Trans-Siberian Railway is 5777 miles long (from Moscow to Vladivostok) and is therefore longer than any of the

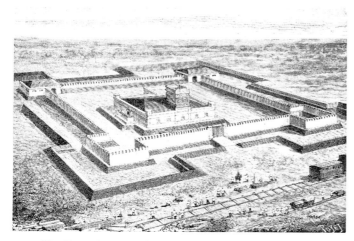

The Trans-Caspian railway; a fort built to protect the work.
(*Nature*, 16 June 1888)

great Trans-Continental lines in North America. Its first section from Samara to Ufa was completed in 1888, but it was not until 17 March 1891 that the line was extended from Ufa to Vladivostok by a decree from the Czar. The next completed section was the Ossouri section, which runs from Vladivostok to Khabarovosk along the Lovat. Many Korean workers died during the construction of this line through swampy land full of poisonous mosquitoes. The heir to the throne, the future Czar Alexander III, inaugurated the line on his return from Japan. The next section, between Samara, Ufa, Zlataoust and Tcheliabinsk faced the difficult problem of crossing the Caucasus mountains, but the inauguration ceremony finally took place in 1892. The line was then extended to Omsk, and in 1894 to Tomsk. This section proved difficult because of shortages of wood and water. Even more difficult was the section between Taiga and Lake Baikal, near the River Ienissei, and to cross the Ienissei a bridge 1000 yards long had to be built on stone piers. In 1904, the line was virtually completed. However, the track was too light and was replaced by heavier track so that train speed could be increased. As far as Baikal, traction was by articulated 'Mallet'-type engines, with four coupled axles and a carrying-axle at the front on passenger trains, and with six coupled axles for goods trains. Beyond this point, compound locomotives with two outside cylinders and five axles, four of which were coupled, were used. Lake Baikal was crossed by ferry-boat which in winter had to be fitted with an ice-breaker. Sometimes, however, the ice was too thick. When this occurred, passengers crossed on sledges and were able to dine in a kind of hotel restaurant in the middle of the lake. During the war between Russia and Japan, the Trans-Siberian Railway proved unable to feed and transport the huge numbers of men required to fight.

Opening of the Cape Town to Wellington Railway.
The first train arrives in Wellington station.
(*Illustrated London News*, 16 January 1864: South African Railways Collection)

Construction work on the Cape-Cairo Railway.
(*Nature*, 28 November 1903)

In Africa, the Ethiopian Railway and the Cape Railway, which was seen as the first section of the Cape to Cairo line, must feature among the most remarkable railways at the beginning of this century. France was directly involved in the building of the former. In 1894, Emperor Menelik granted France the concession to build a line 200 miles in length from Harar on the Abyssinian plateau to the French colony of Djibouti. The arid and hilly nature of the terrain made the work particularly difficult. From sea-level, the line rose to a height of 6000 feet, but gradients in excess of 1 in 33 had to be avoided, as did curves with a radius of less than 500 feet. Water for the workforce and for the building of the Chabele Viaduct had to be fetched by camel from 7–9 miles away. Later, without much difficulty, the line was extended from Harer to Addis Ababa, the capital of Ethiopia, a distance of 90 miles but with an altitude difference of only 3000 feet.

In South Africa, between the Zambezi and the Transvaal, the sole means of transport originally was large trucks pulled by oxen or donkeys. They could travel 6–9 miles per day. When the railway was built in 1896, Cape Town was only a three-day journey from Bulawayo and, by 1903, there ran every Wednesday a luxury train, with restaurant-car, library, saloon-car and bathrooms. On this line, from the Cape to Rhodesia, the train travelled along rails laid straight onto the ground and even across shallow streams. When it reached the Zambezi, passengers could stay in the 500-room hotel from which the famous Falls, three times higher than the Niagara Falls, were visible. The journey to Cairo was completed mainly by water, in particular across Lake Tanganyika and down the Nile.

Generally, South African railway development resulted from the various mining discoveries: the diamond mines in Kimberley, the gold mines in Witwatersrand, and the discovery of coal in Wankie. Another important factor was the need to transport corn and livestock.

The Cape to Cairo Railway – Bulawayo ford.
(*Nature*, 28 November 1903)

Inauguration of the Algiers Railway at Blida, in 1862.

(Florange archive)

FRENCH COLONIAL RAILWAYS

In North Africa, railway engineers found that, before their lines could reach the huge inland plateau, they had to pass, at sea-level, through inhospitable areas and then climb steep gradients. In the north and south were zones which enjoyed a temperate climate, and had a large population of Arabs and Europeans, and it was there that the

African railways began, in Egypt, Algeria, and Tunisia.

In 1844, in Algeria, concessions were granted to build first of all a line which ran parallel to the sea and then lines which linked the main ports to this original line. However, the building programme was not co-ordinated and often the tracks were of different gauge. In 1884, the trunk line from the border of Morocco to the Tunisian border was completed. The first sections of lines

into the Sahara Desert were also built. Colomb Bechar was only reached in 1906, Berrouaghia as early as 1892, Biskra was reached in 1888 and from there a narrow-gauge track was laid as far as Touggourt in 1914. Generally speaking, therefore, the railways in Algeria were the result of its status as a colony, the French building lines into the Sahara to extend their territories. However, there were other commercial factors too, such as trains being needed by the mining industry, and to transport the esparto grass which was farmed.

In Tunisia, the first concession was granted in 1871 for the line from Tunis to La Goulette and La Marsa and from Tunis to Bardo. In 1876, the line from Tunis to Dacha Djanbot was built and then

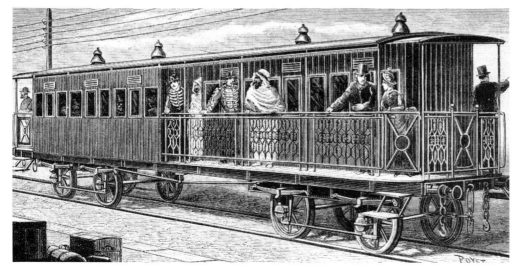

A Bône-Guelma company's coach with an outside corridor.

(*Nature*, 13 August 1887)

East Algerian railway locomotive in 1879.

(Algerian Central Records Collection)

Opening of Tunis station at La Goulette.

This railway was built by a British company.

extended two years later to the Algerian border. In 1894–98, lines were built from Tunis to Bizerta and from Tunis to Sousse. The discovery of phosphates in Southern Tunisia, and the extraordinary success of the Sfax-Gafsa Railway, showed how vital it was to build lines from the coast to the mining areas. Farmers also demanded that lines be built which would link their olive-groves and almond-plantations in Tozeur in the north, to Metlaoui, and in Graiba in the south, to Gabes. This second line was, in a sense, the first section in the rail link with Africa's Italian colonies. Once again, therefore, commercial mining and farming lines followed the building of politico-military lines which had allowed the French to strengthen their position.

Before 1914, the other African railways were in fact colonial lines. Railways were seen as by far the best means of communication and colonial development. Rivers were unreliable, sometimes dry, sometimes turned into torrents, with waterfalls and rapids. Boats had difficulty navigating rivers because of the many rocks and choking plants, and, from the sea, entrance to rivers was often dangerous because of the bar. Roads were expensive to build and often destroyed by torrential rainfall. However, railways in the colonies were unlike their counterparts in Europe, in the sense that they were built before commerce and industry developed, and in fact were the main

contributory factor to this development. In Europe, the reverse tended to be the case. In this respect, African railways were like those built in the Far West of North America; they were the driving force in the building and development of towns. Moreover, colonial railways not only brought a certain prestige to the colonialists but, at the same time, allowed them to deploy their troops more effectively.

The first railway in French West Africa was the Dakar-Saint Louis line, designed in 1878 and opened in 1885. It was built mainly for military transport but also, for economic reasons, to link the port of Dakar and Saint Louis, the capital of Senegal. Dakar was a thriving port but the

First-class coach with gallery on the Dakar-Saint-Louis railway (1900).

(Lachèze archive)

Waggon loaded with peanuts on the Dakar-Saint-Louis railway, about 1900.

(Lachèze archive)

Samory tribesmen working on the railway to the sound of music.

Senegal River to Saint Louis was not open to shipping because of the bar at the river mouth. The line also passed through Rufisque, which was the main centre of the peanut industry. During the 30 years which preceded the First World War, traffic increased twenty-fold. Planned in 1863 by General Faidherbe, the Kayes Niger Railway was also a narrow-gauge line. Work began in 1881,

but it was not completed until 1906 because of all kinds of problems – hilly terrain, warring tribes, yellow fever and the inaccessibility of the Senegal river to seaships transporting materials. These problems are reflected in the route taken by the railway. The result was that traffic did not develop to the extent it did on the Dakar-Saint Louis line.

Work began on the Thiès-Kayes narrow-gauge railway in 1907. In 1914, it was 230 miles long. It was intended to link the Sudan directly with the sea, by-passing the expensive and unreliable Senegal route and running through important centres of peanut production.

The Conakry-Niger Railway was built in 1900 between the Niger and the sea, and it also opened up a route to Guinea. It went through a very hilly region, some of the colony's peaks rising to 4500 feet. It transported products such as bananas, cloth, cola seed, matting, leather, cabbage trees, salt, peanuts and rice.

The Ivory Coast Railway was started in 1903, and by 1912 it was 200 miles long. It leaves the port of Abidjan and runs north, establishing a route to the sea from the Ivory Coast hinterland and from the colony of Upper Volta. After passing through thick forests, which provide woods such as mahogany used in the furniture industry, it reaches Agboville, a centre for cocoa production, and then crosses the savanna and woods and valleys before finally arriving at Bouake. From here, lines run to the Upper Ivory Coast, to the Upper Volta and even to the Sudan.

The Dahomean Central Railway began in Cotonou in 1900, and by 1913 it covered a distance of 180 miles, reaching its terminus in Save. It runs through Allada, a region with an abundance of palm-trees. The area is very hilly and rail-traffic increased remarkably. The East

Laying metal sleepers on the Thiès-Kayes line (1912).
(French West Africa General Agency Collection)

Dahomean Railway was built between 1905 and 1913, and was 50 miles long. Its main use was as a local line carrying almonds, palm oil and corn.

Equatorial Africa is five times the size of France, and a huge reservoir of riches, including rubber, oil-producing plants, copal, coffee, vanilla, cocoa, furs, ivory, copper ore and the highly prized Gabon wood. It also possesses a remarkable network of rivers in the Congo, the Oubangui, the Chari and the Logares. For many years, the Mayumbe mountain range and its foothills made the building of railways there an impossible task. The great explorers, Stanley and Savorgnan de Brazza, realized that the development of the region could not take place without the railway. Before the war, Belgian engineers were alone in attempting to provide a rail link between Stanley Pool and the Atlantic. In 1909, a French plan to link Brazzaville and the Sen was drawn up, and, in 1914, 81,000,000 francs were provided to finance the line's construction.

In 1896, from the earliest days of the colonisation of Madagascar, there were projects to build a railway from the capital Tananarive on the coast to Tamatave. But rather than take the shortest route, engineers decided to follow the pre-colonial Madagascan Tananarive-Andevorante path. This would enable them to reduce costs by making use of the canal (later called the Panga-

A railway station in Madagascar (1910).

(Madagascar General Agency Collection)

lanes Canal) which passes through the lagoons along the coast between Andevorante and Tamatave. The railway, therefore, only ran between Andevorante and Tamatave, its starting-point being at Brickaville a few miles from Andevorante. It was opened on 1 January 1909. It rises to an altitude of over 4000 feet and is 168 miles long. However, it only partly solved the transport problem, since the train had to be ferried across the Pangalanes Canal. As a result, a 60-mile stretch of track was laid between Brickaville and Tamatave. In 1912, large quantities of graphite and precious stones near Antsirabe led to the building of a line from Tamatave to Antsirabe. At the same time, a line was being built between the fertile region of Lake Alaotra and the Tamatave

General Gallieni and his entourage at the opening of Gallieni Tunnel at Sahampale on the Brickaville-Tananarive line (1900).

(Madagascar General Agency Collection)

Doumer Bridge in Hanoi which crosses the Red River (1902).
(Indo-China General Agency Collection)

line when the First World War broke out and put an end to construction work. One of the features of the Madagascar Railways is the use of wood to fire the locomotive. This, however, resulted in rapid deforestation alongside the Tamatave–Tananarive line.

Of the other French colonial railways, the Réunion Railway must be mentioned. Dating from 1886, it runs for 80 miles along two-thirds of the island's coast. In India, the French Indian Company built a line 7 miles long from Pondicherry to Villapuram on the Great Madras Line at the southern tip of the Indian peninsula, and a second line 9 miles long linking Karikal to the Great Indian network at Peralam. In New Cale-

donia, a railway line ran between Noumea and the River Dumbea, a distance of 18 miles.

Nowhere did railway construction bring greater change to a country's economy than in Indo-China. In 1896, there were only two lines. One, a purely local line 44 miles long, ran from Saigon to Mytho in Cochin-China, via the great city of Cholon and over splendid metal bridges. The other, in Tonkin, ran between Phu Sang Thuong and Lang Son. It was primarily intended for military use and had a 60-centimetre gauge which was later replaced by metre-gauge track. When Paul Doumer became Governor-General, a coordinated programme was drawn up to build a line across the whole of Indo-China from Saigon

to Tonkin, linking the ports and the rich valleys of the Annam, the sea, and the navigable reaches of the Mekong by cross-country trunk lines, and finally entering China along the Red River valley. A rail network was essential, since the forests of Upper Cochin-China, Cambodia, Laos, and the upper valley of the Red River could not be farmed commercially without a means of transport. Cambodian rice and Annam's many products had no access to rivers or ports. The 1898 programme aimed to establish five lines. The first from Hai Phong to Yn Nan Sen in China was opened on 1 April 1910. Construction proved difficult, because the region was extremely mountainous, with peaks rising to 6500–9500 feet and rivers which flowed through narrow valleys. The second line, from Hanoi to Vinh, was 200 miles long and opened in 1905. The third, from Tourane to Hue, ran for a distance of 106 miles and had operated since 1908. The fourth was from Saigon to Khanh Hoa, and the fifth from Mytho to Vinh Long.

Near Hanoi, the Hanoi-Lang Son line crosses the Red River on a magnificent cantilever metal bridge, 1800 yards long. It has nineteen spans, the two end spans each being 260 feet long. There are nine 246-feet spans and these alternate with eight spans each of which is more than 350 feet long.

In the Chinese section of the Yunnan Railway, between Lao Kay and Yun Nan Sen, a 283-mile stretch of track contains 155 tunnels, with a total length of 10½ miles, and 3,422 viaducts, bridges and aqueducts. Like other lines in Indo-China, it is a metre-gauge. Generally, the locomotives have three coupled axles and pull loads of 300 tons at 25 m.p.h. On the very hilly Yunnan Line, the engines have four coupled axles. In Tonkin and Yunnan, the engines are fired by coal, whereas on the South Annam and Central Annam Railways wood is used, with the attendant problem of deforestation.

Bridge on the Yunnan line (1903–1906).
(Indo-China General Agency Collection)

Metre-gauge shunting locomotive, with vertical boiler (1886).
(Corpet-Louvet company archive)

METRE-GAUGE

Originally, metre-gauge track was used by industry inside factory buildings, but later it was developed for use by the army and by the public. In 1892, a metre-gauge line was opened in Calvados, between Lion-sur-Mer and Ouistreham, and, in July and August 1892, a similar line on the coast at Royan, Pontaillac and Saint-George carried 400,000 passengers. In factories and factory-yards, shunting-engines ran on metre-gauge, but generally it was used on local lines.

In France, a law of 12 July 1865 and, later, of 11 June 1880, defined its role: it would be limited to local lines, that is, it would link small towns and villages to larger towns and cities; it would run only short distances; it would not carry intensive traffic; and it would have a smaller budget than main-line track. At first, the mistake was made of building such lines as if they were main lines, in other words, at a cost out of all proportion to the

Metre-gauge shunting locomotive, weighing 4 tons (1886).
(Corpet-Louvet company archive)

return that could be expected. At the time there was no law governing which gauge track should be used. In fact, narrow gauge, that is any gauge narrower than standard gauge (4 feet 8½ inches), costs less because it is lighter and sharp curves present no problem. Curves become a problem where wheels are interdependent and their axles are aligned. Narrow-gauge track, of course, requires stock which is narrower and shorter. Axles are, therefore, closer together and the wheelbase can negotiate sharp curves more easily. With such a system, the natural life of the land can be followed and the laying of track is less costly. Trains can negotiate curves with a radius of 300 feet and even less in stations. Moreover, since the track formation also is narrower, savings in expenditure can be made of the order of at least fifty per cent compared to the cost of standard-gauge track.

Track costs also depend on track weight, and this in turn depends on the engines which run on

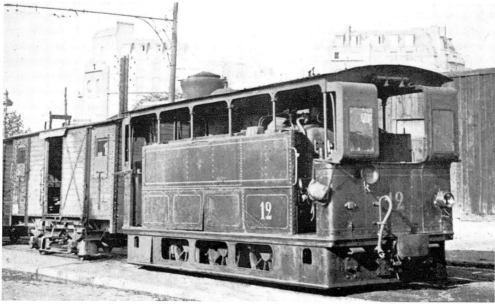

Tramway train on the Paris-Arpajon local line (1914).
(P. Ancel archive)

Tramway train on the Gargan-Livry line.

(Henry archive)

it. Three-axle locomotives weigh between 18 and 22 tons, 25 tons being the maximum limit. This means a 7–8 ton axle loading, with rails weighing 13 lbs per foot needed to carry such a weight. Other factors in reduced costs are: sleepers are shorter and less thick; station buildings can be dispensed with completely if so wished; the station-master's duties can be performed by someone from the village employed in a part-time capacity.

The 58-mile Anvin to Calais line cost 122,000 francs per mile. Other metre-gauge lines, covering a distance of 520 miles, cost 133,000 francs per mile. The 19-mile line from Le Mans to Grand-Lucé cost only 71,000 francs per mile because the route follows the roadway and there are no station buildings at all. About 1895, it was estimated that maintenance, renewal, traction and running costs were approximately fifty per cent lower than on standard gauge, and that the annual running cost was between 4,800 and 6,400 francs per mile. By contrast, a standard-gauge line

Metre-gauge locomotive on the Anvin-Calais line.

(*Nature*, 30 December 1882)

Uzerche-Argentat metre-gauge railway.

(Villain archive).

would cost 270,000–290,000 francs per mile to build.

Of course, metre-gauge track had its limitations, but these were acceptable on small lines. First, trains could not travel faster than 15–18 m.p.h. because of the sharp bends. On such a line, however, this speed was perfectly adequate. Second, local trains had to be transferred across main-line junctions, but since at the time traffic was not intensive, this caused little disruption. Finally, in France about 1895, it was generally thought that local lines should run on narrow gauge since most other countries had already adopted this system. Besides, the cost to government and municipal councils would be reduced, since installation and running costs would better reflect the amount of traffic using the line. Unfortunately such logic has not always been applied in the development of local lines in France.

TRAM RAILS

Between 1600 and 1650, mine owners in the Newcastle area were trying to secure lower transport costs from their mines to the port on the Tyne. Accordingly, they laid rows of wooden beams along the route to be taken, along which coal-trucks could run. About 1803, Woodhouse filed a patent to lay slightly concave iron beams on stone blocks or lengths of wood along ordinary roads. They were level with the ground, and cross-beams were used to ensure that they did not move. In 1821, between Gloucester and Cheltenham, a horse-tram carried passengers along lines of iron beams. Later, the beams were flanged. Various experiments followed, for example in Birmingham, where two of the coach's four wheels were fitted with tenons which engaged in holes in the rail. This system replaced the grooved rail. Eventually the double-flanged rail was adopted.

In 1852, M. Loubat, who had seen the use which was made of tramways in the United States, obtained permission to lay a track from the Place de la Concorde to Passy for the purposes of passenger transport. The American type of

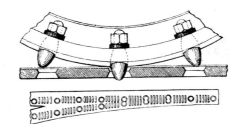

Top: Tramway wheel engaging with rail.
Above: Branching on a tramway rack rail.

(*Nature*, 19 February 1881)

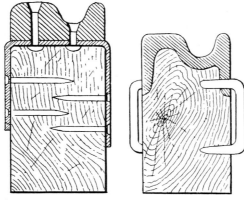

Left: An early rail on the Courbevoie-Suresnes line, about 1875.
Right: North Tramway network rail about 1875.

(Graffigny and Dumas Tramways)

These single-heel rails were fastened to the beams by vertical pins. About 1871, Lansen, a British engineer, who had built the Southern line in Paris, used double-heel rails weighing 20 lbs per foot.

About 1875, in Paris, the early Loubat rail was replaced by several types of rail, some without a heel, some with a double heel. On the Etoile and Suresnes lines, rails without heels were fixed to the beam as follows: first of all, holes were made in the rail and groove, but not in the beam itself. Screw-spikes were then riveted to a plate on the wooden beam. Finally, nails were driven through the sides of the plate into the beam itself. This was a complicated type of fixing and so, on the Northern Tramway line, the double-heel rail was fastened by side clamps which were hammered into the sides of the beam, with the top spike being driven through the corresponding heel of the rail.

From 1881 onwards, the Broca rail became widely used in Paris and many other towns. It was a grooved Vignole rail made of iron and was laid directly onto the ground. Since the base plate of the rail was broader than the wooden beams, the latter were no longer used. The correct distance between the Broca rails was maintained by oval stays which fitted neatly between the cobble-

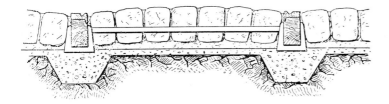

Cross-section of track on an early London tramway, about 1858.
(Graffigny and Dumas Tramways)

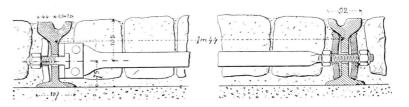

Cross-section of Broca-type track in Paris, in 1881.
(Graffigny and Dumas Tramways)

grooved rail was used. In 1854, this line was extended from Passy to Sèvres and in 1855 from Sèvres to Versailles. These 'American railways', as they were called at the time, ran at a loss until 1872, and did not begin to make a profit until their point of departure was transferred from the Place de la Concorde to the Louvre. In 1854, laying a 'Loubat track' cost 44,000 francs per mile and 48,000 francs on cobbled roadways.

About 1858, George Train built an 'American tramway' in London. The rails were laid in the following way: cobble-stones and tarmac were first of all taken up across the full width of the track and a hole was dug to about the depth of the cobbles. Along the line of the wooden beams a trench was excavated and concrete poured in up to ground level. Then, at regular intervals, iron blocks were sunk into the concrete and the wooden beams laid in them. Metal stays were used to maintain the distance between the two rails. The cobbles were then placed back in position. The rails weighed about 15 lbs per foot.

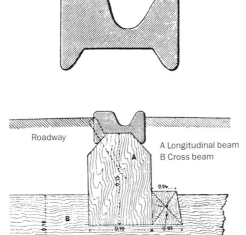

Roadway

A Longitudinal beam
B Cross beam

Centre: Cross-section of an early Loubat rail, and beam and sleeper supporting a Loubat tramway rail.

(*Nature*, 28 April 1877)

stones. A nut at each end of the stay enabled it to be tightened by the desired amount, and this made the system stronger and more solid than its predecessor since it was better able to withstand the coach's lateral thrust. Although more expensive, it was safer and easier to maintain, and particularly suited to mechanical traction. Track strength, in fact, became a problem as soon as animal-traction was replaced by steam-traction. In an article published on 23 February 1877 in *The Engineer*, it was stated that tram rails in London would not be strong enough for steam-traction since engine power on upward gradients would create a pressure of 4,400 lbs per wheel at contact point with the rail. Moreover, at the time, people had the strange idea that a tram should be light enough to leave the track if it was blocked and be able to run on the roadway, returning to the track further along the line. Apparently, this had been a standard procedure with horse-trams but was, of course, not possible when trams were driven by steam.

An open horse-tram 1876.

A closed horse-tram without a top deck (1876).

Tram carrying its own turntable.

Tram on its turntable at the terminus.

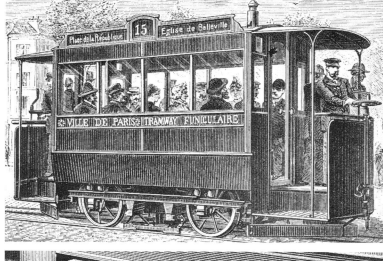

The funicular tram at Belleville.

Top: a coach. *Above*: the cable and brake mechanism.

(*Nature*, 4 October 1890).

The Chicago funicular tram.

Cross-section of coach and roadway showing mechanism. (*Nature*, 15 December 1883)

When horses fell sick in America – a tram pulled by men in a Boston street.

The loads which horses had to pull in the United States.

HORSE AND CABLE TRAMWAYS

The tramway was invented in Britain but was developed to a far greater extent in the United States, in view of the way in which American cities tended to be more spread out than European cities. The width of American streets provided ample space for the laying of tram lines and these, it was noted, reduced traction effort. On a cobbled road, an effort of 66 lbs is required to pull 1 ton, whereas on a smooth road surface an effort of 44 lbs is enough. On a tramway, this is reduced to only 18 lbs. On railways, where the rails are raised, rather than being grooved and consequently often filled with soil and dust, the effort required is a mere 6 lbs. In America, therefore, tramways were seen as a huge step forward.

On the flat, a tram moves far more smoothly than a horse-drawn omnibus. However, when it goes uphill it expends greater energy, both because of the weight it carries and the greater weight of the vehicle. On the other hand, on the downward slope there is a saving of energy, since the vehicle descends under its own weight. In 1893, this was the system used in both Denver,

Colorado and in California, where the tram carried its own horses as it went downhill.

Some tram coaches had a top deck, and some trams were symmetrical. On these, horses could be harnessed at the front and rear, but the trams could not leave the rails. Non-symmetrical trams often had a front set of wheels which could be used when the tram left the rails to travel briefly along the roadway.

The non-symmetrical Paris omnibus tramcar, with a top deck which was reached up a stairway from a platform at the rear of the car, seated 20 passengers on the lower deck and 22 to 24 on the top deck, with 6 more passengers able to travel on the platform. Like a rail-coach, the car had laminated steel springs and weighed 3¼ tons, with a laden weight of 6½ tons. The driver's seat was on the top deck, near to a release mechanism which controlled the front set of wheels. Three or four horses were needed to pull it.

The symmetrical Delettre-type tramcar, with a top deck and a platform at each end, was used on the Southern Tramway network in Paris. The driver stood on the front platform with the vertical brake-handle in front of him. Sixteen passengers could travel on the lower deck, 12 on the platforms and 24 on the upper deck. It had a weight of 2½ tons. The same kind of tram was also in service in Lyons. In Paris, there were also smaller tramcars, pulled by one or two horses: in some cases, these also had a top deck. On the small line from Porte Maillot to the Botanical Gardens, Suc-type open tramcars operated. They resembled charabancs and could hold up to 10 passengers. Two of these cars could be coupled together, and a single pony was sufficient to pull them and their load. This small, narrow-gauge tramway was immediately successful.

In Paris, a depot for tram horses contained stables, a section for sick horses, an area for fodder, a forge, a saddlery, sheds, workshops for

A horse-tram taking advantage of gravity down a steep incline to give the horses a rest.
(*Nature*, 14 December 1895)

repairs, a lamp store, a spare parts store and the depot manager's living-quarters and offices.

Another kind of tram traction, very popular in the United States and Canada but hardly developed at all in Europe, was cable traction. In France, this system operated only in Belleville in Paris, in Bellevue near Meudon, in Croix-Rousse and in Fourvière near Lyons.

By 1896, the United States and Canada had 845 miles of cable lines operated each day by 5,220 tramcars. The best examples of these were in Chicago and San Francisco. The perfectly straight main roads of America's new towns and cities were ideally suited to this type of traction. Problems, however, were encountered where routes crossed. When this happened the 'gripman', or driver, had to release the grip when the tramcar passed beneath the other cable. If he forgot to do this, a stop pin broke the grip. This was, of course, far less serious than breakage of the cable

itself. The track was very strong and weighed 28 lbs per foot.

San Francisco's cable-cars were first built in 1873 and eventually covered a distance of 105 miles. By 1892, the cable tramway there had carried 92,981,606 paying passengers, at speeds of 9 m.p.h. and occasionally even 12 m.p.h. Los Angeles also had a very fine cable system.

A cable tramway is expensive to build, the one in Edinburgh costing 1,368,000 francs per mile. The Belleville cable tramway in Paris which was only 1¼ miles long was built in 1889 and cost 1,300,000 francs. One of the advantages of this type of system is the very low deadweight, particularly on steeply sloping lines. There are no problems of adhesion, and it is a simple matter to increase capacity, since one merely has to add more cars and this involves little extra cost. Moreover, there are no exhaust fumes, no noise and no smell.

Changing horses in mid-journey, about 1895.

Lamm and Francq steam-tram. The locomotive had no firebox.
(*Nature*, 9 November 1878).

STEAM TRAMWAYS

About 1875, the respective merits of the horse-tram and the steam-tram were frequently discussed. In favour of the latter it was argued that the number of cars operating at any one time could be varied to match the number of passengers needing transport and that this system did not require a huge number of horses to be fed all week when they might work only on a Sunday or a Bank Holiday. It was, on the other hand, agreed that the smoke from a steam-tram, the sparks it emitted which could cause fires, and its noise,

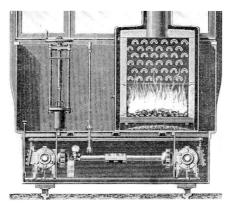

Cross-section of a Serpollet boiler for use on a tram railcar.
(*Nature*, 10 February 1894).

which often terrified horses, were strong arguments against its use.

In fact, a steam locomotive which gave off no smoke and no sparks operated in 1874 in the United States between New Orleans and Carrolton. At normal atmospheric pressure, water boils at 100°C. If the pressure rises, the temperature at which water boils also rises. When water is heated in an enclosed space to 100°C, it cannot boil because steam accumulates and cannot escape. The temperature continues to rise, but the water will boil only if the pressure is reduced as a result of the steam being allowed to escape. This is what occurs when steam is used to drive a piston. The

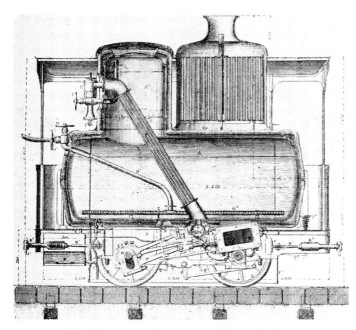

The Francq tram locomotive without a firebox.
(*Les Automobiles*: Farman)

Grantham steam-tram which entered service in London in 1873.
(Model from the Science Museum, London)

Inauguration of steam-trams propelled by a Harding locomotive between Gare Montparnasse and Gare de l'Austerlitz

Lamm locomotive in New Orleans operated on this principle, and with some modifications by Francq it ran in 1878 between Rueil and Marly. At the start of the journey, 395 gallons of water were heated to 200°C. The boiler was covered in insulating materials such as ash, plaster, wood, to prevent its cooling too quickly. In this way sparks and fumes were avoided, and deadweight was reduced since there was no firebox, tender or coal. Such a system could not, however, be used on a journey of more than 9 miles.

Later, the success of the Serpollet boiler, with its instant steam-generation using capillary water-tubes and providing superheated steam, led to the development of a different type of steam-tram. The boiler being much less bulky, it became possible to build steam railcars similar to the tram which was in service in 1890 between the

Interior of the Purrey boiler for use on a steam-tram railcar.

(*Nature*, 14 February 1903).

Madeleine and place Clichy. Its weight, including fuel, was 7½ tons and it could carry 40 passengers. Laden it had a total weight of 13 tons. About 1895, Rowan-type steam railcars, fitted with a steam condenser on top of the car, operated in Paris between the Louvre and Boulogne and also on the Tours–Vouvray line. The bogie had a vertical boiler and the rear of the car rested on a single axle. Coke consumption was just over 10 lbs per mile.

In 1897, the Paris Southern Tramway successfully tested small Purrey-type steam railcars, which carried a much reduced volume of water. Use of this same system was common in 1900 on many lines. On the Bastille–Rapp, Gare de Lyon–Alma, Créteil–Louvre, and Louvre–Vincennes lines it replaced the Blot-type storage-battery electric railcars.

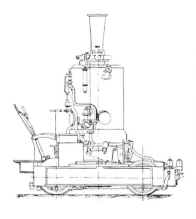

Rowan boiler.

(*Les Automobiles*: Farman)

Rowan's steam-tram railcar built in 1887.

(Ganz company, Budapest)

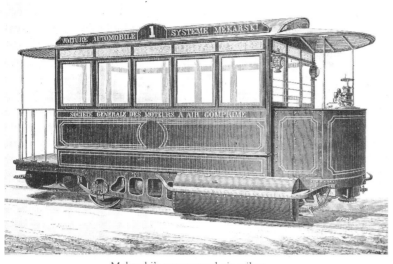

Mekarski's compressed-air railcar.
(*Nature*, 19 February 1876)

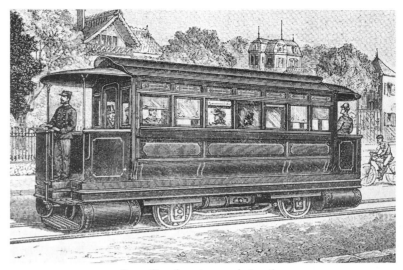

Popp-Conti's compressed-air railcar.
(*Nature*, 22 February 1896)

VARIOUS TRAMWAY MECHANICAL TRACTION SYSTEMS

The first application of compressed-air traction to tramways was in 1879 on the Doulon–Chantenay line near Nantes. A compressed-air railcar was already in operation in 1840. In 1872, Mekarski had started to carry out tests on a type of locomotive being built at Le Creusot. The engine, which might have been a locomotive or a railcar, not only had a supply of compressed air but also a tank filled with hot water. This would be used to heat the air after it had been cooled by expansion and before it arrived at the driving-cylinders. At the terminus, the supply of compressed air was renewed, and the water was reheated by a steam blast from a stationary boiler.

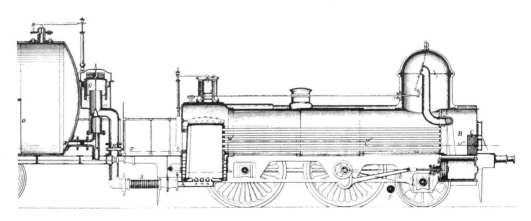

Gas locomotive, without smoke or exhaust steam, built to Charpentier's design (1872).

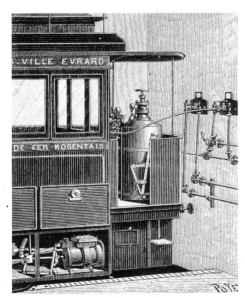

Recharging compressed air.
The compressed air was produced and sent directly from the factory to various points on the track.
(*Nature*, 31 December 1887).

Compressed-air intake on track.

In 1900, on the Passy-Hôtel de Ville line, the water was heated continuously by a firebox inside the tank itself. On the Montrouge-Gare de l'Est line, the compressed air was stored at a pressure of 448 lbs per square inch and its consumption rate was 49 lbs per mile. After travelling 10 miles, pressure was still as high as 26 lbs. To heat the water in the tank, 2 lbs of coke were used per mile. Compressed-air traction was, therefore, more efficient with the continuous-heating system than with Mekarski's system. A further advantage was that it could be used on lines where the terminus station could not accommodate a reheating boiler. The compressed-air plant for the Montrouge, Passy, Auteuil and La Muette lines was next to the Seine in Billancourt, and steel pipes were used to distribute the air to the various depots and stations. On the Montrouge line, these underground pipes were over 4 miles long. The Mekarski system continued to be used on the Nogent Railway between Vincennes and Evrard.

With the Popp-Conti system, compressed-air pressure is lower. The air reservoir is, therefore, lighter and the plant producing compressed air becomes less important even though the railcar has to be recharged every mile or two. Although the system functions more efficiently than Mekarski's, installation costs are higher because a greater number of compressed-air intake points is needed. In fact, compressed-air traction is only moderately effective and consumes a great deal of fuel. However, it is pollution-free and very flexible, coping equally well with hilly areas and irregular use.

The desire to rid urban areas of smoke and fumes led engineers to tak an interest in gas. In 1872, Charpentier argued in favour of a gas locomotive in which the burning residue, after combustion, was directed into the water reservoir where it heated the water to a temperature of 100°C. The reservoir was linked to the water-tanks on the side of the engine and these acted as steam-condensers. As a consequence, there was no exhaustion of steam. Although the design was supported by local councils for use on a metropolitan railway, it was never developed.

However, the invention of the internal combustion engine led to the idea of using gas combustion in the driving-cylinder itself. About 1895, therefore, when Otto's gas engine was fully developed, gas trams ran in Dresden, Dessau and Blackpool. They were fitted with compressed-air tanks and had two driving-axles. The axles were driven by chains which connected to a friction clutch, gears and reverse and forward drives.

As a result the Paris omnibus company decided to test gas traction on the La Villette-Nation line. This was welcome news to gas companies, who had lost a great deal of business as a consequence of the increasing popularity of electric lighting. Nevertheless, electric traction was eventually preferred.

Another system, which was tested unsuccessfully, was Honingmann's lye locomotive. This steam-engine was not fitted with a firebox, the steam being generated by concentrated lye which covered and heated the boiler's water-filled elements. One property of saline solutions is that they absorb steam, and their temperature rises higher than that of the steam they have absorbed. The steam used was in fact exhausted steam. As

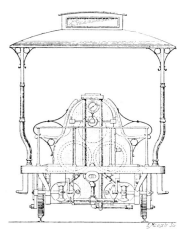

Front view of ammonia tram.
(*Nature*, 13 February 1892)

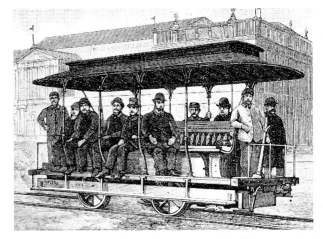

Ammonia-engine tram tested in Chicago.
(*Nature*, 13 February 1892)

Honingmann's lye locomotive for use on tramways.
(*Nature*, 19 December 1885)

this is released, the water in the boiler tends to cool, at which point the lye heats the water and maintains both the temperature of the water and the correct steam-pressure. Moreover, the lye itself remains at a constant temperature by absorbing the exhausted steam. The problem with the steam is that the metal of the boiler is corroded by the lye.

A similar type of system using an ammonia solution was also tested. This was heated to a temperature of 27°C. It released steam at a pressure of 10 atmospheres and this operated a driving-cylinder. Then the steam condensed in the water-tank which contained the tank of liquid ammonia. It heated the ammonia and the cycle repeated itself without any loss of heat. This was the system used in 1892 in Chicago on an ammonia tram built by MacMahon, a former engineer in the American Navy. The results of these tests were fairly satisfactory.

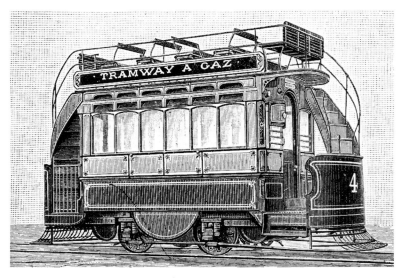

A gas tram.
(*Nature*, 29 August 1896)

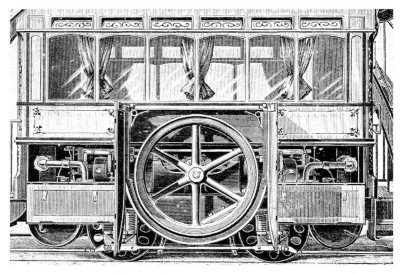

Internal layout of a gas tram showing its flywheel.
(*Nature*, 29 August 1896)

THE BEGINNINGS OF ELECTRIC TRACTION

In 1879, at Sermaize (Marne), tests were carried out by Félix and Chrétien to devise a means of using electric energy to plough a field. As a result of these tests, Siemens and Halske built the first electric railway for the industrial exhibition in Berlin. A small electric locomotive pulled three open waggons round a circular track at a speed of approximately 7½ m.p.h. An uninsulated strap centre-rail, made first of all of iron then later of copper, was laid directly onto the same sleepers as the rails. The current ran along this centre-rail from a dynamo. It was then fed into the locomotive's electric motor through metal brushes which made contact with the centre-rail's two side faces. The current then returned to the dynamo along the outer rails. The Siemens traction engine was like a locomotive fitted with only its driving

The first electric railway, built by Siemens and Halske for the 1879 Berlin Exhibition.
(*Nature*, 24 January 1880).

Testing a trolley in 1881 on a tram
in Charlottenburg.

(*Le Règne de l'électricité*: Gaston Bonnefont, 1895)

mechanism, that is, without a firebox and boiler, and as if steam were being fed to it from a power plant along a pipe. The deadweight was thereby reduced and this explains why the Siemens locomotive appears so small in comparison with the train it pulled.

After the success of these tests, the first electric tram was put into service between Lichterfeld station and the Cadets School near Berlin. The tramway was opened on 16 May 1881, and ran for a distance of 1½ miles on metre-gauge track. Electric power was transmitted very simply, one of the outer rails taking current to the engine, with return current via the other rail.

In streets, the safest system seemed to be to use overhead wiring fixed to posts. The first practical application of this system was by the Siemens brothers at the International Electricity Exhibi-

Testing a trolley in 1890 on a tram in Lichterfeld.

(*50 jahre elektrische Bahnen*: Siemens and Schuckert)

tion in Paris in 1881 on a track which went from the Palace of Industry to the Place de la Concorde. 'Two tubes split' along their bottom length took the current to and from the car. Flexible cables were used to attach these 'tubes' to the engine, and they pulled a sliding shuttle along the inside of the tubes through slots.

The 'twin overhead conductor' was also installed by Siemens and Halske on the Modling to Hinterbrulh line near Vienna in 1883, and on the Frankfurt–Offenbach line in 1884. Insulation was such that a 500-volt current was possible. The same system was used in 1886 on the Vevey–Montreux line.

The single overhead wire, with current returning via the rails, was introduced to Leeds in 1890 by Americans, and then taken to Florence and Brême.

On the Continent, various firms adopted it and in 1890 it was tested on a new section of the Lichterfeld line near Berlin by Siemens and Halske, who used the sliding bow to pick up current since this proved to be a much better system when the car had to pass through a junction.

Siemens electric tramway and electric lighting in the Place de la Concorde.
(*Le Règne de l'électricité*: Gaston Bonnefont, 1895)

Moving from one walkway to the next.

The moving walkway had two sections side by side which progressed at different speeds. One moved at 2½ m.p.h. and the other at 5 m.p.h. There was also a fixed path.

There was much cause for amusement as passengers attempted to move from one to the other.

The moving walkway near the Eiffel Tower.

The slower walkway moved at little more than walking pace. The faster walkway was 2 miles long, and could carry 63,000 passengers an hour.

It was an endless chain of trucks running on rails.

THE MOVING WALKWAY AT THE PARIS EXHIBITION, 1900

(*Le Panorama*, 14 April 1900. Photo: Neurdein Frères)

VARIOUS SYSTEMS OF ELECTRIC TRAMWAYS

What the Lichterfeld tramway, and Edison's experiments in 1880 in his Menle Park laboratory in the United States, focused attention on, was the need to insulate the power lead in order to avoid electric current running to earth. In coal mines this was a simple matter, since the conductor could be fixed to the ceiling of the tunnel as was the case in Zauckeroed in Saxony (1883), in Neu Stassfurt (1883), and in Hohenzollern near Beuthen in Upper Silesia (1884). However, local councils protested against the use of overhead wires, and engineers tried to devise a system of ground-level or underground power transmissions. In 1884, the Blackpool tramway operated with a central duct invented by Holroyd Smith. A single conductor ran along this duct and the current returned via the track. However, maintenance costs were enormous and the system was abandoned. Moreover, in Europe, Plante's storage battery had made its appearance, and the modifications made to it had considerably reduced its weight, so that it became a source of energy which could be used by trams. In 1880, an electric locomotive and its tender, filled with storage batteries, were used to hang out linen in M. Duchesne-Fournet's laundry at Breuil-en-Auge (Calvados).

On 25 May 1881, an electric car, fitted by Raffard with 225 Faure electric cells, was tested on the Vincennes tramway line. It was an ordinary omnibus company 50-seater coach, with a Gramme dynamo at the rear. A countershaft, operated by a drive belt, transmitted power to the two driving-wheels by means of a system of cog-wheels and chains. Storage-battery trams were also tested on the Metropolitan line in London and, following the 1885 Antwerp Exhibition, they ran regularly on commercial lines.

However, the deadweight of storage batteries, their high maintenance costs and their limited power, were all factors which hindered their development. Fortunately for electric traction, the Americans were not discouraged by these European constraints. Moreover, such a means of transport was admirably suited to the American way of life, with its rapid expansion of towns and industrial zones, its constant desire to save time, the generally poor conditions of its roads, the long distances Americans had to travel, their tendency to build homes far from the city centres where they worked, the almost total absence of administrative obstacles, and the extreme ease with which new concessions could be obtained and old ones modified. All these factors resulted in electric traction developing and expanding at a far faster rate in America than in Europe.

In Spring 1883, Van Depoele, a Belgian living

An electric colliery train in 1882.
(Deutsches Museum, Munich)

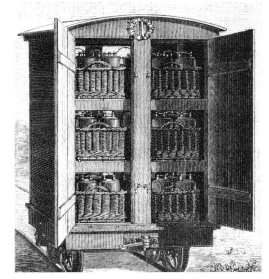

Top: Faure storage-battery tender.
Above: Electric locomotive with rheostat.
ELECTRIC RAILWAY USED AT A FACTORY
IN BRUEIL–EN–AUGE (CALVADOS).
(*Nature*, 6 May 1882)

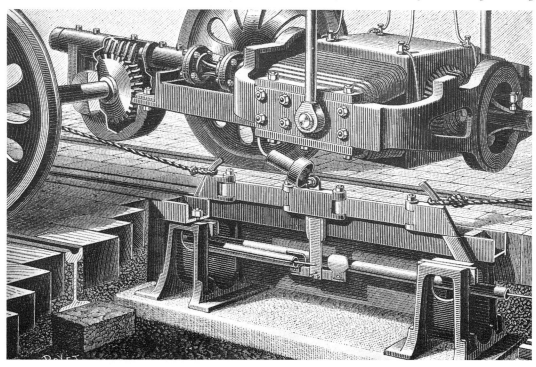

Motor, central conductor and current pick-up system on electric tramway in Blackpool.
(*Nature*, 27 November 1886)

Faure battery tram, built by Raffard, and operating in Paris in May 1881.
(Conservatoire des arts et métriers)

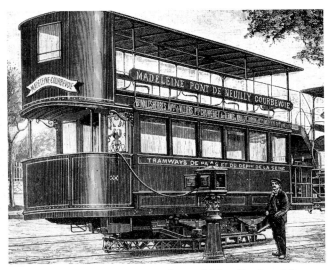

Recharging a battery tram on the Madeleine-Courbevoi line.
(*Nature*, 10 July 1897).

in America, built a car with a 3 h.p. engine which ran on a small test line with overhead wires. A few months later, for the Chicago Exhibition, he built another overhead line, and then a third line with underground wires. A current of 2,500 volts was passed safely through these, the current returning via the rails.

In 1884, in Cleveland, Ohio, Betney and Knight built the first electric tramway and it ran a distance of 1¾ miles. The power lead was laid underground in a duct which ran between the two lines. Current was picked up through a slot in the top of the duct.

At the end of 1886, Henry introduced an interesting variation on a small line in Kansas City. He replaced the tubes used in Europe on the twin overhead conductor by two wires. Current was picked up by a trolley which passed above the wires and was pulled along by a cable connected to the car. Different systems of current pick-up were tested in the United States, and only after several years of unsuccessful experiments was the single-pulley system adopted. In this case, contact was made from below, which reduced pressure

Grooved channel, with continuous contact being made with the trolleys of both inward and outward vehicles.
(*Nature*, 14 March 1896)

on the wire, and the result was a much lighter and more attractive system.

In 1887, Frank Sprague built a tram which succeeded in climbing a 1 in 10 gradient in Richmond. However, the motor overheated and broke down. A new type of motor was therefore fitted to 60 cars and the service resumed in February 1888. But there were more setbacks and Sprague later said that he tested at least 65 diffe-

rent kinds of trolley before finding one which worked.

By the end of 1887, 65 miles of lines were electrified in America, most with overhead wires. Some people still favoured two overhead wires, some one, with current return via the rails. Eventually, the single wire prevailed as a result of the work of Sprague and Van Depoele.

In France, the first electric tramway was installed in Clermont-Ferrand, built by Claret, using Swiss Thury stock. Although the trolley was by now in widespread use in the United States, the old-fashioned split tube with its sliding shuttle was adopted in Clermont. This was followed by tramways running from Marseilles to Saint-Louis (1892), from Bordeaux to Vigan (1893), from Lyons to Le Havre (1894), and in Paris from the Place de la Republique to Romainville (1896). All of these operated using Claret-Vuilleumier's ground-level conductor system. Storage-battery trams then appeared on the Madeleine to Courbevoie and Neuilly to Levallois lines (1897). A mixed traction tram, using storage batteries and overhead wire, ran from Paris to Pantin and Aubervilliers (1898). Finally, a mixed traction electric tramway was built in 1899 in the Bois de Boulogne, making use of trolleys and Vedovelli's ground-level contact system.

The Claret-Vuilleumier tramway on the République-Romainville line.
Current is distributed when vehicles pass over contacts on the ground.
(*Nature*, 11 July 1896)

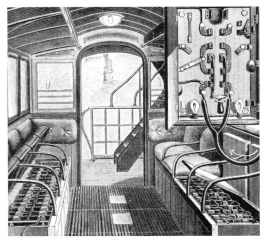

Interior of a battery tram, showing charging panel.
(*Nature*, 10 July 1897).

METROPOLITAN RAILWAYS

Towards the end of the nineteenth century, factors such as rapid, urban expansion in the United States, distances between place of work and home, and the need to reduce travel time from one to the other, contributed to the development of not only electric tramways but also overhead and underground railways.

These rapid means of travel were particularly suited to a city like New York, which had tended to expand lengthwise. In 1878, therefore, its elevated railway was built. The Americans, being less patient than the British, preferred this to the underground system, since it was quicker to build. From its opening, a ticket cost 10 cents, whatever the distance of the journey. Initially, cable traction had been considered, but small steam locomotives were preferred. However, the noise they made and the fumes and steam they gave off made them unpopular and a different form of traction was sought.

So, in 1882, the compressed-air locomotive was tried again. It had been tested in 1879 but not adopted. The new type was based on Mekarski's system. The large metal-plate tanks of the locomotive were filled with air compressed to a pressure of 600 lbs per square inch. The air left the tank and was heated to a temperature of 90°C. It then went to the driving-cylinders and reached there with a pressure of only about 115–130 lbs per square inch. As the air passed over the boiling water in the boiler, it became saturated with steam. The cylinders were therefore driven by a mixture of air and steam. As on Riggenbach's rack locomotives, the driving-cylinders acted as brakes on downhill slopes.

By 1885, electric traction could be found virtually everywhere, and Leo Daft, an American locomotive-builder, constructed the *Ben Franklin*, an electric locomotive which ran from 26 August 1885 for several weeks on the Ninth Avenue elevated line. The engine was 14 feet long and weighed approximately 9 tons. Current was fed to it from an insulated centre-rail, by means of a

New York's elevated railway.
View from Chatam Square at the junction of Second and Third Avenue lines.

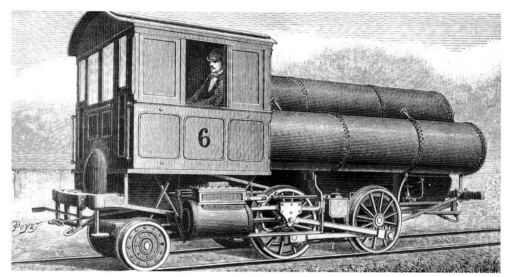

Compressed-air locomotive used on the New York elevated railway.
(*Nature*, 17 June 1882)

phosphor wheel which could be raised or lowered. The steel conductor-rail was laid on cast-iron supports, fixed to hardwood blocks, saturated in asphalt in order to insulate them. In 1888, this locomotive was rebuilt and pulled a train of four coaches. Current of 250 volts came from a centre-rail. Where it crossed other lines, electric feed was from an overhead wire.

By 1881, Berlin also had its elevated railway. The viaducts along which the track was laid were built from stone and not, as in New York, metal, because of the noise made by passing trains. Stations were on two levels, with the ground-floor level being occupied solely by waiting-rooms. The tank-engines were fired by coke to minimise smoke emission, and the exhaust steam was fed into a special condensation cylinder, rather than being released into the atmosphere. The railway crossed the city from east to west, a distance of 6¾ miles. According to the *National Zeitung* of 7 February 1882, the railway had a

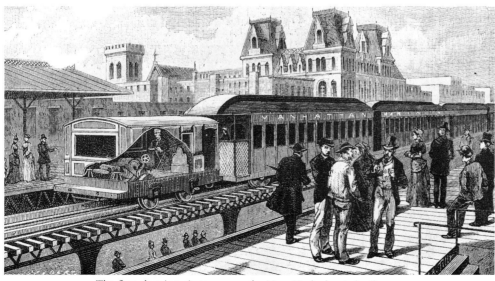

The first electric train to run on the New York elevated railway.
(*Nature*, 26 December 1885)

Layout of track and station on the Liverpool overhead electric railway.
(*Nature*, 29 April 1893)

mainly strategic purpose. 'The Friedrichstrasse Metropolitan Station is a vitally important centre for the strength of Germany and Prussia. When one considers the network of lines which enter and leave it, one sees how essential it is to defence and attack.' In 1902, the Berlin overhead railway was electrified, and was one of the first to use direct current with an average voltage of 800 volts at a time when electric traction had not dared exceed 600 volts elsewhere.

However, the first electric overhead railway was built in 1893 in Liverpool, and was intended to serve the docks which extend along the right bank of the Mersey for more than 6 miles. It replaced a horse tramway line. Steam-traction had been considered but the risk of fire was thought to be too great. The electric feed was by means of a U-iron, with current returning along the rails. Porcelain insulators were placed every 6½ feet on wooden sleepers. Each train consisted of two railcars, 40 feet long, weighing almost 17 tons and carrying 56 passengers. Average speed was more than 30 m.p.h., producing 32 h.p. Using various resistors, speeds of 7, 18, 30 and 47 m.p.h. could be achieved. On 26 January 1893,

First electric locomotive on the City & South London Railway tube line (1890).
(From the original in the Science Museum, London)

when the tramway was tested, the train reached a speed of 50 m.p.h.

In the same year, the Columbian electric overhead metropolitan railway ran at the Chicago Exhibition. At the time, it was the most powerful in the world, since on 4 July, American Independence Day, it carried almost 63,000 passengers. During September, its traffic increased to 1,000,000 passengers. Consequently, between 1895 and 1897, a complete network of electric metropolitan railways with a potential of 600 volts was built in Chicago. They were the Metropolitan West Side Elevated Line, Lake Street Elevated Line, and South Side Elevated Line.

London had had a metropolitan railway since 1863. This was, in fact, the first to be built. However, it was an underground system, and because of the problems caused by smoke from the steam locomotives in the long tunnels, it is not surprising that, in 1890, 7½ miles of double track of the City and South London line, were electrified. Built in 1897, London's electric metropolitan railway preceded Paris's by three years. At that time, London had the most integrated transport system in the world. In 1898, a passenger arriving at Victoria Station had only to cross the station-yard to enter the underground system, from which he could take a train to almost anywhere in the city or its suburbs.

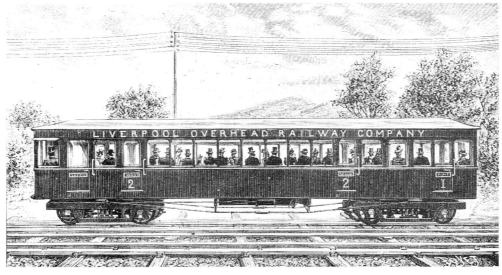

An electric railcar on the Liverpool overhead railway.
(*Nature*, 29 April 1893)

Construction work above ground at the Gare de Lyon in 1900.
(Paris Metro archive)

Shaft used for underground workings about 1905.
(Paris Metro archive)

BUILDING THE PARIS METRO

Though Paris was the last of the great capitals in the world to have its metropolitan railway, it had been the first to plan one. In 1853, Brame and Flachat designed a project to create an underground link between the market at les Halles and the outskirts of the city. In 1871, a network was accepted in principle by the city council, which decided that such a system should meet three requirements. It must link the different parts of the Department of the Seine to a circle line running inside the one already in existence. It must link the districts of Paris to one another and to the centre, the boulevards and the quay sides, and it must link the main-line stations to one another. When, in 1883, the bill was put before Parliament, it accepted in general terms the value and importance of such a scheme, but it did not grant the concession to the City of Paris. This created a great deal of conflict between the State and the city council, a conflict which lasted for twenty years as arguments raged about the merits and demerits of the various schemes. The Government condemned out of hand any system which did not link up directly with the major networks. The city council claimed that without a vast increase in the number of lines it was impossible to build two systems – one based purely on local needs and one which took into account wider issues and requirements – without severely damaging one of the two systems. Moreover, the city council wanted sole control of this new means of transport built on its land, and financed by itself alone without any help from the State.

Finally, on 22 November 1895, the State gave in and accepted that the city had the right to build local lines which served the interests of the city. A law was passed on 30 March 1898 which declared that it was in the public interest that a metropolitan railway consisting of five lines with a total length of 40 miles should be built. Three names will always be associated with the building of this railway. They are Bienvenue, an Inspector in the Department of Transport, Baron Empain, and M.A. Berthelot.

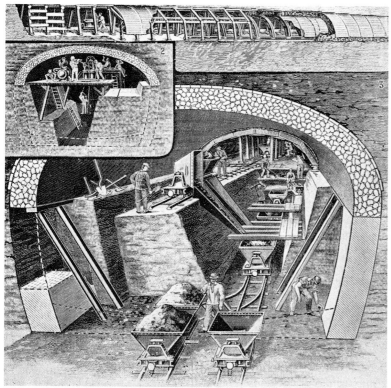

Working underground.
Top: first stages in tunnel building showing excavation, shoring up beams and construction of the arched roof. *Left*: Injection of mortar behind the arched roof. *Bottom*: building the support walls and floor.
(*Nature*, 2 December 1905)

Reinforcing the underground.
Stone supports had to be built where there had been underground quarry workings in Paris. In these areas, where there was a risk of land movement, the tunnel was constructed on stone pillars.
(*Nature*, 29 March 1902)

Austerlitz Bridge on the Metro seen from the Gare d'Orleans (The Gare de Lyon can be seen in the background).

Place Cambronne on the Metro. In the background, can be seen the big wheel and the Eiffel Tower.

Many different plans had already been drawn up purporting to resolve the technical difficulties. A model of an overhead electric railway had been displayed at the Electricity Exhibition in 1881. Its author, Chrétien, was the same man who, in 1879, had tested an electric plough and had demonstrated the possibility of transporting electric energy. He envisaged constructing a railway along the boulevards between the Madeleine and the Bastille. It would run on a double track along a viaduct supported on columns at intervals of 130–160 feet in the middle of the roadway. In 1885, another plan for an overhead metropolitan railway was presented, this time by Jules Garnier. In his system, there were two levels, with the tracks running one above the other rather than side by side. One level would be for outward traffic, the other for return traffic. Supporters of an overhead railway system also argued that the underground alternative would be much more expensive and would force 'travellers to walk around like moles in cold, dark, damp underground passageways'. In fact, victory eventually went to the underground system, mainly on the grounds that it would be less unsightly and would pose fewer problems to town planners. In 1890, the Northern Railway proposed a system of traction using 'train trams' similar to those running on the Paris–Saint–Denis line. To avoid the emission of steam and smoke in the underground tunnels, the locomotives carried a considerable supply of water and condensers. In 1895, the building of the Sceaux Railway's underground track proved to be very instructive since the work was carried out beneath extremely busy roads and above the Paris catacombs.

Work began in 1898 on the Bois de Boulogne–Bois de Vincennes line with electric-traction as the sole means of transport. Two methods of

Paul Bienvenue.
Inspector and President of the Paris underground from its beginnings in 1898. He was nicknamed 'Father of the Metro'.

digging tunnels were adopted: working at ground level, as on the New York Metropolitan Railway, or shoring up tunnels with timber, the method used by the old railway entrepreneurs, but modified and adapted where the nature of the ground so required. This method had the advantage of never interrupting the flow of traffic at ground level, and all that was visible was the occasional shaft used to excavate soil. In 1900, this second solution was adopted except for a few sections of line as, for example, in the vicinity of the Gare de Lyon. The first stage was to dig a heading. This was then widened, timber supports were placed in position, and the arched top of the tunnel was completed. The walls were then built from the ceiling downwards. Where the tunnel passed through sections of loose soil and rocks caused by

old quarry workings, stone pillars were built to support the galleries.

On certain sections, in particular a part of the Vincennes–Maillot line, the tunnel had to be built using water-proof materials since it was below the Seine water-table. At the Opéra, the engineers encountered an underground swamp created by water filtering through from Grange–Batelière. In the very centre of the square, three lines had to be built above one another, the first from Courcelles towards Menilmontant along the rue du 4 Septembre, the second beneath the Palais-Royal towards the place du Danube, and the third beneath the previous two and the boulevards leading to Auteuil. These three underground tunnels were more than 30 feet below the roadway, and the water-table was less than 30 feet below it. Construction work took place, therefore, in an underground swamp, and a huge watertight concrete block had to be built in the very centre of the square outside the Opéra. The three superimposed lines, with two levels of metal bridges, were built inside this concrete block.

The Metro also has sections which are above ground where, for example, it has had to cross main-line railway lines and the Saint-Martin Canal. Any underground section here would have had to run beneath the main lines and would have been so deep that access to nearby stations would have presented considerable difficulty. The line passes, therefore, across a viaduct and, contrary to what was thought at the time, this proved to be more expensive than the underground tunnels. It was a parabolic-span-type viaduct and had to satisfy two basic conditions. It had to be high enough for double-decker trams on the Saint-Augustin–Vincennes line to pass beneath, and it had to ensure minimum disruption to traffic below.

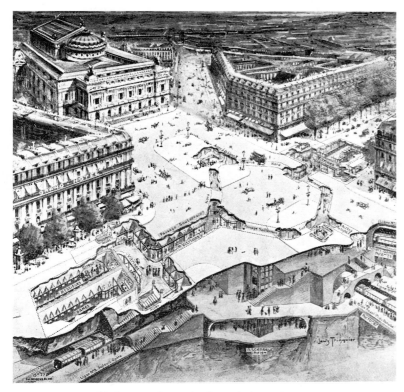

Underground complex beneath the station at the Place de l'Opera.
(L'Illustration, 5 November 1910).

An overhead section of the Metro which crosses La Villette roundabout on a curved viaduct. (L'Illustration, 31 January 1903)

An early type of two-door railcar used
on the Paris Metro.

A three-door railcar with bogies and two 175 h.p. engines (1912).
(Photo: Metro)

RUNNING A METROPOLITAN RAILWAY

The automatic block signal pedal as the train leaves the Gare d'Austerlitz for the Etoile (1905).
(Photo: Metro)

At the same time as the electric-traction Metro was being built in Paris, between 1900 and 1902, the old overhead steam-traction railway in Berlin was being electrified. Water below ground made the building of an underground system impossible. Therefore, in certain streets people had to tolerate the noise of trains running on overhead lines. It was not until the line reached the district round Charlottenburg and Potsdam station that it could pass underground.

This structural difference in the two networks resulted in operational differences. In Paris, lines were not allowed to branch off and so passengers had to change trains. On the other hand, in Berlin, trains could run from each of the three terminals to the other two. Branch lines, forming a kind of triangle, ran in all three directions, and this necessitated a system of points at different heights to prevent lines from cutting across one another.

One particular feature of the Berlin railway was its 800-volt current, which was remarkably high

Cross-section views of different underground tunnels. 1. Sceaux Railway; 2. Central London;
3. Glasgow; 4. Boston; 5. Paris; 6. Berlin.
(*Nature*, 6 September 1902)

'A first-class ticket, please'.

A Parisienne settles down in comfort.

(*Femina* 1903, an article by H. Duvernois)

Dante and Virgil in Hell, watching passengers jostle each other on the underground.

(A painting by Albert Guillaume – photo: Braun)

for the time. The Paris Metro, which was also direct current, was 600 volts. On both railways, the electric circuit consisted of an insulated centre conductor rail connected to a positive pole in the sub-stations. The circuit was completed by the track rails which had a zero earth potential. At first, in Paris, electric energy was provided only by the Rapée power station. Its 5000-volt current was transformed into 600-volt direct current by two sub-stations.

In 1910, the new North–South Metro line was opened from Montmartre to Vaugirard. Berlier, the promoter of the line, had envisaged sinking metal tubes to a considerable depth. However, this idea was abandoned and construction went ahead following the same system as for the rest of the Metro, that is, double-track stone tunnels, elliptical in shape and not far below ground level. The famous 'Berlier' tube, a type of metal tunnel favoured in London, was used only where the railway passed under the Seine.

Direct current was also used on the North–South line but electric equipment was different from that of the Metro. A positive 600-volt insulated rail, a negative 600-volt overhead wire, and a zero potential track constituted 'three conductor and two bridge distribution', which was equivalent to 1,200-volt two-wire ordinary distribution.

In 1911, the tunnel through Montmartre on the North–South line was a remarkably bold piece of engineering. The hill was in fact riddled with gypsum workings which followed no set pattern. In some areas, the tunnel had to be built beneath the old quarries, and cement had to be injected into the ground above the tunnel while the tunnel roof was under construction.

The Paris Metro and the North–South line were the first railways in France to use the luminous automatic block system. An electric current running continuously along the line keeps the signals in the 'track clear' position. The current is broken when a train makes contact with the end of a pedal at the side of the rail and the signal then shows 'Stop'.

Traction on both these railways was by 'multiple motive-power units with synchronised controls'. Before the current is fed into the motor, it passes through control monitors in the driver's cab at the front of the car. These monitors are not operated manually since this would require the presence of a driver in each car. A weak auxiliary current, called a control current, operates a remote control system. The current is carried from coach to coach by cable and is itself controlled by the driver at the front of the train. This explains why passengers often see the electro-magnetic contactors moving in the empty driver's cab. In the event of any possible danger, the brakes are applied and the current reversed, and the train stops almost dead. Such an action, however, considerably damages the rolling-stock and may result in passengers and staff sustaining serious injury.

Obligado Metro station in 1903.

Bac station on the North–South line in 1910.

THE VARIOUS STAGES IN THE TRANSMISSION OF ELECTRIC ENERGY FOR USE ON THE RAILWAYS

Top left: Water runs from an artificial lake down pipes to a power station. Here high-tension electricity (150,000 to 200,000 volts) is produced, since high tension is cheaper to transport over a long distance (considerable savings are made on the wires needed). In the three-phase form (a line with three wires), this alternating energy goes to the distribution centre (in the middle of the picture). Here the tension of the current is reduced to 15,000 volts and it is then sent to various sub-stations.

In the foreground: in one of the sub-stations rotary current converters transform the three-phase current to 600-volt direct current.

Bottom left: the wire from the sub-station feeds the catenary contact line above the track. (Drawing by M. A. Jahan).

FIRST TESTS OF SELF-PROPELLING ELECTRIC TRACTION

Distance transmission of electric energy had always been seen as complicated and costly and many engineers therefore sought to invent a system of self-propelling electric traction. The invention of storage batteries raised many hopes.

In 1894 and 1897, an engineer called Heilmann carried out various tests to build a self-propelling electric locomotive for the Western Railway. It was, in fact, a steam locomotive which drove a dynamo which in turn fed current to motors fitted to the locomotive's eight axles. The axles were in groups of four per bogie. It was a maximum adhesion locomotive weighing 125 tons. Since connecting rods were not needed for the axles, it was easier for the locomotive to negotiate curves in the track. Apart from its flexibility, this locomotive had a further advantage in that the absence of connecting rods reduced considerably sideways and rocking movement, and this led to considerable savings on track maintenance costs. The Belpaire-type fire-tube boiler fed a twelve-cylinder vertical steam motor. The cylinders drove two dynamos which were excited by a special small dynamo. The locomotive pulled a 45-ton tender-guard's van which carried 20 tons of water. Together, they weighed 170 tons and produced 1,000 h.p. Generally, steam locomotives of the time developed the same power but with a weight of only 80 tons, thus producing the same power at only half the weight. That is why Heilmann's engines were not developed. To obtain greater flexibility, manoeuvrability and adhesion, a motor to produce electricity had been fitted between the steam-engine and the driving-axle. It was this motor which caused the increase in deadweight.

About the same time, in 1899, the P.L.M. Company carried out tests on an electric locomotive between Paris and Laroche. Current was from storage batteries weighing 20 tons and kept in a van designed specifically for this purpose. The system was invented by Auvert, an engineer working for the company. The locomotive had three axles and weighed 46 tons. The special van

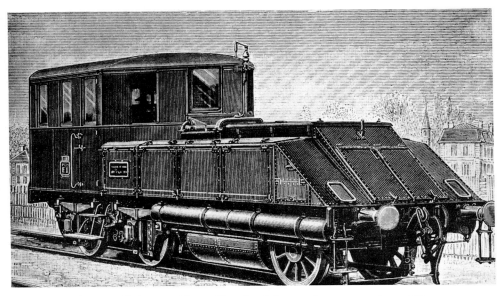

The P.L.M.'s Auvert self-propelling electric locomotive. (*Nature*, 4 February 1899).

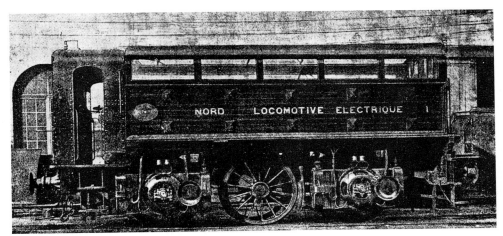

The Northern Railway's experimental self-propelling electric locomotive.
(*Le Génie civil*, 1 April 1893)

weighed 45 tons. Pulling a 100-ton load, it reached a speed of 46 m.p.h. However, a steam locomotive of the same weight was more efficient, and so the system was abandoned.

Because further expansion of the Metro was being considered, in 1893 the Northern Railway also tested a self-propelling electric locomotive, with current supplied once again by storage batteries. The aim was to build an engine which did not give off smoke, would travel at a moderate speed, and be able to maintain this speed on gradients. Its motors and generators were to be of a moderate size. These tests were carried out on a branch line, but did not prove to be successful.

A Heilmann self-propelling electric locomotive.
(*L'Illustration*, 21 January 1893).

Interior view of the Heilmann electric locomotive.
(Conservatoire des arts et métiers)

THE BEGINNINGS OF REMOTE-POWERED MAIN-LINE ELECTRIC TRACTION

In the use of remote-powered electric traction, Europe lagged far behind America. The cause of this was, without doubt, the invention of the Plante storage battery and the subsequent improvements to it which made it much lighter. In America, as we have already seen, the electric tramway had developed considerably and this in turn led to the use of remote-powered electric traction on main lines.

In 1883, after earlier tests carried out by Edison between 1880 and 1882, an electric locomotive pulling a 16-seater coach on 90 centimetre narrow-gauge track was exhibited in Chicago and then in Louisville by the Electric Railway Company, under the names of T.A. Edison and Stephen D. Field. Current was fed to the locomotie along a centre-rail, and returned via the running rail, where a copper conductor was used to increase conductibility.

In the same year, Leo Daft built a kind of electric locomotive which ran on the Saratoga and Mount MacGregor Railroad. The 12 h.p. engine pulled a 10-ton coach with 68 passengers on board at a speed of 10 m.p.h. up a gradient of 1 in 57. The current was fed along a centre-rail laid on hardwood blocks impregnated with resin. It was collected by phosphor wheels which were pushed lightly against the rail by springs. Speed was

A modified version of an Edison electric locomotive in 1882.

A type of steam locomotive was used on this test.

(*Electric Traction for Railway Trains*: Edward P. Burch, 1911)

controlled by inductance coil commutation. The engine was fitted with an electric brake consisting of electro-magnets which the wheels pulled against themselves when current was fed into them.

In 1885, Leo Daft built an electric locomotive for New York's elevated railway.

In the United States, there were so many experiments and inventions that it is difficult to make a clear distinction between inter-city and suburban lines at that time. The early electric lines evolved from the tramways and railroads and were built between Minneapolis and Saint-Paul, around Cleveland, between Buffalo and Niagara

Falls, and between Washington and Alexandria and Mount Vernon. These lines operated between 1890 and 1892.

In Europe, some of the early lines showing influences of the tramway, railway and American electric lines were the Bochum network in Westphalia, the Upper Silesia tramways, the Budapest–Neupost–Rakespalota line, the South Staffordshire tramways and, in France, the mountain line from Fayet to Saint-Gervais built by the P.L.M. Company in 1900, the Pierrefitte to Cauterets line operating at the same time, and the Grenoble–Chapareillan line built in 1901. Four hydro-electric plants were envisaged for the

Plan for an electric railway from St-Louis to Chicago.

Illustration from *Electrical World* of windbreak locomotives which achieve speeds of 100–155 m.p.h.

The picture gives a glimpse of the strange views which people had at the time concerning main-line electric traction.

One of the first electric locomotives.
This engine was tested in Baltimore in 1895 by the General Electric Company on a Baltimore & Ohio Railroad branch line.

Fayet–Chamonix line. A current of 550 volts was fed along a side rail and was collected by brushes. A dynamotor was fitted to each coach and, thanks to an ingenious device invented by Auvert, an engineer working for the P.L.M. Company, a pneumatic servomotor made it possible for the driver at the front of the train to operate the controls in each of the coaches. On steep inclines, a centre-rail was used for extra braking power.

The Pierrefitte to Cauterets railway has a 750-volt current fed to the coaches by two overhead wires. The coaches are fitted with trolleys and run on two bogies, each of which is driven by two dynamotors, one on each axle. Each coach has therefore four 25 h.p. motors and three brakes: a handbrake which presses brake shoes on to the eight wheels, a tempered steel slipper brake which bears on the rails, and an electric brake consisting of dynamotors which operate on downhill sections. The particular feature of the Grenoble–Chapareillan line is that its two overhead wires have a potential difference, not of 750 volts, but of 1,200 volts, one wire carrying a positive 600-volt current, the other a negative 600-volt current. Two trolleys are therefore required. The running track has a zero earth potential. Such equipment was remarkable for the time, since the increase in voltage is similar in some respects to the increase in pressure on steam locomotives, with insulation replacing the mechanical resistance of the boiler's tubes and metal plate. This

system was installed ten years before a similar one on the North–South line in Paris, the only difference being that on the latter, one of the two wires acts as a third conductor rail.

It was only after 1895 that there was any noticeable increase in the number of electric lines in Europe but this increase was still far from being as rapid as that in the United States. Between 1 January 1891 and 1 January 1898, throughout the

Edison's electric locomotive in 1880, with current fed through the track, one rail being positive, the other negative

(*Electric Traction for Railway Trains*: Edward P. Burch, 1911)

whole of Europe, electrification increased from 44 miles of line to 1,400 miles, with 700 miles in Germany, 246 miles in France and 83 in Britain.

Railcars with both a traction and carrying capacity ran on all these lines, which doubled as tramways and railways. The electric locomotive proper, that is, one hauling a train in the same way as a steam locomotive on main lines and over long distances, operated for the first time in 1895 on the Baltimore & Ohio Railroad. The 7-mile section of track called the 'Bet Line' ran through the city of Baltimore, partly above ground, partly underground, and linked several lines. It inspired a famous experiment by the General Electric Company in Schenectady, in which ordinary locomotives emitting toxic fumes and unpleasant smells were not used at all on the underground section. Thus the 96-ton four-axle locomotive was created. Each axle had its own motor, with current fed to it from a rigid overhead line and return current via the eight wheels and rails. Current was collected by a copper plate sliding along a groove between the two Z bars which made up the line, the plate resting on the two horizontal bottom sections of the Z bar. Self-adjusting hinged joints, which responded immediately to any variation in the overhead line and the track, linked the track and the locomotive. This early electric locomotive employing a 550-volt direct current gave very satisfactory results.

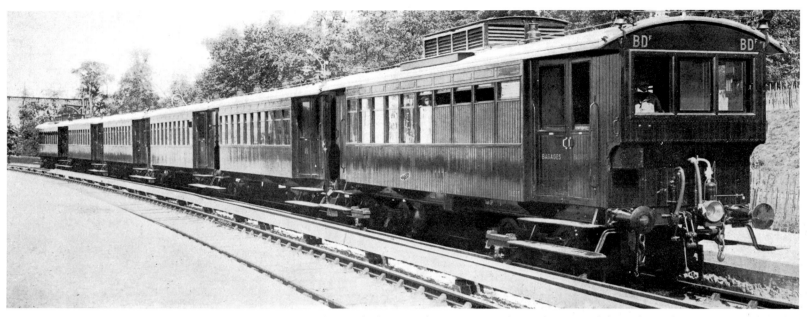

Sprague's multiple drive-unit train with a single driving-cab. It ran in 1901 between Les Invalides and Meudon.

DIRECT CURRENT FOR MAIN-LINE ELECTRIC TRACTION

On main lines, direct-current electric traction was used at first only for suburban services. Thus, in August 1901, the famous Sprague trains which were then widely used in the United States, and particularly on the Chicago elevated line, ran on the new Paris Invalides to Meudon line. Frank Sprague was an American engineer who, in 1885, had invented a special system in which the axle-hung electric motors are geared directly to the axles. This 'nose support' suspension is found in all motors today. The motor is supported on one side by two bearings on the axle and on the opposite side by a nose support on some part of the waggon. Springs or rubber pads allow the motor some freedom of movement while maintaining wheel alignment and distance between the motor's axis and that of the axle. The Sprague train was above all a 'motor-coach train', made up of railcars. This gave the train considerable adhesion since the number of motors was proportionate to the weight pulled. Acceleration from rest

was therefore rapid and this represented an appreciable saving of time on a line with many stations close together. Finally, on these trains all the motors were controlled by a single driver in the leading car, using special low-voltage circuits.

About the same time, on the Western and P.O. networks (between Orsay and Gare d'Austerlitz), tests were carried out on the so-called multiple-unit Thomson-Houston trains on which a similar system of synchronised control operated.

After many difficulties, such as the instability of the sandy soil, the Meudon Tunnel was completed, and in 1902 the electric line from Invalides to Meudon was extended to Versailles. In the tunnel, electric traction was necessary since a continuous gradient of 1 in 125 over a distance of 2¼ miles made ventilation extremely difficult. With steam engines, the air soon became unpleasant to breathe. A three-phase 5,000-volt current was fed to this electric traction line from the power station in Issy. Three sub-stations transformed the current into 550-volt direct current and this was sent along a raised insulated rail at the side of the track.

In 1903, the P.O. Railway decided to extend its Orsay to Austerlitz electric line as far as Juvisy.

More and more electric locomotives began to operate, but still in the form of a motor-coach. So, side by side with multiple-unit trains, which had proved so valuable on suburban lines where stations were very close together and trains had frequent stops and starts, one found the single traction train. As had happened in the case of steam, power was once again being concentrated rather than dispersed. The reason for this was that most stations were by now electrified and main-line rolling stock could be taken by electric power to the section of track where their steam locomotive was waiting. This led to the creation, not of electric locomotives as such, but of what could only be described as motor-coaches, since they still incorporated a guard's van. The result was that there were two drivers' cabs, and the driver had to move from one to the other to drive the train. The P.O. Railway quickly replaced this arrangement with a single cab from which the driver could see in both directions. Since this vehicle now had only one function, it was in fact a locomotive.

In 1905, a locomotive of this type, but much more powerful, weighing 93 tons, operated a service similar to the one between Orsay and

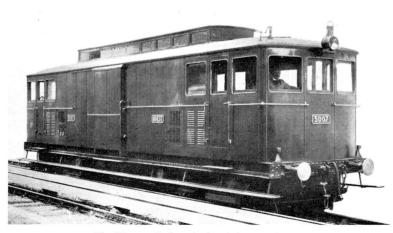

The Western Railway's electric locomotive on the Paris-Versailles Left Bank line.

The entrance to Meudon Tunnel and the Versailles track with its electric third rail.

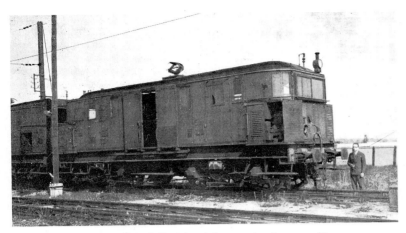

The P.O. Railway's first electric locomotive. It operated in
1903 between Paris and Juvisy.
(Photo: A. Dubois)

The first high-tension (2,400 volts) locomotive
on the Saint-Georges-de-Commiers to La Mure-d'Isère
metre-gauge railway.

Austerlitz in the 2-mile-long tunnel in the heart of New York on the New York Central Railroad. One of its lines ran to Chicago and the Great Lakes. The engine's four electric motors drove the four corresponding driving-axles with no loss of speed, and were attached to the axles in such a way that it was not possible to fit shock-absorber springs. Axle-weight therefore increased, and constant repairs to the track and the locomotive were required because of lack of shock absorption. Moreover, the engine's weight at axle level lowered considerably the train's centre of gravity and this made high-speed travel much less comfortable. A further consequence of the lack of engine space was a reduction in engine power.

Engines were therefore built with fewer motors. They were placed in a higher position and by means of connecting rods and cranks they drove an untrue axle which, on the same level as the driving-axles, drove two coupled axles. This was the arrangement on the Pennsylvania Railroad's enormous electric locomotive which was built in 1910. It weighed 149 tons and generated 4,000 h.p. It had eight axles, four of which were driving-axles, and operated in the tunnels of the huge Pennsylvania Railroad station.

Of all the direct-current locomotives, mention must be made of the one which ran from 1903 on the Saint-Georges-de-Commiers–La Mure d'Isère line. It had a 2,400 voltage. Its twin-wire electric

The 93-ton electric locomotive which hauled trains through the 2-mile tunnel to
Grand Central Station in New York.
Each driving-axle had its own motor attached to it. (*Nature*, 22 April 1905)

distribution was similar to that on the Grenoble–Chapareillan line in 1901, except that the latter had a limit of 1200 volts.

The advantage of direct current is that the motor has great flexibility and adapts automatically to the resistance it meets. Moreover, when the train sets off from rest the motor produces a very powerful torque. However, since it is not really suited to high tension, current strength has to be increased and this means the supply conductor must be strengthened. This in turn leads logically to the use of the third rail.

The driving-axle controls on the Pennsylvania Railroad's huge 149-ton electric locomotive.
There are fewer motors than axles, the motors being positioned above the axles and controlling them by a system of connecting-rods, cranks and untrue axles.
This locomotive ran from the Pennsylvania Station at New York via the tunnels beneath the Hudson River and East River.

ALTERNATING CURRENT FOR ELECTRIC TRACTION

By its nature electric current is 'alternating' rather than, as people might think, 'direct'. All current-producing motors rotate. A coil rotating in a magnetic field returns regularly to the same position in the field. This is where the current oscillating between maximum and minimum is produced. If, as the coil turns, current is collected at 120 degree intervals this is called 'three-phase alternating current'. If these three phases are fed to a motor at generating speed, the motor will continue to turn at that speed. Obviously, therefore, a three-phase electric track generally consists of two overhead wires (for two trolleys) with the running rails acting as the third 'wire'. The first three-phase traction tests were carried out in 1892 in Charlottenburg by Siemens and Halske. The

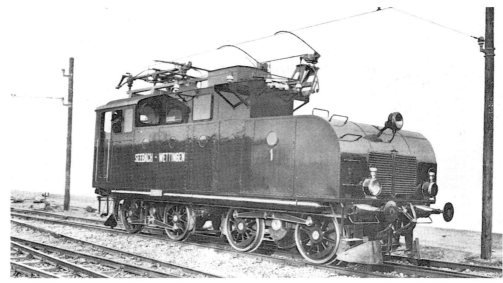

Single-phase current test-locomotive on the Seebach-Wettingen line in 1904.
(Swiss Federal Railway archive)

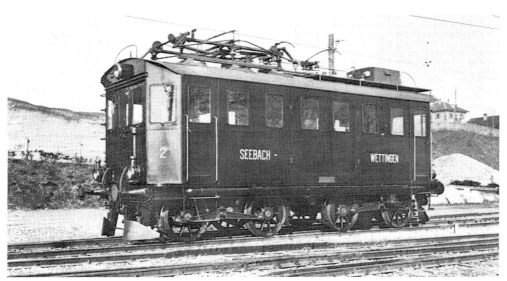

Single-phase current test-locomotive on the Seebach-Wettingen line in 1905.
(Swiss Federal Railway archive)

number of overhead wires which it requires, and for its lack of flexibility, since its motors turn at about the same speed on gradients as they do on the flat. As a result, in the United States and Switzerland, single-phase current was tested. This has the advantage of three-phase current with regard to the use of high tension, but, like direct current, needs only one overhead wire.

Considerable energy can easily be transmitted long distances to the locomotive by high-tension single-phase current. The locomotive's static transformer reduces the tension without changing the current's form. It can then be used on single-phase motors. This was the system applied in 1910 on the Lotschberg locomotives and the French Southern Railway's locomotives. In 1911, the P.L.M. Railway tested Auvert and Ferrand's device between Cannes and Grasse. This first of all lowered the single-phase voltage on the locomotive itself, and then transformed it from alternating to direct current.

result was the application of this system in 1895 to the tramways in Lugano, then, in 1898, to the rack lines in Gornergratt and Jungfrau and, in 1900, to the Valteline Railway. Italy then rapidly became the country which led the way with three-phase traction. Ganz electric locomotives with con rod drive, pulling goods trains, ran for the first time in 1904 on the Valteline Railway. Whereas in the past there had been as many motors as axles, which, of course, had increased axle-weight and given a hard and uncomfortable ride, now only two motors were used. In 1906, electric locomotives based on the Valteline experience ran on the Simplon line, hauling 350-ton passenger trains at 40 m.p.h.

Further support for the three-phase current came in 1902 at the famous Zossen-Marienfelde electric railcar trials. Here, a track with three overhead wires and three trolleys replaced the old system of two overhead wires and conductor running rail, and a staggering speed of 120 m.p.h. was achieved for the first time.

Three-phase current can be criticised for the

A single-phase current electric locomotive, modified by Auvert and Ferrand, being tested between Cannes and Grasse on the P.L.M. line. (*Nature*, 10 June 1911)

Electric car on the Schlucht rack railway.

Points on a rack railway, seen from the driver's cabin on an electric car (1913). (Federal Swiss Railways)

ELECTRIFIED RACK RAILWAYS

The first electrified rack railway had a three-phase current of 750 volts and ran from Zermatt to the Gornergrat, at an altitude of just over 10,000 feet.

(Gornergrat Railway archive)

The electric cars, using the Abt system, on the Gornergrat Railway.

(Gornergrat Railway archive)

The Gornergrat Railway in winter, at the foot of Mont Cervin.

(Photo: A. Klopfenstein)

THE GORNERGRAT RAILWAY (1898)

THE HIGHEST ELECTRIFIED RACK RAILWAY IN EUROPE
(Jungfrau Railway archive)

The Jungfrau Railway (the view here is from near the Eigergletscher station) has a three-phase current of 750 volts and employs the Strub System. It was built in 1893 by Adolphe Guyer-Zelles, an industrialist from Zurich. Two phases are picked up from the overhead wires and the third phase from the rail. Leaving from the little Scheidegg (at 6,770 feet), the train climbs over a distance of 5½ miles to the Jungfraujoch station (at 11,332 feet) – which was opened in 1912 – in less than an hour.

Italian railcar on the Valteline line (1902). This operates on three-phase current at 3000 volts.
(Italian State Railways)

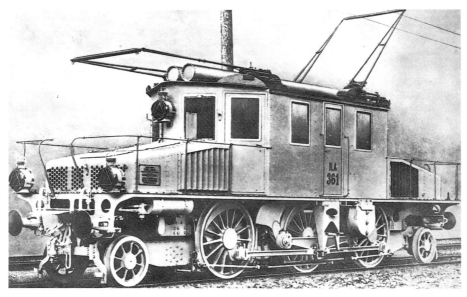

Italian locomotive on the Valteline line (1904).
(Italian State Railways)

Swiss locomotive on the Simplon line (1906). Three-phase current at 3000 volts.

RAILCARS AND LOCOMOTIVES EMPLOYING THREE-PHASE CURRENT

With three-phase current, two phases come via overhead wires, the third is picked up from the rail.

Erecting a rigid rail on the overhead electric track between Perpignan and Bourg-Madame.
(*Nature*, 25 May 1912)

OVERHEAD ELECTRIC SUPPLY AND ELECTRIC AXLE-DRIVE

In France, it was not until 1912 that electric traction began to be used on long-distance trains. Until then its application had been limited to suburban services. However, alternating current made it easier to insulate high tension and this reduced loss of energy to a minimum. As a result, electric current became feasible on long-distance traction. In 1912, the French Southern Railway was the first to develop a new system of collecting current. Until then, on suburban lines, the third electric side-rail had performed this function, but it was impossible to run 15,000 volts through a conductor which was so close to the ground. It was dangerous for staff working on the track and for passengers if the train was derailed. On high-tension lines, therefore, an overhead supply was essential.

Overhead wires, however, had a tendency to sag considerably between supports, and at high speeds contact with the trolley was poor. This problem was solved by catenary suspension: the electric wire was suspended from another wire which was stronger and insulated. However, variations in temperature changed the amount of sag on the suspension wire, and this meant that the electric line did not remain perfectly horizontal. Apart from this, there were fears at the time that the wire might snap and that this could result in dangerous short-circuiting on the ground. Fortunately, Paul, the chief engineer of the Southern Railway, invented a rigid overhead electric rail which would give perfect contact with the trolley. Moreover, if breakage occurred, it was constructed in such a way that a complete section of it would fall to the ground, and since it had no contact with the rest of the line, there would be absolutely no danger.

This type of rail had the appearance of a lattice girder. In cross-section it was triangular, with its point facing downwards, and it was with this

bottom section that the trolley made contact. It weighed only 4 lbs per foot, and to avoid the possibility of strong side winds causing it to break, it was supported horizontally in the following way: two parallel wires at the same height as the rail ran along each side of it; these were fastened at each end to the tops of posts positioned at regular intervals and then linked to the overhead rail by horizontal chains. The arrangement was therefore somewhat similar on a horizontal plane to the system used to maintain rigidity on a suspension bridge roadway.

This type of overhead rigid rail was used on the line between Perpignan and Bourg-Madame and signalled the beginning of a vast programme of track electrification undertaken by the Southern Railway. It aimed to electrify more than 300 miles of track, by building five plants which would produce 60,000-volts single-phase current. This would then be transformed and distributed as 12,000-volt current by five sub-stations. This electrification programme occurred at the same time as the first development of hydro-electric power in the Pyrenees.

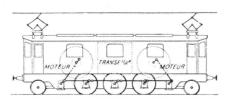

Pennsylvania R.R. direct-current electric locomotive.

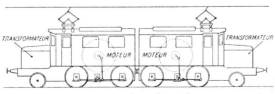

Simplon three-phase electric locomotive.

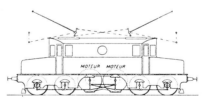

Lotschberg single-phase electric locomotive.

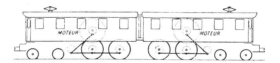

French Southern Railway single-phase electric locomotive.

A COMPARISON OF DIFFERENT KINDS OF POWER TRANSMISSION BETWEEN TWO ELECTRIC MOTORS AND THREE OR FOUR DRIVING-AXLES ON VARIOUS TYPES OF ELECTRIC LOCOMOTIVES (1905–12)

Rigid overhead electric rail with horizontal catenary support.
(*Nature*, 25 May 1912)

When current enters the locomotive from either an overhead or ground-level source, it drives the electric motors. These in turn drive the axles. In the case of electric railcars, axle-drive is individual, with each axle driven by its own motor or motors. In the case of very powerful locomotives, axle-drive is collective, with two or more axles driven by one motor. Such locomotives by definition require a number of adhesion axles. In general, when the number of adhesion axles exceeds that of the motors, in other words when power together with savings in cost and weight are important considerations, connecting-rods are essential. Connecting-rod drive can be achieved in a variety of ways. First, horizontal con-rods may be driven by an untrue axle with gear drive from the motor, the other axles being connected to the driving-axle by horizontal con-rods. Second, a single axle may be driven by two motors by means of a triangular rod sometimes called 'a Kando Frame', with the other axles connected to the driving-axle by horizontal rods. This is the most common form of drive, with widespread application in Switzerland and Italy (the Valteline Railway), and is the normal form of drive on the three-phase locomotive. Finally, there is untrue-axle drive by oblique con-rods, with the untrue axle linked by gears or horizontal rods to one of the axles. Where there are two motors, there are two untrue axles with con-rods used to link them together.

In general, collective drive by connecting-rods, as opposed to individual drive where no rods are used, gives a weight reduction of the order of fifty per cent.

Maudslay Motor Company gasoline locomotive.
(*Nature*, 20 May 1905)

Diesel locomotive at Winterthur.
(*Nature*, 27 September 1913)

EARLY DIESEL LOCOMOTIVES

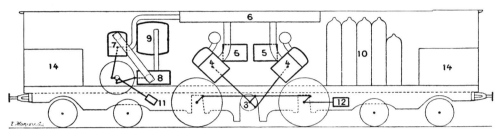

Longitudinal section of the Sulzer diesel locomotive in Winterthur, with direct coupling to the driving-axles.
(See text for explanation of the numbers)
(*Nature*, 22 June 1912)

The forerunner of the diesel engine dates from 1888, when a small tram propelled by a Daimler-type oil engine ran in Cannstadt near Stuttgart. A small locomotive propelled by an automobile engine was tested in 1901. Engine movement was transmitted to the leading axle by a set of gears similar to that on a car. Ignition of the oil injected into the carburettor was by incandescent platinum tubes, with burners used to avoid any drop in temperature. A flywheel ensured that speed remained constant. In 1905, the North Eastern Railway tested a railcar propelled by an 80 h.p. combustion engine which drove an electric generator. Direct current from the generator propelled the vehicle as in an electric-traction system. This was, in fact, an early attempt at traction by combustion engine with electric transmission. In the same year the Maudslay Motor Company of Coventry tested an 80 h.p. gasoline locomotive for London County Council. In 1913, the Schneider Company tested a 70 h.p. naphtha light rail motor tractor with power transmission to the axles by compressed-air, using a device invented by M. Hautier.

It was, in fact, drive-power transmission to the axles which was the main problem encountered in using combustion engines for rail traction. Such engines are not as flexible as steam engines, their acceleration not being as smooth and their need for a high level of adhesion creating weaknesses in driving-axle couplings.

Lack of smoothness proved to be an even greater problem with the diesel engine than it had been with the oil engine. The diesel engine first appeared in 1897. Its basic principle was that ignition of the mixture of air and fuel was no longer by electric spark as with the internal combustion engine but by sudden compression causing a rapid rise in temperature – similar to the heat generated when a bicycle-pump is compressed in order to inflate an inner tube. In the diesel engine, this rise in temperature causes spontaneous combustion of the mixture of air and fuel. The advantage of such an engine is that it can run on diesel oil, which is less flammable and combustible than petrol or fuel oil. Thus the diesel engine is better suited to more powerful locomotives than the oil-fired engine, but is heavier.

In 1912, in Winterthur, the Sulzer company tested a diesel locomotive with direct coupling from the engine to the adhesion axles. An untrue axle (3) (see the figure above) operated the driving-wheels by connecting-rods and was driven by four motors (4) coupled in pairs and fitted at an angle of 45°. The pumps (5) expelled the burned gases along the pipe (6). Two auxiliary diesel engines (7) drove two air compressors (8). This air passed through the cooler (9) and was then injected with the fuel into the motors (4) when the train set off. For normal running further injection was not required. The compressed-air tanks (10) could replace the auxiliary diesel engines (7). The water pumps (11) and (12) were used in the cooling process and the tanks (14) contained water and fuel. This 1,200 h.p. 85-ton locomotive was only a first step in the development of diesel locomotives, since it weighed 187 lbs per horse power and was mechanically much more complicated than the steam engine which, with its tender included, weighed only 143 lbs per horse power. However, at the time it was seen as a locomotive which could be used in areas where there was no coal or water and was talked of as the locomotive which would be able to haul trains across the Sahara Desert.

A Schneider naphtha locomotive.
A. Naphtha reservoir; B. Engine; C. Driving cab.
(*Nature*, 31 May 1913)

Steam, electric and diesel.

(Drawing by E.A. Schefer)

CHAPTER THREE

RAILWAYS

BETWEEN THE TWO WORLD WARS

The modern railway.

(Drawing by E.A. Schefer)

MODERN TRACK

Since the earliest years of the railways, rails have increasingly become longer and heavier because of the increasing weight of trains. As a result, mechanical means are now used to renew track, particularly on lines where there is intensive traffic, since work has to be carried out quickly, often between the passage of one train and another.

With modern methods of track-laying and renewal, hoists take the rails from the stockyard and lay them on the sleepers, to which they are then fixed by mechanical means. In this way, whole sections of new track are prepared and are then taken to where they are to be laid by mobile crane, travelling either along the track which already exists or along a parallel track.

Special trains bring the ballast, whose thickness and strength will provide the elasticity necessary to support the heavy trains which pass along the track at high speeds. If the same ballast is to be used again, a digger scoops up the old ballast and it is transferred to a rotating sifter which separates the clean stone from any impurities and any stones which are too small. When the new track is laid, each sleeper is positioned mechanically, using special equipment.

The tangle of rails at the entrance to a station.

These shining lines of steel, which carry heavy trains travelling at speed, do not appear to be parallel. In fact they seem to cut across each other, to meet and to separate to such a degree that an inexperienced eye would see only an inexplicable tangle. And yet chance plays no part here. Everything is planned both spatially and temporally. They only appear tangled, and in time they are totally separate from one another since no train can ever cross at the same place at the same moment. These invisible routes which never meet are planned by a network of electric currents which control the points. The points control each other. As soon as one is set, all those which complete the route are set, and any which may cut across this route automatically close.

(Photo: Sougez)

P.L.M. rail joint in 1871.

P.L.M. rail joint in 1889.

P.L.M. rail joint in 1933.

(P.L.M. Railway archive)

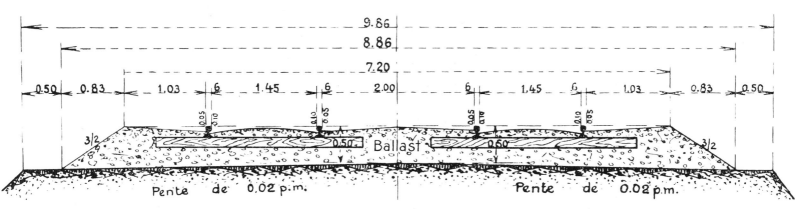

Cross-section of P.L.M. Railway track before 1914.

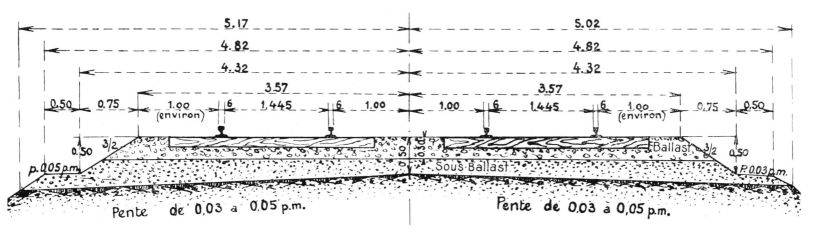

Cross-section of P.L.M. Railway track after 1918.

(P.L.M. Railway archive)

Welding rails by thermoaluminium.
(Photo: Northern Railway).

Sawing through a rail in a few minutes, using a portable machine.
(Photopress)

WELDING AND SOUNDING RAILS

Where the ends of rails butt together, the joints are subject to stress when a train passes over them. To avoid the effects of the constant pounding, a system of welding them together by aluminothermy was devised. Aluminium has the property of combining with the oxygen in metallic oxides to produce an enormous release of heat greater than 3,000°C. At this temperature, the two rail ends weld together inside a container of compressed magnesia which is fitted round the rails.

The purity of the steel is of vital importance in preventing rails breaking and avoiding the disasters which could result from such breakage. Internal faults are barely visible to the naked eye. Track inspection is continually carried out by staff who walk along the lines and strike the rails with a hammer so as to detect any fault from the sound the rails make. Such work, however, can only be done by men with many years' experience.

For this reason, in the United States, where the

Sections of rail showing internal cracks.
(State Railway archive)

quality of the rails left a great deal to be desired, Sperry, a railway enginer, developed an electro-magnetic, highly sensitive method of sounding track. This method is in use [1935] on French railways. It involves a specially equipped waggon propelled by a railcar. The waggon is fitted with slide contacts which feed a low-voltage electric current into the rail. The slightest internal crack causes a break in the current. This is immediately revealed by an electro-magnetic variation which is amplified by valves and shows up in the line traced by pens which traverse a moving roll of paper. Simultaneously, a device sprays a small amount of white paint on to the break in the rail. The operator then stops the railcar, returns to the broken rail, and using a manually-operated machine which works on the same principle, completes the sounding and checks for any longitudinal cracks, since the waggon's machine cannot detect these as accurately as transverse faults. To determine how sensitive this device was, checks were carried out on rails marked as being defective. The rails were sawn through and the hidden cracks were revealed – yet another method of ensuring safety on the railways.

Sounding a rail.
(State Railway archive)

Electro-magnetic sounding of a rail.

Marshalling yards at Longueau station, near Amiens.

Lens station with annexes, engine-sheds, and workers' houses built to a plan by M. Dautry.

BIRD'S EYE VIEW OF RECONSTRUCTED RAILWAY STATIONS

Entrance and concourse at Pennsylvania Station in New York.
(Pennsylvania Railroad archive)

The famous Grand Central Station concourse in New York.
The floor and walls are made of the finest white marble. The ceiling represents the sky filled with stars which twinkle in the electric lighting. (New York Central R.R. archive)

INTERIORS OF TWO OF THE LARGEST AMERICAN STATIONS

Sint-Pieters station at Ghent, with its impressive tower.
(Belgian State Railway archive)

The huge station at Leipzig seen from the air.
The station incorporates 26 tracks and contains two concourses, together with buffets, post-offices, slipper-baths, and shops, much as in American stations. (Bildarchiv der Pressestelle der D.R.G.)

TWO DIFFERENT TYPES OF EUROPEAN STATIONS

Principal façade of Milan station.

The building looks out on to the Piazza Andrea Doria and is 700 feet long and 300 feet deep. Inside on the ground floor, is a roadway 600 feet long and 80 feet wide. (Italian Ministry of Communications)

Milan station concourse next to the platforms.

The hall is 700 feet long and 80 feet wide, and has an artificial-stone arched roof 80 feet high, with large glass windows. (Italian Ministry of Communications)

MILAN TERMINAL STATION. A TYPICAL LARGE ITALIAN STATION

Platforms at Rotterdam's Deftsiche Poort Station. It was modernised in 1934

(Dutch Railways archive)

MODERN STATIONS

Leipzig station is one of the largest to have been built anywhere in the world in war time. It was completed shortly after New York's Grand Central Terminal which, with its cathedral-like con-

Platforms at Euston Station.

(Photo London, Midland & Scottish Railway)

course and star-studded ceiling, has an almost magical appearance at night when all the lights are on. The façade of Leipzig station is nearly 1000 feet long. The arrival and departure hall contains 26 tracks, with 30-feet wide platforms between each track. Separate areas exist for passenger and luggage movement. As in British stations, pas-

senger access is along platforms which are level with the floor of the coaches, whereas luggage access areas are set at a lower level so that the truck's platform is at the same height as the floor of the luggage vans. The departure hall is 850 feet long. Luggage is carried mechanically to a series of lifts at the end of the 13 underground corridors.

Milan Station, built in 1931, is a magnificent example of a modern station and offers passenger, express, goods and mail services. It is in two parts; the first is uncovered and contains 63 tracks between 650 and 1000 feet long; it has all the equipment required to clean engines and coaches, batteries can be recharged, water and steam can be supplied, and staff have all the facilities they may need; the second part is under the glazed arrival and departure hall. Here there are 22 tracks and, as in Leipzig station, each has a platform specially reserved for passenger use and another area solely for luggage movement. The façade of the station is nearly 700 feet long and looks out on to the Piazza Andrea Doria. At ground level is an access road for vehicles. From there, passengers enter the ticket hall beneath the arched roof, whose highest point is 135 feet above the ground. On the upper level, where the platforms are situated, is the concourse with its various offices and services. The platforms are located in a hall which is 670 feet wide and 1100 feet long. It is a station whose grandeur and beauty cannot fail to impress.

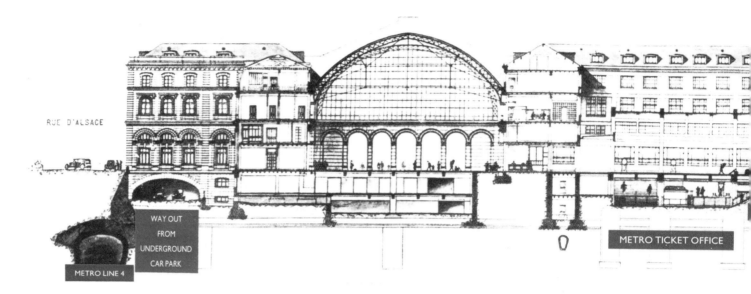

RUE D'ALSACE

WAY OUT FROM UNDERGROUND CAR PARK

METRO LINE 4

METRO TICKET OFFICE

Cross-section at right angles to the tracks.

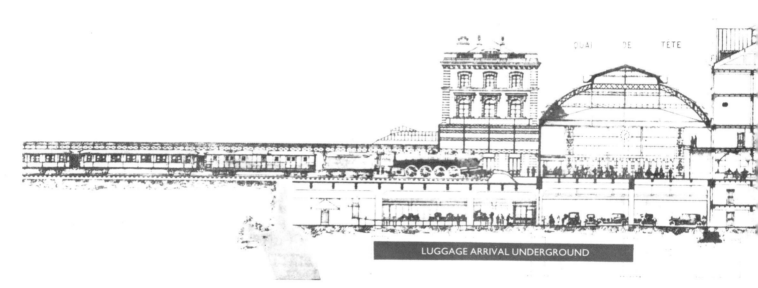

QUAI DE TETE

LUGGAGE ARRIVAL UNDERGROUND

Cross-section parallel to the tracks.

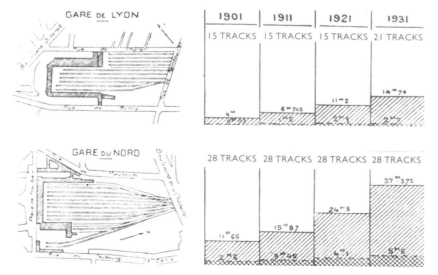

GARE DE LYON

1901	1911	1921	1931
15 TRACKS	15 TRACKS	15 TRACKS	21 TRACKS

GARE DU NORD

28 TRACKS	28 TRACKS	28 TRACKS	28 TRACKS

Numbers (in millions of passengers) departing annually from stations in Paris.
The shaded section indicates (in millions) the number of passengers per kilometre of platform.

The façade of the station.

THE NEW GARE DE L'EST. THE MO

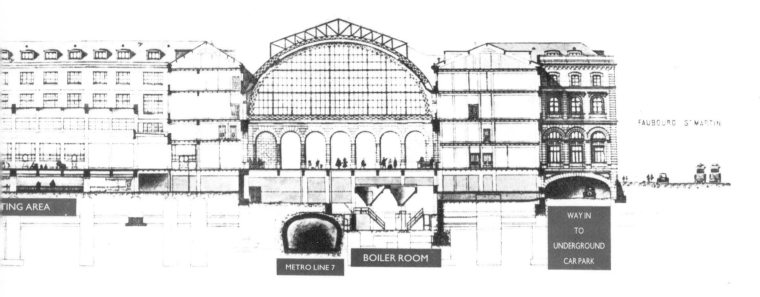

TING AREA

METRO LINE 7 | BOILER ROOM

FAUBOURG S? MARTIN

WAY IN
TO
UNDERGROUND
CAR PARK

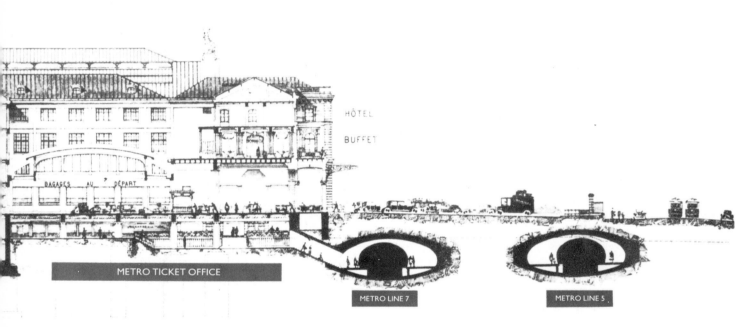

HÔTEL

BUFFET

BAGAGES AU DÉPART

METRO TICKET OFFICE

METRO LINE 7 | METRO LINE 5

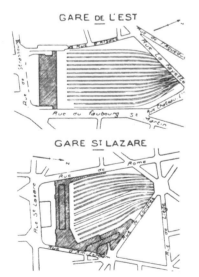

GARE DE L'EST

GARE S? LAZARE

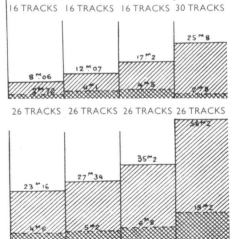

1901	1911	1921	1931
16 TRACKS	16 TRACKS	16 TRACKS	30 TRACKS

| 26 TRACKS | 26 TRACKS | 26 TRACKS | 26 TRACKS |

Numbers (in millions of passengers) departing annually from stations in Paris.

The shaded section indicates the number (in millions) of passengers per kilometre of platform.

(Eastern Railway archive)

ODERN STATION IN PARIS (NOVEMBER 1931)

Night view of platforms at Vienna's Western station.
(Photo: Otto-Zell, Vienna)

Night view from the Pont de l'Europe of platforms at the Gare Saint-Lazare.
(Photo: State Railway)

LIGHTING IN MODERN STATIONS

The most widely used types of French railway tickets [1935].
Left: Three ready-printed tickets of the old type. Right: Three tickets prepared as required by a special machine. (Northern Railway)

The old type of ticket service, using ready
printed tickets.
(Northern Railway)

New system of ticket service, with special
machines printing tickets as required.
(Northern Railway)

PASSENGER SERVICES

To avoid people having to queue unnecessarily at ticket offices, companies had for a long time employed a system of printing tickets for later use so that they had only to be punched after purchase. However, this proved expensive and, to reduce costs, special machines were invented which would print tickets as they were required.

Automatic timetable at Victoria Station, London
(*Illustrated London News*, 30 March 1935)

Again, in order to save passenger time, an automatic timetable was tested at Victoria Station in London. The passenger had only to press a button and the time of his train was shown. Travel agencies, some of which were well-known and long-established, became common features in large stations, providing travellers with information about journeys, luggage, etc, and offering a wide variety of services.

The many services a travel agency can offer to arriving passengers.
(Photo: Brodsky)

Water-tower in 1917.
(Photo: Czechoslovakian Railways)

(Photo: Belgian State Railway)

Reinforced-concrete water-tower at Saint-Quentin.
(Photo: Northern Railway).

The quality of water is very important to minimise damage to the locomotive's boiler. Whenever possible, station water-towers are filled with natural spring water. If they are built out of metal, they are encased as a protection from frost. Nowadays [1935], they are frequently built from reinforced concrete. So that they do not obstruct the driver's view, they are positioned at some distance from the track and the water is fed to the hydraulic water-feeders along underground pipes. These cast-iron feeders stand about 10 feet high and resemble pivoting gallows.

Modern reinforced concrete water-tower fitted with an electric motor and hydraulic feeding cranes; note, on the right, one of the cranes (1930).
Above, centre: An old water-feed system using wind-power (about 1900). (Photo: Swedish Railways)

UNIFORMS FROM AROUND THE WORLD

1. British guard   2. British stationmaster   3. Swedish stationmaster   4. Dutch guard   5. Dutch stationmaster   6. Swiss stationmaster   7. An employee at a large German station
8. Italian stationmaster   9. Polish stationmaster   10. Chechoslovac guard   11. Chechoslovac stationmaster   12. Chechoslovac signal man   13. American porter
14. Austrian traffic controller.

FRENCH RAILWAY UNIFORMS

1. Guard (Paris–Orléans–Midi line)   2. Pullman car attendent   3. A porter at the Gare d'Orsay   4. A ticket collector on the Paris–Orléans–Midi line)   5. A sleeping car attendent
6. A driver in town uniform 7. Station master (P.L.M.)   8. A ticket collector (Northern Railway)   9. Chief porter (State Railway) 10. A booking clerk (State Railway)
11. Porter at the Gare St-Lazare   12. Ticket collector (East Railway)

Storage-battery motor-tractor used for shunting.
(Photo: Czechoslavakian Railways)

100 h.p. diesel motor-tractor used for shunting.
(State Railway archive)

STATION APPROACHES

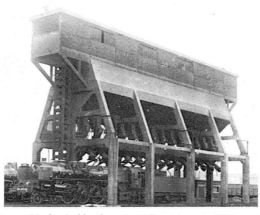

For reasons of cost, motor tractors were preferred to shunting locomotives for moving waggons about inside the station. These tractors, which were at first all oil-fired, are now fitted [1935] with diesel engines. The running cost of a steam shunting-locomotive was 60 francs per hour. The oil-fired motor tractor cost 42 francs per hour and the diesel engine a mere 20 francs per hour. When electricity is readily available, a battery-operated motor tractor is even cheaper to run, since current

Mechanical loader at La Villette depot in 1932, used for loading coal into locomotives.
(Henry Collection)

is needed only in sufficient quantity to shunt waggons within the station.

Beside the tracks near major railway stations other new machines were to be seen, such as the mechanical coal-loader. The tender is positioned beneath the loader while coal is mechanically fed into it.

Flyovers were constructed to permit non-stop express trains to pass through stations without hindering or endangering the activities of local trains or shunting engines. The construction of these flyovers involved the railway companies in considerable expense.

The flyovers at Longueau.
(Photo: Northern Railway)

Cedar Hill marshalling yards fitted with brake rails.
(Photo: New York & New Haven R.R. – General Signals Company)

LARGE MARSHALLING YARDS

Marshalling and assembly yards are vital if rail transport is to be economical and efficient. Immediately after the First World War, the Northern Railway introduced the most modern equipment and machines to provide these services in its station at Lille-la-Délivrance.

First, there is the sorting area, which is a huge set of sidings on a slope where waggons are uncoupled and left on one of the many parallel tracks. Each train to be split up is brought here, the brakes are then applied, and the locomotive returns to the depot. At the far end of this area is the marshalling yard, and finally at the end of that is the assembly yard. This yard is the longest of all and almost entirely on the flat except at its two ends.

The waggons, then, are processed through the system in one direction only and, by force of gravity, they run from the sorting area to the marshalling yard. At the far end of this yard, waggons are received from different sidings and the new train is assembled. For the waggons to move under their own weight, steep gradients of 1 in 66 are needed, since prevailing winds or low temperatures which can freeze the grease on the

Operator in rail brake-control box on
the Pennsylvania R.R.
(Photo: General Signals Company)

wheels of the waggons may impede movement. A locomotive would have some difficulty hauling a heavy train back up such gradients. Therefore at Lille-la-Délivrance the newly-assembled trains pass through a loop at the bottom of the slope as they leave the marshalling and assembly yards.

This arrangement ensures that they do not obstruct the entry of other trains into the sorting area. It is, therefore, possible to maintain a continuous flow of traffic at the rate of one waggon every ten or twenty seconds giving a total of some 3,000 to 4,000 waggons per day.

However, once they are on the incline a means must be found of preventing them from running into waggons already in the marshalling yard. The previous system had consisted of men placing brake blocks on the rails. Not only was this dangerous but it was also a very inefficient way to attempt to stop 30-ton waggons moving at speeds of 12–18 m.p.h. M. Deloison, the depot head at Lille-la-Delivrance, invented a device in which a brake-shoe mounted on a stand slides along a channel at the side of the rail. When necessary, the stand can be diverted into an 'alley' at the side of the track. The stand is also attached to an endless cable which is driven by a winch fitted with an electric motor. The cable pulls the brake-shoe along the rail until it meets the waggon. The waggon's wheel then activates a trip-lever which disconnects the shoe and the cable. The brakes are then applied until the brake-shoe is ejected into the alley. Here it reconnects with the cable and the process begins again. With this system, the man controlling the operation remains in his box and simply pulls a lever which causes the electric

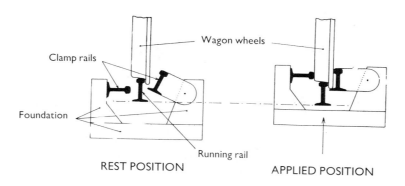

How the brake rails operate in Trappes station.
(Photo: State Railway)

motor to drive the cable.

This process was improved by Rabourdin, the chief engineer with the Eastern Railway. Under his system, six brake-blocks automatically move along the rail away from the waggon as it arrives. If the waggon is moving too quickly it catches them up and the brakes are brought into operation. The blocks act as a kind of filter since the only waggons which they allow to pass are those whose speed is lower than the speed which the guard considers safe. As the waggon moves down the track, it makes contact with a series of pedals. It is this contact which causes the brake-blocks to move down the line away from the oncoming waggon.

At Trappes station, remote-controlled hydro-pneumatic or electro-pneumatic devices were in use in 1935 to operate rail-brakes. These clamp on to the wheels of the waggons as they pass along. Since light waggons may be derailed if this braking action is too harsh, the system was modified by Frolich, an engineer on the Reichsbahn, so that braking force was proportional to the weight of the vehicle. It was the weight which the flange on the wheel brought to bear upon the rail which determined how tightly the brake was applied.

As the waggons move down towards the sorting area, the points are switched from a central signal-box controlling the whole operation. The pointsman has simply to watch a control panel on

Points control desk in Trappes signal-box.
(Photo: State Railway)

which the layout of the yard is reproduced. Each set of points is represented by a tiny lever, at the side of which a small red indicator lights up when a waggon moves across the points, in other words, when there is danger. To avoid the need to move each lever individually, Descubes, an engineer with the Eastern Railway, invented 'route boxes', with one lever controlling all the

points on a particular route. This method was applied in Trappes by Robert Levi, the chief engineer on the State Railway, in the following way: inside a special apparatus, marbles, representing the waggons moving along by the force of gravity, drop into tubes which correspond to the track destination of the waggons. The marbles move along the tubes at the same time as the waggons move along the lines and trigger the automatic lever for each set of points at exactly the right moment. If one waggon catches up another waggon, the switch triggered off by the second waggon is cancelled and the waggon is sent into a siding. In this way any possible danger is averted.

At Trappes, another system involves the use of infra-red beams of light striking a photo-electric cell. In the illustration on this page can be seen, on the left-hand side, the two parallel barriers, one each side of the track. One is fitted with the device which sends the invisible beam, the other with the receiver which has an electric circuit running through it. When a waggon intercepts the beam as it passes by, the variation which occurs in the circuit moves an indicator which returns to its original position as soon as the beam is no longer intercepted. An advantage of this system is that the movement of the indicator is proportional to the length of the waggon's wheelbase.

Brake-block turnout alley in the marshalling yards at Lille-la-Délivrance.
(Photo: Northern Railway)

Infra-red beam points-control for waggons on sloping track at Trappes.
(*Railway Gazette*, 10 November 1933 – Photo: Fenino)

The new points-box at Thirsk. It replaced five old signal-boxes and controlled 20 miles of track.
(London & North Eastern Railway)

Signal box No 1 at Saint-Denis, protected from derailments by a reinforced concrete shield.

THE DEVELOPMENT OF AUTOMATIC SIGNAL BOXES

The use of automatic controls in points and signal-boxes was becoming more and more widespread even before the First World War. In a sense, railway points are similar to rudders on ships. Because the latter have become so huge that human strength is no longer capable of moving them, engineers have had to find a third force which will act as a kind of intermediary between manpower and the mass which is to be moved. They turned to such sources of energy as compressed-air, water, and electricity, which can

Maintenance of an electric points-motor
(Dutch Railways)

be used to drive the machines which will carry out the task. Where points are concerned, a simple movement of a valve can send compressed air or water into a cylinder where a piston movement controls the points. Effort is thus reduced to a minimum. Two sources may be used, for example electricity to control the valve from a distance, and compressed air to operate the points.

In the modern signal-box, the only source of energy is electricity. The first thing one sees on entering a signal-box is the control centre, with its switches which send current to the motors on the ground next to the points. On the control-panel, the relays reveal schematically the geographical position of the points, each relay corres-

Signal-box No 1 at Lens.

Reinforced-concrete signal-box at Delft (1931).
(Dutch Railways)

The points-room in the new electro-dynamic signal-
box at the Gare de Lyon, Paris.
(P.L.M. Railway archive)

The new electro-dynamic signal box at the
Gare de Lyon, Paris.
(P.L.M. Railway Archive)

ponding to one set. The system operates in such a
way that a current cannot pass unless the relays
reproduce on a small scale one of the many
permanently-set routes. Each of these routes is
controlled by a single lever called the 'route
lever'. These are located on the first floor, on a
switchboard in the middle of a large glazed room
which looks out onto the tracks.

In this room are rows of small route levers,
each one controlling the ten or so sets of points
and signals which make up a particular route.
These levers are interlocked and can be moved
only when it is safe to do so.

Above the switchboard is a panel showing the
physical layout of the track. At any given time,
flashing coloured lights reveal the situation on the
track.

The relays in the control-room also reveal on
the panel the position of the points and confirm
that they are locked. Some relays are connected to
the semaphore signals, and these are not allowed
to move until the points are correctly positioned.

Manually-operated signals in Holland.
(Dutch Railways)

If a set of points happens to move from its correct
position, the relays automatically close the
semaphore signal. This system ensures that the
signals at the route entrance cannot indicate the
track is clear unless all the points on the route are
in place and have been checked.

There is a further check. The train has its own
safety control which operates as soon as the train
enters a set route. It then automatically operates a
series of switch bolts in the signal-box. These
immobilise any lever which could allow a train to
cut across the route which the first train will take.
The bolts remain immobilised until the route-
entry semaphore has blocked off the track to any
other train.

This automatic control system, with its
schematic panel showing the track and its sets of
points, is so safe that there is no longer any need
to build signal-boxes from which the track is
visible. A striking example of this is the 'remote
central control' operating at the Gare Saint-
Lazare.

At the Gare de Lyon in Paris; interior of the old
Saxby signal-box with its 200 levers.

The old Saxby signal-box at the Gare de Lyon in
Paris. By 1935 it had been replaced by an electro-
dynamic box.
(P.L.M. Railway archive).

Despatcher on the Houilles-Sartrouville section. From the Gare Saint-Lazare he not only controlled traffic but also operated centrally 22 sets of points and 14 checkboard signals.

THE DESPATCHING SYSTEM AND CENTRAL TRAFFIC CONTROL

The despatching system was introduced to France by the Americans during the First World War. Troop transportation from the Gare Saint-Nazaire to Is-sur-Tille caused serious disruption to rail traffic, and the American military administration suggested to the P. & O. Railway that they should try their despatching system.

In fact, this system had existed for a long time. In 1887, Roederer, a deputy manager with the P.L.M., analysed the American system of centralisation in which one man, the despatcher, has overall charge of all trains stopping, leaving, and remaining in a particular section. All traffic is controlled by the despatcher, who originally communicated with other despatchers by Morse. At the same time, these Morse messages went to all stations in the immediate area, the stations retaining only those messages which were of concern to them.

More recently, the telephone and the loudspeaker have replaced the telegraph. All stations on a particular section are on the same telephone circuit. The station simply has to announce itself and the despatcher on duty listens to the message being sent. The station gives all information concerning the arrival, departure and movement of any train or locomotive. All this information is recorded by the despatcher on a sheet of paper which contains a vertical list of the names of stations and signal-boxes and a horizontal list of train times.

The time at which a train will pass through a station is indicated by a dot at the point where the horizontal line showing the station and the vertical line showing the time intersect. When the dots are joined together the movement of traffic from station to station is clearly revealed. All that is then required is to compare this line with the planned line on the table in front of the despatcher, and he is then immediately able to see whether the train is late and which lines must be blocked off. If this needs to be done, he calls the relevant station directly and informs them of the measures to be taken. There is only one telephone circuit for all the stations. Each station has its own selection key which the despatcher enters. This key releases a set of electro-magnetic impulses which are different for each station. These interlock with the selector of the station which is being called and that station is the only one to receive the information being transmitted.

In fact, it is as if the despatcher is sitting in an observation balloon from which he can actually see the trains running along their respective lines and can guide them to their destination by his instructions. The system solves effectively the problem of trains which are not time-tabled. Detours, counter-flow traffic, single-line traffic can all be organised promptly so as to avoid any delay. The responsibility is no longer left to individual station-masters along the line but is the sole concern of one man who supervises the whole section and thus improves traffic flow.

Since September 1933, a central traffic-control system which originated in America, has been in operation at the Gare Saint-Lazare. It was the first to be used in Europe to control intensive traffic-flow. On the Paris–Le Havre line, traffic flow between Houilles and Sartrouville had presented so many problems that engineers had considered the possibility of quadrupling existing tracks to solve the situation. However, a special feature of suburban traffic is that it is one-way traffic, since the rush hour occurs in each direction at a different time of day, traffic moving to Paris in the morning and out to the suburbs in the evening. Central traffic control of this section meant that the tracks did not have to be quadrupled and that only one extra line, a centre line which could be used for traffic moving in either direction, had to be built. The equipment available to the despatcher allows him to control the 22 sets of points and 14 checkboard signals on a section from the Gare Saint-Lazare to a point 37 miles away. Above him is the topographical plan of the track, with white lights indicating the track is free and red lights indicating the track is occupied. Below, is a row of levers which operate the points. A second row operates the signals. This central traffic-control system has meant that at Houilles and Sartrouville pointsmen are no longer needed.

THE MODERN SIGNALS SYSTEM AND THE AUTOMATIC BLOCK SYSTEM

If, in the case of sets of points, the problem at any given moment is to separate trains spatially, where signals are concerned the problem is to separate them temporally. After the First World War, railway networks tried to adapt their signals to the needs of traffic and carried out research into automatic block equipment on heavily used lines. A commission set up in 1926 developed a new system of signals called 'Verlant' after its president, a manager with the P.L.M. Railway.

This system functions on the following principles: the white aspect to show the track is clear is

Old type of French pivoting disc.
(Photo: General Signals Company)

Luminous electric signal-board.
(Photo: General Signals Company)

Old type of American pivoting disc.
(Photo: General Signals Company)

no longer used; certain pennants have been modified; a 'Slow Down' reminder system has been introduced and signals generally are simplified.

In future, on French networks, a green aspect will mean the track is clear, since the disadvantage of the white aspect is that a 'Stop' signal shows white when the red glass is broken. The red and white checkboard will continue to show two red aspects at night. The semaphore will have only one red aspect instead of one red and one green. The checkered green and white warning signal will be one yellow aspect instead of two green aspects. The 'Slow Down' signal will change from its present green disc to show two yellow aspects. The red disc will have one red and one yellow aspect instead of simply one red. When open, all these signals will show a green aspect to indicate the track is clear.

Some people may be surprised that the

German signal.
(Photo: Vereingte Signalwerke)

British signal.
(Photo: Sims and Company)

semaphore and warning signals will show only one aspect rather than two, whereas the green and red discs will show two rather than one. This is because the Verlant commission wished to use lights on both day and night signals.

In France, the first daytime light signals were those on the Paris–Saint-Germain line. They were the same as the night signals, and proved to be much more visible and effective than the pivoting signals since the driver sees only one signal at any one time. Moreover, with light signals, the driver can be sure the signal will not be showing 'Track Clear' just because the signal is stuck in that position since the flexibility of electric current means it can monitor itself and even anticipate a malfunction.

Where pennants are concerned, the green and white check distant signals will have a yellow pennant but they will still be set on their pointed end. The present green disc will be yellow and will have a triangular pennant which will point downwards. The triangle was, in fact, the only simple geometrical figure which remained available for use. In many cases there is no direction indicator. It remains, however, important to remind the driver, as he arrives at the open checkboard sign, that he must slow down to 10–20 m.p.h. as indicated by the green disc he has already passed. Therefore a new signal, a 'Slow Down' reminder signal was created. It was a yellow triangle, pointing downwards and looking like a finger showing that it is 'here' that the driver must slow down. At night, this signal will consist of two yellow aspects, one above the other. This new signal simplifies the system at a junction where there are two possible directions, since the direction indicator is no longer required.

The Verlant system aimed to limit the most commonly-used signals to one light only. A further simplification was to discontinue the use of the red disc on automatic block main lines equipped with luminous signal boards. This meant the driver would only see a luminous signal board every mile or so. They would show only one signal, either a green aspect for 'Proceed', a single or double red signal for 'Stop', a single semaphore for 'Proceed with Caution', and

Group of signals showing 'stop'. A warning disc, a 'Sem' signal and a semaphore signal.

(Photo: Northern Railway)

a double aspect for 'Stop until Signals Change'. Finally, yellow still meant 'Slow Down'. One single yellow meant 'Slow Down and obey the next semaphore or checkboard'. Two yellow aspects side by side meant 'Slow Down to 8–10 m.p.h. as from the next point after the signal'. Two yellow aspects, one beneath the other, meant 'Slow Down immediately'. This new system of signals will certainly be much simpler but

at the time of writing [1935] it would appear that several years will be needed before it operates fully throughout France, since 70,000 signals have to be changed and a programme for retraining of drivers has to be devised. Such changes always demand a great deal of reorganisation.

The automatic block system was first applied in the United States in 1879, when electric current was fed for the first time along the track. The rails are linked by copper strips except at the entrance to the block section where the track is insulated by a fishplate. The two rails become conductors of direct or alternating current, low-voltage current being used to avoid it running to earth. When the train enters the section, its axles short circuit the rails and the signal closes, since the relay which kept the signal open is no longer excited. This arrangement means the section's size can be reduced, traffic increased, and any special staff to operate the old system manually no longer needed. In 1913, luminous block signal boards made their first appearance in the United States.

In 1926, in France, the Southern Railway installed the first automatic block system on its Bordeaux to Sète line, and on certain sections of its lines running between Toulouse and Bayonne, Toulouse and Auch, and Bordeaux and Dax. Then the Eastern network applied the block system on its Paris–Saint-Germain line, together with luminous signal boards which had the same daytime and night-time signals.

'Sem' signal, showing 'track clear' to an express train in Chantilly Forest.

(R. Floquet Collection)

A 2–8–4-class Austrian passenger locomotive, showing steam exhaustion as the locomotive sets off.

(Austrian Federal Railway)

THE DEVELOPMENT OF THE LOCOMOTIVE UP TO 1935

Between 1918 and 1935, the principal tendency in the evolution of the steam locomotive was the adoption of four coupled axles for passenger trains and five coupled axles for goods trains. For high-speed locomotives, an improved version of the Pacific-class engine was generally preferred. The Northern Railway had in service a Super-Pacific, with improved steam distribution and capable of pulling 500-, 600- and even 650-ton

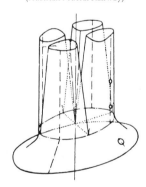

Kylala pipes to widen and standardise locomotive exhaust (1919).

(*Railways Review*, September 1928)

express trains on the flat at almost 75 m.p.h. Similarly the P.L.M. had a Pacific-class engine with twin water reheating and twin exhaustion, and on the Alsace–Lorraine network a similar engine operated with the addition of a booster. However, side by side with this pre-1914 class of engine, the P.L.M., Eastern, and State Railways also had in service the famous 4–8–2 Mountain-class. This had a total weight (on the P.L.M. and State Railways) of 126 tons and produced 3,500 h.p. capable of pulling 630 tons up a gradient of 1 in 125 at 60 m.p.h.

Of the suburban tank engines and the slower goods engines, the 2–8–2 Mikado-class, weighing

120-ton 4–8–4-class compound tank engine (1927), used later on suburban lines.

(P.L.M. Railway)

Polish goods locomotive, with six coupled axles for use primarily on track with few curves. (Photo: Cegielski company)

Smoke obscuring the driver's view; to combat this, smoke-deflector side pannels were fitted to the front of locomotives.

(Photo: Floquet)

up to 96 tons (and even 122 tons on the Northern line) proved especially popular as did the 122-ton 4–8–4 class on the Alsace–Lorraine and P.L.M. networks. The weight of these locomotives comes from the size of their water tanks which can carry up to 2,600 gallons of water.

One of the most remarkable of the five-coupled-axle goods engines was the P.L.M.'s 2–10–2 class. This Sante Fé-class engine could haul a 2,000-ton train of coal waggons at 34 m.p.h. up a 1 in 200 gradient. The special feature of this class of compound engine is that it has four rather than two cylinders outside the underframe. The high-pressure cylinders drive the trailing driving-axle while the low-pressure cylinders are in their normal position at the front of the engine and drive the second driving-axle. On other networks, the usual goods engine was the 2–10–0 class. These, then, are the principal external changes which have occurred in locomotives since the First World War. Remarkable internal changes have also taken place.

Superheat has risen to 350°C and even 400°C. Before the water enters the boiler to become steam, it is now reheated by combustion gases or, as is more frequently the case now, by exhaust steam.

The most remarkable changes stemmed from the work carried out by Chapelon, an engineer working for the P.O. Railway, who specialised in modifications to the Pacific-class locomotive. The way in which the idea of transforming the Pacific developed illustrates perfectly the value of the

Top: The modified 'Pacific'-class locomotive with valve distribution, twin steam exhaust and superheat (1930).
Above: 'Pacific'-class locomotive transformed into 4–8–0 class to achieve maximum power in relation to weight: 3,500 h.p. with a weight of 107 tons (1932).

(P.O. Railway archive)

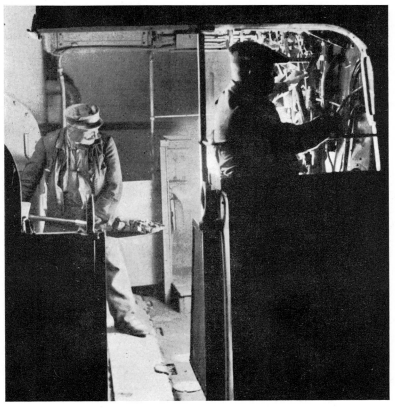

Stoking the fire manually. 70 lbs of coal are required per mile, that is almost every 70 seconds.
(Photo: Otto-Zell)

Set of controls on a 4–6–4 'Hudson'-class American locomotive, hauling the '20th Century Limited'.
(New York Central Railroad archive)

study of technology. When in 1908 and 1909 the Pacific class replaced the Atlantic class on the Bordeaux line, the Pacific's driving-axle only produced between 565 and 655 h.p. whereas the Atlantic had produced on average 800 h.p. The Pacific, therefore, in spite of its overall greater power (1,970 h.p. as opposed to 1,600) was by comparison an inferior engine to the Atlantic. By studying the reasons for this apparent loss of power, the P.O. came to recognise the importance of making better use of steam expansion by improving not only steam distribution and flow to the cylinders but also steam exhaustion.

Because slide-valve distribution presented lubrication problems at the high temperatures required for superheat, it was replaced by lift-valve distribution, since lift valves remain airtight at such high temperatures and are not prone to wire-drawing leaks, the inlet area being much larger. This same system of distribution was applied on other networks, being used for example by the State Railway on a non-compound Mountain-class engine. In this way, the locomotive was influenced by the internal combustion engine, which uses lift valves to admit and exhaust fuel gases. Moreover, the P.O. Railway

Twin steam exhaust to reduce counter-pressure.
(*The Railway Gazette*, 28 September 1934)

doubled steam-pipe capacity and considerably widened the exhaust pipes by adoption of the Kylchap exhaust system. This standardised draught counter-pressure and at the same time reduced it by fifty per cent. The result was a modified Pacific-class engine which was much more powerful and economical simply because of the way steam energy was used. The P.O. then went one step further and replaced the trailing carrying-axle by a fourth driving-axle, thus transforming the old 4–6–2 Pacific into a 4–8–0 class, with greater adhesion and less weight than the Mountain class (109 as against 126 tons). Producing 4,000 h.p., it was just as powerful as the Mountain-class engine and twice as powerful as the original Pacific, being able to pull 650 tons at 87 m.p.h. on the flat.

Unfortunately, the widening of the steam-

Tender corridor for changeover of staff in mid-journey.
(Photo: *Wide World*)

Oil-fired heating controls on a 'Pacific'-class locomotive.

exhaust pipes was counter-balanced by a reduction in the speed at which the smoke was emitted from the chimney. It no longer, therefore, cleared the driver's cab and obscured considerably his view of the signals. As a result, modern locomotives are fitted with smoke deflectors which drive the air and smoke upwards and over the driver's cab.

As the locomotive improves, it becomes more complicated to drive. In the driver's cab of a

Tender modified for oil-fired engine.

Hudson-class American engine there were at least 30 controls which the driver must supervise and operate. On some sections of a journey, a locomotive may consume up to 70 lbs of coal per mile while taking only 50 seconds to complete this distance. On average, the fireman may, therefore have to shovel 7½ tons of coal over a period of almost five hours, in other words 55 lbs per minute continuously for nearly 300 minutes. To avoid the vast effort needed in such a process

the mechanical loader was invented. A worm-screw (1) (see previous page) driven (2) by a steam-reversal (4) two-cylinder engine (3) sends the crushed coal along a draw tube to a distribution plate. An ejector pump (5) then drives the fuel into the firebox. Stoking is controlled by a horizontal-screw (6), and a shield (7) protects the air as it arrives at the pump. The coal enters the firebox to the rear of the firebed (8) and combustion is such that there is no possibility of the tubes (9) becoming blocked. Although the fireman no longer has to expend physical energy, his total concentration is required to control the ejector pump and ensure the coal is spread evenly over the heating surface.

Recently, to fire the engine, there has been a return to the heavy oil used for engines in the Navy. It is essential if the engine is to fire correctly that this oil is reheated by steam. Sometimes the steam is sprayed on to the burners, in which case they are located opposite the feeding gate, sometimes they are sprayed mechanically, in which case they are at the side of the gate. Where steam is used, the steam and oil pass along different pipes and do not mix until they are in the combustion chamber. This system produces a much larger flame. Water wastage, in the form of steam-injection, is estimated at fifty per cent of that of fuel. In the reheating process, 11 lbs of steam are sufficient to raise the temperature of 20 lbs of oil from 15°C to 65°C.

Long-distance tests were carried out in France in the 1930s on coal-fired Pacific-class engines incorporating all the latest improvements in superheat distribution and exhaustion. It was found that coal consumption exceeded 5 lbs per 100 tons, whereas in the oil-fired engine, consumption was about 3½ lbs.

Delaware & Hudson R.R. high-pressure triple-expansion locomotive and booster tender.
(Photo: *The Sphere*, 15 December 1934)

SPECIAL LOCOMOTIVES

The advantages of superheat are readily accepted, but opinions differ as to whether it is appropriate to use it on compound engines, or whether its use should be limited to the simple expansion engine. The Germans and the Americans favoured the latter, while in France both systems were in use. Whatever the truth of the matter, it seems to be the case that at high speeds the compound engine is less successful that the simple expansion engine but it is more successful at lower speeds on gradients, and when accelerating from rest. For some years, therefore, the Americans used boosters to compensate for the inadequacy of simple expansion. The booster, an auxiliary steam engine, is mounted on the locomotive's rear pony truck or on one of the tender's bogies. When the train sets off, or as it climbs a gradient, a clutch system is used to engage this additional motor. When normal running conditions are resumed, the clutch is disengaged.

Some countries have also experimented with high-pressure locomotives, the pressure being increased from 284 lbs per square inch to 853 lbs. The Delaware & Hudson Railroad's locomotive, the *Loree*, has a pressure of 500 lbs per square inch. Its tender is fitted with a booster, and it is the first locomotive to have triple expansion. It

Alsace-Lorraine Railway: booster for trailing carrying-axle on a 'Pacific'-class locomotive.
(Archive of Société alsacienne de constructions mécaniques)

can, in fact, operate as either a simple- or a triple-expansion engine.

For some years, tests were also carried out in an effort to create a steam-turbine locomotive, one which 'recycles its steam'. The problem is to devise a system of condensation which will create the vacuum required for a steam turbine to func-

tion successfully. It will probably be a steam locomotive without pistons and without any water consumption. During the 1930s, the Federal Swiss Railway and the Krupp company were testing the Zoelly locomotive and the Swedish State Railway was testing the Ljungstrom locomotive.

Zoelly-system steam-turbine locomotive without pistons.
(Archive of the Société de construction de locomotives de Winterthur)

'Santa-Fé', on the Paris–Lyon–Midi line, with five coupled driving wheels, capable of reaching 30 m.p.h. with a 2,000 ton train on an upward gradient of 1 in 200

'Mountain', a Paris–Lyon–Midi locomotive with four coupled driving wheels, able to quickly accelerate the heavy passenger trains on the upward slopes such as that at Blaisy-Bas between Laroche and Dijon.

MODERN FRENCH LOCOMOTIVES

The 'pure breed'
Three locomotives getting up steam to leave New York for Chicago with the famous '20th Century' train

A Czechoslovak locomotive taking on water
A 'Mountain' type with three cylinders and weighing 163 tons which can reach 38 m.p.h. on an upward gradient of 1 in 100

SOME FOREIGN LOCOMOTIVES

New York Central R.R. 'Hudson'-class locomotive pulling the famous '20th Century Limited'.

This class had first appeared in 1910 as a 'Baltic'-class locomotive on the French Northern Railway. Intended to haul heavy trains and passenger express trains, the American locomotive is fitted with a booster on the last wheel of the trailing carrying-bogie for faster acceleration from rest on a sloping track. (New York Central Railroad archive)

Two 'Flying Scotsman' trains meet.
When these two trains meet, travelling at 68 m.p.h., their combined speed relative to each other is 136 m.p.h.

(Photo: *The Times*)

GREAT EXPRESSES

The famous 110-ton 'Mikado'-class locomotive, the *Cock o'the North*, which ran on the London & North Eastern Railway's Edinburgh–Aberdeen line, on the test-bed at Vitry.

LOCOMOTIVE TEST BEDS

All progress in locomotive design and construction is a result of tests which have to be increasingly accurate in order to match the ever-improving performance of locomotives. For the engineer to have a precise knowledge of locomotive test conditions, the locomotive must run without any variation over a long period of time, and the energy it expends and its speed must remain constant. On an open track it is difficult to create the best conditions possible, since tests are always liable to be interrupted by signals or traffic movement. The dynometric coaches which are coupled to the rear of the test locomotive only partially resolve the problem. Engineers therefore looked increasingly to the possibility of testing engines under controlled conditions.

Such tests are not new. In 1881, De Borodine carried out static tests in the Kiev workshops of the South West Russian Railway as did Perdue University at Lafayette in the United States in 1891, the Chicago & North Western Railroad in 1895, and New York's Columbia University in 1899. However, it was not until 1919 that the test bed as such made its first appearance. It was built at Vitry-sur-Seine by the Central Office concerned with the development of rolling-stock, and incorporated all the latest refinements.

A locomotive tested under these conditions is an impressive sight. The locomotive arrives backwards, running not on its tyres but on its flanges, as if walking on tiptoe. When each of its wheels is level with a roller bar, the deck which carries the locomotive slowly descends until the tyres are

New type of German test bed at Grunewald near Berlin.
(Bildarchiv der Pressestelle der D.R.G.)

resting on the corresponding roller. The locomotive is attached to a dynamometer, and when the regulator is opened the wheels turn and, because of adhesion, turn the rollers in the opposite direction. So that the revolution speed of the wheels can be controlled and will reflect the tractive effort which corresponds to the engine's power, hydraulic brakes are fitted to the rollers.

277

1840 train with 14 carriages weighing 90 tons and travelling at 22 m.p.h. (250 h.p. locomotive)

1854 train with 24 carriages weighing 185 tons and travelling at 22 m.p.h. (380 h.p. locomotive)

1867 train with 24 carriages weighing 210 tons and travelling 27 m.p.h. (570 h.p. locomotive)

1878 train with 24 carriages weighing 255 tons and travelling at 27 m.p.h. (600 h.p. locomotive)

1889 train with 9 carriages weighing 224 tons and travelling at 42 m.p.h. (770 h.p. locomotive)

1900 train on the Bordeaux line with 11 carriages weighing 255 tons travelling at 50 m.p.h. (1000 h.p. locomotive)

1900 train on the Toulouse line with 15 carriages weighing 280 tons travelling at 44 m.p.h. (1000 h.p. locomotive)

1906 train on the Bordeaux line with 14 carriages weighing 350 tons travelling at 50 m.p.h. (1500 h.p. locomotive)

1925 train on the Bordeaux line with 11 carriages weighing 460 tons travelling at 42 m.p.h. (2000 h.p. locomotive)

1935 train with 15 all-metal carriages weighing 760 tons and capable of travelling at 72 m.p.h. on the level (4,000 h.p. locomo

These pages show how the power of the P.O.'s passenger engines and the size of its coaches have changed over one hundred years. In 1840, engines had single driving-axles and coaches were small, with first-class coaches still resembling the old stage-coach, and third-class coaches being open to the sky. By 1854, although engines still had single driving-axles, coaches had already acquired their modern appearance. In 1867, engines had four coupled wheels and, by 1878, the distance between axles had increased considerably. The first appearance of inter-communicating coaches, and coaches fitted with bogies, took place in 1889. In 1900, four-cylinder compound locomotives appeared, and coaches had two axles and up to

A HUNDRED YEARS OF CHANGES IN ROLLIN

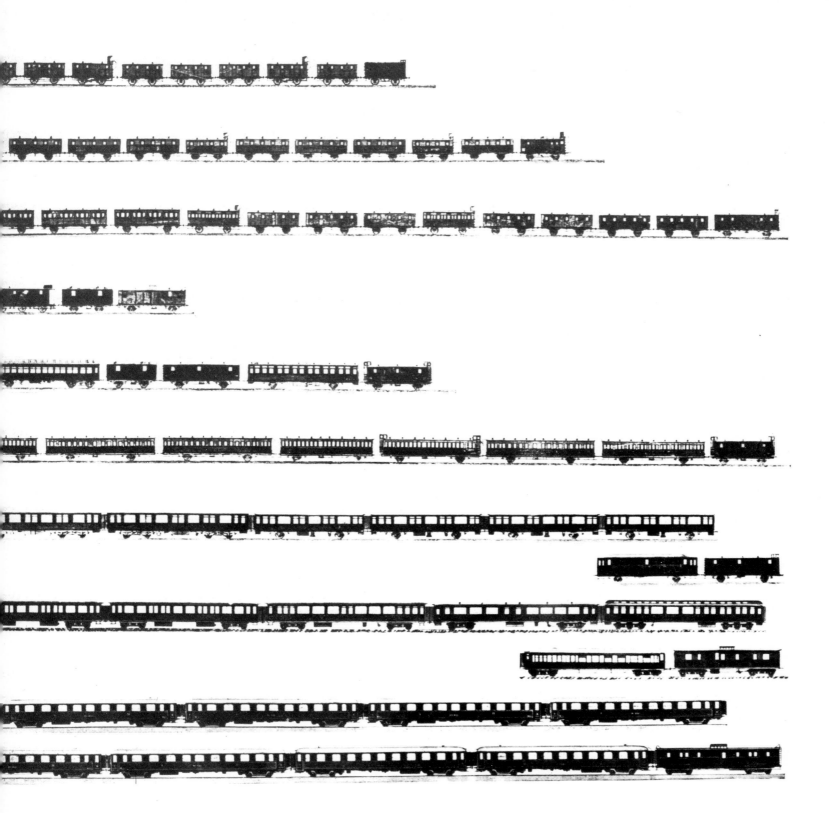

nine compartments. On long-distance trains, coaches were either inter-communicating or had a corridor which gave access to a washroom. By 1925, trains were more or less similar, all coaches and guards' vans being fitted with bogies. By 1935, all rolling-stock was made of metal.

Between 1900 and 1906 engine power increased by 50 per cent and engines could pull trains of 350 tons at 56 m.p.h. Between 1906 and 1935, power more than doubled and 760-ton trains could be pulled at speeds of up to 80 m.p.h. on the flat. The number of coaches per train remained approximately the same but their weight doubled for reasons of safety and comfort. At the end of the period, electric tractions begins to rival steam traction.

ТOCK ON THE PARIS– ORLEANS NETWORK

A derailment on the Southern R.R. near Washington. Although the rails have been ripped out in the accident, the metal coaches have remained intact.

(Photo: *Topical*)

METAL COACHES IN RAILWAY ACCIDENTS

Railway accidents are not solely a result of mistakes or signalling faults. More often than not, the train is derailed for one of a variety of mechanical reasons – broken tyres, broken rails, lack of stability at high speed – and, since the cause of the crash is often destroyed in the crash, it is difficult to ascertain exactly why the accident occurred. While the improvements in signalling are, of course, essential, it is also true that attention must be paid to the strengthening of rolling stock.

If we look at some accidents which have occurred we will see that passenger safety is certainly better assured in metal coaches. In 1932, at Cerences in Normandy and in the military train disaster at Turenne in Algeria, many passengers died because the coaches were made from a variety of materials. When the Basle express was derailed in Villepatour station at a speed of 68 m.p.h., the modern metal rolling-stock saved the lives of many passengers and of the staff in the mail-van. The locomotive and its tender left the rails, and the metal luggage-van behind them turned over. The metal mail-van, which was the next coach, described a complete somersault and came to rest after demolishing one of the walls of the station, causing the roof to collapse. The other end of the mail-van struck a wooden waggon filled with sugar beet and completely destroyed it. The passenger-coaches which were also made of metal finished up criss-crossing the track, which had been ripped from its bed over a distance of 320 yards. Amazingly only a few passengers were injured. In the same year, when the Vintimille to Paris express overturned near Marseilles, on a raised section of track over 20 feet high, not one passenger inside the metal coaches was injured.

In 1933, many passengers died in the train which was derailed near Nantes at a speed of 55 m.p.h. The coaches of this train were only part metal. When the Paris–Bordeaux express was derailed at 75 m.p.h. near Montmoreau in Charente, it provided further evidence that metal coaches offer passengers much greater security.

A comparison between the derailment from a 30-foot high embankment of the Cherbourg to Paris express at Saint-Helier near Conches, and a similar incident on the Vintimille–Paris express, underlines once again the dangers of non-metal coaches. It is interesting to note that, on this occasion, the metal guard's van immediately behind the tender withstood the enormous impact when it ran into the heavy locomotive, which had come to an almost instant stop as it sank into the soft ground, and when, at the same time, it was struck from behind by the mass of coaches travelling at 60 m.p.h.

On 24 December 1933, the disaster at Lagny, when the heavy steel coaches of an express train collided with the old metal coaches of a local train, confirmed these findings. Finally, in April 1935, the accident at Marcheprime on an electrified line showed that passengers run less risk of being electrocuted if they are travelling in metal coaches.

The remains of non-metal coaches crushed in the Lagny catastrophe on 24 December 1933.

The 'crocodile' which makes contact with the metal brush even in frosty conditions.
(*Railway Gazette*, 28 December 1934)

REPETITION OF TRACK SIGNALS ON THE LOCOMOTIVE

One of the devices intended to protect drivers from their own mistakes is the Flaman sealed roll, which records the train's speeds and the signals it passes through. Another device is the 'crocodile', the ribbed version of which always gives good electrical contact even when there is severe ground frost.

In the United States, companies did not hesitate to create a system of automatic signals which bypass the driver. This led to the creation of 'train control'. In the first tests, in 1880, mechanical devices caused the train to stop automatically if signals were ignored. From 1892 onwards, both the block system and train control were developed using both electrical and mechanical de-vices. On high-speed lines, however, these often failed to operate in poor weather conditions. Therefore, in 1907, the Interstate Commerce Commission, a body created to oversee technical and financial rail matters, carried out further research into train control. The result was that in 1930, along more than 18,000 miles of single track, 9,201 locomotives were fitted with electric-al devices. These gave far greater flexibility than the old mechanical versions and controlled train speed by linking it to the amount of traffic ahead.

At the present time three control systems are in operation. First, there is cab signalling, which basically dispenses with automatic braking and makes the driver fully responsible. Signals are repeated continuously in the cab by a coded alternating current fed along the rail and amplified by a kind of radio set. The code varies according to the amount of traffic on the track. The advantage of this system is that the track signal con-tinues to be repeated on the locomotive as far as the next signal. It is, therefore, impossible for the driver not to be aware of the signals.

The second system is the automatic train stop system, which again works by induction and amplification. If the driver fails to see the warning signal or stop signals, the train is automatically brought to a halt. If the driver has seen the signals he intervenes and prevents the brakes being ap-plied.

Finally, automatic speed control is a system which offers complete safety. If the driver does not react within seconds of passing a warning signal, the device operates the brakes and reduces the train's speed so that it can stop immediately if required. If, for some reason, the driver fails to see the stop signal the device causes the train to stop. The introduction of this system on the Chicago & North Western network enabled the company to dispense with all its signals along 500 miles of track.

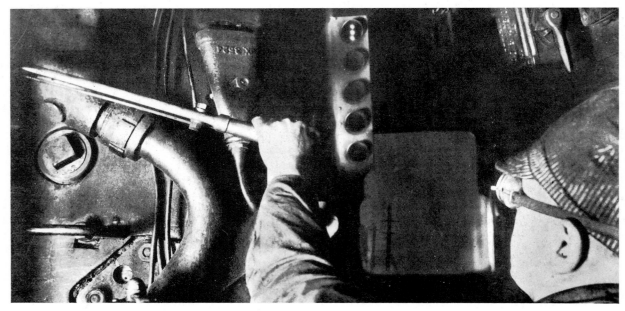

American cab signal reproducing track signals in the locomotive. The picture shows the 'track clear' signal being repeated.
(Pennsylvania R.R. archive)

Construction of tubular-type metal coaches for the French Northern network.
(Archive of the Société Lorraine de Lunéville)

NEW IDEAS IN PASSENGER-COACH CONSTRUCTION

When metal coaches first appeared in Europe, they were based on the old concepts used in the construction of wooden coaches, that is, a light body fixed to a rigid underframe which gave the coach its strength. (See page 000). Since it was the underframe alone and not the body which was intended to withstand shock, the coach was extremely heavy.

New thinking, therefore, involved the use of metal girders to create a product in which all the parts contributed to its overall strength. The coach was no longer a body set on an underframe but a tubular girder resting at each end on bogies, like a bridge on its piers, with the walls, the floor and even the roof all playing a vital part in the coach's strength. The tubular girder, which in fact later became simply a single sheet of metal, was reinforced only by strengthening rings. These rings were, in fact, the walls separating the compartments, and apart from them the coach had no frame as such. Metal coaches used on the State network main lines and metal coaches used on the Northern Railway suburban lines were all built in this way.

Another concept was based on the metal-frame girder as opposed to the tubular girder. The strength comes from prefabricated ribs which form a kind of lattice-work of beams. This is, therefore, a return to the idea of an underframe, but made up of a horizontal lattice girder and two sides consisting of vertical lattice girders linked together by the roof. The function of the metal facing on the sides of the coach is simply to ensure that the coach will not buckle. It, therefore, does not need to be as thick as on the box girder coach. This was the type of coach used on the Belgian State Railway lines and the State suburban lines.

Another idea centred on the construction of coaches with a collapsible compartment at each end. This was intended to reduce the effects of telescoping.

Experience has proved the value of these new ideas, metal coaches having withstood considerable impact in those rail accidents which have occurred since their introduction. They have the further advantage, particularly where electric traction is concerned, of being more fire-resistant and of protecting passengers from electrocution, since the coach acts as a kind of 'Faraday cage'.

First-class bogie coach with a riveted metal body for the P.L.M. line.
(Archive of the Société franco-belge de matériel de chemin de fer)

State suburban network double-decker coach with a lowered centre section (1933).
(Archive of the Entreprises industrielles charentaises)

THE WEIGHT AND CARRYING CAPACITY OF MODERN COACHES

The replacement of old coaches by modern metal coaches raises immediately the difficult problem of their weight and capacity. Since the very beginnings of the railways, the deadweight of passenger coaches has continued to increase, not only because the search to provide greater safety has led to stronger coaches, but also because of demands for ever-increasing levels of comfort. In simple terms, comfort is the amount of space available to each passenger. If there are fewer passengers, there is more room available to each of them, but this, of course, also increases the deadweight per passenger. In fact, compared to the older type of coach made of different materials, the modern metal coach has proved to be far more comfortable. The increased weight of coaches is actually a result of the higher level of comfort provided rather than of the material used in its construction. It must also be remembered that, weight for weight, steel is thirty times more durable than wood.

Metal coaches are as comfortable as wooden coaches without being appreciably heavier. In 1930, at the International Railway Congress, it was stated that in France first-class steel coaches weighed just under 1 ton, second-class just over ½ ton and third-class about ½ ton, while wooden coaches weighed only about three or four per cent less in each case. The difference in deadweight per passenger is therefore relatively low, but the strength of a steel coach is incomparably greater.

It is possible that coaches could be made lighter still by the use of pressed metal and moulded steel parts as in the automobile industry, by welding rather than riveting, and by using high tensile steel and light alloys. This would, however, raise construction costs. Metal corrosion must also be taken into account, since this weakens the coach's strength. Rail coaches must last much longer than cars, and riveting is in many ways preferable to welding as it is much easier to detach a riveted section and replace it by a new unit.

The conflict between, on the one hand, comfort and, on the other, weight and capacity, proved an even greater problem on suburban services. On the State network, the length of the platforms in the Gare Saint-Lazare limited the length of a train to nine coaches. In an effort to cope with intensive traffic flow, engineers looked to South African railways, where trains running on metre-gauge track managed to carry as many passengers as French trains running on standard track. As a result, double-decker coaches started to appear, the centre section of which between the bogies was at a lower level than the rest of the coach, in order both to give it greater stability and to reduce its height to enable it to pass beneath bridges. Passengers who enter these coaches at one end see two staircases, one leading to the top deck, the other leading down to a level not much higher than the track. These coaches offer exceptional carrying capacity. A train of eight such coaches is no longer than an ordinary suburban six-coach train, and can carry 2,112 passengers as against 1,524, with an average deadweight per passenger as low as 440 lbs.

View from the entrance of the upper and lower decks on a French State Railway suburban double-decker coach.

Passengers reach the upper deck from the lower deck's central corridor.
Interior of an American double-deck coach

Restaurant-car on Japanese Railways.
(Photo: Tetsudosho)

A fourth-class train on the Lung-Hai line in China.
(Photo: Republic of China State Railway)

COMFORT ON MODERN TRAINS

In the matter of passenger comfort, the Compagnie internationale des wagons-lits has played a vital part. It was formed in Brussels in 1876 and,

up to the outbreak of the First World War, instigated improved travelling conditions, not only on the continent of Europe but also in Russia, Egypt and North Africa. The doyen of trains is the Orient Express which was inaugurated in 1883. This was followed by the Sud Express running between Paris, Madrid and Lisbon, the Mediterranean Express, the Ostend–

Interior of a Swedish third-class sleeping-car at night.
(Swedish State Railways. Photo: Ifa)

Vienna Express, whose route, like that of the Orient Express, was extended to Istanbul in 1895, the Nord Express and the Riviera Express.

After 1918, the first to resume service was the Paris–Rome Express, followed a short time later by the Orient Express and the Bombay Express. The first metal sleeping-cars, with their underframe, roof, frame and outer walls all made of steel, were introduced in 1922. In 1925, the first metal restaurant-cars appeared.

After 1918, the most important innovation was the Simplon–Orient Express linking Western Europe with Bucharest, Sofia, Athens and Istanbul via Switzerland, Italy and Yugoslavia. Later, this service was further improved by the introduction of the Anatolia Express and the Taurus Express, with the result that the journey from Paris to Cairo in the 1930s could be completed in six days, from Paris to Baghdad in six and a half days, Paris to Teheran in eight days, Paris to Basra in seven and a half days, and Paris to Karachi in twelve days. In Basra, passengers joined a ferry connection to Bombay, which could be reached in fourteen days.

In order to offer daytime passengers a level of comfort comparable with that found on sleeping-cars, the wagons-lits company built trains equipped with Pullman saloon and restaurant-cars. The first of these trains entered service in 1925 between Milan and Cannes. In 1926, two other metal Pullman-coach trains were in operation, the Golden Arrow Express running between Paris and Calais and connecting with the Dover–London Pullman train, and the Sud Express running to the Basque Coast and Spain. On these trains, pairs of coaches work in tandem, with one coach containing a kitchen which provides food to passengers on both the coaches. Later, second-class Pullman coaches were built in which bench seats replaced armchairs. This stock was put into service on the North Star running between Paris, Brussels and Amsterdam, on the Bluebird between Paris, Brussels and Antwerp, on the Côte d'Azur Pullman Express between Paris and Nice, and on various other routes linking industrial towns and tourist areas.

In 1930, the State Railway built all-steel coaches which showed a marked American influence. Their interiors were particularly attractive and offered a variety of facilities without any increase

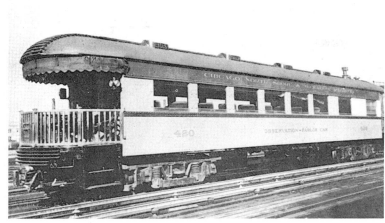

Chicago & Milwaukee R.R. observation car with enamelled panels.
(Photo: Armco)

Interior of an observation saloon-car at the rear of a South African train.
(South African Railway)

in weight, the deadweight per passenger being only 1¾ tons whereas on the old stock it had been 2 tons. Following the world-wide financial crisis of 1931, the wagons-lits company launched a programme to extend its services to a wider public. Except in certain countries where a third-class sleeping-car facility was available, initially only first-class passengers could travel in sleeping-cars and on luxury trains. Since 1927, on all great international trains and even on ordinary services, second-class passengers have been able to enjoy this facility too. In 1932, in Austria, Holland, Romania and Yugoslavia, a third-class sleeping-car service was made available, and on 1 April 1933, in France, between Paris, Marseilles and the Côte d'Azur. Each compartment contained a washbasin and wardrobe and, at night, three bunk beds with sheets, pillow and blanket. A buffet-car was also introduced, giving a cheaper alternative to the restaurant-car. Finally, in France and certain Central European countries, a restaurant-cum-bar car offered a more informal service.

Two basic factors in rail comfort are heating and ventilation. Many of the older-type coaches were generally heated too efficiently, except at times of extreme cold. The tiredness experienced by overnight passengers can be explained in two ways. First, the temperature in the compartment often exceeds 25°C; second, ventilation is inadequate and frequently non-existent. As time passes, the amount of breathable air decreases, and conditions for passengers become progressively unpleasant. In modern coaches, heating is either regulated automatically or controlled from within the compartment.

In the United States, air-conditioning has proved to be particularly popular. Since the windows on aerodynamic trains cannot be opened, a special device automatically renews the air between 20 and 30 times per hour with fresh pure air, cool in summer and warm in winter, replacing the stale air inside the compartment. Because of the sealed system, smoke and dust cannot enter the coach and external noise is considerably reduced. Moreover 'rubber heels' are fitted to the coaches and this reduces vibration. All the underframe's carrying points and the ends of springs are similarly fitted with rubber pads, there being at least 51 of these on a twelve-wheel coach (two

three-axle bogies). Some American companies see air-conditioning as the main reason for the traffic increase which occurred in the summer of 1934.

Although air-conditioning is thought to have been invented in the United States, it existed in France in 1930 when the Paris–Orleans Railway coaches were fitted with a system of ventilation which provided cool, filtered air.

Interior of an air-conditioned Pullman sleeping-car on one of the Union Pacific's aerodynamic trains.
(Photo: Union Pacific Railroad)

Lubricating connecting-rods and
cranks.
(Photo: Dutch Railways)

LUBRICATION

Though the passenger may not be aware of it, an important factor in his or her safety is daily axle lubrication. An overheated bearing can well be the cause of a disaster since steel, when heated, loses much of its strength. Modern rolling-stock is becoming heavier and heavier, and axle-loads have increased to the maximum the track can withstand. At the same time, axle revolution speed has increased. The result is that axle-boxes must be more often and more generously lubricated. Until recently, lubrication was based simply on capillary action, operating in the same way as a wick in an old oil lamp.

Mechanical lubrication became a necessity. One means of minimising friction between two surfaces is to place between the surfaces a layer of oil thick enough to act, not by capillary action or by molecular attraction, but hydrodynamically. This layer of oil is provided by the steel 'Isothermos box'. The oil inside it is distributed by a blade which turns on the axle and gives maximum lubrication at any speed. At a speed of 60–75 m.p.h. the blade distributes 100–110 lbs of oil per hour. This is far more efficient than the best oil pad which could distribute only about ½ lb per hour. Moreover, in the Isothermos box the temperature remains lower and, with its specially designed sealed system, the same oil, without any replenishment, lasts up to 60,000 miles.

Another method of lubrication is to reduce the

S.K.F. bearing-housing parts fitted to axle-spindle.
(Photo: Compagnie d'applications mécaniques)

number of friction surfaces by the use of roller-bearings, as opposed to the ball-bearings used in cars and bicycles. The latter would not be suitable given the heavy loads carried by rail. By this method, lubrication is not by oil but by a special grease injected under pressure. Where S.K.F. roller-bearing boxes are fitted, lubrication is required only every 60,000 miles. Moreover, the temperature hardly exceeds the temperature of the air around them. The only problem which may occur is when too much grease is injected, or when the grease is not thick enough.

Roller-bearing was beginning to be applied [1935] to locomotive linkages. The Delaware & Hudson Railroad successfully tested it on a 4–6–2 class express locomotive, fitted with bearings not only on the main connecting-rod stub ends but also on the coupling-rod heads. The lubrication of a roller-bearing box is achieved by first of all removing the cover, and then screwing in place a special pump with a piston driven by a threaded rod. In bad weather this operation must be carried out under cover to prevent rain thinning the special grease, since this could cause rust to form on the bearings.

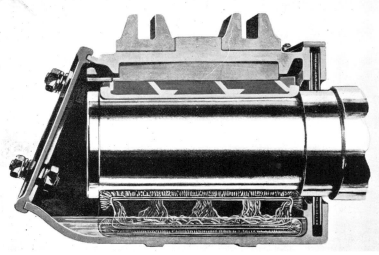

Lubricating-pad type spindle-box.
(Isothermos archive)

'Isothermos'-type mechanical lubrication spindle-box.
(Isothermos archive)

Japanese waggon with ventilation.

(Photo: Tetsudosho)

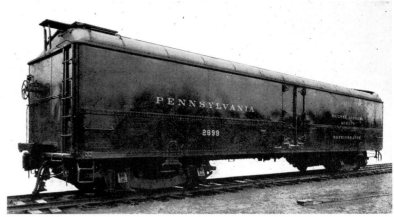

Express refrigeration waggon.

(Pennsylvania R.R.)

French railways standard flat waggon.

(Office central d'étude de matériel de chemin de fer)

40-ton automatic discharge waggon.

(Hungarian State Railways)

THE MODERN WAGGON

Since 1918, the goods waggon has also become heavier and, as capacity has increased, so carriage has become more efficient, in other words, the deadweight per ton of capacity has decreased. This increase in capacity stems principally from the lengthening of the wheelbase, which has resulted in improved maintenance of operating stock and faster movement of goods. A further factor concerning speed of movement is the invention of the continuous brake. The increase in weight has been caused mainly by the replacement of wooden by metal frames in order to strengthen stock. Whereas, before 1914, the usual type of low-speed waggon had a load capacity of 10 tons, it can now carry up to 20 tons and this has become the standard load on the main French networks.

Other stock includes the standard flat bogie waggon, which will carry up to 40 tons, the Northern Railway's high-sided automatic-tipper bogie waggons, with a 60-ton capacity and a 19-ton tare, the Eastern Railway's 50-ton high-sided waggon to transport corn, insulated and refrigerator cars, and waggons to transport fresh vegetables which can run in France, Britain and even Spain, where the axles are changed so that they may operate on the broader gauge.

Large-capacity waggon (63 tons) for transporting ore.

(South African Railways)

Extended all-steel gondola-type waggon.

(Pennsylvania R.R.)

Oil-tanker waggon with a capacity of 4800 gallons.

(Photo Northern Railway)

French railways standard high-sided waggon.

(Office central d'étude de matériel de chemin de fer)

Special flat waggon designed to carry 8 mobile containers. In the illustration, the containers' doors are open.
(Pennsylvania R.R.)

WAGGONS AND CONTAINERS

Since 1918, the capacity and wheelbase of waggons have increased to give improved stability and greater running speed. Everywhere metal has replaced wood. Buffer and traction mechanisms are stronger, capacity has risen to 20 tons per unit instead of the pre-1914 10 tons. This is now used as a basis for standardisation of low-speed two-axle rolling stock. Standard 40-ton bogie stock, with a tare slightly over 20 tons, is now appearing on major networks.

The idea of a continuing increase in carrying capacity per unit is counter-balanced by the development of a new kind of stock based on the idea of the divisibility of traffic and the possibility of door-to-door transportation. Waggons run on rails and rails cannot go everywhere. By contrast, the automobile represents an extremely flexible means of transport, since it can go from door to door without any interruption to its journey and without any assistance from other vehicles. The container is, in fact, simply a metal body containing the goods to be carried which can be loaded on to a lorry or a flat waggon or the deck or hold of a ship. Although it may need to be transferred from one vehicle to another, it allows a signficant reduction in two key areas of distribution costs, packaging and transportation. It is its own packaging, and this packaging is discounted when transportation costs based upon the weight of the goods transported are calculated. In short, a container is a detachable section of a waggon or lorry which is placed on the chassis of a road or rail vehicle fitted with wheels, springs and a platform.

Railway networks are in the process of building container parks which they rent out to commerce and industry. Instead of being airtight, some containers are ventilated to allow them to carry perishable goods such as fruit, vegetables, butter and poultry. Moreover, certain refrigerator-car companies working in close co-operation with the rail networks have started to export insulated containers which can be used to transport solid carbon dioxide and fresh meat.

The cost to an individual company of hiring a container from a rail company is minimal. Transportation costs are the same as for goods loaded directly onto a rail waggon. When the container makes its return journey its deadweight, of course, is extremely low.

Unloading tanker used to transport milk.
(Northern Railway)

Unloading ventilated containers used to transport perishable goods.
(Northern Railway)

Testing brakes on a goods train of almost 100 waggons. Each carry a 20-ton load and, with a 10-ton tare, that gives a total weight of 2500–3000 tons.

(Westinghouse archive)

BRAKING SYSTEMS ON LONG GOODS TRAINS

It is known that the idea of brakes being controlled directly by the driver was first conceived in 1844, and that George Westinghouse, in 1869, was the first to fit compressed-air brakes to rail vehicles. In 1874, the inventor changed his earlier system and gave it the form it now has in North and South America, Asia, Australia and part of Europe. Britain and Spain prefer the vacuum-brake, which was invented and developed about the same time.

At first, the compressed-air automatic continuous brake was used only on passenger trains because it improved safety. About 1905, in the United States, it was applied to goods trains. Because it made stopping easier, trains become longer and heavier. Their speed was increased and traffic became more intensive. Fewer guards were needed, since the system of manual brakes at various points along the train was dispensed with. In the United States, application of the new system of braking caused fewer problems because waggons there had rigid centre coupling. In Europe, however, flexible side buffers are used and goods trains are coupled less rigidly to allow

the train to set off more easily. However, the compressed-air which operates the brakes takes some time to travel from the locomotive to the end of the train. Therefore, when the train sets off, the brakes on the front waggons are released before those on the rear waggons, and the locomotive's traction can cause couplings to fracture. Moreover, the different weights of the vehicles require different braking efforts and this can again damage couplings. So, modifications had to be made to the Westinghouse brake-system on passenger trains, and on goods trains it was changed to give a more gentle braking action and at the same time one that could be transmitted more rapidly along the train.

When brakes are applied on a long downhill stretch, air pressure tends to decrease as a result of the inevitable leaks. A system which maintained the original braking effort had to be devised. The P.L.M. therefore tested an automatic brake which operated in conjunction with a second, direct brake. The direct brake sent compressed air along an auxiliary pipe directly into the brake-cylinders. A few years before the First World War, international tests were carried out in Austria on the Hardy brake and on the auxiliary-pipe Westinghouse brake. However tests were about to begin on the Kunze-Knorr German brake when war broke out.

In 1926, Swiss and Italian engineers found that the Westinghouse brake, which was already in use in France, could be used in conjunction with the Kunze-Knorr brake and the two were adopted by railways throughout the world.

The present goods-train Westinghouse brake has two cylinders beneath each waggon. Though independent from each other, they control the same brake system and operate in different ways, depending on the waggon's load and whether the terrain is hilly or flat. The 'deadweight cylinder' operates whatever the situation. When the waggon is empty, it operates alone, but if the waggon is loaded, the second cylinder, the 'load cylinder', also operates. By moving a special handle on which are the words 'hilly – flat', the triple-valve inlets (see page 000) can be opened and closed.

In the 1930s, passenger-train brakes need to be modified to cope with increased speeds. In fact, brake-shoe friction against the wheel varies according to the revolution speed of the wheel. At high speeds, friction decreases, so that braking is less efficient at first, unless brake-shoe pressure is increased. As the train slows down, the pressure is then gradually reduced so that the train does not come to a sudden stop. The changes required, therefore, a method of giving both greater but more flexible braking-power when the brakes are first applied.

A sight once common in Egypt. Alongside a river in the Nile Delta, the Egypt

RAILWAYS OUTSIDE EUROPE

Fifty-seven per cent of the world's railways were on the American continent [1935], including 43 per cent in the United States, where there were 42,000 miles of rail networks. Since 1893, the Pan-American inter-continental line has been under construction, running from north to south and linking Ottawa, the capital of Canada, and Buenos Aires, the capital of Argentina. This involves a total distance of over 10,500 miles, three-quarters of which had been completed. This dorsal line will eventually have transverse lines running from it to Venezuela, Guiana, Brazil, Paraguay, Uruguay and Chile. The longest of these transverse lines will stand comparison with the New York–San Francisco line running from ocean to ocean. It will link the Chilean port of Antofagasta on the Pacific to Rio de Janeiro on the Atlantic, a distance of 3,000 miles, of which at the time of writing [1935] 800 are to be built.

In Africa, rail development is much less advanced. Parts of a north–south dorsal line are in existence, the famous Cecil Rhodes vision of a Cape to Cairo railway. But the Benguela–Beira line is still the only one to run from east to west, while in the African hinterland there were four regions of commercial importance which in the 1930s neighbouring powers are making efforts to reach by rail.

The first was Abyssinia which had only the Addis Ababa metre-gauge line constructed by the French. This was opened in 1894. The second region was Chad. Before 1914, Germany wanted to extend its lines from the Cameroon to this area. Similarly, France aimed to reach Chad from Gabon and Ubangi Shari as did Britain from Nigeria. Since 1934, the French had built the Congo–Ocean line as a first link and this provided a route to the sea from all the rivers and roads which criss-cross French Equatorial Africa. Almost unsurmountable difficulties had to be overcome in the building of this 300-mile long line, with its 12 tunnels and 92 bridges and viaducts. Standard-gauge track was used, and traction was by a special Golwoe-class articulated

Next to an old tank engine on the right, a 4–8–2 + 2–8–4 'Garratt'-class articulated locomotive on the Blida-Djelfa line (1932).
There is only one locomotive and only one boiler, the two ends of which rest on two driving trucks.

(Algerian General Agency archive)

...al Train passes a palm grove parallel to a road which is a thousand years old.　(Eygptian Railway archive)

locomotive. Operating on the Ivory Coast, it had six coupled axles and an adhesive weight of 72 tons. Only bogie coaches and waggons were used, and all rolling-stock was made of metal and fitted with centre coupling as in America.

The third region was Kimberley and Johannesburg, where there was keen interest to build rail links to the ports of Port Elizabeth, East London, Durban, and Lourenço Marques in Mozambique. The fourth region was Katanga, with its important mines. Here competition between Belgium, Angola, Rhodesia and the West African colonies led to the building of the Benguela–Beira line.

Apart from these sections of track, there are only two networks as such, one in the south in South Africa, the other in the north. Technically,

the South African network is one of the most remarkable in the world. In spite of its narrow-gauge track (3 feet 6 inches), its rolling-stock achieves exceptional efficiency and output through the power and flexibility of its enormous locomotives, the carrying capacity and comfort of its coaches, and the excellent use made of its large waggons. Because of difficulty in hauling these heavy trains up steep gradients and through sharp curves, particularly in Natal where the line rises to almost 6,500 feet above sea-level, special classes of articulated locomotives such as the Garratt were built. Electric traction is used on suburban and mountain lines in the Cape and Natal.

In North Africa, standard gauge is used on the Western and Egyptian networks. Since 1934,

Algeria, Tunisia and Morocco had formed a block of countries which railways had linked more and more closely together along the 1,700 miles of track between Tunis and Marrakesh. Here also the Garratt-class locomotive operated: on standard gauge, where as a 4–6–2+2–6–4 double Pacific it provided an express service from Algiers to Oran, and on the Blida–Djelfa metre-gauge track at an altitude of more than 3,200 feet. Side by side with these powerful articulated steam locomotives, electric traction could be seen not only in Algeria in the district of Bône, but, in particular, in Morocco where electric locomotives solved the problem posed by poor-quality water with its high salt content which would damage a steam locomotive's boilers.

The Sultan of Morocco at the inauguration of the rail link between Tunisia, Algeria and Morocco.

In the newly-built station at Bône, an electric locomotive on the Oued Keberit to Bône mining line.
(Algerian General Agency archive)

AN ELECTRIC TRAIN ON A SUBURBAN LINE

MODERN ELECTRIC TRACTION [1935]

Before 1914, railway companies could not agree on the best type of electric traction. Italy was the champion of three-phase current. Single-phase was preferred in Switzerland, Germany, Sweden and the United States. All other countries which had electric lines preferred direct current (see pages 000 to 000).

A single three-phase current combination, in which the locomotive itself transforms single-phase current into three-phase current, was used [1935] on the Norfolk & Western Railroad and the Virginia Railroad in the United States, while the Pennsylvania Railroad had plans to instal this system on the hilliest part of its New York–Philadelphia–Pittsburg line to haul passenger trains using single-phase current and goods trains using single- and three-phase current across the Allegheny Mountains. In Europe, Hungary was electrifying in similar fashion the 120 miles of line between Budapest and Bruck: a 15,000-volt single-phase current is fed directly into the locomotive, which transforms it into three-phase current using a process developed by the engineer, De Kando. Generally speaking, direct current tends to be more widely used now. It is at present [1935] being introduced on the Naples–Foggia line in Italy. Certain single-phase current lines in America have now changed to direct current. Switzerland, which was one of the first countries to adopt single-phase current, was changing to direct current following its successful use on the Chicago–Milwaukee–St Paul line. In France, about 1910, the Southern Railway had equipped its 15 miles of line between Villefranche-de-Conflent and Ille with 12,000-volt single-phase current, but in 1920 it returned to direct current.

High-tension direct current is tending to be more commonly used. In 1903, high tension was tested on the Saint-Georges-de-Commiers to La Mure line and, in 1910, on the North–South line in Paris. Now voltages in excess of 1,200 are exceeded regularly and on the Turin–Ceres line in Italy 3,600-volt current is used. In 1917, on more than 400 miles of its trans-continental line across the Rocky Mountains, the Chicago–Milwaukee Railroad used 3,000-volt direct current, and plans were in hand to equip a further 880 miles of its network. The success of this system influenced French engineers and the Government when they were considering which current to adopt on the rail networks. In 1919, it was agreed that 1,500 and 3,000 volts would be fed to contact lines, the former on intensive traffic lines and the latter on less intensive lines and on lines used by powerful locomotives. A principal factor in this decision was the financial savings made where high-tension wires are installed. Moreover, 3,000-volt locomotives were equipped to run on both 1,500- and 3,000-volt lines at the same speed and with the same load. Electrification of the French rail networks was based on these principles, and at the present time [1935] approximately 1,200 miles of track have been electrified.

To sum up: half the electric locomotives in the world run off direct current, with a maximum of

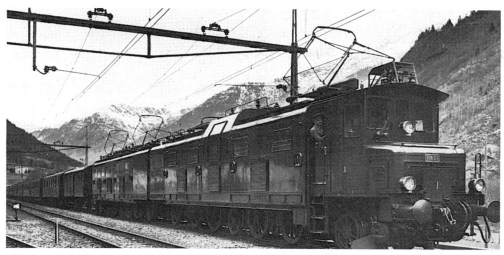

The largest single-phase electric locomotive in Europe, producing 8000 h.p. It has eight driving-axles and ran on the Saint-Gothard line (1932).

(Swiss Federal Railways)

One of the Chicago & Milwaukee R.R. 1-Bo-Do+Do-Bo-1 electric locomotives. Since 1920, these powerful engines, using 3000-volt direct current, have crossed the Rocky Mountains.

(Milkwaukee R.R.)

Single-phase passenger-train electric locomotive capable of speeds of 50 m.p.h. up steep Austrian gradients.

(Austrian Federal Railways)

THE ELECTRIC 'SOUTHERN EXPRESS'
The electric locomotive with four driven axles giving a total of 3,600 h.p. and a top speed of 65 m.p.h.

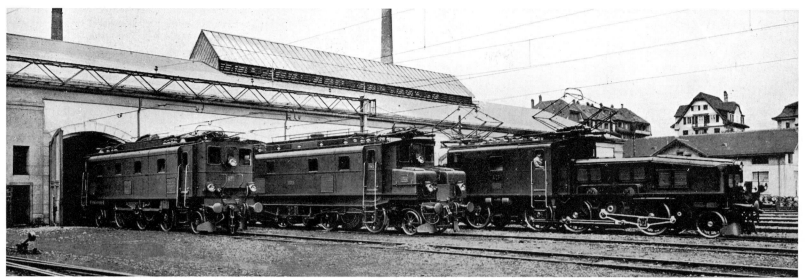

Three different types of single-phase 'Oerlikon'-class electric locomotives at Berne depot.

(Swiss Federal Railway archive)

3600 h.p. 2-Do-2-class P.O. locomotive weighing 140 tons and capable of pulling an 800-ton train at 75 m.p.h.

The engine is seen here coupled to the Sud Express at the Gare d'Austerlitz. (Archive of the Compagnie éléctro-mécanique)

4,000 volts. If this maximum was exceeded, the copper blades on the current collectors fitted to all direct-current motors would very quickly become worn. These motors are very flexible, overheat far less than others and can produce far greater power than motors running off other forms of current.

The electric locomotive, which does not produce its own energy, has both the advantage and disadvantage of being dependent on an outside source of power. There is a disadvantage in that it is immediately affected by any problem at the power station or in the distribution network. However, with the creation of a network of power stations linked together, this disadvantage is minimised. The advantage is that it does not have to haul a heavy tender carrying fuel and water, and this reduces its deadweight when it has to climb steep gradients. The electric locomotive is lighter and less bulky relative to its power and can therefore pull away and accelerate quickly, provided, of course, it has sufficient adhesion. Since electric energy can be distributed to a greater number of driving-axles, track adhesion is guaranteed and it is this ability to accelerate rapidly from rest that enables such engines to

Electric locomotive capable of pulling a goods train at 37 m.p.h.

(Austrian Federal Railway archive)

97-ton mixed track Japanese locomotive driven by 600-volt direct current.

(Photo: Tetsudosho)

provide a much improved service on city suburban lines where there are frequent stops.

One problem which electric locomotives face is the transmission of power to the adhesion-axles from the huge motors into which the current is fed. The Americans, using a gearless system divided the motor in two. There was the inductor fixed to the bogie, and there was the armature fixed to the axle. The disadvantage of this system is that axle-weight is increased, and smoothness of ride is therefore reduced. Sometimes, also, electric energy is lost because of the gap between the inductor and the armature.

Until the introduction of the American system, connecting-rods had been preferred (see page 000), and this meant that motors were positioned higher and that the locomotive's centre of gravity rose. This gave a somewhat smoother ride, in spite of the sideways and rocking movements which caused driver-fatigue and track wear. The

Electric test train with single-phase traction and dynamometric coach in Erstfeld station, Switzerland.

(Swiss Federal Railways)

Goods train single-phase electric locomotive, capable of speeds of 25 m.p.h. up steep gradients in Austria.

(Austrian Federal Railways)

1-Co+Co-1 electric goods locomotive. Using 1500-volt direct current, it ran on the P.L.M. line between Culoz and Modane.

(Photo: Compagnie eléctro-mécanique)

solution appears to lie in the system of gearing known as 'nose support', which has always been a feature of electric trams. On locomotives, the logical answer seems to be to encase the driving-axle in a hollow tube or concentric untrue axle, to which the gear ring is fitted and which drives the centre axle. Gearing takes place on the wheels by means of springs and spherical link rods.

One problem encountered by the electric locomotive is the continuous need to cool those parts of the engine where electric energy is transformed into mechanical energy. This is done by fans which inject cold air even when the train is stationary. Another problem is the operation of the controls. Because of the power involved, this cannot be done manually. A low current is therefore used, to drive the valves which distribute compressed-air to the cylinders. In the cylinders, pistons drive the traction current-contactors.

One advantage of electric traction is that electric energy can be generated as the train runs downhill, the direct current motor being reversible. Instead of current being fed to the train, the train feeds current to the line, at the same time creating resistance which acts as a powerful and continuous braking device. In this way, the locomotive as it descends the gradient provides some of the energy needed by the locomotive which passes it on its uphill journey. It is almost as if the second locomotive is being hauled uphill by an invisible cable.

As on steam locomotives, the axle layout is described by the use of symbols, these being capital letters whose position in the alphabet shows the number of driving-axles: A = 1, B = 2, C = 3, etc. If these are individual drive-axles the letters are followed by O. An electric locomotive with two individual-drive bogies will have the symbols Bo-Bo. If they were coupled it would be BB. If the electric locomotive has a carrying bogie at the front and rear, with, between them, two groups of two driving-axles coupled beneath the same underframe, its symbol will be 2-B-B-2. In the case of a double locomotive, the + sign is used to link the symbols describing each unit. Thus the P.O.'s gearless direct-drive locomotive with six coupled axles and a double unit has the symbols 2-C+C-2.

Alignment supports on the Bordeaux to Hendaye 1500-volt
direct-current catenary line.
(Drouard Frères)

1500-volt direct-current catenary line from Dax to Toulouse. The
support posts take the line round a curve in the track.
(Drouard Frères)

ELECTRIC TRACK

Initially, electric track was fitted with a centre rail from which the locomotive collected current. Later, for example on the Paris Metro, this centre rail became a side rail, and on Paris suburban lines current was collected by slide contacts fitted to the underside of the rail to reduce problems caused by frost and ice. The third rail continued to be used solely for low-voltage (600–1,500 volts) direct current. As this system posed an element of danger for track personnel, and given the increasing use of electrified lines, companies began to adopt overhead feed, with a single line for direct- and single-phase current and a double line for three-phase current. To ensure that the locomotive makes good contact with the overhead feed line, even at high speed, it is fitted with two pantographs in place of the tramways' 'sliding bow'. These are hinged and in the shape of a pentagon and are operated by compressed-air. At the top, they have two aluminium bars, which oscillate transversely as they make contact with the wire. A slot in the bars is filled with grease to improve contact.

Since electric locomotives travel at high speed and collect high-voltage current they must make continuous contact on an almost horizontal plane, otherwise the pantograph is subjected to excessive movement and can break. Catenary lines (from the Latin word 'catena', meaning a small chain)

have therefore been installed. These consist of steel cables which maintain the feed line on an almost horizontal plane by means of vertical supports or suspension wires of unequal length. This system ensures that the line is almost perfectly straight in spite of the distance between pylons. Between Vierzon and Brive, for example, the catenary line was as follows: two hard, copper, contact wires running on the same horizontal plane and connected to an auxiliary copper carrying-wire by suspension wires every 7 feet or so. The auxiliary carrying-wire in turn is connected by a second series of suspension wires to a

main carrying-cable made of copper or cadmium. The catenary system is flexible, and fully insulated by porcelain insulators fixed to horizontal brackets. Bracing-wire with an adjuster unit runs to the upper part of each bracket. In spite of the strength of this system, the possibility of damage from side winds led engineers to limit the intervals between pylons to 200 feet.

On double track, two independent catenary lines are installed. A similar arrangement is found in stations, but since trains pass through stations at lower speeds, and collect weaker currents, the catenary lines are lighter.

Overhead wires at Juvisy station.
(Drouard Frères)

ELECTRIFICATION OF SUBURBAN SERVICES AND REVERSIBLE STEAM TRAINS

Nothing shows better the carrying capacity of a railway line than a suburban service. For example, in the 1930s the suburban services from the Gare Saint-Lazare carried 285,000 passengers daily on weekdays, and in summer 300,000 daily on Sundays and Bank Holidays. At the busiest time of day, between 6.15 and 7.15 pm, 800 passengers leave the station every minute. On the Paris–Saint-Germain line, one of the oldest in the world, the number of trains running each day in both directions in 1837 was 16. A hundred years later it was 310.

How has the rail service coped with this vast increase without increasing the number of tracks and without building longer platforms? First of all, by adopting an automatic block system which increases considerably the flow of traffic along a line. Second, by electrification and, third, on non-electric lines, by the use of reversible steam trains. The engine no longer has to be turned round or to leave the rear of the train to take its place at the front. As we have seen, electric traction started in towns where savings could be made on boiler-maintenance, and costs of fuel and water, and where smoke and fumes had previously been unpleasant factors in the lives of the people living in the town. Electric traction then spread out from city centres and was extended to provide main-line services.

Thanks to its flexibility, and its capacity to feed an increasing number of driving-axles, electric energy offers financial gains, not only where the locomotive is concerned, but also for the train itself. Trains can be shortened or lengthened to

The 'Brighton Belle', an electric Pullman train, running between London and Brighton in the 1930s at speeds of 50 m.p.h.

(Photo: Nofée)

include one, two or three units. The trains' composition can therefore be linked closely to demand. In 1935, on the Saint-Lazare suburban lines, with a service operated 50 per cent by electricity and 50 per cent by steam, the number of passenger places available was as high as 68,802 per hour. With complete electrification, there could be as many as 147,316.

Reversible trains, which can either be pulled or pushed by the locomotive, have run from the Gare Saint-Lazare since 1929. When the engine is at the rear, the driver moves to a cab at the front of the train. There he can operate a continuous brake and, using compressed-air from the locomotive's pump, he controls a servo-motor which drives the regulator. By a simple movement of a valve he can control the speed. If the air-pipe breaks, the regulator closes automatically. An intercom system enables driver and fireman to contact each other if the need arises.

Driver's cab on a reversible train.

(Photoschall).

A reversible train with double-decker metal coaches and the locomotive at the front.

(Photoschall).

The same reversible train but, running in the opposite direction, with the engine at the rear.

(Photoschall)

A Canadian diesel electric locomotive of the 1930s.

(Photo: Canadian National Railway)

THE DIESEL ELECTRIC LOCOMOTIVE – A MOBILE POWER-STATION

Unlike the steam engine, the oil- or diesel-fired engine does not need a boiler or water since fuel burns directly in the cylinders. It is, therefore, lighter. Fuel in its liquid form is less bulky and easier to store. This again makes the engine lighter. However, oil, with its very fine droplets, is too flammable for powerful engines. Diesel fuel, which is lighter and less volatile, is preferred. But the mixture of air and the heavy droplets of fuel cannot be ignited by an electric spark. The mixture needs to be rapidly compressed so that its temperature is raised. This compression requires a stronger, and therefore heavier, mechanism. As a result, although the diesel engine produces greater horse-power than the oil-fired engine, it is heavier relative to the power it generates.

Like the oil engine, the diesel engine cannot be coupled directly to the driving-axles. A transmission system is needed. However, the power of such an engine means that mechanical transmission, as on a car, is out of the question. Electrical power, which is more flexible, is therefore used. By means of a horizontal drive-shaft parallel to the track, the diesel engine drives a dynamo. The current generated drives electric motors suspended from the locomotive's axles in the same way as on an electric locomotive. The system, in fact, involves a kind of electric power-station on wheels.

Unfortunately, this transformation of heat, and electric and mechanical energy involves a considerable weight factor. While engine weight is as low as 20 lbs per horse-power, electric transmission alone can weigh 44 lbs and sometimes even as much as 65–75 lbs per horse-power. To provide the same power, therefore, the diesel electric locomotive proves to be heavier than the steam locomotive. It does, however, given better traction. It consumes fuel only during running time, whereas the steam locomotive at rest continues to burn coal to maintain its pressure. Moreover, not needing water, the diesel locomotive can complete long journeys non-stop.

For these reasons, the P.L.M. Railway and the Paris Circle line were, during the 1930s, testing a diesel electric locomotive. It offered real savings on goods services and as a shunting engine. Tests carried out by the P.L.M. on a train travelling non-stop at an average speed of 60 m.p.h. on the 535-mile journey between Paris and Marseilles – which would normally require three steam locomotives and three stops – proved that on a future trans-Sahara line the diesel electric locomotive, operating without water, may well turn out to be 'the future camel of the desert'.

A P.L.M. 600-h.p. shunting engine, showing the interior of a diesel electric locomotive.

Slightly to the left of centre: the diesel engine. On the right: the dynamo and its exciter.

(Photo: Compagnie électro-mécanique)

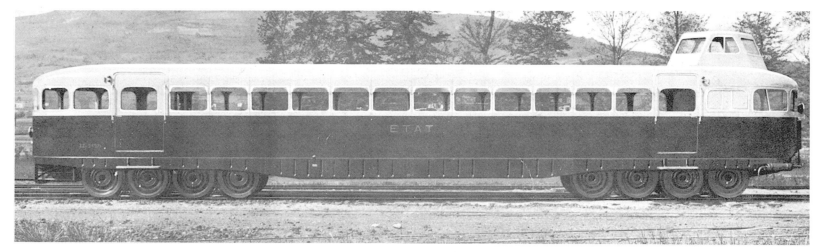

The Micheline, with seats for 36 passengers, on the Lille-Valenciennes-Lens-Bethune line (1935).
(Micheline archive)

THE RAILCAR

In July 1931, the appearance of the 'Micheline' produced a revolution in coach design. At the time, the situation was as follows: on secondary lines traffic was decreasing; the old-fashioned rolling-stock – 30, 40, and sometimes 50 years old – was unattractive when compared with the splendid new coaches now introduced on the roads. Moreover, the older type of trains had become relatively slow and infrequent. Even when almost empty they weighted over 1 ton per passenger.

On main lines traffic had not declined. Trains were now heavier and longer. Locomotives were more powerful and could carry more passengers in greater comfort. On luxury trains, where attempts to improve amenities led to a loss of space, the deadweight remained as high as 1½ tons per passenger, whereas heavy express trains pulled by Mountain-class locomotives had a deadweight as low as ¾ ton per passenger, including the weight of the locomotive and its tender.

On suburban lines subject to dense traffic, where comfort was less important in view of shorter journey times, the weight of the State

The first 'Micheline' with pneumatic tyres (1933).
(Michelin archive)

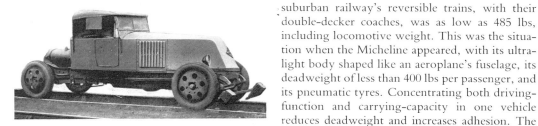

The Michelin rail tyre, with adhesion three times greater than that of a steel tyre.

suburban railway's reversible trains, with their double-decker coaches, was as low as 485 lbs, including locomotive weight. This was the situation when the Micheline appeared, with its ultra-light body shaped like an aeroplane's fuselage, its deadweight of less than 400 lbs per passenger, and its pneumatic tyres. Concentrating both driving-function and carrying-capacity in one vehicle reduces deadweight and increases adhesion. The tyres make this adhesion even more efficient, and this is a vital factor in the acceleration and deceleration speeds, particularly with a powerful engine. So the Micheline was the ideal solution for light-traffic stopping lines. Unfortunately, its tyres were too narrow for the rail and this limited load capacity. The only answer seemed to be to increase the number of wheels, but this would have the effect of raising deadweight per passenger. The problem was solved by the invention of the steel tyre and the cushioned wheel. However, some adhesion was lost, since the steel rails came into contact with the steel tyres. To minimise to some extent this loss of adhesion, an electro-magnetic braking system was devised. An electric current causes a magnetic field to form from a collector-shoe parallel to the rail, and the magnetic field creates a multitude of tiny currents (Foucauld currents). These attract the shoe and act

The tube of the tyre is inside a steel casing. This protection reduces wear and increases efficiency.

(Lorraine-Dietrich archive)

De Dietrich and Company railcar bogie, fitted with electro-magnetic brake. The brake block can be seen between the wheels.

(Jourdain-Monneret archive)

The rubber on the wheel is compressed between the wheel's two faces. This prevents the metal from making complete contact, thus cushioning shocks and providing a smoother ride.

(Somua archive)

Renault railcar with three two-axle bogies, the end bogies being driving-bogies and the middle bogie being a carrying-bogie.

(Renault archive)

as a powerful braking agent on the vehicle. The braking system thus owes more to magnetic attraction than to friction on the rail.

However, passenger safety could not be guaranteed in what was basically an aeroplane body. Heavier and larger metal railcars were built. Deadweight per passenger increased to more than 550 lbs, except in the case of the Pauline class where, thanks to the use of the alloy Duralumin, it was as low as 300 lbs.

A second factor in weight-increase was the replacement of the oil-fired engine, with its highly flammable oil, by the heavier but equally powerful diesel engine, with its electric transmission system. As with an automobile, a surge of power is needed if the railcar is to accelerate

The 'Pauline', a Duralumin diesel-engine railcar, which could carry 55 seated passengers, with a deadweight of 300 lbs per passenger.

(Archive of the Enterprises industrielles charentaises)

quickly from rest. Such motive power means that journey time between stations and overall journey times can be reduced.

A further development was the use on main lines of railcars intended originally to run only on secondary lines. They were capable of providing an express service. The steam express, therefore, had yet another competitor, not in terms of comfort or capacity, but in terms of speed. Furthermore, on long journeys a comfortable armchair is no longer enough to satisfy the passenger. He needs space to stretch his legs, a washroom, a toilet, a bar. The train was therefore in a sense re-invented, since the railcar could not provide more room without becoming heavier and longer as it changed gradually to become a 'railcar train'.

Diesel-engine mechanical-transmission Renault railcar.

(Northern Railway archive)

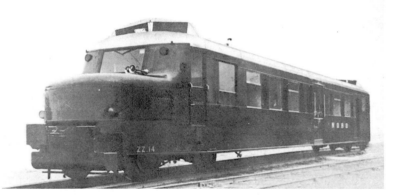

Mechanical-transmission Saurer diesel twin-motor Decauville railcar.

(Northern Railway archive)

Electric-transmission diesel-engine Northern Steelworks railcar.

(Northern Railway archive)

De Dietrich diesel-engine railcar with synchronised permanently-engaged gears.

(Dietrich archive)

The 'Zephyr', an aerodynamic railcar train on the Chicago, Burlington & Quincy R.R. It had three 72-seater stainless steel coaches and buffet and observation cars.

(Photo: Burlington R.R.)

Installing a 900 h.p. diesel-electric engine on a Pullman aerodynamic railcar train on the Union Pacific R.R.

(Photo: Union Pacific R.R.)

AERODYNAMIC RAILCARS

The diesel electric railcar train, propelled by two railcars separated by a single coach, made its first appearance in July 1934 in France on the Northern Railway network. With a deadweight per passenger of 1,800 lbs, it could carry 150 passengers at nearly 90 m.p.h. Its predecessors were the famous 'Fliegender-Hamburger', running between Berlin and Hamburg, and the 'Flying Dutchman' in Holland.

In the United States, where journeys were much longer, greater standards of comfort were demanded and, as a result, deadweight increased. On the Chicago, Burlington & Quincy Railroad's stainless steel 'Zephyr' train, with its buffet, grill-room and observation-car, there was a limit of 72 passengers in the three coaches, with a deadweight per passenger of over 1½ tons. The Union Pacific Railroad also built a three-car train, in this case made of Duralumin, to carry 116 passengers with a deadweight per passenger of only just under 1 ton in spite of carrying 11 tons of mail. Since there is sufficient power to haul four cars, a Pullman coach with multiple sleeping-berths was envisaged. Tests were carried out on a second six-unit, five-bogie Duralumin railcar train to carry 102 passengers and with three sleeping-cars containing 34 berths. Its deadweight was just over 2 tons per passenger. In October 1934, journey time for the 3,440 miles between New York and Los Angeles was reduced from 84 hours to 56 hours 55 minutes by the world's fastest train. The Rocky Mountains were crossed at a speed of 63 m.p.h.

When long distances have to be covered non-stop, the main function of power must be to overcome the air resistance. That is why aerodynamic design is of south vital importance to the modern train.

The Union Pacific R.R.'s new [1935] aerodynamic Duralumin railcar train, with mail-coach, luggage-van, three 34-bed Pullman sleeping-cars and a restaurant-car.

(Photo: Union Pacific R.R.)

THE BUGATTI TRAIN ON THE PARIS-VICHY LINE IN 1934
Four oil-fired motors giving 200 h.p. drive the axles via an hydraulic gearbox

A DIESEL-ELECTRIC TRAIN ON THE PARIS-LILLE LINE (1934)
A pair of diesel motors each giving 400 h.p. drive an electric generator which power the axles.

AERODYNAMIC TRAINS DRIVEN BY INTERNAL COMBUSTION ENGINES

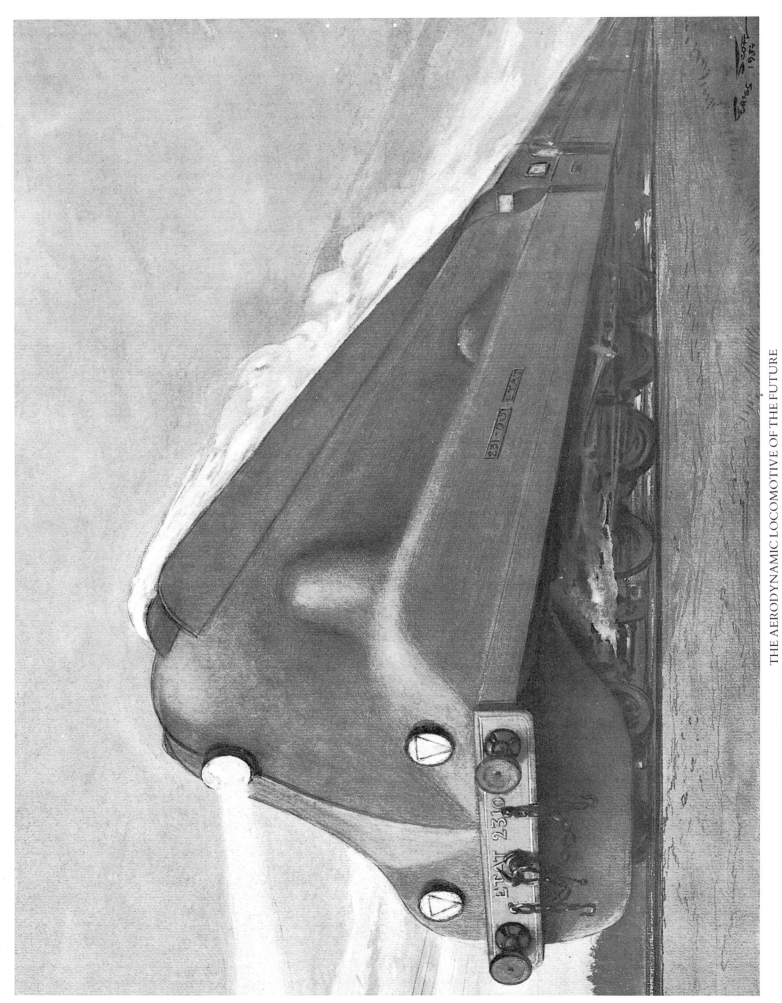

THE AERODYNAMIC LOCOMOTIVE OF THE FUTURE
Wind tunnel tests on models show that wind resistance at 55 m.p.h. can be reduced by 60% by streamlining. In this example, State Railways locomotive 231 is clothed in a metal casing to cover up all the protruberances

The P.L.M.'s 'Atlantic'-class aerodynamic steam locomotive with an average speed of 65 m.p.h.

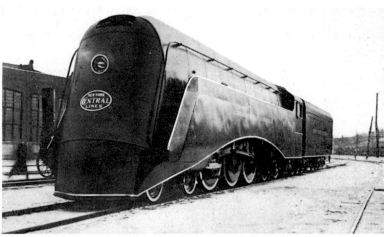

The *Commodore Vanderbilt*, New York Central R.R.'s aerodynamic steam locomotive.
(*The Sphere*, 12 January 1935).

THE RETURN TO STEAM AND THE AERODYNAMIC TRAIN

In the 1930s, steam traction was rapidly changing to meet competition from the diesel engine. Before the First World War, there had been attempts to propel railcars by steam (see page 000), but the small steam engine did not have enough water to generate instant steam and development was abandoned. However, a Sentinel-Cammell class steam railcar operated for several years with great success on a line on the south coast of Jersey. It is driven by a high-pressure water-tube vertical boiler with superheat and feed-water reheating. This class is becoming increasingly popular, and the London & North Eastern Railway tested it on its secondary lines.

Even on long-distance express lines, the streamlined steam train is now a rival to the railcar train. It is beginning to take on an aerodynamic shape. Smoke deflector panels are fitted to disperse wind and smoke and thus improve the driver's visibility. The window through which the driver peers to make out track signals and which attracts grime has been replaced [1935] on the Northern Railway by an airflow moving vertically downwards and creating a current of air strong enough to prevent rain, snow or soot entering the cab. The windscreen remains clear whatever the weather and conditions. The steam locomotive is beginning now to abandon completely its classic shape. German locomotive-builders tested a new type of locomotive in an effort to lighten and streamline wheels, boiler and tender. Any external projecting part liable to create air turbulence has disappeared. Some engines even have the driver's cab at the front of the engine, returning in this way to an older design (see page 000).

In the United States and France, the tendency was rather to breathe new life into old shapes. The *Commodore Vanderbilt*, which was in passenger service for several years on the New York Central Railroad, was fitted with an aerodynamic shell which, after December 1934, gave a saving in power of approximately 30 per cent. The

Applied aerodynamics.
Replacing the window by an air-shield to create a downward air-flow improves signal visibility for the driver. (Northern Railway)

P.L.M. Railway went one step further. Taking a much older locomotive, the 4–4–2 Atlantic-class, and modifying it to incorporate all the latest developments in superheat, reheating and pressure lubrication, it encased it in metal sheeting. This hid completely its wheels and mechanism, and enabled it to pull a train of three modern metal coaches which, together with the tender, were also streamlined. Looking more like a caterpillar than a train, it reduced air-resistance to a minimum. This return to lighter steam trains is reminiscent of the Austrian trials in 1873. At that time, a Stock Exchange crash provoked a crisis on the railways, and Elbel, an Austrian engineer, built very light steam locomotives specifically for secondary lines. They had two driving-axles, in some cases only one, and hauled a maximum of two or three waggons. These locomotives saved the day where secondary lines were concerned. Perhaps the present crisis may required us to break with the errors of the past and adopt similar measures on our main lines and on an even larger scale. Perhaps the time has arrived to develop a lighter, faster, steam train which will offer a more frequent service, and attract back to the railways travellers who have come to prefer other means of transport. A frequent service is not, however, the only answer. Greater comfort is vital if railways are to rediscover their past.

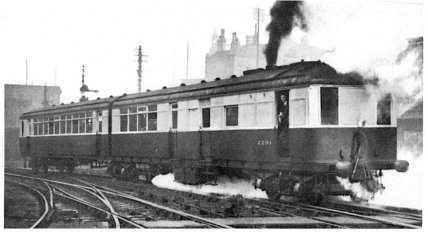

An articulated steam railcar in service on the London & North Eastern Railway.
(Copyright: Express Photos Ltd)

An example of a modern station at the Brussels Exhibition, 1935.

THE BRUSSELS EXHIBITION 1935

To celebrate the centenary of the first railway network in the world, Belgium built a modern station to be shown at the World Exhibition in Brussels in 1935. Its beauty and grandeur made it the star of this magnificent display.

Beneath a concrete arch, with an extraordinary span and a great feeling of lightness, stood modern rolling-stock from a number of the world's great nations. They stood on tracks on either side of their Belgian forerunner – that same train which on 5 May 1835 took George Stephenson and numerous guests from Brussels to Malines.

Here were engines representing the three modern forms of traction – steam, electric and diesel.

To the left, on the first two tracks, where electric-line pylons had been erected stood electric locomotives from the Italian railways. They bore witness to the fact that the country where three-phase current once reigned supreme was in the process of changing to direct current. Beside them were Fiat and Breda diesel-engine railcars, an oil-fired railcar luggage-van, a first-class coach, refrigerator-cars, and waggons to transport fresh produce.

On the next four tracks stood French rolling-stock, steam locomotives – the P.L.M.'s Sante Fé-class, the State Railway's Mountain-class, the Northern suburban line's Mikado-class – a P.O.

Southern Railway's electric locomotive, suburban metal coaches, special waggons, and, on tracks five and six, Renault, Bugatti, Micheline, De Dietrich and Northern steel works railcars, all creating a striking impression on account of their power, range and comfort.

On the other side of the 1835 Belgian train stood 1930s Belgian rolling-stock: on track seven, a streamlined Pacific with metal coaches; on track eight, the new Brussels–Antwerp electric train; on the remaining tracks, the Belgian 'Franco' class which is a huge articulated locomotive, a Belgian steam-railcar, a Swedish sleeping-car offering a level of comfort never before seen, and, finally, tramcars belonging to Belgian local railway companies.

CHRONOLOGY OF RAILWAY HISTORY

*This chronology lists the principal developments in the period covered by the book
and also in the period since the Second World War.*

1758 *9 June:* first railway authorised by Parliament in Britain (Middleton colliery to Leeds). This was first line on which steam locomotives were used commercially: two rack engines built by Matthew Murray for John Blenkinsop first ran on 12 August 1812.

1767 First recorded use (at Coalbrookdale, Shropshire) of cast-iron bars fitted to the tops of wooden rails.

1778–9 First railway in France (to serve an ordnance factory at the mouth of the Loire) built by an Englishman, William Wilkinson.

1784 First recorded use of French term 'chemin de fer' by de Givry.

1787 Iron flanged rails first used underground at Duke of Norfolk's Sheffield collieries. First used on the surface in 1788 at Ketley, Shropshire.

1790 Cast-iron edge rails suitable for flanged wheels first used in South Wales.

1792 'Fish-bellied' cast-iron rails designed by William Jessop. First laid in 1793–4 for railway from Nanpantan to Loughborough, Leicestershire.

1794 First recorded use of flanged (wooden) wheels at the Otaviga Mines in Hungary.

1795 First wooden track railroad in North America laid at Beacon Hill, Boston to carry building materials.

1803 *26 July:* Surrey Iron Railway opened. This was the first public goods railway in Britain and ran from Wandsworth to Croydon.

Richard Trevithick designed first railway locomotive at Coalbrookdale ironworks in Shropshire. This employed high-pressure steam unlike James Watt's low-pressure or atmospheric steam engines.

1804 Trevithick built his second locomotive for the Penydarran ironworks near Merthyr Tydfil in Wales.

29 June: First railway to carry fare-paying passengers incorporated by Act of Parliament. The horse-drawn Oystermouth Railway (also known as the Swansea & Mumbles Railway) opened in April 1806 and carried passengers from 25 March 1807.

1805 First locomotive with flanged wheels, built by John Whinfield, tested unsuccessfully at Wylam colliery, Northumberland. Built in Gateshead.

1806 Introduction by Matthew Murray of short 'D'-pattern slide-valve.

1808 *27 May:* First railway in Scotland (Kilmarnock & Troon) incorporated. Opened in July 1812. Horse-drawn until 1817, when it was converted to steam.

Trevithick's fourth locomotive *Catch me who can* built in Shropshire, for demonstration on circular track in London.

1812 *12 August:* Matthew Murray's engine, built for John Blenkinsop at Middleton colliery, Leeds, began operating.

Spring-loaded safety valve introduced by James Fenton.

1813 Patent for locomotive bogie taken out by William Chapman.

William Hedley, Timothy Hackworth and Jonathan Forster built first engine at Wylam colliery, Northumberland, named *Grasshopper*.

1814 *25 July: Blücher,* George Stephenson's first locomotive, completed at Killingworth, near Newcastle-upon-Tyne.

1816 First use of George Stephenson's loose-eccentric valve gear.

1823 *21 March:* Pennsylvania Railroad incorporated. First section opened in 1829, and complete line opened on 16 April 1834.

1825 *February:* First steam locomotive in North America built by John Stevens at Hoboken.

First iron railway-bridge, for Stockton & Darlington Railway.

First public railway to use steam from its beginning opened on 27 September. Stockton & Darlington Railway ran only goods trains at first, but introduced passenger steam trains in 1833.

Locomotion No. 1 built by George Stephenson for Stockton & Darlington Railway. First locomotive to have coupled wheels.

1826 First scheduled railway passenger service on the Stockton & Darlington Railway. Originally horse-drawn.

1827 First coal-carrying railway in Canada built at Picton, Nova Scotia. It was horse-drawn.

First iron tramway in Australia, to carry coal from Newcastle.

Multi-tubular boiler patented in France by Marc Seguin.

7 September: First railway opened in Austria–Hungary (Budweiss to Linz). Horse-drawn until 1872.

1828 George Stephenson's *Lancashire Witch* was the first locomotive in which wheels were driven direct from the piston-rod.

1 October: First public railway in France opened between Saint-Etienne and Andrézieux. Horse-drawn passenger trains commenced on 1 March 1832.

1829 *8 August: Stourbridge Lion* tested on Delaware & Hudson Railroad (line built by J.B. Jervis).

October: Rainhill Trials won by the *Rocket*, built by George and Robert Stephenson.

7 November: First French steam locomotive, built by Marc Seguin, tested on Saint-Etienne–Lyons Railway.

1830 George Stephenson's *Planet* built for Liverpool & Manchester Railway. It had inside cylinders.

3 May: Canterbury & Whitstable Railway opened. First regular steam passenger service. Locomotive was Stephenson's *Invicta.*

4 May: First tunnel for passenger traffic opened on Canterbury & Whitstable Railway.

24 May: Baltimore & Ohio Railroad opened for passenger and freight traffic. First railroad in the USA to offer a regular public service.

25 August: Peter Cooper's *Tom Thumb* was the first steam locomotive to run on the Baltimore & Ohio Railroad.

15 September: Liverpool & Manchester Railway opened. First public railway operated entirely by locomotives and first to have double track throughout.

15 September: Liverpool Road Station in Manchester opened. Now closed, it was the world's oldest railway station.

11 November: Mail first carried by train on Liverpool & Manchester Railway.

1831 *15 January:* Opening of first regular steam railroad in the USA (South Carolina Railroad).

9 August: De Witt Clinton pulled first steam train in New York State on the Mohawk & Hudson Railroad.

30 August: Train on the Baltimore & Ohio Railroad ran at 30 m.p.h.

November: US mail first carried by rail on the South Carolina Railroad.

12 November: Stephenson's *Planet*-type locomotive *John Bull* started operating in the USA on the Camden & Amboy Railroad.

1832 *Experiment* was the first indigenous American-type locomotive, built by J.B. Jervis for the Mohawk & Hudson Railroad.

1833 Robert Stephenson introduced steam-brake.

1834 *17 December:* First railway in Ireland (Dublin & Kingstown).

1835 Bells first fitted on American locomotives.

5 May: First railway opened in Belgium (Brussels to Malines).

7 December: First railway opened in Germany (Nuremberg to Furth).

1836 *8 February:* First railway in London opened (London & Greenwich Railway).

21 July: First steam railway in Canada opened (Laprairie to St John).

9 October: First railway opened in Russia (Pavlovsk to Tsarskoe Selo).

1837 First primitive sleeping-car in operation on Cumberland Valley Railroad, Pennsylvania.

26 August: Opening of first public steam railway in France from Paris to le Pecq.

17 November: First railway opened in what is now modern Austria. First railway in Austria to use steam locomotives (the Kaiser Ferdinand Nordbahn).

1838 First 0-6-0 locomotive, *Nonpareil*, built in the USA.

6 January: First travelling post-office introduced between Birmingham and Liverpool.

4 June: First section of Great Western Railway (engineer: I.K. Brunel) opened from London (Paddington) to Maidenhead.

17 September: London & Birmingham Railway opened from London (Euston) to Birmingham.

Electric telegraph first used on Great Western Railway between Paddington and West Drayton.

1839 Erie & Ontario Railway opened in Canada. Horse-drawn until 1854.

First coal-burning locomotives in Canada, *Samson*, *Hercules* and *John Buddle*, operated on Pictou line in Nova Scotia.

Superheater introduced by R. & W. Hawthorn of Newcastle-upon-Tyne.

20 September: First railway opened in Holland (Amsterdam to Haarlem).

4 October: First railway opened in Italy (Naples to Portici).

1840 Disc and crossbar signals introduced on Great Western Railway.

1841 Semaphore signals introduced on the London & Croydon Railway.

1842 *8 May:* Express from Versailles to Paris crashed and caught fire, killing 48 people. First large-scale railway accident.

1843 *25 March:* First underwater railway tunnel built, under the Thames. Used originally for pedestrians, it was taken over for use by the East London Railway on 7 December 1869.

1844 Walschaerts invented his valve-gear, first used in Belgium in 1848.

24 May: Baltimore & Ohio Railroad introduced use of telegraph in USA.

15 June: First railway opened in Switzerland (Basle to St Ludwig). This crossed the frontier into Europe. The first railway completely within the Swiss borders was the Zurich–Baden railway opened on 9 August 1847.

1845 *June:* Great Western 2-2-2 *Ixion* set speed record of 61 m.p.h. between London and Didcot.

25 June: Royal Commission appointed to consider railway gauges in Britain. In 1846, recommended that with exception of Great Western Railway (which used a 7 ft gauge until 1892) standard gauge (4 ft 8½ in) should always be adopted in Britain.

1846 During the 'Railway Mania' in Britain, 272 railway Acts of Parliament were passed in this year.

1 June: 2-2-2 *Great Western* achieved speed of 74 m.p.h. on the Great Western main line in Wiltshire.

1847 First 4-6-0 locomotive, the *Chesapeake*, built in the USA.

'Fish-plates' to join the ends of rails together introduced in Britain.

26 June: First railway opened in Denmark (Copenhagen to Roskilde).

1847–52 Gare de l'Est, Paris built.

1848 Completion of through route from London to Edinburgh.

11 May: Great Western 4-2-2 *Great Britain* reached 78 m.p.h. in Wiltshire.

25 October: *Pioneer* (built by Mathias Baldwin of Philadelphia) was the first locomotive to operate from Chicago.

28 October: First railway opened in Spain (Barcelona to Matero).

3 November: First railway opened in South America, in British Guiana (now Guyana).

1849 Camden & Amboy Railroad in USA first used containers for freight traffic.

1850 Compound cylinders introduced by James Samuel on the Eastern Counties Railway in England.

Oil-lamps used in passenger-coaches in USA.

1 April: Completion of through route from London to Aberdeen.

1851 Fairlie 0-4-4-0 articulated locomotive built in Belgium for Semmering trials in Austria.

Krupp of Essen produced all-steel tyres for locomotive wheels.

16 August: First international rail link in North America, from Quebec, Canada to New York State.

25 December: First railway opened in Chile.

1851–2 King's Cross station, London, built.

1852 Great Northern Railway in Britain introduced 'foot-warmers', the first method of heating carriages.

9 December: The *Pacific* was the first locomotive to run west of the Mississippi (from St Louis to Cheltenham).

1853 Two railways in Canada (Great Western and the Ontario, Simcoe and Union) opened, and used steam locomotives from the outset.

18 April: First railway opened in India (Bombay to Thana).

1854 *16 January:* Brunel's Paddington Station in London opened.

30 April: First railway opened in Brazil.

15 May: First railway opened over the Alps, via the Semmering Pass.

18 May: Australia's first passenger railway opened (Port Elliot & Goolwa Railway, South Australia). It was originally horse-drawn.

June: 4-2-4 tank engine of Bristol & Exeter Railway achieved speed of 81 m.p.h. in Somerset.

1 September: First railway opened in Norway (Christiana – the original name for Oslo – to Eidsvoll).

12 September: Opening of Australia's first steam railway (Melbourne to Sandridge, Victoria).

1855 Vignier responsible for installing system interlocking points and signals on French Western Railway.

28 January: Panama Railroad opened, linking the Atlantic and the Pacific.

1856 *January:* First railway opened in Africa (Alexandria to Cairo).

22 February: First railroad opened on Pacific coast of USA (Sacramento to Folsom, California).

1856 cont

28 October: First railway opened in Portugal (Lisbon/Carregado).

1 December: The first sections of the Swedish State Railways opened (Gothenburg to Joosered and Malmö to Lund).

1857

21 June: Baltimore & Ohio Railroad ran first through service from the Atlantic to the Mississippi.

First steel rails laid in Britain, at Derby on the Midland Railway.

30 August: First railway opened in Argentina.

31 August: Mount Cenis, the first of the Alpine tunnels, opened.

1859

First Pullman sleeping-car ran from Bloomington to Chicago.

Steam injector, invented by Henri Giffard, first used.

1860

First British 4-4-0 locomotive with bogie built for Stockton & Darlington Railway.

First 2-6-0 Mogul class built in USA by Mathias Baldwin.

First installation of water-troughs (on the Chester–Holyhead line).

26 June: First railway opened in South Africa (Durban to The Point).

1861–5 Gare du Nord, Paris built.

1862

3 February: First railway opened in New Zealand (the horse-drawn Dun Mountain Railway in South Island).

1863

First restaurant-cars in operation between Philadelphia and Baltimore.

First steel rails laid in the USA, on the Pennsylvania Railroad.

Gas-lighting introduced for passenger-coaches on North London Railway.

10 January: First section of London's Metropolitan Railway opened – the world's first underground passenger railway.

1 December: First steam railway opened in New Zealand (Christchurch to Ferrymead in South Island).

1865

First 2-8-0 Consolidation class built at Baldwin locomotive works, Philadelphia.

1868

Railway opened over the Mount Cenis Pass, employing Fell's centre-rail friction drive system.

1 October: St Pancras station in London opened. It has the largest station roof in Britain.

1869

Experiments in France with oil-fired locomotives.

10 May: First transcontinental railroad in America completed at Promontory, Utah, linking Central Pacific and Union Pacific Railroads.

3 July: First mountain rack railway opened at Mount Washington, New Hampshire.

1870

May: First through train from Atlantic to Pacific in the USA.

1871

First use of compressed-air brake, by Caledonian Railway in Scotland.

23 May: Vitznau–Rigi mountain rack trailway opened in Switzerland, employing Riggenbach's rack system, patented in 1863.

1872

12 June: First railway in Japan opened (Yokohama to Sinagawa).

1872–3 Westinghouse braking system introduced.

1873

2 April: First purpose-built sleeping-car operated in Britain (between Glasgow, Edinburgh and London).

1874

1 June: Pullman cars introduced into Britain.

1876

Anatole Mallet built first successful compound locomotives for Bayonne–Biarritz Railway in France.

First railway opened in China (Shanghai to Woosung). Dismantled a year later. First permanent railway opened in 1880.

1878

First 2-6-0 Mogul class built in Britain ran on Great Eastern Railway.

Vacuum brake introduced in Britain.

1879

Werner von Siemens built first electric railway for Berlin Trades Exhibition.

1 November: First restaurant-cars operated in Britain (London to Leeds).

28 December: Tay Bridge disaster.

1881

Electric-lighting for passenger-coaches first introduced in UK.

Steam-heating of passenger-coaches introduced in the USA.

12 May: Opening of first public electric railway, at Lichterfelde near Berlin.

December: First all-Pullman train in Britain (London to Brighton).

1882

1 January: St Gotthard Tunnel opened to goods traffic (and to passenger traffic on 1 June).

1883

4 August: Opening of first public electric railway in Britain (Volk's Electric Railway at Brighton).

1884 Anatole Mallet's articulated locomotive patented.

1885

Abt rack system employed for first time on railway in Harz Mountains.

7 November: Canadian Pacific Railway completed transcontinental link.

1886

First 4-6-2 Pacific class built in the USA by Vulcan ironworks, Wilkes Barr, Pennsylvania.

1 February: Mersey Railway opened under River Mersey, between Liverpool and Birkenhead.

1 September: Severn Tunnel, the longest railway tunnel in Britain (4¼ miles long), opened by the GWR between England and Wales.

1888

First 4-4-2 Atlantic class built in USA by Vulcan for Lehigh Valley Railroad.

1889

4-2-0 Crampton locomotive achieved a speed of 89 m.p.h. on the Paris–Dijon line in France.

4 June: Mount Pilatus Railway opened in Switzerland, using Locher's rack system.

1890

4 March: Forth Bridge, the oldest cantilever railway bridge, opened.

18 December: First electric underground railway opened (City & South London).

1892

7 March: First corridor trains in Britain (Great Western Railway).

20 May: Last broad-gauge trains ran on Great Western Railway. Gauge converted by 23 May.

1893

6 March: Opening of Liverpool Overhead Railway, the first electric elevated railway.

1894 First 4-6-0 locomotive in Britain ran on the Highland Railway.

1895

Opening of Chicago Elevated Railway.

28 June: First electric train service in USA, on the New York, New Haven & Hartford Railroad.

1897

First 2-8-2 Mikado class built by Baldwin locomotive works in the USA for Japanese Railways.

1898

First 4-4-2 Atlantic class in Britain introduced on the Great Northern Railway.

20 August: Gornergrat Railway, the first electric mountain rack railway, opened at Zermatt, Switzerland.

1899

21 July: First three-phase ac overhead electric railway opened (Burgdorf to Thun, in Switzerland).

1900

First 2-6-2 Prairie type built by Baldwin locomotive works in USA for the Chicago, Burlington & Quincy Railroad.

First streamlined passenger train ran on Baltimore & Ohio Railroad.

Underground railway opened in New York.

10 July: First section of Paris Metro opened.

1902 Opening of Berlin Elevated Railway.

15 June: 'The Twentieth Century Limited' introduced between New York and Chicago, covering the 961 mile journey in 20 hours.

1903 First 2-10-2 Santa Fe class started operating on Atchison, Topeka & Santa Fe Railroad in the USA.

1903–13 Building of Grand Central Terminal, New York, the world's largest station.

1904 First single-phase ac electric railway (Seebach to Wettingen, Switzerland).

May: 4-4-0 *City of Truro* reached a speed of 100 m.p.h. between Plymouth and Bristol.

1905 First all-steel passenger coaches in the USA (Long Island Railroad).

1906 *1 June:* First single-line Simplon Tunnel opened between Switzerland and Italy. Second tunnel was opened on 16 October 1922 (12¼ miles long).

1907 First 4-6-2 Pacific class in Europe ran on the Paris–Orleans line.

1908 First 4-6-2 Pacific locomotive in Britain built at Swindon for Great Western Railway.

1909 First Garratt articulated locomotives built.

First 2-10-0 locomotive in France went into service on Paris–Orleans line.

1 December: Electric trains first ran on South London line of London, Brighton & South Coast Railway.

1911 First 4-8-2 Mountain class introduced on the Chesapeake & Ohio Railroad in the USA.

1912–13 First experimental diesel locomotive built in Germany.

1915 *22 May:* Britain's worst rail disaster. 227 were killed in collision followed by fire near Carlisle.

1921 *19 August:* 123 railway companies in Britain amalgamated into four companies – LMS, LNER, GWR and Southern.

1925 First main-line diesel-electric locomotives built for German State Railways.

1926 *12 September: Golden Arrow* express (London to Paris) introduced. Became all-Pullman in 1929.

1928 Completion of trans-Africa route from Benguela on the Atlantic to Beira on the Indian Ocean.

1929 *12 January:* Cascade Tunnel, the longest through tunnel in the USA (7½ miles long), opened in Washington State.

1930 Air-conditioned coaches went into regular use in the USA.

Milan Central station completed.

April: First air-conditioned restaurant-car on the Baltimore & Ohio Railroad.

1931 Railcars with pneumatic tyres introduced in France.

21 June: Petrol railcar in Germany achieved speed of 143 m.p.h.

1932 *Flying Hamburger*, first high-speed diesel train, ran between Berlin and Hamburg.

1933 First diesel railcar built for Great Western Railway.

1 January: All-Pullman 'Brighton Belle' (known originally as 'Southern Belle') ran for first time (London to Brighton).

1 January: First main-line electrification in Britain (London to Brighton and Worthing, Southern Railway).

1934 Britain's first 2-8-2 locomotive *Cock o' the North* built at Doncaster for the LNER.

First streamlined diesel-electric train, *Burlington Zephyr*, went into service on Chicago, Burlington & Quincy Railroad in USA.

1935 *May:* Germany claimed world record for steam locomotive when a 4-6-4 achieved 124 m.p.h. on a test run between Berlin and Hamburg.

1938 *1 January:* Major French railway companies merged into French National Railways (SNCF).

3 July: LNER locomotive *Mallard* reached speed of 125 m.p.h. between Grantham and Peterborough. This remains steam record.

27 July: Electric train between Rome and Naples achieved average speed of 96 m.p.h. and maximum of 125 m.p.h.

1939 *23 June:* Record speed for diesel-electric locomotive established in Germany (133 m.p.h.).

1946 *31 March:* First regular sleeping-car service between Atlantic and Pacific in the USA.

1948 *1 January:* British Railways nationalised.

1955 Main line between Valenciennes and Thionville in France electrified.

1960 *March:* Last steam-engine introduced by British Railways (No. 92220 *Evening Star*).

1961 First British Rail 'Deltic' diesel locomotives delivered.

1965 *1 November:* Japan Railways introduced 'bullet' trains between Tokyo and Osaka on a regular scheduled run at over 100 m.p.h.

1971 *1 May:* 'Amtrak' took over passenger services of 22 major railroads in the USA.

1976 *1 April:* 'Conrail' (Consolidated Rail Corporation) combined activities of Penn Central and other leading US railroads, covering an area from the Mississippi to Canada and the Atlantic Coast.

1977 *7 May:* British Rail's High Speed Train between Bristol and London achieved average speed of 103 m.p.h. and maximum of 128 m.p.h.

1981 *26 February:* French TGV electric train achieved speed of 236 m.p.h. on test run, near Tonnerre. Maximum speeds on Paris–Lyons TGV trains 162–186 m.p.h.

1984 *30 August:* High Speed Train between London and Bristol achieved average speed of 112 m.p.h.

GENERAL INDEX

INDEX OF TYPES OF LOCOMOTIVE CLASSIFIED BY WHEEL ARRANGEMENT

1. STEAM LOCOMOTIVES

319

---

2. ELECTRIC TRACTION

Locomotives, electric units and tractors

---

3. MIXED TRACTION